ANTE-NICENE CHRISTIAN LIBRARY : TRANSLATIONS OF THE WRITINGS OF THE FATHERS DOWN TO A. D. 325 (VOLUME 10)

ANTE-NICENE CHRISTIAN LIBRARY : TRANSLATIONS OF THE WRITINGS OF THE FATHERS DOWN TO A. D. 325 (VOLUME 10)

Roberts, Alexander, 1826-1901 and donaldson, James, Sir, 1831-1915

www.General-Books.net

Publication Data:

Title: Ante-Nicene Christian Library : Translations of the Writings of the Fathers Down to A. D. 325
Volume: 10
Author: Roberts, Alexander, 1826-1901 and Donaldson, James, Sir, 1831-1915
Publisher: Edinburgh : T. and T. Clark
Publication date: 1867
Subjects: Christian literature, Early
Christian literature, Early = Bibliography

1

ANTE-NICENE CHRISTIAN LIBRARY : TRANSLATIONS OF THE WRITINGS OF THE FATHERS DOWN TO A. D. 325 (VOLUME 10)

THE WRITINGS . TRANSLATED BY

BEY. FREDERICK CROMBIE, M. A.,

PROFESSOR OF BIBLICAL CRITICISM, ST. MARY'S COLLEGE. ST. AN-DREWS.

VOL. I.

EDINBURGH: T. T. CLARK, 38, GEORGE STREET.)NDON: HAMILTON CO. DUBLIN: JOHN ROBERTSON CO.

MDCCGLXIX.

CONTENTS.

HE name of the illustrious Origen comes before us in this volume in connection
with his works De Principiisy Epistola ad Africcmicmy and Contra Celsum. Of these,
the first two have been given entire, while of the third we have been able at present
only to give the first book. A full account of the life and writings of the author will be
prefixed to our next volume of his works. Meanwhile, we restrict ourselves to a brief
notice of the three which have been mentioned.

It is in his treatise Ilepl Ap wv or, as it is commonly known under the Latin
title, De Principiisy that Origen most fully develops his system, and brings out his
peculiar principles. None of his works exposed him to so much animadversion in
the ancient church as this. On it chiefly was based the charge of heresy which some
vehemently pressed against him, a charge from which even his firmest friends felt it
no easy matter absolutely to defend him. The points on which it was held that he
had plainly departed from the orthodox faith, were the four following: First, That the
souls of men had existed in a previous state, and that their imprisonment in material
bodies was a punishment for sins which they had then committed. Second, That
the human soul of Christ had also previously existed, and been united to the Divine
nature before that incarnation of the Son of God which is related in the Gospels.
Third, That our material bodies shall be transformed into absolutely ethereal ones at
the resurrection; and fourth, That all men, and even devils, shall be finally restored
through the mediation of Christ. His principles of interpreting Scripture are also
brought out in this treatise; and while not a little ingenuity is displayed in illustrating
and maintaining them, the serious errors into which they might too easily lead will be
at once perceived by the reader.

It is much to be regretted that the original Greek of the De Principiis has for the
most part perished. We possess it chiefly in a Latin translation by Rufinus. And there
can be no doubt that he often took great liberties with his author. So much was this
felt to be the case, that Jerome undertook a new translation of the work; but only
small portions of his version have reached our day. He strongly accuses Kufinus of
unfaithfulness as an interpreter, while he also inveighs bitterly against Origen himself,
as having departed from the catholic faith, specially in regard to the doctrine of the
Trinity. There seems, however, after all, no adequate reason to doubt the substantial
orthodoxy of our author, although the bent of his mind and the nature of his studies
led him to indulge in many vain and unauthorized speculations.

The Epistle to Africanus was drawn forth by a letter which that learned writer had addressed to Origen respecting the story of Susanna appended to the book of Daniel. Africanus had grave doubts as to the canonical authority of the account. Origen replies to his objections, and seeks to uphold the story as both useful in itself, and a genuine portion of the ancient prophetical writings.

The treatise of Origen Against Celsus is, of all his works, the most interesting to the modern reader. It is a defence of Christianity in opposition to a Greek philosopher named Celsus, who had attacked it in a work entitled 'AXrjorjc; A6yo;, that is. The True Word, or The True Discourse. Of

INTRODUCTORY NOTICE.

this work we know notliing, except from tlie quotations contained in the answer given to it by Origen. Nor has anything very certain been ascertained respecting its author. According to Origen, he was a follower of Epicurus, but others have regarded him as a Platonist. If we may judge of the work by those specimens of it preserved in the reply of Origen, it was little better than a compound of sophistry and slander. But there is reason to be grateful for it, as having called forth the admirable answer of Origen. This work was written in the old age of our author, and is composed with great care; while it abounds with proofs of the widest erudition. It is also perfectly orthodox; and, as Bishop Ball has remarked, it is only fair that we should judge from a work written with the view of being considered by the world at large, and with the most elaborate care, as to the mature and finally accepted views of the author.

The best edition of Origen's works is that superintended by Charles and Charles Vincent de la Kue, Paris 1783, 4 vols, fob, which is reprinted by Migne. There is also an edition in 25 volumes, based upon that of De la Rue, but without the Latin translation, by Lommatzsch, Berlin 1831-1848. The De Princijiis has been separately edited by Redepenning, Leipzig 1836. Spencer edited the Contra Celsurriy Cambridge 1677.

PEOLOGUE OF KUFINUS TO THE DE PEINCIPIIS.

KNOW that very many of the brethren, induced by their thirst for a knowledge of the Scriptures, have requested some distinguished men, well versed in Greek learning, to translate Origen into Latin, and so make him accessible to Roman readers. Among these, when our brother and colleague had, at the earnest entreaty of Bishop Damasus, translated two of the Homihes on the Song of Songs out of Greek into Latin, he prefixed so elegant and noble a preface to that work, as to inspire every one with a most eager desire to read and study Origen, saying that the expression, "The King hath brought me into his chamber," was appropriate to his feelings, and declaring that while Origen in his other works surpassed all writers, he in the Song of Songs surpassed even himself. He promises, indeed, in that very preface, that he will present the books on the SoucT of Soncrs, and numerous others of the works of Origen, in a Latin translation, to Eoman readers. But he, finding greater pleasure in compositions of his own, pursues an end that is attended with greater fame, viz. in being the author rather than the translator of works. Accordingly we enter upon the undertaking, which was thus begun and approved of by him, although we cannot compose in a style of elegance Jerome is the person alluded to. 2 Cant. i. 4.

equal to that of a man of such distinguished eloquence; and therefore I am afraid lest, through my fault, the result should follow, that that man, whom he deservedly esteems as the second teacher of knowledo-e and wisdom in the church after the apostles, should, through the poverty of my language, appear far inferior to what he is. And this consideration, which frequently recurred to my mind, kept me silent, and prevented me from yielding to the numerous entreaties of my brethren, until your influence, my very faithful brother Macarius, which is so great, rendered it impossible for my unskilfulness any longer to offer resistance. And therefore, that I might not find you too grievous an exactor, I gave way, even contrary to my resolution; on the condition and arrangement, however, that in my translation I should follow as far as possible the rule observed by my predecessors, and especially by that distinguished man whom I have mentioned above, who, after translating into Latin more than seventy of those treatises of Origen which are styled Homilies and a considerable number also of his writings on the apostles, in which a good many " stumbling-blocks" are found in the original Greek, so smoothed and corrected them in his translation, that a Latin reader would meet with nothing which could appear discordant with our belief. His example, therefore, we follow, to the best of our abiuty; if not with equal power of eloquence, yet at least with the same strictness of rule, taking care not to reproduce those expressions occurring in the works of Origen which are inconsistent with and opposed to each other. The cause of these variations we have explained more freely in the Apologelicits, which Pamphilus wrote in defence of thc works of Origen, where we added a brief tract, in which we showed, I think, by unmistakeable proofs, that his books had been corrupted in numerous places by heretics and malevolent persons, and especially those books of which you now require me to undertake the translation, i. e. the books which may be entitled De Principiis or De Principatihusy and which are indeed in other respects full of obscurities and difficulties. For he there discusses those subjects with respect to which philo- sophers, after spending all their lives upon them, have been unable to discover anything. But here our author strove, as much as in him lay, to turn to the service of religion the belief in a Creator, and the rational nature of created beings, which the latter had degraded to purposes of wickedness. If, therefore, we have found anywhere in his writings, any statement opposed to that view, which elsewhere in his works he had himself piously laid down regarding the Trinity, we have either omitted it, as being corrupt, and not the composition of Origen, or we have brought it forward, agreeably to the rule which we frequently find affirmed by himself. If, indeed, in his desire to pass rapidly on, he has, as speaking to persons of skill and knowledge, sometimes expressed himself obscurely, we have, in order that the passage might be clearer, added what we had read more fully stated on the same subject in his other works, keeping explanation in view, but adding nothing of our own, but simply restoring to him what was his, although occurring in other portions of his writino; s.

These remarks, therefore, by way of admonition, I have made in the preface, lest slanderous individuals perhaps should think that they had a second time discovered matter of accusation. But let perverse and disputatious men have a care what they are about. For we have in the meantime undertaken this heavy labour, if God should aid your prayers, not to shut the mouths of slanderers (which is impossible, although

God perhaps will do it), but to afford material to those who desire to advance in the knowledge of these things. And, verily, in the presence of God the Father, and of the Son, and of the Holy Spirit, I adjure and beseech every one, who may either transcribe or read these books, by his belief in the kingdom to come, by the mystery of the resurrection from the dead, and by that everlasting fire prepared for the devil and his angels, that, as he would not possess for an eternal inheritance that place where there is weeping and gnashing of teeth, and where their fire is not quenched and their worm dieth not, he add nothing to Scripture, and take nothing away from it, and make no insertion or alteration.

but that he compare liis transcript with the copies from which he made it, and make the emendations and distinctions according to the letter, and not have his manuscript incorrect or indistinct, lest the difficulty of ascertaining the sense, from the indistinctness of the copy, should cause greater difficulties to the readers.

OEIGEN DE PRINCIPIIS.

PKEFACE.

ILL wlio believe and are assured tliat grace and truth were obtained through Jesus Christ, and who know Christ to be the truth, ao-reeablv to His own declaration, "I am the truth," derive the knowledge which incites men to a good and happj life from no other source than from the very words and teaching of Christ. And by the words of Christ we do not mean those only which He spake when He became man and tabernacled in the flesh: for before that time, Christ, the. Word of God, was in Moses and the prophets. For witliout) the Word of God, how could they have been able to pro- phesy of Christ And were it not our purpose to confine the present treatise within the limits of all attainable brevity, it would not be difficult to show, in proof of this statement, out of the Holy Scriptures, how Moses or the prophets botli spake and performed all they did through being filled with the Spirit of Christ. And therefore I think it sufficient to quote this one testimony of Paul from the Epistle to the Hebrews, in v diich he says: ' By faith Moses, when he was come to years, refused to be called the son of Pharaoh's daughter; choosing rather to suffer affliction with the people of God, than to enjoy the pleasures of sin for a season; w esteeming the reproach of Christ greater riches than the treasures of the Egyptians." Moreover, that after His ascension into heaven He spake in His apostles is shown 1 John xiv. G. 2 Ifd), xi. 24-26.

by Paul ill these words: " Or do you seek a proof of Christ, vvho speaketh in me?"

2. Since many, however, of those who profess to believe in Christ differ from each other, not only in small and trifling matters, but also on subjects of the highest importance, as e. g. regarding God, or the Lord Jesus Christ, or the Holy Spirit; and not only regarding these, but also regarding others which are created existences, viz. the powers and the holy virtues; it seems on that account necessary first of all to nx a definite limit and to lay down an unmistakeable rule regarding each one of these, and then to pass to the investigation of other points. For as we ceased to seek for truth (notwithstanding the professions of many among Greeks and yBarbarians to make it known) among all who claimed it for erroneous opinions, after we had come to believe that Christ was the Son of God, and were persuaded that we must learn it from Himself; so, seeing there are many wdio think they hold the opinions of Christ, and yet some of these think differently from their predecessors, yet as the teaching

of the church, transmitted in orderly succession from the apostles, and remaining in the churches to the present day, is still preserved, that alone is to be accepted as truth which differs in no respect from ecclesiastical and apostolical tradition.

3. Now it ought to be known that the holy apostles, in preaching the faith of Christ, delivered themselves with the utmost clearness on certain points which they believed to be necessary to every one, even to those who seemed somewhat dull in the investigation of divine knowledge; leaving, however, the grounds of their statements to be examined into by those who should deserve the excellent gifts of the Spirit, and who, especially by means of the Holy Spirit Himself, should obtain the gift of language, of wisdom, and of knowledge: while on other subjects they merely stated the fact that things were so, keeping silence as to the manner or origin of their existence; clearly in order that the more zealous of their successors, who should be lovers of wisdom, might have a subject of exercise on which to display the fruit of their 1 2 Cor. xiii. 3. Dominationes. Virtutes.

talents, those persous, I mean, who should prepare themselves to be fit and worthy receivers of wisdom.

4. The particular points clearly delivered in the teaching of the apostles are as follow:

First, That there is one God, who created and arranged all things, and who, when nothing existed, called all things into being God from the first creation and foundation of the world the God of all just men, of Adam, Abel, Seth, Enos, Enoch, Noc, Scm, Abraham, Isaac, Jacob, the twelve patriarchs, Moses, and the prophets; and that this God in the last days, as He had announced beforehand by His prophets, sent our Lord Jesus Christ to call in the first place Israel to Himself, and in the second place the Gentiles, after the unfaithfulness of the people of Israel. This just and good God, the Father of our Lord Jesus Christ, Himself gave the law, and the prophets, and the gospels, being also the God of the apostles and of the Old and New Testaments.

Secondly, That Jesus Christ Himself, who came into the world, was born of the Father before all creatures; that, after He had been the servant of the Father in the creation of all things ' For by Him were all things made"" He in the last times, divesting Himself of His glory, became a man, and was incarnate although God, and while made a man remained the God which He was; that He assumed a body like to our own, differing in this respect only, that it was born of a virgin and of the Holy Spirit: that this Jesus Christ was truly born, and did truly suffer, and did not endure this death common to man in appearance only, but did truly die; that He did truly rise from the dead; and that after His resurrection He conversed with His disciples, and was taken up into heaven.

Then, thirdly, the apostles related thatjthe Holy Spirit was associated in honour and dignity with the Father and the Son. But in His case it is not clearlv distinguished whether He is to be re i: arded as born or innate, 'or also as a Son of

Species. John i. 3.

Innatus. Tlie words which Rufinus has rendered " natus an innatus " are rendered by Jerome in his Epistle to Avitus (O'i alias 59), "factus

God or not: for these are points which have to be inquu'ed into out of sacred Scripture according to the best of our abihty, and which demand careful investigation.

And that Ithis Spirit inspired each one of the saints whether prophets or apostles; and that there was not one Spirit in the men of the old dispensation, and another in those who were inspired at the advent of Christ, is most clearly taught throughout the churches.

5. After these points, also, the apostolic teaching is that the soul, having a substance and life of its own, shall, after its departure from the world, be rewarded according to its deserts, being destined to obtain either an inheritance of eternal life and blessedness, if its actions shall have procured this for it, or to be delivered up to eternal fire and punish- ments, if the guilt of its crimes shall have brought it down to this: and also, that there is to be a time of resurrection from the dead, when this body, which now " Is sown in corruption, shall rise in incorruption," and that which " is sown in dis-, honour will rise in glory."'" This also is clearly defined in the teaching of the church, that every rational soul is pos-I sessed of free-will and volition; that it has a struggle to maintain with the devil and his angels, and opposing influences, because they strive to burden it with sins; but if we live rightly and wisely, we should endeavour to shake ourselves free of a burden of that kind. From which it follows, also, that we understand ourselves not to be subject to necessity, so as to be compelled by all means, even against our will, to do either good or evil. For if we are our own masters, some influences perhaps may impel us to sin, and others help us to salvation; we are not forced, however, by any necessity either to act rightly or wrongly, which those an infectus." Criticising the errors in the first book of the Principles, he says: " Origen declares the Holy Spirit to be third in dignity and honour after the Father and the Son; and although professingignorance whether he were created or not (factus an infectus), he indicated afterwards his opinion regarding him, maintaining that nothing was uncreated except God the Father." Jerome, no doubt, read yivmog n dyhviro;, and Rufinus yiyumrog 3 dysuu rog. R.

1 Substantia. 1 Qqj. xv. 42. " Virtutes.

persons think Is the case who say that the courses and movements of the stars are the cause of human actions, not only of those which take place beyond the influence of the freedom of the will, but also of those which are placed within our own power. But with respect to the soul, whether it is derived from the seed by a process of traducianism, so that the reason or substance of it may be considered as placed in the seminal particles of the body themselves, or whether it has any other beginning; and this beginning itself, whether it be by birth or not, or whether bestowed upon the body from without or no, is not distinguished with sufficient clearness in the teaching of the church.

6. Regarding the devil and his angels, and the opposing influences, the teaching of the church has laid down that these beings exist indeed; but what they are, or how they exist, it has not explained with sufficient clearness. This opinion, however, is held by most, that thedevil was an angel, and that, having become an apostate, he induced as many of the angels as possible to fall away with himself, and these up to the present time are called his angels.

7. This also is a part of the church's teaching, that the world was made and took its bemnnino; at a certain time, and is to be destroyed on account of its wickedness. But what existed before this w orld, or what will exist after it, has not become certainly

known to the many, for there is no clear statement regarding it in the teaching of the church.

8. Then, finally, that the Scriptures were written by the Spirit of God, and have a meaning, not such only as is apparent at first sight, but also another, which escapes the notice of most. For those words which are written are the forms of certain mysteries,- and the images of divine things. Ee-specting which there is one opinion throughout the whole church, that the whole law is indeed spiritual; but that the spiritual meaning which the law conveys is not known to all, but to those only on whom the grace of the Holy Spirit is bestowed in the word of wisdom and knowded e.

The term aacojlarov, i. e. incorporeal, is disused and un- Sacramentorum.

known, not only in many other writings, but also in our own Scriptures. And if any one should quote it to us out of the little treatise entitled The Doctrine of Peter in which the Saviour seems to say to His disciples, "I am not an incorporeal demon,"" I have to reply, in the first place, that that work is not included among ecclesiastical books; for we can show that it was not composed either by Peter or by any other person inspired by the Spirit of God. But even if the point were to be conceded, the word aacojiatov there does not convey the same meaning as is intended by Greek and Gentile authors wdien incorporeal nature is discussed by philosophers. For in the little treatise referred to he used the phrase "incorporeal demon" to denote that that form or outline of demoniacal body, whatever it is, does not resemble this-gross and visible body of ours; but, agreeably to the intention of the author of the treatise, it must be understood to mean that He had not such a body as demons have, wdiich is naturally fine, and thin as if formed of air (and for this reason is either considered or called by many incorporeal), but that He had a solid and palpable body. Now, according to human custom, everything which is not of that nature is called by the simple or ignorant incorporeal; as if one w ere to say that the air which we breathe was incorporeal, because it is not a body of such a nature as can be grasped and held, or can offer reslstance to pressure.

9. We shall inquire, however, whether the thing which Greek philosophers call do-oyjlarov, or " incorporeal," is found 1 Eusebius (Eccles. Hist. iii. c. 36), treating of Ignatius, quotes from his Epistle to the Church of Smyrna as follows: "Writing to the Smyrnseans, he (Ignatius) has also employed words respecting Jesus, I know not whence they are taken, to the following effect: ' But I know and believe that He was seen after, the resurrection; and when He came to Peter and his companions, He said to them, Take and handle me, and see that I am not an incorporeal spirit." " Jerome, in his catalogue of ecclesiastical writers, says the words are a quotation from the Gospel of the Nazarenes, a work which he had recently translated. Origen here quotes them, however, from The Doctrine of Peter on which Ruseus remarks that the words might be contained in both of these apocryphal works.

2 Dsemonium. Subtib.

in holy Scripture under anotiier name. For it is also to be a subject of investigation how God Himself is to be understood, whether as corporeal, and formed according to some shape, or of a different nature from bodies, a point which is not clearly indicated in our teaching. And the same inquiries have to be made regarding Christ and the

Holy Spirit, as well as respecting every soul, and everything possessed of a rational nature.

10. This also is a part of the teaching of the church, that there are certain angels of God, and certain good influences, vs'hicli are His servants in accomplishing the salvation of men. When these, however, were created, or of what nature they are, or how they exist, is not clearly stated. Regarding the sun, moon, and stars, whether tliey are living beings or without life, there is no distinct deliverance.

Every one, therefore, must make use of elements and foundations of this sort, according to the precept, ' Enlighten yourselves with the light of knowledge," if he would desire to form a connectcd series and body of truths agreeably to the reason of all these things, that by clear and necessary statements he may ascertain the truth regarding each individual topic, and form, as we have said, one body of doctrine, by means of illustrations and arguments, either those which he has discovered in holy Scripture, or which he has deduced by closely tracing out the consequences and following a correct method.

Hos. X. 12. The words in the text are not the rendering of the authorized version, but that of the Septuagint, which has (parigocri koivrolg cpag yyiatu;. Where the Masoretic. text has riy l (e tempiis) Origen evidently read np'H (scientia) the similarity of Van and Daletli 1. Jsr Mj KNOW that some will attempt to say that, even according to the declarations of our own Sciip-tures, God is a body, because in the, vrit aigs of Moses they find it said, that " our God is a fire;" and in the Gospel according to John, that " God is a Spirit, and they who worship Him must worship Him in spirit and in truth." Fire and spirit, according to them, are to be regarded as nothing else than a body. Now, I should like to ask these persons what they liave to say respecting that passage where it is declared that God is light; as John writes in his epistle, "God is light, and in Him there is no darkness at all." Truly He is that light which illuminates the whole understanding of those who are capable of receiving truth, as is said in the thirty-sixth Psalm, "In Thy light we shall see light." For what other light of God can be named, "in which any one sees light," save an influence of God, by which a man, being enlightened, either thoroughly sees the truth of all things, or comes to know God Himself, who is called the truth Such is the meaning of the expression, "In Thy light we shall see light;" i. e. in Thy word and wisdom, which is Thy Son, in Himself we shall see Thee the Father. Because He is called light, shall He be supposed to have any resemblance to the light of the sun? Or how should there be the 1 Deut. iv. 24.-John iv. 24.

3 1 John i. 5. Fs. xxxvi. 9.

Book i. OPJGEN DE PPJNCIPIIS, g slightest ground for imagining, that from that corporeal light any one could derive the cause of knowledge, and come to the understanding of the truth?

2. If, then, they acquiesce in our assertion, which reason, itself has demonstrated, regarding the nature of light, and acknowledge that God cannot be understood to be a body in the sense that liiiht is, similar reasonino; will hold true of the expression " a consuming fire." For what will God consume in respect of His being fire? Shall He be thought to consume material substance, as w ood, or hay, or stubble? And what in this view can be called Vv orthy of the glory of God, if He be a fire, consun ing materials

of that kind? But let us reflect that God does indeed consume and utterly destroy; that He consumes evil thoughts, wicked actions, and sinful desires, when they find their way into the minds of believers; and that, inhabiting along with His Son those souls which are rendered capable of receiving His word and wisdom, according to His own declaration, "I and the Father shall come, and we shall make our abode with him," He makes them, after all their vices and passions have been consumed, a holy temple, worthy of Himself. Those, more-ovev, vho, on account of the expression " God is a Spirit," think that Pie is a body, are to be answered, I think, in the following manner. It is the custom of sacred Scripture, when it wishes to designate anything opposed to this gross and solid body, to call it spirit, as in the expression, "The letter killeth, but the spirit giveth life," where there can be no doubt that by " letter" are meant bodily things, and by "spirit" intellectual things, which w e also term "spiritual." The apostle, moreover, says, "Even unto this day, when Moses is read, the veil is upon their heart: nevertheless, when it shall turn to the Lord, the veil shall be taken away: and where the Spirit of the Lord is, there is liberty." For so long as any one is not converted to a spiritual understanding, a veil is placed over his heart, with which veil, i. e. a gross understanding, Scripture itself is said or thought to be covered: and this is the meaning of the statement that a 1 John xiv. 23.- 2 Cor. iii. 6. 9 Cor. iii. 15-17.

veil was placed over the countenance of Moses when he spoke to the people, i. e. when the law was publicly read aloud. But if we turn to the Lord, where also is the word of God, and where the Holy Spirit reveals spiritual knowledge, then the veil is taken away, and with unveiled face we shall behold the glory of the Lord in the holy Scriptures. 3. And since many saints participate in the Holy Spirit, He cannot therefore be understood to be a body, which being divided into corporeal parts, is partaken of by each one of the saints; but He is manifestly a sanctifying power, in which all are said to have a share who have deserved to be sanctified by His grace. And in order that what we say may be more easily understood, let us take an illustration from things very dissimilar. There are many persons who take a part in the science or art of medicine: are we therefore to suppose that those who do so take to themselves the particles of some body called medicine, which is placed before them, and in this way participate in the same? Or must we not rather understand that all who with quick and trained minds come to understand the art and discipline itself, may be said to be pertakers of the art of healing? But these are not to be deemed altogether parallel instances in a comparison of medicine to the Holy Spirit, as they have been adduced only to establish that that is not necessarily to be considered a body, a share in which is possessed by many individuals. For the Holy Spirit differs widely from the method or science of medicine, in respect that the Holy Spirit is an intellectual existence, and subsists and exists in a peculiar manner, whereas medicine is not at all of that nature.

4. But we must pass on to the language of the Gospel itself, in which it is declared that " God is a Spirit," and where we have to show how that is to be understood agreeably to what we have stated. For let us inquire on what occasion these w ords were spoken by the Saviour, before whom He uttered them, and what was the subject of investigation. We find, without any doubt, that He spoke these words to Disciplina.- Subsistentia.

the Samaritan woman, saying to her, who thought, agreeably to the Samaritan view, that God ought to be worshipped on Mount Gerizim, that " God is a Spirit." For the Samaritan woman, beheving Him to be a Jew, was inquiring of Him whether God ought to be worshipped in Jerusalem or on this mountain; and her words were, "All our fathers w or-shipped on this mountain, and ye say that in Jerusalem is the place where we ought to worship." To this opinion of the Samaritan woman, therefore, who imagined that God was less rightly or duly worshipped, according to the privileges of the different localities, either by the Jews in Jerusalem or by the Samaritans on JMount Gerizim, the Savio. ur answered that he who would follow the Lord must lay aside all preference for particular places, and thus expresse d Him-self: " The hour is coming when neither in Jerusalem nor on this mountain shall the true worshippers worship-the Father. God is a Spirit, and they who worship Him must worship Him in spirit and in truth."- And observe how logically He has joined together the spirit and the truth: He called God a Spirit, that He might distinguish Him from bodies; and He named Him the truth, to distinguish Him from a shadow or an image. For they who worshipped in Jerusalem worshipped God neither in truth nor in spirit, being in subjection to the shadow or image of heavenly things; and such also was the case with those who worshipped on Mount Gerizim.

5. Having refuted, then, as well as we could, every notion which might suggest that we were to think of God as in any degree corporeal, we go on to say that, according to strict truth, God is incomprehensible, and incapable of being measured." For whatever be the knowledo; e which we are able to obtain of God, either by perception or reflection, we must of necessity believe that He is by many degrees far better than what we perceive Him to be. For, as if we were to see any one unable to bear a spark of light, or the flame of a very small lamp, and were desirous to acquaint such a one, whose vision could not admit a greater degree of 1 John iv. 20.- John iv. 23, 24. u Ingestimabilem."

liojht than what we have stated, with the brio; htness and splendour of the sun, would it not be necessary to tell him that the splendour of the sun was unspeakably and incalculably better and more glorious than all this light which he saw? So our understanding, when shut in by the fetters ' of flesh and blood, and rendered, on account of its participation in such material substances, duller and more obtuse, although, in comparison with our bodily nature, it is esteemed to be far superior, yet, in its efforts to examine and behold incorporeal things, scarcely holds the place of a spark or lamp. But among all intelligent, that is, incorporeal beings, what is so superior to all others so unspeakably and incalculably superior as God, whose nature cannot be grasped or seen by the power of any human understanding, even the purest and brightest?

6. But it will not appear absurd if we employ another similitude to make the matter clearer. Our eyes frequently cannot look upon the nature of the light itself that is, upon the substance of the sun; but when we behold his splendour or his rays pouring in, perhaps, through windows or some small openings to admit the light, we can reflect how great is the supply and source of the light of the body. So, in like manner, the works of Divine Providence and the plan of this whole world are a sort of rays, as it were, of the nature of God, in comparison with His real substance and being. As, therefore, our understanding is unable of itself to behold God Himself as He is, it

knows the Father of. the world from the beauty of His works and the comeliness)f His creatures. God, therefore, is not to be thought of as being either a body or as existing in a body, but as an un-compounded intellectual nature,- admitting within Himself no addition of any kind; so that He cannot be believed to have within Him a greater and a less, but is such that He is in all parts Mom?, and, so to speak, 'Evd, and is the mind and source from which all intellectual nature or mind takes its beginning. But mind, for its movements or operations, needs no physical space, nor sensible magnitude, nor bodily shape " Simplex intellectualis natura."

nor colour, nor any other of those adjuncts which are the properties of body or matter. Wherefore that simple and wholly intellectual nature can admit of no delay or hesitation in its movements or operations, lest the simplicity of the divine nature should appear to be circumscribed or in some degree hampered by such adjuncts, and lest that which is the beginning of all things should be found composite and differing, and that which ought to be free from all bodily intermixture, in virtue of being the one sole species of Deity, so to speak, should prove, instead of being one, to consist of many things. That mind, moreover, does not require space in order to carry on its movements agreeably to its nature, is certain from observation of our own mind. For if the mind abide within its own limits, and sustain no injury from any cause, it will never, from diversity of situation, be retarded in the discharge of its functions; nor, on the other hand, does it gain any addition or increase of mobility from the nature of particular places. And here, if any one were to object, for example, that among those who are at sea, and tossed by its waves, the mind is considerably less vigorous than it is wont to be on land, we are to believe that it is in this state, not from diversity of situation, but from the commotion or disturbance of the body to which the mind is joined or attached. For it seems to be contrary to nature, as it were, for a human body to live at sea; and for that reason it appears, by a sort of inequality of its own, to enter upon its mental operations in a slovenly and irregular manner, and to perform the acts of the intellect with a duller sense, in as m'eat degree as those who on land are prostrated with fever; with respect to whom it is certain, that if the mind do not discharge its functions as well as before, in consequence of the attack of disease, the blame is to be laid not upon the place, but upon the bodily malady, by which the body, being disturbed and disordered, renders to the mind its customary services under by no means the well-known and natural conditions: for we human beings are animals composed of a union of body and soul, and in this way only was it possible for us to live upon the earth. But God, "Natura ila simplex et tota mens."

who is the beginning of all things, is not to be regarded as a composite being, lest perchance there should be found to exist elements prior to the beginning itself, out of which everything is composed, whatever that be which is called composite. Neither does the mind require bodily magnitude in order to perform any act or movement; as when the eye by gazing upon bodies of larger size is dilated, but is compressed and contracted in order to see smaller objects. The mind, indeed, requires magnitude of an intellectual kind, because it grows, not after the fashion of a body, but after that of inteuigence. For the mind is not enlarged, together with the body, by means of corporal additions, up to the twentieth or thirtieth year of life; but the intellect is sharpened by exercises of learning, and the powers implanted within it for intelligent purposes are called forth; and it is rendered capable of greater intellectual efforts, not being increased by bodily additions, but carefully polished by learned exercises. But these it cannot receive immediately from boyhood, or from birth, because the framework of limbs which the mind employs as organs for exercising itself is weak and feeble; and it is unable to bear the weight of its own operations, or to exhibit a capacity for receiving training.

7. If there are any now who think that the mind itself and the soul is a body, I wish they would tell me by way of answer how it receives reasons and assertions on subjects of such importance of such difficulty and such subtlety? Whence does it derive the power of memory? and whence comes the contemplation of invisible things? How does the body possess the faculty of understanding incorporeal existences? How does a bodily nature investigate the processes of the various arts, and contemplate the reasons of things? How, also, is it able to perceive and understand divine truths, which are manifestly incorporeal? Unless, indeed, some should happen to be of opinion, that as the very bodily shape and form of the ears or eyes contributes something to hearing and to sight, and as the individual members, formed by God, have some adaptation, even from the very quality of their Some read " visible."

form, to the end for which they were naturally appointed; so also he may think that the shape of the soul or mind is to be understood as if created purposely and designedly for perceiving and understanding individual things, and for being set in motion by vital movements. I do not perceive, however, who shall be able to describe or state what is the colour of the mind, in respect of its being mind, and acting as an intelligent existence. Moreover, in confirmation and explanation of what we have already advanced regarding the mind or soul to the effect that it is better than the whole bodily nature the following remarks may be added. There underlies every bodily sense a certain peculiar sensible substance, on which the bodily sense exerts itself. For example, colours, form, size, underlie vision; voices and sound, the sense of hearing; odours, good or bad, that of smell; savours, that of taste; heat or cold, hardness or softness, roughness or smoothness, that of touch. Now, of those senses enumerated above, it is manifest to all that the sense of mind is much the best. How, then, should it not appear absurd, that under those senses which are inferior, substances should have been placed on which to exert their powers, but that under this power, which is far better than any other, i. e. the sense of mind, nothing at all of the nature of a substance should be placed, but that a power of an intellectual nature should be an accident, or consequent upon bodies? Those who assert this, doubtless do so to the disparagement of that better substance which is within them; nay, by so doing, they even do wrong to God Himself, when they imagine He may be understood by means of a bodily nature, so that according to their view He is a body, and that which may be understood or perceived by means of a body; and they are unwilling to have it understood that the mind bears a certain relationship to God, of whom the mind itself is an intellectual image, and that by means of this it may come to some knowledge of the nature of divinity, especially if it be purified and separated from bodily matter.

8. But perhaps these declarations may seem to have less " Substantia qusedam sensibilis propria."

weight with those who wish to be instructed in divine things out of the holy Scriptures, and who seek to have it proved to them from that source how the nature of God surpasses the nature of bodies. See, therefore, if the apostle does not say the same thing, when, speaking of Christ, he declares, that " He is the image of the invisible God, the first-born of every creature." Not, as some suppose, that the nature of God is visible to some and invisible to others: for the apostle does not say " the image of God invisible " to men or ' invisible" to sinners, but with unvarying constancy pronounces on the nature of God in these words: " the image of the invisible God." Moreover, John in his Gospel, when asserting that "no one hath seen God at any time," manifestly declares to all wdio are capable of understanding, that there is no nature to which God is visible: not as if He were a being who was visible by nature, and merely escaped or baffled the view of a frailer creature, but because by the nature of His being it is impossible for Him to be seen. And if you should ask of me what is my opinion regarding the Only-begotten Himself, whether the nature of God, which is naturally invisible, be not visible even to Him, let not such a question appear to you at once to be either absurd or impious, because we shall give you a logical reason. It is one thing to see, and another to know: to see and to be seen is a property of bodies; to know and to be known, an attribute of intellectual being. Whatever, therefore, is a property of bodies, cannot be predicated either of the Father or of the Son; but what belongs to the nature of deity is common to the Father and the Son. Finally, even He Himself, in the Gospel, did not say that no one has seen the Father, save the Son, nor any one the Son, save the Father; but His words are: " No one hiowetli the Son, save the Father; nor any one the Father, save the Son." By which it is clearly shown, that whatever among bodily natures is called seeing and being seen, is termed, between the Father and the Son, a knowing and being known, by means of the power of knowledge, not
1 Col. i. 15. 2 John i. 18.

s " Constat inter Patrem et Filium." Matt. xi. 27.

by (lie fiailness of the sense of sight. Because, then, neither see pg nor being seen can be properly applied to an incorporeal and invisible nature, neither is the Father, in the Gogpel, said to be seen by the Son, nor the Son by the Father, but the one is said to be known by the other.

9. Here, if any one lay before us the passage where it is said, "Blessed are the pure in heart, for they shall see God," from that very passage, in my opinion, will our position derive additional strength; for what else is seeing God in heart, but, according to our exposition as above, understanding and knowing Him wuth the mind? For the names of the organs of sense are frequently applied to the soul, so that it may be said to see with the eyes of the heart, i. e. to perform an intellectual act by means of the power of intelligence. So also it is said to hear with the ears when it perceives the deeper meaning of a statement. So also we say that it makes use of teeth, when it chews and eats the bread of life which cometli down from heaven. In like manner, also, it is said to employ the services of other members, which are transferred from their bodily appellations, and applied to the powers of the soul, according to the words of Solomon, "You will find a divine sense." For he knew that there were within us two kinds of senses: the one mortal, corruptible, human; the other immortal and intellectual, which he now termed divine. By this divine sense, therefore, not of the

eyes, but of a pure heart, which is the mind, God may be seen by those who are worthy. For you will certainly find in all the Scriptures, both old and new, the term " heart" repeatedly used instead of "mind," i. e. intellectual power. In this manner, therefore, although far below the dignity of the subject, have we spoken of the nature of God, as those who understand it under the limitation of the human understanding. In the next place, let us see what is meant by the name of Christ.

1 Matt. V. 8. 2 cf. Prov. ii. 5.

OEIG.

CHAPTER 11.

ON CHRIST.

1. In the first place, we must note that the nature of that deity which is in Christ in respect of His being the only-fee-gotten Son of God is one thing, and that human nature whicii He assumed in these last times for the purposes of the dispensation of grace is another. And therefore we have first to ascertain what the only-begotten Son of God is, seeing He is called by many different names, according to the circumstances and views of individuals. For He is termed Wisdom, according to the expression of Solomon: " The Lord created me the beginning of His ways, and among His works, before He made any other thing; He founded me before the ages. In the beginning, before He formed the earth, before He brought forth the fountains of waters, before the mountains were made strong, before all the hills. He brought me forth." He is also styled First-born, as the apostle has declared: "who is the first-born of every creature." The first-born, however, is not by nature a different person from the Wisdom, but one and the same. Finally, the Apostle Paul says that " Christ is the power of God and the wisdom of God."' 2. Let no one, however, imagine that we mean anything impersonal when we call Him the wisdom of God; or suppose, for example, that we understand Him to be, not a living being endowed w-ith wisdom, but something whicli makes men wise, giving itself to, and implanting itself in, the minds of those who are made capable of receiving His virtues and intelligence. If, then, it is once rightly understood that the only-begotten Son of God is His wisdom hypostatically existing, I know not whether our curiosity ought to advance beyond this, or entertain any suspicion that that viroatacri 1 Prov. viii. 22-25. The reading in the text differs considerably from that of the Vulgate.

2 Col. i. 15. " 1 Cor. i. 24.

Aliquid insubstantivum. Substantialiter.

bstantia contains anything of a bodily nature, since inching that is corporeal is distinguished either by form,-toiiour, or magnitude. And who in his sound senses ever ed i for form, or colour, or size, in wisdom, in respect of ial s' ' wisdom? And who that is capable of entertaining wcj j A de i thoughts or feelings regarding God, can suppose jcs j-rrecth ti t God the Father ever existed, even for a moment cj time, without havino; L enerated this Wisdom? For in that case he must say either that God was unable to generate Wisdom before He produced her, so that He afterwards called into being her who formerly did not exist, or that He possessed the power indeed, but what cannot be said of God without impiety was unwilling to use it; both of which suppositions, it is patent to all, are alike absurd and impious: for they amount to this, either that God advanced from a condition of inability to one of ability, or that, although possessed of the power, He concealed it, and delayed the generation of Wisdom. AVherefore we have always held that God is the Father of His only-begotten Son, wdio was born indeed of Him, and derives from Him what He is, but without any beginning, not only such as may be measured by any divisions of time, but even that which the mind alone can contemplate within itself, or behold, so to speak, with the naked powers of the understanding. And therefore we must believe that Wisdom was generated before any beginning that can be either comprehended or expressed. And since all the creative power of the coming creation was included in this very existence of Wisdom (whether of those things which have an original or of those which have a derived existence), having been formed beforehand and arranged by the power of foreknowledge; on account of these very creatures which had been described, as it were, and prefigured in Wisdom herself, does W isdom say, in the words of Solomon, that she was created the beginning of the ways of God, inasmuch as she contained within herself either the beginnings, or forms, or species of all creation.

Ad punctum alicujus momenti.

2 Omnis virtus ac deformatio futurse creaturcc.

3. Now, in tlie same way in which we have under i that Wisdom was the beginning of the ways of God, f said to be created, forming beforehand and containing yi herself the species and beginnings of all creatures, m I underslana h r. Ji)-bfilthe Woid o because of)f that closing to all other beings, i. e. to universal crea only-he-nature of the mysteries and secrets which are ire whicb within the divine wisdom; and on this account s'Of is called the Word, because she is, as it were, the interpreter of the secrets of the mind. And therefore that language which is found in the Acts of Paul where it is said that "here is the Word a living being," appears to me to be rightly used. John, however, with more sublimity and propriety, says in the beginning of his Gospel, when defining God by a special definition to be the Word, "And God was the Word," and this was in the beginning with God." Let him, then, who assigns a beginning to tlie Word oi Wisdom of Ood, take care that he be not guilty of impiety against the unbegotten Father Himself, seeing he denies that He had always been a Father, and had generated the Word, and had possessed wisdom in all preceding periods, whether they be called times or ages, or anything else that can be so entitled.

4. This Son, accordingly, is also the truth and life of all things which exist. And with reason. For how could those things which were created live, unless they derived their being from life? or how could those things Avhich are, truly exist, unless they came down from the truth? or how could rational beings exist, unless the Word or reason had previously existed? or how could they be wise, unless there were wdsdom? But since it was to come to pass that some also should fall away from life, and bring death upon themselves by their declension for death is nothing else than a 1 This work is mentioned by Eusebius, Hist. Eccles. B. iii. cb. iii. and XXV., as among the spurious writings current in the church. The Acts of Paid and Thecla was a different work from the Acts of Paul. The words quoted, "Hie est verbum animal vivens," seem to be a corruption from Heb. iv. 12, l au ycip 6 T oyog roll Qeou.

2 Or, " and the Word was God."

de "e from life and as it was not to follow that tliose be. hich had once been created by God for the enjoy- me life should utterly perish, it was necessary that, be death, there should be in existence such a power as wc X destroy the coming death, and that there should be a re. rrection, the type of which was in our Lord and Saviour, and that this resurrection should have its. ground in the wisdom and word and life of God. And then, in the next place, since some of those who were created were not to be always willing to remain unchangeable and unalterable in the calm and moderate enjoyment of the blessings which they possessed, but, in consequence of the good which was in them being theirs not by nature or essence, but by accident, were to be perverted and changed, and to fall away from their position, therefore was the Word and Wisdom of God made the Way. And it was so termed because it leads to the Father those who walk along it.

Whatever, therefore, we have predicated of the wisdom of God, will be appropriately applied and understood of the Bon of-God, ia virtue of His being the Life, and the Word, and the Truth, and the Eesurrection: for all these titles are derived from His power and operations, and in none of them is there the slightest ground for understanding anything of a corporeal nature which might seem to denote either size, or form, or colour; for those children of men which appear among us, or those descendants of other living beings, correspond to the seed of those by whom they were begotten, or derive from those mothers, in whose wombs they are formed and nourished, whatever that is, which they bring into this life, and carry with them when they are born. But it is monstrous and unlawful to compare God the Father, in the generation of His only-begotten Son, and in the sub-

"Quoniam hi qui videntur apud nos hominmn filii, vel ceterorum animaliiim, semini eoruni a quibus seminati sunt respondent, vel earum quarum in utero formantur ac nutriuntur, habent ex his quidquid ilhid est quod in lucem banc assumunt, ac deferunt processuri." Probably the last two words should be "deferunt processuris" " and hand it over to those who are destined to come forth from them," i. e. to their descendants.

stance- of the same, to any man or other living thing f xl in such an act; for we must of necessity hold that is something exceptional and worthy of God which c lot admit of any comparison at all, not merely in thin, t which cannot even be conceived by thought or disco. d by perception, so that a human mind should be able to ap e-hend how the unbecjotten God is made the Father of ihe only-begotten Son. Because His generation is as eternal and everlasting as the brilliancy which is produced from tljie sun. For it is not by receiving the breath of life that Hje is made a Son, by any outward act, but by His own nature.

5. Let us now ascertain how those statements which we have advanced are supported by the authority of holy Scripture. The Apostle Paul says, that the only-begotten Son is the " image of the invisible God," and " the first-born of every creature." And when writing to the Hebrews, he says of Him that He is " the brightness of His glory, and the express image of His person." Now, we find in the treatise called the Wisdom of Solomon the following description of the wisdom of God: " For she is the breath of the power of God, and the purest efflux of the glory of the Almighty."" Nothing that is polluted can therefore come upon her. For she is the splendour of the eternal light, and the stainless mirror of God's working, and the image of His goodness. Now we say, as before, that Widomjias her existence nowhere else save in Him who is the beginning

f all things: from whom also is derived everything that is wise, because He Himself is the only one who is by nature a Son, and is therefore termed the Only-begotten.

6. Let us now see how we are to understand the expression " invisible image," that we may in this way perceive how God is rightly called the Father of His Son; and let

Subsistentia. Some would read liere, " substantia."

2 Per adoptionem Spiritus. The original words here were probably dgtTo'nnaii rov 7rvsvf, c!, Tog and Rufinus seems to have mistaken the allusion to Gen. ii. 7. To " adoption," in the technical theological sense, tlio words in the text cannot have any reference. Schnitzee.

3 Col. i. 15. Heb. i. o. cl? r6ppo c:. Ykd. vii. 25.

us, in the first place, draw our conclusions from what are customarily called images among men. That is sometimes called an image which is painted or sculptured on some material substance, such as wood or stone; and sometimes a child is called the image of his parent, when the features of the child in no respect belie their resemblance to the father. I think, therefore, that that man who was formed after the image and likeness of God may be fittingly compared to the first illustration. Kespecting him, however, we shall see more precisely, God willing, when we come to expound the passage in Genesis. But the image of the Son of God, of whom we are now speaking, may be compared to the second of the above examples, even in respect of this, that He is the invisible image of the invisible God, in the same manner as we say, according to the sacred history, that the image of Adam is his son Seth. The words are, "And Adam begat Seth in his own likeness, and after his own image." Now this image contains the unity of nature and substance belonging to Father and Son. For if the Son do, in like manner, all those things which the Father doth, then, in virtue of the Son doing all things like the Father, is the image of the Father formed in the Son, who is born of Him, like an act of His will proceeding from the mind. And I am therefore of opinion that the will of the Father ought alone to be sufficient for the existence of that which He wlshes to exlst. For lll the exercise of Hls wlll He employs no other way than that which is made known by the counsel of His will. And thus also the existence" of the Son is generated by Him. For this point must above all others be maintained by those who allow nothing to be unbegotten, i. e. unborn, save God the Father only. And we must be careful not to fall into the absurdities of those who picture to themselves certain emanations, so as to divide the divine nature into parts, and vho divide God the Father as far as they can, since even to entertain the remotest suspicion of such a thing regardin r an incorporeal being is not only the height of impiety, but a mark of the greatest folly, it being most remote from any in-1 Gen. V. 3. 2 Subsistentia.

telligent conception that there should be any physical division of any incorporeal nature. Rather, therefore, as an act of the will proceeds from the understanding, and neither cuts off any part nor is separated or divided from it, so after some such fashion is the Father to be supposed as having begotten the Son, His own image; namely, so that, as He is Himself invisible by nature, He also begat an image that was invisible. For the Son is the Word, and therefore we are not to understand that anything in Him is cognisable by the senses. He is wisdom, and in wisdom there can be no suspicion of anything corporeal. He is the true light, which enlightens every man that cometh into this world; but He has nothing in common with the light of this sun. Our Saviour, therefore, is the image of the invisible God, inasmuch as compared with the Father Himself He is the truth: and as compared with us, to whom He reveals the Father, He is the image by which we come to the knowledge of the Father, whom no one knows save the Son, and he to whom the Son is pleased to reveal Him. And the method of revealing Him is through the understanding. For He by whom the Son Himself is understood, understands, as a consequence, the Father also, according to His own words: " He that hath seen me, hath seen the Father also."- 7. But since v e quoted the language of Paul regarding Christ, where he says of Him that He is " the brightness of the glory of God, and the express figure xdf his person," let us see what idea we are to form of this. According to John, "God is light." The only-begotten Son, therefore, is the glory of this light, proceeding inseparably from God Himself, as brightness does from light, and illuminating the whole of creation. For, agreeably to what we have already explained as to the manner in which He is the Way, and conducts to the Father; and in which He is the Word, interpreting the secrets of wisdom, and the mysteries of knowledge, making them known to the rational creation; and is also the Truth, and the Life, and the Eesurrection, in the same way ought we to understand also the meaning of 1 John xiv. 9. Heb. i. 3.

His being the brightness: for it is by its splendour tliat we understand and feel what light itself is. And this splendour, presenting itself gently and softly to the frail and weak eyes of mortals, and gradually training, as it were, and accustoming them to bear the brightness of the light, when it has put away from them every hindrance and obstruction to vision, according to the Lord's own precept, "Cast forth the beam out of thine eye," renders them capable of enduring the splendour of the light, being m. ade in this respect also a sort of mediator between men and the light.

8. But since He is called by the apostle not only the brightness of His glory, but also the express figure of His person or subsistence ' it does not seem idle to inquire how there can be said to be another figure of that person besides the person of God Himself, whatever be the meaning of person and subsistence. Consider, then, whether the Son of God, seeing He is His Word and Wisdom, and alone knows the Father, and reveals Him to whom He will i. e. to those vv'ho are capable of receiving His word and wisdom), may not, in regard of this very point of niaking God to be understood and acknowledged, be called the figure of His person and subsistence; that is, when that Wisdom, which desires to make known to others the means by which God is acknowledged and understood by them, describes Plimself first of all, it may by so doing be called the express figure of the person of God. In order, however, to arrive at a fuller understand-in of the manner in which the Saviour is the figure of the person or subsistence of God, let us take an instance, which, although it does not describe the subject of which we are treating either fully or appropriately, may nevertheless be seen to be employed for this purpose only, to show that the Son of God, who was in the form of God, divesting Himself of His glory, makes it His object, by this very divesting of Himself, to demonstrate to us the fulness of His deity. For instance, suppose that there were a statue of so enormous a size as to fill the whole world, and which on that account could be seen by no one; and that another statue were

Luke vi. 4,-2. Heb. i. 3. Substantise vel siifcsistentise.

formed altogether resembling it in the shape of the limbs, and in the features of the countenance, and in form and material, but without the same immensity of size, so that those who were unable to behold the one of enormous proportions, should, on seeing the latter, acknowledge that they had seen the former, because it preserved all the features of its limbs and countenance, and even the very form and material, so closely, as to be altogether undistinguishable from it; by some such similitude, the Son of God, divesting Himself of His equality with the Father, and showing to us the w ay to the knowdedge of Him, is made the express image of His person: so that we, who w ere unable to look upon the glory of that marvellous light when placed in the greatness of His Godhead, may, by His being made to us brightness, obtain the means of beholding the divine light by looking upon the brightness. This comparison, of course, of statues, as belonging to material things, is employed for no other purpose than to show that the Son of God, though placed in the very insignificant form of a human body, in consequence of the resemblance of His works and power to the Father, show ed that there was in Him an immense and invisible greatness, inasmuch as He said to His disciples, ' He who sees me, sees the Father also;" and, "I and the Father are one." And to these belong also the similar expression, "The Father is in me, and I in the Father."

9. Let us see now what is the meaning of the expression which is found in the Wisdom of Solomon, where it is said of Wisdom that " it is a kind of breath of the power of God, and the purest efflux of the glory of the Omnipotent, and the splendour of eternal light, and the spotless mirror of the w orking or power of God, and the image of His goodness." These, then, are tlie definitions which He gives of God, pointing out by each one of them certain attributes which belong to the Wisdom of God, calling wisdom the power, and the glory, and the everlasting light, and the working, and the goodness of God. He does not say, however, that wisdom is the breath of the glory of the Almighty, nor of 1 Wisd. vii. 25, 26.

tlie everlasting liglit, nor of the working of the Father, nor of IIis goodness, for it was not appropriate that breath should be ascribed to any one of these; but, with all propriety, ho says that wisdom is the breath of the power of God. Now, by the power of God is to be understood that by which He is strong; by which lie appoints, restrains, and governs all things visible and invisible; which is sufficient for all those things which He rules over in His providence; among all which He is present, as if one individual. And although the breath of all this mighty and immeasurable power, and the vigour itself produced, so to speak, by its own existence, proceed from the power itself, as the will does from the mind, yet even this will of God is nevertheless made to become the power of God.

Another power accordingly is produced, which exists with properties of its own, a kind of breath, as Scripture says, of the primal and unbegotten power of God, deriving from Him its "being, and never at any time non-existent. For if any one were to assert that it did not formerly exist, but came afterwards into existence, let him explain the reason why the Father, who gave it being, did not do so before. And if he shall grant that there was once a beginning, when that breath proceeded from the power of God, we shall ask him again, why not even before the beginning, which he has allowed; and in this way, ever demanding an earlier date, and going upwards with our interrogations, we shall arrive at this conclusion, that as God was always possessed of power and will, there never was any reason of propriety or otherwise, why He may not have always possessed that blessing which He desired. By which it is shown that that breath of God's power always existed, having no beginning save God Himself. Nor was it fitting that there should be any other beginning save God Himself, from whom it derives its birth. And according to the expression of the apostle, that Christ

"Hujus ergo totius virtutis tantse et tarn immensce vapor, et, iit ita dicam, vigor ipse in propria subsistentia effectus, quamvis ex ipsa virtuto velut voluntas ex mente procedat, tamen et ipsa vokiutas Dei nihilominiis Dei virtus efficitur."

"is the power of Gocl," it ought to be termed not only the breath of the power of God, but power out of power.

10. Let us now examine the expression, "Wisdom is the purest efflux of the glory of the Almighty;" and let us first consider what the glory of the omnipotent God is, and then we shall also understand what is its efflux. As no one can be a father without having a son, nor a master without possessing a servant, so even God cannot be called omnipotent unless there exist those over whom He may exercise His power; and therefore, that God may be shown to be almighty, it is necessary that all things should exist. For if any one would have some ages or portions of time, or whatever else he likes to call them, to have passed away, while those things which were afterwards made did not yet exist, he vrould undoubtedly show that during those ages or periods God was not omnipotent, but became so afterwards, viz. from the time that He began to have persons over whom to exercise power; and in this way He will appear to have received a certain-increase, and to have risen from a lower to a higher condition; since there can be no doubt that it is better for Him to be omnipotent than not to be so. And now how can it appear otherwise than absurd, that when God possessed none of those things which it was befitting for Him to possess, He should afterwards, by a kind of progress, come into the possession of them? But if there never was a time when He was not omnipotent, of necessity those things by which He receives that title must also exist; and He must always have had those over whom He exercised power, and which were governed by Him either as king or prince, of which we shall speak more fully in the proper place, when we come to discuss the subject of the creatures. But even now I think it necessary to drop a word, although cursorily, of warning, since the question before us is, how wisdom is the purest efflux of the glory of the Almighty, lest any one should think that the title of Omnipotent was anterior in God to the birth of Wisdom, through whom He is called Father, seeing that Wisdom, which is the Son of God, is the purest efflux of the 1 1 Cor. i. 24.

glory of-the Almighty. Let him who is inclined to entertain this suspicion hear the undoubted declaration of Scripture j ronouncing, "In wisdom hast Thou made them all," and the teaching of the gospel, that "by Him were all things made, and without Him nothing was made;"" and let him understand from this that the title of Omnipotent in God cannot be older than that of Father; for it is through the Son that the Father is almighty. But from the expression " glory of the Almighty," of which glory Wisdom is the efflux, this is to be understood, that Wisdom, through which God is called Omnipotent, has a share in the glory of the Almighty. For through Wisdom, which is Christ, God has power over all things, not only by the authority of a ruler, but also by the voluntary obedience of subjects. And that you may understand that the omnipotence of Father and Son is one and the same, as God and the Lord are one and the same with the Father, listen to the manner in which John speaks in the Apocalypse: " Thus saitli the Lord God, which is, and which was, and which is to come, the Almighty." For who else was "He which is to come" than Christ? And as no one ought to be offended, seeing God is the Father, that the Saviour is also God; so also, since the Father is called omnipotent, no one ought to be offended that the Son of God is also called omnipotent. For in this w-ay will that saying be true which He utters to the Father, "All mine are Thine, and Thine are mine, and I am glorified in them." Now, if all things wdiich are the Father's are also Christ's, certainly among those things which exist is the omnipotence of the Father; and doubtless the only-begotten Son ought to be omnipotent, that the Son also may have all things wdiich the Father possesses. "And I am glorified in them," He declares. For " at the name of Jesus every knee shall bow, of things in heaven, and things in earth, and things under the earth; and every tongue shall confess that the Lord Jesus is in the glory of God the Father." Therefore He is the efflux of the glory of God in this respect, that He is 1 Ps. civ. 24. 2 joiin i. 3. 3 Rev. i. g.

4 John xvii. 10. Phil. ii. 10, 11.

so ORIGEN BE PRINCIPIIS, Book r.

omnipotent the pure and limpid Wisdom herself glorified as the efflux of omnipotence or of glory. And that it may be more clearly understood what the glory of omnipotence is, we shall add the following. God the Father is omnipotent, because He has piower overfall things, i. e. over heaven and earth, sun, moon, and stars, and all things in them. And He exercises His power over them by means of His Word, because at the name of Jesus every knee shall bow, both of things in heaven, and things on earth, and things under the earth. And if every knee is bent to Jesus, then, without doubt, it is Jesus to whom all things are subject, and He it is who exercises powei ovei all diings, and through whom all things are subject to the Father; for through wisdom, i. e. by word and reason, not by force and necessity, are all things subject. And therefore His glory consists in this very thing, that He possesses all things, and this is the purest and most limpid glory of omnipotence, that by reason and wisdom, not by force and necessity, all things are subject. Now the purest and most limpid glory of wisdom is a convenient expression to distinguish it from that glory which cannot be called pure and sincere. But every nature which is convertible and changeable, although glorified in the works of righteousness or wisdom, yet by the fact that righteousness or wisdom are accidental qualities, and because that which is accidental, may also fall away, its glory cannot be called sincere and pure. But the Wisdom of God, which is His only-begotten Son, being in all respects incapable of change or alteration, and every good quality in Him being essential, and such as cannot be changed and converted. His glory is therefore declared to be pure and sincere.

11. In the third place, wisdom is called the splendour of eternal light. The force of this expression we have explained in the preceding pages, when we introduced the similitude of the sun and the splendour of its rays, and showed to the best of our power how this should be understood. To what we then said we shall add only the following

remark. That is properly termed everlasting or eternal which neither had a beginning of existence, nor can ever cease to be what it is.

And tills Is the idea conveyed by John vhen he says that "Godis Light." Now His wisdom is the splendour of that light, not only in respect of its being light, but also of being everlasting light, so that His wisdom is eternal and everlasting splendour. If this be fully understood, it clearly shows that the existence of the Son is derived from the Father, but not in time, nor from any other beginning, except, as we have said, from God Himself.

12. But wisdom is also called the stainless mirror of the ii epyeia or working of God. We must first understand, then, what the working of the power of God is. It is a sort of vigour, so to speak, by which God operates either in creation, or in providence, or in judgment, or in the disposal and arrancrement of individual thino; s, each in its season. For as the image formed in a mirror unerringly reflects all the acts and movements of him who gazes on it, so would Wisdom have herself to be understood when she is called the stainless mirror of the power and working of the Father: as the Lord Jesus Christ also, who is the Wisdom of God, declares of Himself when He says, "The works which the Father doeth, these also doeth the Son likewise." And again He says, that the Son cannot do anything of Himself, save what He sees the Father do. As therefore the Son in no respect differs from the Father in the power of His works, and the work of the Son is not a different thing from that of the Father, but one and the same movement, so to speak, is in all things. He therefore named Him a stainless mirror, that by such an expression it might be understood that there is no dissimilarity whatever between the Son and the Father. How, indeed, can those things which are said by some to be done after the manner in which a disciple resembles or imitates his master, or according to the view that those things are made by the Son in bodily material which were first formed by the Father in their spiritual essence, agree with the declarations of Scripture, seeing in the Gospel the Son is said to do not similar thinojs, but the same thincrs in a similar manner?

13. It remains that we inquire what is the " image of His 1 John V. 19.

goodness;" and here, I think, we must understand the same-thing which we expressed a httle ago, in speaking of the image formed by the mirror. For He is the primal goodness, doubtless, out of which the Son is born, who, being in all respects the image of the Father, may certainly also be called with propriety the image of His goodness. For there is no other second goodness existing in the Son, save that which is in the Father. And therefore also the Saviour Himself rightly says in the Gospel, "There is none good save one only, God the Father," that by such an expression it may be understood that the Son is not of a different goodness, but of that only which exists in the Father, of whom He is rightly termed the image, because He proceeds from no other source but from that primal goodness, lest there might appear to be in the Son a different goodness from that which is in the Father.) Nor is there any dissimilarity or difference of goodness in the Son. And therefore it is not to be imagined that there is a kind of blasphemy, as it were, in the words, "There is none good save one only, God the Father," as if thereby it may be supposed to be denied that either Christ or the Holy Spirit was good. But, as we have already said, the primal goodness is to be understood as residing in God the Father, from whom both the Son is born and the Holy Spirit proceeds, retaining within them, without any doubt, the nature of that goodness which is in the source whence they are derived. And if there be any other things which in Scripture are called good, whether angel, or man, or servant, or treasure, or a good heart, or a good tree, all these are so termed cata-chrestically, having in them an accidental, not an essential goodness. But it would require both much time and labour to collect together all the titles of the Son of God, such e. g. as the true light, or the door, or the righteousness, or the sanctification, or the redemption, and countless others; and to show for what reasons each one of them is so given. Satisfied, therefore, with what we have already advanced, we go on with our inquiries into those other matters which follow.

1 Abusive.

1. The next point is to investigate as briefly as possible the subject of the Holy Spirit. All who perceive, in whatever manner, the existence of Providence, confess that God, who created and disposed all things, is unbegotten, and recognise Him as the parent of the universe. Now, that to Him belongs a Son, is a statement not made by us only; although it may seem a sufficiently marvellous and incredible assertion to those who have a reputation as philosophers among Greeks and Barbarians, by some of whom, however, an idea of His existence seems to have been entertained, in their acknow-ledmno; that all things were created bv the word or reason of God. We, however, in conformity with our belief in that doctrine, which we assuredly hold to be divinely inspired, believe that it is possible in no other way to explain and bring-within the reach of human knowledge this higher and diviner reason as the Son of God, than by means of those Scriptures alone which were inspired by the Holy Spirit, i. e. the gospels and epistles, and the law and the prophets, according to the declaration of Christ Himself. Of the existence of the Holy Spirit no one indeed could entertain any suspicion, save those who were familiar w ith the law and the prophets, or those who profess a belief in Christ. For although no one is able to speak with certainty of God the Father, it is nevertheless possible for some knowledge of Him to be gained by means of the visible creation and the natural feelings of the human mind; and it is possible, moreover, for such knowledge to be confirmed from the sacred Scriptures. But with respect to the Son of God, although no one knoweth the Son save the Father, yet it is from sacred Scripture also that the human mind is taught how to think of the Son; and that not only from the New, but also from the Old Testament, by means of those things wdiich, although done by the saints, are figuratively referred to Christ, and from which both His divine

ORIG. C nature, and that human nature which was assumed by Him, may be discovered.

2. Now, what the Holy Spirit is, we are taught in many passages of Scripture, as by David in the fifty-first Psalm, when he says, "And take not Thy Holy Spirit from me;" and by Daniel, where it is said, "The Holy Spirit which is in thee." And in the New Testament we have abundant testimonies, as when the Holy Spirit is described as having descended upon Christ, and when the Lord breathed upon His apostles after His resurrection, saying, 'Receive the Holy Spirit;" and the saying of the angel to Mary, "The Holy Spirit will come upon thee;'" the declaration by Paul, that no one can call Jesus Lord, save by the Holy Spirit. In the Acts of the Apostles, the Holy

Spirit was given by the imposition of the apostles' hands in baptism. From all which wo learn that the person of the Holy Spirit was of such authority and dignity, that saving baptism was not complete except by the authority of the most excellent Trinity of them all, i. e. by the naming of Father, Son, and Holy Spirit, and by joining to the unbegotten God the Father, and to Plis only-begotten Son, the name also of the Holy Spirit. Who, then, is not amazed at the exceeding majesty of the Holy Spirit, when he hears that he who speaks a word against the Son of man may hope for forgiveness; but that he who is guilty of blasphemy against the Holy Spirit has not forgiveness, either in the present world or in that which is to come!

3. That all things were created by God, and that there is no creature which exists but has derived from Him its being, is established from many declarations of Scripture; those assertions being refuted and rejected which are falsely alleged by some respecting the existence either of a matter co-eternal with God, or of unbegotten souls, in which they w ould have it that God implanted not so much the power of existence, as equality and order. For even in that little treatise called The Pastor or Angel of Repentance, composed by Hermas, we 1 Ps. li. 11. 2 Dan. iv. 8.

3 John XX. 22. i j 35 5 1 Cqj., xii. 3.

c Acts viii. 18. " Cf. Matt. xii. o2 and Luke xii. 10.

have the following: ' First of all, believe that there is one God who created and arranged all things; who, when nothinj!; formerly existed, caused all things to be; who Himself contains all things, but Himself is contained by none." And in the book of Enoch also we have similar descriptions. But up to the present time we have been able to find no statement in holy Scripture in which the Holy Spirit could be said to be made or created," not even in the way in which we have shown above that the divine wisdom is spoken of by Solomon, or in which those expressions which we have discussed are to be understood of the life, or the word, or the other appellations of the Son of God. The Spirit of God, therefore, which was borne upon the waters, as is written in the beginning of the creation of the world, is, I am of opinion, no other than the Holy Spirit, so far as I can understand; as indeed we have shown in our exposition of the passages themselves, not according to the historical, but according to the spiritual method of interpretation.

4. Some indeed of our predecessors have observed, that in the New Testament, whenever the Spirit is named without that adjunct which denotes quality, the Holy Spirit is to be understood; as e. g. in the expression, "Now the fruit of the Spirit is love, joy, and peace;" and, ' Seeing ye began in the Spirit, are ye now made perfect in the flesh? " We are of opinion that this distinction may be observed in the Old Testament also, as when it is said, "He that giveth His Spirit to the people who are upon the earth, and Spirit to them who walk thereon."" For, without doubt, every one who walks upon the earth (i. e. earthly and corporeal beings) is a partaker also of the Holy Spirit, receiving it from God. My Hebrew master also used to say that those two seraphim in Isaiah, which are described as having each six wings, and calling to one another, and saying, "Holy, holy, holy is the Lord God of hosts," were to be understood of the only-begotten Son of God and of the Holy Spirit. And we

Cf. Hermx Past. Yis. v. Mandat. 12.

- Per quern Spiritus Sanctus factura esse vel creatura diceretiir.

2 Gal. V. 22. Gal. iu. 3. isa. xlii. 5. jga. vi. 3.

think that that expression also which occurs in the hymn of Habakkuk, "In the midst either of the two Hving things, or of the two Hves, Thou wilt be known," ought to be understood of Christ and of the Holy Spirit. For all knowledge of the Father is obtained by revelation of the Son through the Holy Spirit, so that both of these beings wdiich, according to the prophet, are called either " living things" or " lives," exist as the ground of the knowledge of God the Father. For as it is said of the Son, that " no one knoweth the Father but the Son, and he to whom the Son will reveal Him," the same also is said by the apostle of the Holy Spirit, wdien he declares, ' God hath revealed them to us by His Holy Spirit; for the Spirit searcheth all things, even the deep things of God;" and again in the Gospel, when the Saviour, speaking of the divine and profounder parts of His teaching, which His disciples were not yet able to receive,-thus addresses them: " I have yet many things to say unto you, but ye cannot bear them now; but when the Holy Spirit, the Comforter, is come. He will teach you all things, and will bring all things to your remembrance, w hatsoever I have said unto you." We must understand, therefore, that as the Son, who alone knows the Father, reveals Him to whom He will, so the Holy Spirit, who alone searches the deep things of God, reveals God to whom He will: " For the Spirit bloweth where He listeth." We are not, however, to suppose that the Spirit derives His knowledge through revelation from the Son. For if the Holy Spirit knows the Father through the Son's revelation. He passes from a state of ignorance into one of knowledge; but it is alike impious and foolish to confess the Holy Spirit, and yet to ascribe to Him ignorance. For even although something else existed before the Holy Spirit, it was not by progressive advancement that He came to be the Holy Spirit; as if any one should venture to say, that at the time when He w as not yet the Holy Spirit He w'as ignorant of the Father, but that after He had received knowledge He was made the Holy 1 Hab. iii. 2. 2 Luke x. 22. " 1 Cor. ii. 10.

4 Cf. Julm ʌvi. 12, 13, and ʌiv. 26. John iii. 8.

Chap, hi. ORIGEN BE PPJNCIPIIS.

Spirit. For if this were the case, the Holy Spirit would never be reckoned in the unity of the Trinity, i. e. along with the unchangeable Father and His Son, unless He had always been the Holy Spirit. When we use, indeed, such terms as " always" or " was," or any other designation of time, they are not to be taken absolutely, but with due allow ance; for while the significations of these words relate to time, and those subjects of w hich we speak are spoken of by a stretch of language as existing in time, they nevertheless surpass in their real nature all conception of the finite understanding.

5. Nevertheless it seems proper to inquire what is the reason why he who is regenerated by God unto salvation has to do both with Father and Son and Holy Spirit, and does not obtain salvation unless with the co-operation of the entire Trinity; and why it is impossible to become partaker of the Father or the Son without the Holy Spirit. And in discussing these subjects, it will undoubtedly be necessary to describe the special working of the Holy Spirit, and of the Father and the Son. I am of opinion, then, that the working of the Father and of the Son takes place as well in saints as in sinners, in rational beings and in dumb animals; nay, even in those things which are without life, and in all things universally which exist; but that the operation of

the Holy Spirit does not take place at all in those things which are without life, or in those which, although living, are yet dumb; nay, is not found even in those who are endued indeed with reason, but are engaged in evil courses, and not at all converted to a better life.- In those persons alone do I think that the operation of the Holy Spirit takes place, who are already turning to a better life, and walking along the way which leads to Jesus Christ, i. e. who are engaged in the performance of good actions, and who abide in God.

6. That the working of the Father and the Son operates both in'saints and in sinners, is manifest from this, that all who are rational beings are partakers of the word, i. e. of reason, and by this means bear certain seeds, implanted within them, of wisdom and justice, which is Christ. Now, in Him who truly exists, and wlio said by Moses,-1 am what I am," all tilings, whatever they are, participate; which participation in God the Father is shared both by just men and sinners, by rational and irrational beings, and by all things universally which exist. The Apostle Paul also shows truly that all have a share in Christ, wdien he saj s, "Say not in thine heart. Who shall ascend into heaven? (i. e. to bring Christ down from above;) or who shall descend into the deep? (that is, to bring up Christ again from the dead.) But what saith the Scripture? The word is nigh thee, even in thy mouth, and in thy heart." By which he means that Christ is in the heart of all, in respect of His being the word or reason, by participating in which they are rational beings. That declaration also in the Gospel, "If I had no t come and spoken unto them, they had not had sin; but now they have no excuse for their sin," renders it manifest and patent to all who have a rational knowled je of how Ion a; a time man is without sin, and from what period he is liable to it, how, by participating in the word or reason, men are said to have sinned, viz. from the time they are made capable of understanding and knowledge, when the reason implanted within has suggested to them the difference between good-and evil; and after they have already begun to know what evil is, they are made liable to sin, if they commit it. And this is the meaning of the expression, that "men have no excuse for their sin," viz. that, from the time the divine word or reason has begun to show them internally the difference between good and evil, they ought to avoid and guard against that which is wicked: " For to him who knoweth to do good, and doeth it not, to him it is sin." V Moreover, that all men are not without communion with God, is taught in the Gospel thus, by the Saviour's words: " The kingdom of God cometli not with observation; neither shall they say, Lo here! or, lo there I but the kingdom of God is within you." But here we must see whether this does not bear the same meaning with the expression in 1 Ex. iii. 14. 2 j ouj. x. 6-8. ' John xv. 22.

Jas. iv. 17. fi Luke xvii. 20, 21. '

Genesis: " And lie breathed into his face the breath of Hfo, and man became a living soul." For if this be understood, as applying generally to all men, then all men have a share X in God.

7. But if this is to be understood as spoken of the Spirit of God, since Adam also is found to have prophesied of some things, it may be taken not as of general application, but as confined to those who are saints. Finally, also, at the time of the flood, when all flesh had corrupted their way before God, it is recorded that God spoke thus, as of undeserving men and sinners: " My Spirit shall not abide with those

men for ever, because they are flesh."" By whicli it is clearly shown that the Spirit of God is taken away from all who are unworthy. In the Psalms also it is written: " Thou wilt take away their spirit, and they will die, and return to their earth. Thou wilt send forth Thy Spirit, and they shall be created, and Thou wilt renew the face of the earth;" which is manifestly intended of the Holy Spirit, who, after sinners and unworthy persons have been taken away and destroyed, creates for Himself a new people, and renews the face of the earth, when, laying aside, through the grace of the Spirit, the old man with his deeds, they begin to walk in newness of life. And therefore the expression is competently applied to the Holy Spirit, because He w ill take up His dw elling, not in all men, nor in those who are flesh, but in those wdiose land" has been renewed. Lastly, for this reason was the grace and revelation of the Holy Spirit bestowed by the imposition of the apostles' hands after baptism. Our Saviour also, after the resurrection, when old things had already passed away, and all things had become new". Himself a new man, and the first-born from the dead. His apostles also being renewed by faith in His resurrection, says, "Receive the Holy Spirit." This is doubtless what the Lord the Saviour meant to convey in the Gospel, when He said that new wine cannot be put into old bottles, but commanded that the bottles should be 1 Gen. ii. 7. 2 Qen. vi. 3. Vs. civ. 29, 30.

4 Terra. John xx. 22.

made new, i. e. that men should walk in newness of life, that they might receive the new wine, i. e. the newness of grace of the Holy Spirit. In this manner, then, is the working of the power of God the Father and of the Son extended without distinction to every creature; but a share in the Holy Spirit we find possessed only by the saints. And therefore it is said, "No man can say that Jesus is Lord, but by the Holy Ghost." And on one occasion, scarcely even the apostles themselves are deemed worthy to hear the words, "Ye shall receive the power of the Holy Ghost coming upon you." For this reason, also, I think it follows that he who has committed a sin against the Son of man is deserving of forgiveness; because if he who is a participator of the word or reason of God cease to live agreeably to reason, he seems to have fallen into a state of ignorance or folly, and therefore to deserve forgiveness; whereas he who has been deemed worthy to have a portion of the Holy Spirit, and who has relapsed, is, by this very act and work, said to be guilty of blasphemy against the Holy Spirit. Let no one indeed suppose that we, from having said that the Holy Spirit is conferred upon the saints alone, but that the benefits or operations of the Father and of the Son extend to good and bad, to just and unjust, by so doing give a preference to the Holy Spirit over the Father and the Son, or assert that His dignity is greater, which certainly would be a very illogical conclusion. For it is the peculiarity of His grace and operations that we have been describing. Moreover, nothing in the Trinity can be called greater or less, since the fountain of divinity alone contains all things by His word and reason, and by the Spirit of His mouth sanctifies all things which are worthy of sanctification, as it is written in the Psalm: " By the word of the Lord were the heavens strengthened, and all their power by the Spirit of His mouth." There is also a special working of God the Father, besides that by which He bestowed upon all things the gift of natural life. There is also a special ministry of the Lord Jesus Christ to those upon whom He confers by nature the 1 1 Cor. xii. 3. 2 cts i. 8. pg, xxxiii. 6.

gift of reason, by means of wliich they are enabled to be rightly what they are. There is also another grace of the Holy Spirit, which is bestowed npon the deserving, through the ministry of Christ and the working of the Father, in proportion to the merits of those who are rendered capable of receiving it. This is most clearly pointed out by the Apostle Paul, when demonstrating that the power of the Trinity is one and the same, in the words, "There are diversities of gifts, but the same Spirit; there are diversities of administrations, but the same Lord; and there are diversities of operations, but it is the same God who worketh all in all. But the manifestation of the Spirit is given to every man to profit withal." From which it most clearly follows that there is no difference in the Trinity, but that which is called the gift of the Spirit is made known through the Son, and operated by God the Father. " But all these worketh that one and the self-same Spirit, dividing to every one severally as He will."

8. Having made these declarations regarding the unity of the Father, and of the Son, and of the Holy Spirit, let us return to the order in which we began the discussion. God the Father bestows upon all, existence; and participation in Christ, in respect of His being the word of reason, renders them rational beings. From which it follows that they are deserving either of praise or blame, because capable of. virtue and vice. On this account, therefore, is the grace of the Holy Ghost present, that those beings which are not holy in their essence may be rendered holy by participating in it. Seeing, then, that firstly, they derive their existence from God the Father; second!, their rational nature from the Word; thirdly, their holiness from the Holy Spirit, those who have been previously sanctified by the Holy Spirit are again made capable of receiving Christ, in respect that He is the righteousness of God; and those who have earned advancement to this grade by the sanctification of the Holy Spirit, will nevertheless obtain the gift of wisdom according to the power and working of the Spirit of God. And this I 1 1 Cor. xii. 4-7. 2 1 Cor. xii. 11.

consider is Paul's meaning, when he says that to " some is given the word of wisdom, to others the word of knowledge, according to the same Spirit." And while pointing out the individual distinction of gifts, he refers the whole of them to the source of all things in the words, "There are diversities of operations, but one God who worketh all in all." Whence also the working of the Father, which confers existence upon all things, is found to be more glorious and magnificent, wdiile each one, by participation in Christ, as being wisdom, and knowledge, and sanctification, makes progress, and advances to higher degrees of perfection; and seeing it is by partaking of the Holy Spirit that any one is made purer and holier, he obtains, when he is made worthy, the grace of wisdom and knowledge, in order that, after all stains of pollution and ignorance are cleansed and taken away, he may make so great an advance in holiness and purity, that-the nature which he received from God may become such as is worthy of Him who gave it to be pure and perfect, so that the being which exists may be as worthy as He who called it into existence. For, in this way, he who is such as his Creator wished him to be, will receive from God power always to exist, and to abide for ever. That this may be the case, and that those whom He has created may be unceasingly and inseparably present with Him, who IS, it is the business of wisdom to instruct and train them, and to bring them to perfection by confirmation of His Holy Spirit and unceasing sanctification, by which alone are they capable of receiving God.

In this way, then, by the renewal of the ceaseless working of Father, Son, and Holy Spirit in us, in its various stages of progress, shall we be able at some future time perhaps, although with difiiculty, to behold the holy and the blessed life, in which (as it is only after many struggles that we are able to reach it) we ought so to continue, that no satiety of that blessedness should ever seize us; but the more we perceive its blessedness, the more should be increased and intensified within us the longing for the same, while we ever more eagerly and freely receive and hold fast the 1 Cor. xii. 6.

Father, and the Son, and the Holy Spirit. But if satiety should ever take hold of any one of those who stand on the hio-hest and perfect summit of attainment, I do not think that such an one would suddenly be deposed from his position and fall away, but that he must decline gradually and little by little, so that it may sometimes happen that if a brief lapsus take place, and the individual quickly repent and return to himself, he may not utterly fall away, but may retrace liis steps, and return to his former place, and again make good that which had been lost by his negligence.

CHAPTEK ly.

ON DEFECTION, OR FALLING AWAY.

1. To exhibit the nature of defection or falling away, on the part of those who conduct themselves carelessly, it will not appear out of place to employ a similitude by way of illustration. Suppose, then, the case of one who had become gradually acquainted with the art or science, say of geometry or medicine, until he had reached perfection, having trained himself for a lengthened time in its principles and practice, so as to attain a complete mastery over the art: to such an one it could never happen, that, when he lay down to sleep in the possession of his skill, he should awake in a state of ignorance. It is not our purpose to adduce or to notice here those accidents which are occasioned by any injury or weakness, for they do not apply to our present illustration. According to our point of view, then, so long as that geometer or physician continues to exercise himself in the study of his art and in the practice of its principles, the knowledge of his profession abides with him; but if he withdraw from its practice, and lay aside his habits of industry, then, by his neglect, at first a few things will gradually escape him, then by and by more and more, until in course of time everything will be forgotten, and be completely effaced from the memory. It is possible, indeed, that when he has first begun to fall away, and to yield to the corrupting influence of a negligence which is small as yet, he may, if he be aroused and return speedily to his senses, repair those losses which up to that time are only recent, and recover that knowledge which hitherto had been only slightly obliterated from his mind. Let us apply this now to the case of those who have devoted themselves to the knowledge and wisdom of God, whose learning and diligence incomparably surpass all other training; and let us contemplate, according to the form of the similitude employed, what is the acquisition of knowledge, or what is its disappearance, especially when we hear from the apostle what is said of those who are perfect, that they shall behold face to face the glory of the Lord in the revelation of His mysteries.

2. But in our desire to show the divine benefits bestowed upon us by Father, Son, and Holy Spirit, which Trinity is the fountain of all holiness, we have fallen, in what we have said, into a digression, having considered that the subject of the soul, which

accidentally came before us, should be touched on, although cursorily, seeing we were discussing a cognate topic relating to our rational nature. We shall, however, with the permission of God through Jesus Christ and the Holy Spirit, more conveniently consider in the proper place the subject of all rational beings, which are distinguished into three genera and species.

CHAPTER V.

ON EATIONAL NATUEES.

1. After the dissertation, which we have briefly conducted to the best of our ability, regarding the Father, Son, and Holy Spirit, it follows that we offer a few remarks upon the subject of rational natures, and on their species and orders, or on the offices as well of holy as of malignant powers, and also on those which occupy an intermediate position between these good and evil powers, and as yet are placed in a state of struggle and trial. For we find in holy Scripture numerous names of certain orders and offices, not only of holy beings, but also of those of an opposite description, which we shall bring before us, in the first place; and the meaning of which we shall endeavour, in the second place, to the best of our ability, to ascertain. There are certain holy angels of God whom Paul terms " ministering spirits, sent forth to minister for them who shall be heirs of salvation." In the writincrs also of St. Paul himself we find him designating them, from some unknown source, as thrones, and dominions, and principalities, and powers; and after this enumeration, as if knowing that there were still other rational offices" and orders besides those which he had named, he says of the Saviour: "Who is above all principality, and power, and might, and dominion, and every name that is named, not only in this world, but also in that which is to come."" From which he shows that there were certain beings besides those which he had mentioned, which may be named indeed in this world, but were not now enumerated by him, and perhaps were not known by any other individual; and that there were others which may not be named in this world, but will be named in the world to come.

2. Then, in the next place, we must know that every being which is endowed with reason, and transgresses its statutes and limitations, is undoubtedly involved in sin by swerving from rectitude and justice. Every rational creature, therefore, is capable of earning praise and censure: of praise, if, in conformity to that reason which he possesses, he advance to better things; of censure, if he fall away from the plan and course of rectitude, for which reason he is justly liable to pains and penalties. And this also is to be held as applying to the devil himself, and those who are with him, and are called his angels. Xow the titles of these beings have to be explained, that we may know what they are of whom we have to speak. The name, then, of Devil, and Satan, and Wicked One, who is also described as Enemy of God, is mentioned in many passages of Scripture. Moreover, certain angels of the devil are mentioned, and also a prince of this 1 Heb. i. 14.- Officia. 3 Ep, j. 21.

world, who, whether the devil himself or some one else, is not yet clearly manifest. There are also certain princes of this world spoken of as possessing a kind of wisdom which will come to nought; but whether these are those princes who are also the principalities with whom we have to wrestle, or other beings, seems to me a point on which it is not easy for any one to pronounce. After the principalities, certain powers also are named with whom we have to wrestle, and carry on a struggle even against the princes of this world and the rulers of this darkness. Certain spiritual powers of wickedness also, in heavenly places, are spoken of by Paul himself. What, moreover, are we to say of those wicked and unclean spirits mentioned in the gospel? Then we have certain heavenly beings called by a similar name, but which are said to bend the knee, or to be about to bend the knee, at the name of Jesus; nay, even things on earth and things under the earth, which Paul enumerates in order. And certainly, in a place where we have been discussing the subject of rational natures, it is not proper to be silent regarding ourselves, who are human beings, and are called rational animals; nay, even this point is not to be idly passed over, that even of us human beings certain different orders are mentioned in the words, ' The portion of the Lord is His people Jacob; Israel is the cord of His inheritance." Other nations, moreover, are called a part of the angels; since "when the Most High divided the nations, and dispersed the sons of Adam, He fixed the boundaries of the nations according to the number of the angels of God." " And therefore, with other rational natures, we must also thoroughly examine the reason of the human soul.

3. After the enumeration, then, of so many and so important names of orders and offices, underlying which it is certain that there are personal existences, let us inquire whether God, the creator and founder of all things, created certain of them holy and happy, so that they could admit no element at all of an opposite kind, and certain others so that they were made 1 Deut. xxxii. 9.

"Deut. xxxii. 8. The Scptuagint here differs from the Masoretic text.

capable both of virtue and vice; or whether we are to suppose that He created some so as to be altogether incapable of virtue, and others again altogether incapable of wickedness, but with the power of abiding only in a state of happiness, and others again such as to be capable of either condition. In order, now, that our first inquiry may begin with the names themselves, let us consider whether the holy angels, from the period of their first existence, have always been holy, and are holy still, and will be holy, and have never either admitted or had the power to admit any occasion of sin. Then in the next place, let us consider whether those who are called holy principalities began from the moment of their creation by God to exercise power over some who were made subject to them, and whether these latter were created of such a nature, and formed for the very purpose of being subject and subordinate. In like manner, also, whether those which are called powers were created of such a nature and for the express purpose of exercising power, or wdiether their arriving at that power and dignity is a reward and desert of their virtue. Moreover, also, whether those which are called thrones or seats gained that stability of happiness at the same time with their coming forth into being,- so as to have that possession from the will of the Creator alone; or whether those which are called dominions had their dominion conferred on them, not as a reward for their proficiency, but as the peculiar privilege of their creation, so that it is something which is in a certain degree inseparable from them, and natural. Now, if we adopt the view that the holy angels, and the holy powers, and the blessed seats, and the glorious virtues, and the magnificent dominions, are to be regarded as possessing those powers and dignities and glories in virtue of their nature, it will doubtless appear to follow that those beinf s which have been mentioned as holding offices of an opposite kind must be regarded in the same manner; so that those principalities with whom we have 1 Simul cum siibstantise siise prolatione at tlie same time with the emanation of their substance.- Conditionis prserogativa, Substantialiier.

to struggle are to be viewed, not as liavlng received that spirit of opposition and resistance to all good at a later period, or as falling away from good through the freedom of the will, but as having had it in themselves as the essence of their being from the beginning of their existence. In like manner also will it be the case with the powers and virtues, in none of which was wickedness subsequent or posterior to their first existence. Those also whom the apostle termed rulers and princes of the darkness of this world, are said, with respect to their rule and occupation of darkness, to-fall not frprnj er-verslty of intention, but from the necessity of their creation. Logical reasoning will compel us to take the same view with regard to wicked and malignant spirits and unclean demons. But if to entertain this view regarding malignant and opposing powers seem to be absurd, as it is certainly absurd that the cause of their wickedness should be removed from the purpose of their own will, and ascribed of necessity to their Creator, why should we not also be obliged to make a similar confession regarding the good and holy powers, that, viz., the good which is in them is not theirs by essential being, which we have manifestly shown to be the case with Christ and the Holy Spirit alone, as undoubtedly with the Father also? For it was proved that there was nothing compound in the nature of the Trinity, so that these qualities might seem to belong to it as accidental consequences. From which it follows, that in the case of every creature it is a result of his own works and movements, that those powers which appear either to hold sway over others or to exercise power or dominion, have been preferred to and placed over those whom they are said to govern or exercise power over, and not in consequence of a peculiar privilege inherent in their constitutions, but on account of merit.

4. But that we may not appear to build our assertions on subjects of such importance and difficulty on the ground of inference alone, or to require the assent of our hearers to Avhat is only conjectural, let us see whether we can obtain any declarations from holy Scripture, by the authority of which these positions may be more credibly maintained. And, firstly, we shall adduce what holy Scripture contains regarding wicked powers; we shall next continue our investigation with reo-ard to the others, as the Lord shall be pleased to enhghten us, that in matters of such difficulty wo may ascertain what is nearest to the truth, or what ought to be our opinions agreeably to the standard of religion. Now we find in the prophet Ezekiel two prophecies written to the prince of Tyre, the former of which might appear to any one, before he heard the second also, to be spoken of some man who was prince of the Tyrians. In the meantime, therefore, we shall take nothing from that first prophecy; but as the second is manifestly of such a kind as cannot be at all understood of a man, but of some superior power which had fallen away from a higher position, and had been reduced to a lower and worse condition, we shall from it take an illustration, by which it may be demonstrated with the utmost clearness, that those opposing and malignant powers were not formed or created so by nature, but fell from a better to a worse position, and were converted into wicked beings; that those blessed powers also were not of such a nature as to be unable to admit what was opposed to them if they were so inclined and became negligent, and did not guard most carefully the blcsscdness of their condition. For

if it is related that he who is called the prince of Tyre was am. ongst the saints, and was without stain, and was placed in the paradise of God, and adorned also with a crown of comeliness and beauty, is it to be supposed that such an one could be in any degree inferior to any of the saints? For he is described as having been adorned with a crown of comeliness and beauty, and as having walked stainless in the paradise of God: and how can any one suppose that such a being was not one of those holy and blessed powers which, as being placed in a state of happiness, we must believe to be endowed with no other honour than this? But let us see what we are taught by the words of the prophecy themselves. " The word of the Lord," says the prophet, " came to me, saying. Son of man, take up a lamentation over the prince of Tyre, and say to him. Thus saith the Lord God, Thou hast been orjg. D the seal of a similitude, and a crown of comeliness amono-the delights of paradise; thou wert adorned with every good stone or gem, and wert clothed with sardonyx, and topaz, and emerald, and carbuncle, and sapphire, and jasper, set in gold and silver, and with agate, amethyst, and chrysolite, and beryl, and onyx: with gold also didst thou fill thy treasures, and thy storehouses within thee. From the day when thou wert created along wdth the cherubim, I placed thee in the holy mount of God. Thou wert in the midst of the fiery stones: thou wert stainless in thy days, from the day when thou wert created, until iniquities were found in thee: from the greatness of thy trade, thou didst fill thy storehouses with iniquity, and didst sin, and wert wounded from the mount of God. And a cherub drove thee forth from the midst of the burning stones; and thy heart was elated because of thy comeliness, thy dlscq lina was corrupted along with thy beauty: on account of the multitude of thy sins, I cast thee forth to the earth before kings; I gave thee for a show and a mockery on account of the multitude of thy sins, and of thine iniquities: because of thy trade thou hast polluted thy holy places. And I shall bring forth fire from the midst of thee, and it shall devour thee, and I shall give thee for ashes and cinders on the earth in the sight of all who see thee: and all who know thee among the nations shall mourn over thee. Thou hast been made destruction, and thou shalt exist no longer for ever." Seeing, then, that sr. ch are the words of the prophet, who is there that on hearing, "Thou wert a seal of a similitude, and a crown of comeliness among the delights of paradise," or that " From the day when thou wert created with the cherubim, I placed thee in the holy mount of God," can so enfeeble the meaning as to suppose that this language is used of some man or saint, not to say the prince of Tyre? Or what fiery stones can he imagine in the midst of which any man could live? Or who could be supposed to be stainless from the very day of his creation, and wickedness being afterwards discovered in him, it be said of him then that he was cast i Ezek. xxviii. 11-19.

forth upon the earth? For the meaning of this is, that He Yho was not yet on the earth is said to be cast forth upon it: Avhose holy places also are said to be polluted. We have shown, then, that what we have quoted regarding the prince of Tyre from the prophet Ezekiel refers to an adverse power, and by it it is most clearly proved that that power was formerly holy and happy; from which state of happiness it fell from the time that iniquity was found in it, and was hurled to the earth, and was not such by nature and creation. We are of opinion, therefore, that these words are spoken of a certain angel who had received the office of governing the nation of the Tyrians, and to whom also their souls had been entrusted to be taken care of. But what Tyre, or what souls of Tyrians, Ave ought to understand, whether that Tyre which is situated within the boundaries of the province of Phoenicia, or some other of which this one which we know on earth is the model; and the souls of the Tyrians, whether they are those of the former or those wdiicli belong to that Tyre which is spiritually understood, does not seem to be a matter requiring examination in this place; lest perhaps we should appear to investigate subjects of so much mystery and importance in a cursory manner, whereas tliey demand a labour and work of their own.

5. Again, we are taught as follows by the prophet Isaiali regarding another opposing power. The prophet says, "Plow is Lucifer, who used to arise in the morning, fallen from heaven! He who assailed all nations is broken and beaten to the ground. Thou indeed saidst in thy heart, I shall ascend into heaven; above the stars of heaven shall I place my throne; I shall sit upon a lofty mountain, above the lofty mountains which are towards the north; I shall ascend above the clouds; I shall be like the Most High. Now shalt thou be brought down to the lower world, and to the foundations of the earth. They who see thee shall be amazed at thee, and shall say. This is the man who harassed the whole earth, who moved kings, who made the whole world a desert, who destroyed cities, and did not unloose those who were in chains. All the kings of the nations have slept in honour, every one in his own house; but thou shalt be cast forth on the mountains, accursed with the many dead who have been pierced through with swords, and have descended to the lower world. As a garment clotted with blood, and stained, will not be clean; neither shalt thou be clean, because thou hast destroyed my land and slain my people: thou shalt not remain for ever, most wicked seed. Prepare thy sons for death on account of the sins of thy father, lest they rise again and inherit the earth, and fill the earth with wars. And I shall rise against them, saith the Lord of hosts, and I shall cause their name to perish, and their remains, and their seed." Most evidently by these words is he shown to have fallen from heaven, who formerly was Lucifer, and who used to arise in the morning. For if, as some think, he was a nature of darkness, how is Lucifer said to have existed before? Or how could he arise in the morning, who had in himself nothing of the light? Nay, even the Saviour Himself teaches us, saying of the devil, "Behold, I see Satan fallen from heaven like lightning." For at one time he was light. Moreover our Lord, who is the truth, compared the power of His own glorious advent to lightning, in the words, "' For as the lightning shineth from the height of heaven even to its height again, so will the coming of the Son of man be." And notwithstanding He compares him to lightning, and says that he fell from heaven, that He might show by this that he had been at one time in heaven, and had had a place among the saints, and had enjoyed a share in that light in which all the saints participate, by which they are made angels of light, and by which the apostles are termed by the Lord the light of the world. Li this manner, then, did that being once exist as light before he went astray, and fell to this place, and had his glory turned into dust, which is peculiarly the mark of the wicked, as the prophet also says; whence, too, he was called the prince of this world, i. e. of an earthly habitation: for he exercised power over those who were obedient to his wickedness, since "the whole of this world" for I term this place of earth, world " lieth in the wicked one," and in this apostate. That he is an 1 Isa. xiv. 12-22, 2 1 j. 18. Matt. xxiv. 27. 1 John v. 19.

apostate, i. e. a fugitive, even the Lord in the book of Job says, Thou wilt take with a hook the apostate dragon," i. e. a fugitive. Now it is certain that by the dragon is understood the devil himself. If then they are called opposing powers, and are said to have been once without stain, while spotless purity exists in the essential being of none save the Father, Son, and Holy Spirit, but is an accidental quality in every created thing; and since that which is accidental may also fall away, and since those opposite powers once were spotless, and v-ere once among those which still remain unstained, it is evident from all this that no one is pure either by essence V or nature, and that no one was by nature polluted. And the consequence of this is, that it lies within ourselves and in our own actions to possess either happiness or holiness; or by sloth and negligence to fall from happiness into wickedness and ruin, to such a degree that, through too great proficiency, so to speak, in wickedness (if a man be guilty of so great neglect), he may descend even to that state in which he will be changed into what is called an " opposing power."

CHAPTER VL ox THE END OR CONSUMIMATION.

1. An end or consummation would seem to be an indication of the perfection and completion of things. And this reminds us here, that if there be any one imbued with a desire of reading and understanding subjects of such difficulty and importance, he ought to bring to the effort a perfect and instructed understanding, lest perhaps, if he has had no experience in questions of this kind, they may appear to him as vain and superfluous; or if his mind be full of preconceptions and prejudices on other points, he may judge these to be heretical and opposed to the faith of the church, yielding in so doing not so much to the convictions of reason as to the dogmatism of prejudice. These subjects, indeed, are treated bv us with great solicitude and caution, in the manner rather of an investigation and discussion, than in that of fixed and certain decision. For we have pointed out in the preceding pages those questions which must be set forth in clear dogmatic propositions, as I think lias been done to the best of my ability when speaking of the Trinity. But on the present occasion our exercise is to be conducted, as we best may, in the style of a disputation rather than of strict definition.

The end of the world, then, and the final consummation, will take place when every one shall be subjected to punishment for his sins; a time which God alone knows, when He will bestow on each one what he deserves. We think, indeed, that the goodness of God, through His Christ, may recall all His creatures to one end, even His enemies being conquered and subdued. For thus says holy Scripture, "The Lord said to my Lord, Sit Thou at my right hand, until I make Thine enemies Thy footstool." And if the meaning of the prophet's language here be less clear, we may ascertain it from the Apostle Paul, who speaks more openly, thus: " For Christ must reign until He has put all enemies under His feet." But if even that unreserved declaration of the apostle do not sufficiently inform us what is meant by " enemies being placed under His feet," listen to what he says in the following words, "For all things must be put under Him." What, then, is this "putting under" by which all things must be made subject to Christ? I am of opinion that it is this very subjection by which we also wisli to be subject to Him, by which the apostles also were subject, and all the saints who have been followers of Christ. For the name " subjection," by which we are subject to Christ, indicates that the salvation which proceeds from Him belongs to His subjects, agreeably to the declaration of David, "Shall not my soul be subject unto God? From Him cometh my salvation."

2. Seeing, then, that such is the end, when all enemies will be subdued to Christ, when death the last enemy shall be destroyed, and when the kingdom shall be delivered up by Christ (to whom all things are subject) to God the 1 Ps. ex. 1. 2 1 Cor. XY. 25. " Ps. Ixii. 1.

Father; let us, I say, from such an end as this, contemplate the beginnings of things. For the encus, always like the beginning: and, therefore, as there is one end to all things, ought we to understand that there was one beginning; and as there is one end to many things, so there spring from one beginning many differences and varieties, which again, through the goodness of God, and by subjection to Christ, and through the unity of the Holy Spirit, are recalled to one end, which is like unto the beginning: all those, viz., who, bending the knee at the name of Jesus, make known by so doing their subjection to Him: and these are they who are in heaven, on earth, and under the earth: by which three classes the whole universe of things is pointed out, those, viz., who from that one beginning were arranged, each according to the diversity of his conduct, among the different orders, in accordance with their desert; for there was no goodness in them by essential beingj as in God and His Christ, and in the Holy Spirit. For in the Trinity alone, which is the author of all things, does goodness exist in virtue of essential being; while others possess it as an accidental and perishable quality, and only then enjoy blessedness, when they participate in holiness and wisdom, and in divinity itself. But if they neglect and despise such participation, then is each one, by fault of his own slothfulness, made, one more rapidly, another more slowly, one in a greater, another in a less degree, the cause of his own downfall. And since, as we have remarked, the lapse by which an individual falls away from his position is characterized by great diversity, according to the movements of the mind and will, one man falling with greater ease, another with more difficulty, into a lower condition; in this is to be seen the just judgment of the providence of God, that it should happen to every one according to the diversity of his conduct, in proportion to the desert of his declension and defection. Certain of those, indeed, who remained in that beginning which we have described as resembling the end which is to come, obtained, in the ordering and arrangement of the world, the rank of angels; others that of influences, others of principali- ties, others of powers, that they may exercise power over those who need to have power upon their head. Others, again, received the rank of thrones, having the office of judging or ruling those who require this; others dominion, doubtless, over slaves; all of which are conferred by Divine Providence in just and impartial judgment according to their merits, and to the progress which they had made in the participation and imitation of God. But those who have been removed from their primal state of blessedness have not been removed irrecoverably, but have been placed under the rule of those holy and blessed orders which we have described; and by availing themselves of the aid of these, and being remoulded by salutary principles and discipline, they may recover themselves, and be restored to their condition of happiness. From all which I am of opinion, so far as I can see, that this order of the human race has been appointed in order that in the future world, or in ages to fcome, when there shall be the new heavens and new earth, spoken of by

Isaiah, it may be restored to that unity promised by the Lord Jesus in His prayer to God the Father on behalf of His disciples: " I do not pray for these alone, but for all who shall believe on me through their word: that they all may be one, as Thou, Father, art in me, and I in Thee, that they also may be one in us;" and again, when He says: " That they may be one, even as we are one; I in them, and Thou in me, that they may be made perfect in one." And this is further confirmed by the language of the Apostle Paul: " Until we all come in the unity of the faith to a perfect man, to the measure of the stature of the fulness of Christ." And in keeping with this is the declaration of the same apostle, when he exhorts us, who even in the present life are placed in the church, in which is the form of that kingdom which is to come, to this same similitude of unity: " That ye all speak the same thing, and that there be no divisions among you; but that ye be perfectly joined together in the same mind and in the same judgment."

John xvii. 20, 21. 2 John xvii. 22, 23.

3 Eph. iv. 13. 1 Cor. i. 10.

3. It is to be borne in mind, however, that certain beings who fell away from that one beginning of which we have spoken, have sunk to such a depth of nnworthiness and wickedness as to be deemed altogether undeserving of that training and instruction by which the human race, while in the flesh, are trained and instructed with the assistance of the heavenly powders; and continue, on the contrary, in a state of enmity and opposition to those who are receiving this instruction and teaching. And hence it is that the whole of this mortal life is full of struggles and trials, caused by the opposition and enmity of those who fell from a better condition without at all looking back, and who are called the devil and his angels, and the other orders of evil, which the apostle classed among the opposing powers. But whether any of these orders wdio act under the government of the devil, and obey his wicked commands, will in a future world be converted to righteousness because of their possessing the faculty of freedom of will, or whether persistent and inveterate wickedness may be changed by the power of habit into nature, is a result which you yourself, reader, may approve of, if neither in these present worlds which are seen and temporal, nor in those which are unseen and are eternal, that portion is to differ wholly from the final unity and fitness of things. But in the meantime, both in those temporal worlds which are.; seen, as well as in those eternal worlds which are invisible, A all those beings are arranged, according to a regular plan, in the order and degree of their merits; so that some of them in the first, others in the second, some even in the last times, after having undergone heavier and severer punishments, endured for a lengthened period, and for many ages, so to speak, improved by this stern method of training, and restored at first by the instruction of the angels, and subsequently by the powers of a higher grade, and thus advancing through each stage to a better condition, reach even to that which is invisible and eternal, having travelled through, by a kind of training, every single office of the heavenly powers. From which, I think, this will appear to follow as an inference, that every rational nature may, in passing from one order to another, go tlirougli each to all, and advance from all to each, while made the subject of various degrees of proficiency and failure according to its own actions and endeavours, put forth in the enjoyment of its power of freedom of will.

4. But since Paul says that certain things are visible and temporal, and others besides these invisible and eternal, we proceed to inquire how those things which are seen are temporal whether because there will be nothing at all after them in all those periods of the coming world, in which that dispersion and separation from the one beginning is undergoing a process of restoration to one and the same end and likeness; or because, while the form of those things which are seen passes away, their essential nature is subject to no corruption. And Paul seems to confirm the latter view, when he says, "For the fashion of this world passeth away." David also appears to assert the same in the words, "The heavens shall perish, but Thou shalt endure; and they all shall wax old as a c arment, and Thou shalt change them like a vesture, and like a vestment they shall be changed." For if the heavens are to be changed, assuredly that which is changed does not perish, and if the fashion of the world passes away, it is by no means an annihilation or destruction of their material substance that is shown to take place, but a kind of change of quality and transformation of appearance. Isaiah also, in declaring prophetically that there will be a new heaven and a new earth, undoubtedly suggests a similar Vview. For this renewal of heaven and earth, and this trans-' mutation of the form of the present world, and this changing of the heavens, will undoubtedly be prepared for those who are walking along that way which we have pointed out above, and are tending to that goal of happiness to which, it is said, even enemies themselves are to be subjected, and in which God is said to be " all and in all." And if any one imagine that at the end material, i. e. bodily, nature will be entirely destroyed, he cannot in any respect meet my view, how beings so numerous and powerful are able to live and to exist without bodies, since it is an attribute of the divine 1 1 Cor. vii. 31. 2 pg. di. 26.

nature alone i. e. of the Father, Son, and Holy Spirit to exist without any material substance, and vritliout partaking in any degree of a bodily adjunct. Another, perhaps, may say that in the end every bodily substance will be so pure and refined as to be like the aether, and of a celestial purity and clearness. How things will be, how ever, is known with certainty to God alone, and to those w ho are His friends through Christ and the Holy Spirit.

CHAPTER VIL ox INCOKroREAL AND CORPOREAL BEINGS.

1. The subjects considered in the previous chapter have been spoken of in general language, the nature of rational beings being discussed more by way of intelligent inference than strict dogmatic definition, with the exception of the place where we treated, to the best of our ability, of the persons of Father, Son, and Holy Spirit. We have now to ascertain what those matters are which it is proper to treat in the following pages according to our dogmatic belief, i. e. in agreement with the creed of the church. All souls and all rational natures, whether holy or wicked, w ere formed or created, and all these, according to their proper nature, are incorporeal; but although incorporeal, they were nevertheless created, because all things were made by God through Christ, as John teaches in a general w ay in his Gospel, saying, "In the beginning was the Word, and the Word was with God, and the Word vras God. The same was in the beginning with God. All things were made by Him, and without Him was nothing made."- The Apostle Paul, moreover, describing created things by species and numbers and orders, speaks as follows, when showing that all things were made

through Christ: " And in Him were all things created, that are in heaven, and that are in earth, visible and invisible, wdiether they be thrones, or dominions, or principalities, or powers: all things were created by Him, and in Him: and He is before all, and He is the head."" He therefore mani-1 John 1. 1-3. 2 Col. i. 16-18.

festly declares that in Christ and through Christ were all things made and created, whether things visible, which are corporeal, or things invisible, which I regard as none other than incorporeal and spiritual powers. But of those things which he had termed generally corporeal or incorporeal, he seems to me, in the words that follow, to cnumerate the various kinds, viz. thrones, dominions, principalities, powers, influences.

These matters now have been previously mentioned by us, as we are desirous to come in an orderly manner to the investigation of the sun, and moon, and stars by way of logical inference, and to ascertain whether they also ought properly to be reckoned among the principalities on account of their being said to be created in Ap a;, i. e. for the government of day and night; or whether they are to be regarded as having only that government of day and night which they discharge by performing the oflice of illuminating them, and are not in reality chief of that order of principalities.

2. Now, when it is said that all things were made by Him, and that in Him were all things created, both things in heaven and things on earth, there can be no doubt that also those things which are in the firmament, which is called heaven, and in which those luminaries are said to be placed, are included amongst the number of heavenly things. And secondly, seeing that the course of the discussion has manifestly discovered that all things were made or created, and that amongst created things there is nothing which may not admit of good and evil, and be capable of either, what are we to think of the following opinion which certain of our friends entertain regarding sun, moon, and stars, viz. that they are unchangeable, and incapable of becoming the opposite of what they are? Not a few have held that view even regarding the holy angels, and certain heretics also regarding souls, which they call spiritual natures.

In the first place, then, let us see what reason itself can discover respecting sun, moon, and stars, whether the opinion, entertained by some, of their unchangeableness be correct, and let the declarations of holy Scripture, as far as possible, be first adduced. For Job appears to assert that not only may the stars be subject to sin, but even that they are actually not clean from the contagion of it. The follovv-ing are his words: " The stars also are not clean in Thy sight." Nor is this to be understood of the splendour of their physical substance, as if one were to say, for example, of a garment, that it is not clean; for if such were the meaning, then the accusation of a want of cleanness in the splendour of their bodily substance would imply an injurious reflection upon their Creator. For if they are unable, through their own diligent efforts, either to acquire for themselves a body of greater brightness, or through their sloth to make the one they have less pure, how should they incur censure for being stars that are not clean, if they receive no praise because they are so?.

3. But to arrive at a clearer understanding on these matters, we ought first to inquire after this point, whether it is allowable to suppose that they are living and rational beings; then, in the next place, whether their souls came into existence at the same time with their bodies, or seem to V be anterior to them; and also whether,

after the end of the world, we are to understand that they are to be released from their bodies; and whether, as we cease to live, so they also will cease from illuminating the world. Although this inquiry may seem to be somewhat bold, yet, as we are incited by the desire of ascertaining the truth as far as possible, there seems no absurdity in attempting an investigation of the subject agreeably to the grace of the Holy Spirit.

We think, then, that they may be designated as living beings, for this reason, that they are said to receive commandments from God, which is ordinarily the case only with rational beings. " I have given a commandment to all the stars,"" says the Lord. What, now, are these commandments? Those, namely, that each star, in its order and course, should bestow upon the world the amount of splendour which has been entrusted to it. For those which are Job XXV. 5. 2 isa. xlv. 12.

C2 ORIGEN BE PPJNCIPIIS. Book i.

called "planets" move in orbits of one kind, and those which are termed aifkavet are different. Now it manifestly follows from this, that neither can the movement of that body take place without a soul, nor can living things be at any time without motion. And seeing that the stars move with such order and regularity, that their movements never appear to be at any time subject to derangement, would it not be the height of folly to say that so orderly an observance of method and plan could be carried out or accomplished by irrational beings? In the writings of Jeremiah, indeed, the moon is called the queen of heaven. Yet if the stars are living and rational beings, there will undoubtedly appear among them both an advance and a falling back. For the la-nguage of Job, " the stars are not clean in His sight," seems to me to convey some such idea.

4. And now we have to ascertain whether those beings which in the course of the discussion we have discovered to possess life and reason, were endowed with a soul along with their bodies at the time mentioned in Scripture, when " God made two great lights, the greater light to rule the day, and the lesser light to rule the night, and the stars also," or whether their spirit was implanted in them, not at the creation of their bodies, but from without, after they had been already made. I, for my part, suspect that the spirit was implanted in them from without; but it will be worth while to prove this from Scripture: for it will seem an easy matter to make the assertion on conjectural grounds, while it is more difficult to establish it by the testimony of Scripture. Now it may be established conjecturally as follows. If the soul of a man, which is certainly inferior while it remains the soul of a man, was not formed along with his body, but is proved to have been implanted strictly from without, much more must this be the case with those living beings which are called heavenly. For, as regards man, lhow could the soul of him, viz. Jacob, who supplanted his brother in the womb, appear to be formed along wath his body? Or how could his soul, or its images, be formed along i Jer. vii. 18. 2 Qen. i. 16.

vith his body, who, while lying in his mother's womb, was' filled with the Holy Ghost? I refer to John leaping in his mother's womb, and exulting because the voice of the salutation of Mary had come to the ears of his mother Elisabeth. ' IIow could his soul and its images be formed along with his body, who, before he was created in the womb, is said to be known to God, and was sanctified by Him before his birth? Some, perhaps, may think that God fills individuals with His Holy Spirit, and bestows upon them sanctification, not on grounds of justice and according to their deserts, but undeservedly. And how shall we escape that declaration: " Is there unrifrhteousness with God? God forbid!" or this: " Is there respect of persons with God?" For such is the defence of those who maintain that souls come into existence with bodies. So far, then, as we can form an opinion from a comparison with the condition of man, I think it follows that we must hold the same to hold good with heavenly beings, which reason itself and scriptural authority show us to be the case with men.

5. But let us see whether we can find in holy Scripture any indications properly applicable to these heavenly existences. The following is the statement of the Apostle Paul: " The creature was made subject to vanity, not willingly, but by. reason of Plim who subjected the same in hope, because the creature itself also shall be delivered from the bondage of corruption into the glorious liberty of the children of God." ' To what vanity, pray, w as the creature made subject, or what creature is referred to, or how is it said " not willingly," or " in hope of what?" And in w hat way is the creature itself to be delivered from the bondage of corruption? Elsewhere, also, the same apostle says: " For the expectation of the creature waiteth for the manifestation of the sons of God."" And again in another passage, "And not only we, but the creation itself groaneth together, and is in pain until now."' And hence we have to inquire wdiat are the groanings, and what are the pains. Let us see then, in the first place, what 1 Rom. ix. U.-' Rom. ii. 11. qi Rq. viii. 20, 21.

4 Rom. viii. 19. Rom. viii. 22, cf. 23.

is the vanity to wliich the creature is subject. I apprehend y that it is nothing else than the body; for although the body of the stars is ethereal, it is nevertheless material. Whence also Solomon appears to characterize the whole of corporeal y nature as a kind of burden which enfeebles the vigour of the soul in the following language: " Vanity of vanities, saith the Preacher; all is vanity. I have looked, and seen all the works that are done under the sun; and, behold, all is vanity." To this vanity, then, is the creature subject, that creature especially which, being assuredly the greatest in this world, holds also a distinguished principality of labour, i. e. the sun, and moon, and stars, are said to be subject to vanity, because they are clothed with bodies, and set apart to the office of giving light to the human race. " And this creature," he remarks, " was subjected to vanity not willingly." For it did not undertake a voluntary service to vanity, but because it was the will of Him who made it subject, and because of the promise of tlie Subjector to those who were reduced to this unwilling obedience, that when the ministry of their great work was performed, they were to be freed from this bondage of corruption and vanity when the time of the glorious redemption of God's children should have arrived. And the whole of creation, receiving this hope, and looking for the fulfilment of this promise now, in the meantime, as having an affection for those whom it serves, groans along with them, and patiently suffers with them, hoping for the fulfilment of the promises. See also whether the following words of Paul can apply to those who, although not willingly, yet in accordance with the will of Him who subjected them, and in hope oi the promises, were made subject to vanity, when he says, "For. I could wish to be dissolved," or " to return and be V with Christ, which is far better."- For I think that the sun might say in like manner, "I would desire to be dissolved," or ' to return and be with Christ, which is far better." Paul indeed adds, "Nevertheless, to abide in the flesh is more needful for you;" while the sun may say, "To abide in this bright and heavenly body is more necessary, on account of 1 Eccles. i. 1,14. 2 phil. i. 23.

Chap, yiil ORIGEN DE PRINCIPHS. G5 the manifestation of the sons of God." The same views are to be believed and expressed regarding the moon and stars.

Let us see now what is the freedom of the creature, or the termination of its bondage. When Christ shall have delivered up the kingdom to God even the Father, then also those living things, when they shall have first been made the kingdom of Christ, shall be delivered, along with the whole of that kingdom, to the rule of the Father, that when God shall be all in all, they also, since they are a part of all things, may have God in themselves, as He is in all things.

CHAPTEIi VIIL ox THE ANGELS.

1. A similAPw method must be followed in treatins; of the angels; nor are we to suppose that it is the result of accident that a particular office is assigned to a particular angel: as to Raphael, e. g., the work of curing and healing; to Gabriel, the conduct of wars; to j Iichael, the duty of attending to the prayers and supplications of mortals. For we are not to imagine that they obtained these offices otherwise than by their own merits, and by the zeal and excellent qualities wdiich ttiey severally displayed before this world was formed; so that afterw ards, in the order of archangels, this or that office was assigned to each one, while others deserved to be enrolled in the order of angels, and to act under this or that archangel, or that leader or head of an order. All of which things were disposed, as I have said, not indiscriminately and fortuitously, but by a most appropriate and just decision of God, who arranged them according to deserts, in accordance with His own approval and judgment: so that to one angel the church of the Ephesians was to be entrusted; to another, that of the Sm 'rnseans; one angel was to be Peter's, another Paul's; and so on through every one of the little ones that are in the church, for such and such angels as even daily

GQ OBIGEN BE PRINCIPIIS, Book i.

behold the face of God must be assigned to each one of them; and there must also be some angel that encampeth round about them that fear God. All of which things, assuredly, it is to be believed, are not perform. ed by accident or chance, or because they the angels were so created, lest on that view the Creator should be accused of partiality; but it is to be believed that they were conferred by God, the just and impartial Ruler of all things, agreeably to the merits and good qualities and mental vigour of each individual spirit.

2. And now let us say something regarding those who maintain the existence of a diversity of spiritual natures, that we may avoid falling into the silly and impious fables of such as pretend that there is a diversity of spiritual natures both among heavenly existences and human souls, and for that reason allege that they were called into being by different creators; for while it seems, and is really, absurd that to one and the same creator should be ascribed the creation of different natures of rational beings, they are nevertheless ignorant of the cause of that diversity. For they say that it seems inconsistent for one and the same creator, without any existing ground of merit, to confer upon some beings the power of dominion, and to subject others again to authority; to bestow a principality upon some, and to rcnder others subordinate to

rulers. Which opinions indeed, in my judgment, are completely rejected by following out the reasoning explained above, and by which it was shown that the cause of the diversity and variety among these beings is due to their conduct, which has been marked either with greater earnest-Vness or indifference, according to the goodness or badness of their nature, and not to any partiality on the part of the Disposer. But that this may more easily be shown to be the case with heavenly beings, let us borrow an illustration from what either has been done or is done among men, in order that 1 Matt, xviii. 10.

- Ps. xxxiv. 7. Turn demum per singulos minimorum, qui sunt in ecclesla, qui vel qui adscribi singulis debeant angeli, qui etiam quotidie videant faciem Dei; sed et quis debeat esse angelus, qui circumdet in circuitu timentium Deum.

from visible things we may, by way of consequence, behold also things invisible.

Paul and Peter are undoubtedly proved to have been men of a spiritual nature. When, therefore, Paul is found to have acted contrary to religion, in having persecuted the church of God, and Peter to have committed so grave a sin as, when questioned by the maid-servant, to have asserted with an oath that he did not know who Christ was, how is it possible that these who, according to those persons of whom we speak, were spiritual beings should fall into sins of such a nature, especially as they are frequently in the habit of saying that a good tree cannot bring forth evil fruits? And if a good tree cannot produce evil fruit, and as, according to them, Peter and Paul were sprung from the root of a good tree, how should they be deemed to have brought forth fruits so wicked? And if they should return the answer which is generally invented, that it was not Paul who persecuted, but some other person, I know not whom, who was in Paul; and that it was not Peter who uttered the denial, but some other individual in him; how should Paul say, if he had not sinned, that " I am not worthy to be called an apostle because I persecuted the church of God?" Or why did Peter weep most bitterly, if it were another than he who sinned? From which all their silly assertions will be proved to be baseless.

3. According to our view, there is no rational creature which is not capable both of good and evil. But it does not follow, that because we say there is no nature which may not admit evil, we therefore maintain that every nature has admitted evil, i. e. has become wicked. As we may say that the nature of every man admits of his being a sailor, but it does not follow from that, that every man will become so; or, again, it is possible for every one to learn grammar or medicine, but it is not therefore proved that every man is either a physician or a grammarian; so, if we say that there is no nature which may not admit evil, it is not necessarily indicated that it has done so. For, in our view, not even the 1 1 Cor. XV. 9.

G8 ORIGEN BE rrINCIPIIS. Book r.

devil himself was incapable of good; but although capable of admitting good, he did not therefore also desire it, or make any effort after virtue. For, as we are taught by those quotations which w e adduced from the prophets, there was once a time when he was good, when he walked in the paradise of God between the cherubim. As he, then, possessed the power either of receiving good or evil, but fell away from a virtuous course, and turned to evil with all the powers of his mind, so also other creatures, as having a capacity for either condition, in the exercise of the freedom of their will, flee from evil, and cleave to good. There is no nature, then, which may not admit of good or evil, except the nature of God the fountain of all good things and of Christ; for it is wisdom, and wisdom assuredly cannot admit folly; and it is righteousness, and righteousness will never certainly admit of unrighteousness; and it is the Word, of Reason, which certainly cannot be made irrational; nay, it is also the hvht, and it is certain that the darkness does not receive the light. In like manner, also, the nature of the Holy Spirit, being holy, does not admit of pollution; for it is holy by nature, or essential being. If there is any other nature which is holy, it possesses this property of being made holy by the reception or inspiration of the Holy Spirit, not having it by nature, but as an accidental quality, for which reason it may be lost, in consequence of being accidental. So also a man may possess an accidental righteousness, from wdiich it is possible for him to fall away. Even the wisdom which a man has is still accidental, although it be within our own power to become wise, if we devote ourselves to wisdom with the zeal and effort of our life; and if we always pursue the study of it, we may always be participators of wisdom: and that result will follow either in a greater or less deo-ree, according; to the desert of our life or the amount of our zeal. For the goodness of God, as is worthy of Him, incites and attracts all to that blissful end, where all pain, and sadness, and sorrow fall aw ay and disappear.

4. I am of opinion, then, so far as appears to me, that the preceding discussion has sufficiently proved that it is neither

Chap, viil ORIGEN BE PRINCIPIIS. C9 from want of discrimination, nor from any accidental cause, cither that the " principalities" hold their dominion, or the other orders of spirits have obtained their respective offices; but that they have received the steps of their rank on account, of their merits, although it is not our privilege to know or." inquire what those acts of theirs were, by which they earned a place in any particular order. It is sufficient only to know this much, in order to demonstrate the impartiality and righteousness of God, that, conformably with the declaration of the Apostle Paul, " there Is no acceptance of persons with Him," who rather disposes everything according to the deserts and moral progress of each individual. So, then, the angelic office does not exist except as a consequence of their desert; nor do "powers " exercise power except in virtue of their moral progress; nor do those which are called " seats," i. e. the powers of judging and ruling, administer their powers unless by merit; nor do " dominions " rule undeservedly, for that great and distinguished order of rational creatures among celestial existences is arranged in a glorious variety of offices. And the same view is to be entertained of those opposing influences which have given themselves up to such places and offices, that they derive the property by which they are made " principalities," or " powers," or rulers of the darkness of the world, or spirits of wickedness, or malignant spirits, or unclean demons, not from their essential nature, nor from their being so created, but have obtained these degrees in evil in proportion to their conduct, and the progress which they made in wickedness. And that Is a second order of rational creatures, who have devoted themselves to wickedness in so headlong a course, that they are unwilling rather than unable to recall themselves; the thirst for evil being already a passion, and imparting to them pleasure. But the third order of rational creatures is that of those who are judged fit by God to replenish the human race, i. e. the souls of men, assumed in consequence of their moral progress into the order of angels; of whom we see some assumed into the number: those, viz., who have been made the sons of 1 Cf. Rom. ii. 11.

God, or the clilldren of the resurrection, or who have abandoned the darkness, and have loved the light, and have been made children of the light; or those who, proving victorious in every struggle, and being made men of peace, have been the sons of peace, and the sons of God; or those who, morti-y- fying their members on the earth, and, rising above not only their corporeal nature, but even the uncertain and fragile movements of the soul itself, have united themselves to the Lord, being made altogether spiritual, that they may be for ever one spirit with Him, discerning along with Him each individual thing, until they arrive at a condition of perfect spirituality, and discern all things by their perfect illumination in all holiness through the word and wisdom of God, and are themselves altogether undistinguishable by any one.

We think that those views are by no means to be admitted, which some are wont unnecessarily to advance and maintain, viz. that souls descend to such a pitch of abasement ythat they forget their rational nature and dignity, and sink into the condition of irrational animals, either large or small; and in support of these assertions they generally quote some pretended statements of Scripture, such as, that a beast, to which a woman has unnaturally prostituted herself, shall be deemed equally guilty with the woman, and shall be ordered to be stoned; or that a bull which strikes with its horns, shall be put to death in the same way; or even the speaking of Balaam's ass, when God opened its mouth, and the dumb beast of burden, answering with human voice, reproved the madness of the prophet. All of which assertions wc not only do not receive, but, as being contrary to our belief, we refute and reject. After the refutation and rejection of such perverse opinions, we shall show, at the proper time and place, how those passages which they quote from the sacred Scriptures ought to be understood.

FRAGMENT FEOM THE FIRST BOOK OF THE DE PRINCIPIIS. Translated by Jerome in his Epistle to Avitus.

"It is an evidence of great negligence and sloth, that each one should fall down to such (a pitch of degradation), and be so emptied, as that, in coming to evil, he may be fastened to the gross body of irrational beasts of burden."

ANOTHER FRAGMENT FROM THE SAME. Translated in the same Epistle to Avitus.

"At the end and consummation of the world, when souls and rational creatures shall have been sent forth as from bolts and barriers, some of them walk slowly on account Y of their slothful habits, others fly with rapid flight on account of their diligence. And since all are possessed of free-will, and may of their own accord admit either of good or evil the former will be in a worse condition than they are at present, while the latter will advance to a better state of things; because different conduct and varying wills will admit of a different condition in either direction, i. e. angels may become men or demons, and again from the latter they may rise to be men or angels."

De quibusdam repagnlis atqiie carceribus. There is an allusion hero to the race-course and the mode of starting the chariots.

LTHOUGH all the discussions in the preceding book have had reference to the world and its arrangements, it now seems to follow that we should specially re-discuss a few points respecting the world itself, i. e. its beginning and end, or those dispensations of Divine Providence which have taken place between the beginning and the end, or those events which are supposed to have occurred before the creation of the world, or are to take place after the end.

In this investigation, the first point which clearly appears is, that the world in all its diversified and varying conditions is composed not only of rational and diviner natures, and of a diversity of bodies, but of dumb animals, wild and tame beasts, of birds, and of all things which live in the waters; then, secondly, of places, i. e. of the heaven or heavens, and of the earth or water, as well as of the air, which is intermediate, and which they term sether, and of everything which proceeds from the earth or is born in it. Seeing, then," there is so great a variety in the world, and so great a diversity among rational beings themselves, on account of which every other variety and diversity also is supposed to have 1 The words "in aquis " are omitted in Redepenning's edition.

- The original of this sentence is found at the close of the Emperor Justinian's epistle to Menas, patriarch of Constantinople, and, literally-translated, is as follows: "The world being so very varied, and containing so many different rational beings, what else ought we to say was the come into existence, what other cause than this ought to be assigned for the existence of the world, especially if we have regard to that end by means of which it was shown in the preceding book that all things are to be restored to their original condition? And if this should seem to be logically stated, what other cause, as we have already said, are we to imagine for so great a diversity in the world, save the diversity and variety in the movements and declensions of those who fell from that primeval unity and harmony in which they were at first created by God, and who, being driven from that state of goodness, and drawn in various directions by the harassing influence of different motives and desires, have changed, according to their different tendencies, the single and undivided goodness of their nature into minds of various sorts? 2. But God, by the ineffable skill of His wisdom, transforming and restoring all things, in whatever manner they are made, to some useful aim, and to the common advantage of all, recalls those very creatures which differed so much from each other in mental conformation to one agreement of labour and purpose; so that, although they are under the influence of different motives, they nevertheless complete the fulness and perfection of one world,, and the very variety of minds tends to one end of perfection. For it is one power which grasps and holds together all the diversity of the world, and leads the different movements towards one work, lest so immense an undertaking as that of the world should be dissolved by the dissensions of souls. And for this reason w e think that God, the Father of all things, in order to ensure the salvation of all His creatures through the ineffable plan of His word and wisdom, so arranged each of these, that every spirit, whether soul or rational existence, however called, should not be compelled by force, against the liberty of his own will, to any other course than that to which the motives of his own mind led cause of its existence than the diversity of the falling away of those who decline from unity (rij? buuios) in different ways? " RuieUS. Lom-matzsch adds a clause not contained in the note of the Benedictine editor: ' and sometimes the soul selects the life that is in water " (suvopo'). Lit. "into various qualities of minds."

him (lest by so doing the power of exercising free-will should V iseem to be taken away, which certainly would produce a change in the nature of the being itself); and that the varying purposes of these would be suitably and usefully adapted to the harmony of one world, by some of them requiring help, and others being able to give it, and others again being the cause of struggle and contest to those who are making progress, amongst whom their diligence would be deemed more worthy of approval, and the place of rank obtained after victory be held with greater certainty, which should be established by the difficulties of the contest.- 3. Although the whole world is arranged into offices of different kinds, its condition, nevertheless, is not to be supposed as one of internal discrepancies and discordances; but as our one body is provided with many members, and is held together by one soul, so I am of opinion that the whole world also ought to be regarded as some huge and immense animal, which is kept together by the power and reason of God as by one soul. This also, I think, is indicated in sacred Scripture by the declaration of the prophet, "" Do not I fill heaven and earth? saith the Lord;" and again, "The heaven is my throne, and the earth is my footstool;" and by the Saviour s words, when He says that we are to swear ' neither by heaven, for it is God's throne; nor by the earth, for it is His footstool." To the same effect also are the words of Paul, in his address to the Athenians, when he says, "In Him we live, and move, and have our being." For how do we live, and Vmove, and have our being in God, except by His comprehending and holding together the whole world by His power? And how is heaven the throne of God, and the earth His footstool, as the Saviour Himself declares, save by His power

"Et diversi motus propositi earum (rationabilium subsistentiarum) ad unius mimdi consonantiam competenter atque utiliter aptarentur, dum alise juvari indigent, alise juvare possunt, alise vero proficientibus cer-tamiua atque agones movent, in quibus eorum probabilior haberetur industria, et certior post victoriam reparati gradus static teneretur, quae per difficultates laborantium constitisset."

- Jer, xxiii. 24. s jg, ixvi. 1.

Matt. V. 34. 5 Acts xvii. 28.

filling all things both in heaven and earth, according to the Lord's own words? And that God, the Father of all things, fills and holds together the world with the fulness of His power, according to those passages which we have quoted, no one, I think, will have any difficulty in admitting. And now, since the course of the preceding discussion has shown that the different movements of rational beings, and their varying opinions, have brought about the diversity that is in the world, we must see whether it may not be appropriate that this world should have a termination like its beginning. For there is no doubt that its end must be sought amid much diversity and variety; which variety, being found to exist in the termination of the world, will again furnish ground and occasion for the diversities of the other world which is to succeed the present.

4. If now, in the course of our discussion, it has been ascertained that these things are so, it seems to follow that we next consider the nature of corporeal being, seeing the diversity in the world cannot exist without bodies. It is evident from the nature of things themselves, that bodily nature admits of diversity and variety of change, so that it is capable of undergoing all possible transformations, as e. g. the conversion of wood into fire, of fire into smoke, of smoke into air, of oil into fire. Does not food

itself, whether of man or of animals, exhibit the same ground of change? For whatever we take as food, is converted into the substance of our body. But how water is changed into earth or into air, and air again into fire, or fire into air, or air into water, although not difficult to explain, yet on the present occasion it is enough merely to mention them, as our object is to discuss the nature of bodily matter. By matter, therefore, we understand that which is placed under bodies, viz. that by which, through the bestowing and implanting of qualities, bodies exist; and we mention four qualities heat, cold, dryness, humidity. These four qualities being implanted in the Xt;, or matter (for matter is found to exist in its own nature without those qualities before mentioned), produce the different kinds of bodies. Although this matter is, as we have said above, according to its own proper nature without qualities, it is never found to exist without a quality. And I cannot understand how so many distinguished men have been of opinion that this matter, which is so great, and possesses such properties as to enable it to be sufficient for all the bodies in the world which God willed to exist, and to be the attendant and slave of the Creator for whatever forms and species He wished in all things, receiving into itself whatever qualities He desired to bestow upon it, w as uncreated, i. e. not formed by God Himself, who is the creator of all things, but that its nature and power were the result of chance. And I am astonished that they should find fault with those who deny either God's creative power or His providential administration of the world, and accuse them of impiety for thinking that so great a work as the world could exist without an architect or overseer; while they themselves incur a similar charge of impiety in saying that matter is uncreated, and co-eternal with the uncreated God. According to this view, then, if we suppose for the sake of argument that matter did not exist, as these maintain, saying that God could not create anything when nothing existed, without doubt He vvould have been idle, not having matter on which to operate, wdiich matter they say was furnished Him not by His own arrangement, but by accident; and they think that this, which was discovered by chance, was able to suffice Him for an undertaking of so vast an extent, and for the manifestation of the power of His might, and by admitting the plan of all His wisdom, might be distinguished and formed into a world. Now this appears to me to be very absurd, and to be the opinion of those men who are altogether ignorant of the power and intelligence of uncreated nature. But that we may see the nature of things a little more clearly, let it be granted that for a little time matter did not exist, and that God, when nothing formerly existed, caused those things to come into existence which He desired, why are we to suppose that God would create matter either better or greater, or of another kind, than that which He did produce from His own power and wisdom, in order that that might exist which formerly did not? Would He create a worse and inferior matter, or one tlie same as that which they cull uncreated ' Now I think it will very easily appear to any one, that neither a better nor inferior matter could have assumed the forms and species of the world, if it had not been such as that which actually did assume them. And does it not then seem impious to call that uncreated, which, if believed to be formed by God, would doubtless be found to be such as that which they call uncreated?

5. But that we may believe on the authority of holy Scripture that such is the case, hear how in the book of Maccabees, where the mother of seven martyrs exhorts

her son to endure torture, this truth is confirmed; for she says, "I ask of thee, my son, to look at the heaven and the earth, and at all things which are in them, and beholding these, to know thatm3fod made all these things when they did not exist." In the book of the Shepherd also, in the first commandment, he speaks as follows: " First of all believe that there is one God who created and arranged all things, and made all things to come into existence, and out of a state of nothingness."" Perhaps also the expression in the Psalms has reference to this: " He spake, and they were made; He commanded, and they were created." For the words, "He spake, and they were made," appear to show that the substance of those things which exist is meant; while the others, "He commanded, and they were created," seem spoken of the qualities by which the substance itself has been moulded.

CHAPTER II.

ON THE PEEPETUITY OF BODILY NATUEE.

1. Ox this topic some are wont to inquire whether, as the Father generates an uncreated Son, and brings forth a Holy Spirit, not as if He had no previous existence, but because 1 2 Mac. vii. 28.

2 Hermx Past. B, ii.; cf. Apostolic Fathers (Ante-Nicene Library), p. 349.

"Ps. cxlviii. 5.

the Father is the origin and source of the Son or Holy Spirit, and no anteriority or posteriority can be understood as existing in them; so also a similar kind of union or relationship can be understood as subsisting between rational natures and bodily matter. And that this point may be more fully and thoroughly examined, the commencement of the discussion is generally directed to the inquiry whether this very bodily nature, which bears the lives and contains the movements of spiritual and rational minds, will be equally eternal with them, or will altogether perish and be destroyed. And that the question may be determined with greater precision, we have, in the first place, to inquire if it is possible for rational natures to remain altogether incorporeal after they have reached the summit of holiness and happiness (which seems to me a most difficult and almost impossible attainment), or whether they must always of necessity be united to bodies. If, then, any one could show a reason why it was possible for them to dispense wholly with bodies, it will appear to follow, that as a bodily nature, created out of nothing after intervals of time, w as produced when it did not exist, so also it must cease to be when the purposes which it served had no longer an existence.

2. If, however, it is impossible for this point to be at all maintained, viz. that any other nature than the Father, Son, and Holy Spirit can live without a body, the necessity of logical reasoning compels us to understand that rational natures were indeed created at the beginning, but that material substance was separated from them only in thought and understanding, and appears to have been formed for them, or after them, and that they never have lived nor do live without it; for an incorporeal life will rightly be considered a prerogative of the Trinity alone. As we have remarked above, therefore, that material substance of this world, possessing a nature admitting of all possible transformations, is, when dragged down to beings of a lower order, moulded into the crasser and more solid condition of a body, so as to distinguish those visible and varying forms of the world; but when it becomes the servant of more perfect and

more blessed beings, it shines in the splendour of celestial bodies, and adorns either the angels of God or the sons of the resurrection with the clothing of a spiritual body, out of all which will be filled up the diverse and varying state of the one world. But if any one should desire to discuss these matters more fully, it will be necessary, with all reverence and fear of God, to examine the sacred Scriptures with greater attention and diligence, to ascertain whether the secret and hidden sense within them may perhaps reveal anything regarding these matters; and something may be discovered in their abstruse and mysterious language, through the demonstration of the Holy Spirit to those who are worthy, after many testimonies have been collected on this very point.

CHAPTER III.

ON THE BEGINNING OF THE WORLD, AND ITS CAUSES.

1. The next subject of inquiry is, whether there was any other world before the one which now exists; and if so, whether it was such as the present, or somewhat different, or inferior; or whether there was no world at all, but something: like that which we understand will be after the end of all things, when the kingdom shall be delivered up to God, even the Father; which nevertheless may have been the end of another world, of that, namely, after which this world took its beginning; and whether the various lapses of intellectual natures provoked God to produce this diverse and varying condition of the world. This point also, I think, must be investigated in a similar way, viz. whether after this world there will be any system of preservation and amendment, severe indeed, and attended with much pain to those who were unwilling to obey the word of God, but a process through which, by means of instruction and rational training, those may arrive at a fuller understanding of the truth who have devoted themselves in the present life to these pursuits, and who, after having had their minds purified, have advanced onwards so as to become capable of attaining divine wisdom; and after this the end of all things will immediately follow, and there will be again, for the correction and improvement of those who stand in need of it, another world, either resembling that which now exists, or better than it, or greatly inferior; and how long that world, whatever it be that is to come after this, shall continue; and if there will be a time when no world shall anywhere exist, or if there has been a time when there was no world at all; or if there have been, or will be several; or if it shall ever come to pass that there will be one resembling another, like it in every respect, and indistino-uishable from it.

2. That it may appear more clearly, then, whether bodily matter can exist during intervals of time, and whether, as it did not exist before it was made, so it may again be resolved into non-existence, let us see, first of all, whether it is possible for any one to live without a body. For if one person can live without a body, all things also may dispense with them; seeing our former treatise has shown that all things tend towards one end. Now, if all things may exist w ithout bodies, there will undoubtedly be no bodily substance, seeing there will be no use for it. But how shall we understand the words of the apostle in those passages, in which, discussing the resurrection of the dead, he says, "This corruptible must put on incorruption, and this mortal must put on immortality. X When this corruptible shall have put on incorruption, and this mortal shall have put on immortality, then shall be brought to pass the saying which is written. Death is swallowed up in victory! Where, O death, is thy victory? O death,

thy sting has been swallowed up: the sting of death is sin, and the strength of sin is the law." Some such meaning, then, as this seems to be suggested by the apostle. For can the expression which he employs, " this corruptible," and " this mortal," with the gesture, as it were, of one who touches or points out, apply to anything else than to bodily matter? This matter of the body, then, which is now corruptible shall put on incorruption when a perfect soul, and one 1 1 Cor. XV. 53-56: cf. Hos. xiii. 14 and Isa. xxv. 8.

furnished with the marks of incorruption, shall have begun to inhabit it. And do not be surprised if we speak of a perfect soul as the clothing of the body (which, on account of the Word of God and His wisdom, is now named incorruption), when Jesus Christ Himself, who is the Lord and Creator of the soul, is said to be the clothing of the saints, according to the language of the apostle, "Put ye on the Lord Jesus Christ." As Christ, then, is the clotliing of the soul, so for a kind of reason sufficiently intelligible is the soul said to be the clotliing of the body, seeing it is an ornament to it, covering and concealing its mortal nature. The expression, then, "Tliis corruptible must put on incorruption," is as if the apostle had said, "This corruptible nature of the body must receive the clothing of incorruption a soul possessing in itself incorruptibility," because it has been clothed with Christ, who is the Wisdom and Word of God. But when this body, which at some future period we shall possess in a more glorious state, shall have become a partaker of life, it will then, in addition to being immortal, become also incorruptible. For whatever is mortal is necessarily also corruptible; but whatever is corruptible cannot also be said to be mortal. We say of a stone or a piece of wood that it is corruptible, but we do not say that it follows that it is also mortal. But as the body partakes of life, then because life may be, and is, separated from it, w e consequently name it mortal, and according to another sense also we speak of it as corruptible. The holy apostle therefore, with remarkable insight, referring to the general first cause of bodily matter, of which matter, whatever be the qualities with which it is endowed (now indeed carnal, but by and by more refined and pure, which are termed spiritual), the soul makes coijstant use, says, "This corruptible must put on incorruption." And in the second place, looking to the special cause of the body, he says, ' This mortal must put on immortality." tnow, what else w ill incorruption and immortality be, save the wis- 1 Dogmatibus. Schiiitzer says that " dogmatibiis" here yields no sense. He conjectures hiyi aai and renders "proofs," "marks."

2 Rom. xiii. 14.

OEIG. P dom, and the word, and the righteousness of God, which mould, and clothe, and adorn the soul? And hence it happens that it is said, "The corruptible will put on incorruption, and the mortal immortality." For although we may now make great proficiency, yet as we only know in part, and prophesy in part, and see through a glass, darkly, those very things which we seem to understand, this corruptible does not yet put on incorruption, nor is this mortal yet clothed with immortality; and as this training of ours in the body is protracted doubtless to a longer period, up to the time, viz., when those very bodies of ours with which we are enveloped may, on account of the word of God, and His wisdom and perfect righteousness, earn incorruptibility and immortality, therefore is it said, "This corruptible must put on incorruption, and this mortal must put on immortalit"

3. Bat, nevertheless, those who think that rational creatures can at any time lead an existence out of the body, may here raise such questions as the following. If it is true that this corruptible shall put on incorruption, and this mortal put on immortality, and that death is swallowed up at the end; this shows that nothing else than a material nature is to be destroyed, on which death could operate, while the mental acumen of those who are in the body seems to be blunted by the nature of corporeal matter. If, however, they are out of the body, then they will altogether escape the annoyance arising from a disturbance of that kind. But as they will not be able immediately to escape all bodily clothing, they are just to be considered as inhabiting more refined and purer bodies, which possess the property of being no longer overcome by death, or of being wounded by its sting; so that at last, by the gradual disappearance of the material nature, death is both swallowed up, and even at the end exterminated, and all its sting completely blunted by the divine grace which the soul has been rendered capable of receiving, and has thus deserved to obtain incorruptibility and immortality. And then it will be deservedly said by all, "O death, where is thy victory? O death, where is thy sting? The sting of death is sin." If these conclusions, then, seem to hold good, it follows that we must believe our condition at some future time to be incorporeal; and if this is admitted, and all are said to be subjected to Christ; this incorporeity also must necessarily be bestowed on all to whom the subjection to Christ extends; since all who are subject to Christ will be in the end subject to God the Father, to whom Christ is said to deliver up the kingdom; and thus it appears that then also the need of bodies will cease. And if it ceases, bodily matter returns to nothing, as formerly also it did not exist.

Now let us see what can be said in answer to those who make these assertions. For it will appear to be a necessary consequence that, if bodily nature be annihilated, it must be again restored and created; since it seems a possible thing that rational natures, from whom the faculty of free-will is never taken away, may be again subjected to movements of some kind, through the special act of the Lord Himself, lest perhaps, if they w ere always to occupy a condition that was unchangeable, they should be ignorant that it is by the grace of God and not by their own merit that they have been placed in that final state of happiness; and these movements

This passage is found in Jerome's epistle to Avitus; and, literally translated, his rendering is as follows: " If these (views) are not contrary to the faith, we shall perhaps at some future time hve without bodies. But if he who is perfectly subject to Christ is understood to be without a body, and all are to be subjected to Christ, we also shall be without bodies when we have been completely subjected to Him. If all have been subjected to God, all will lay aside their bodies, and the whole nature of bodily things vrill be dissolved into nothing; but if, in the second place, necessity shall demand, it will again come into existence on account of the fall of rational creatures. For God has abandoned souls to struggle and wresthng, that they may understand that they have obtained a full and perfect victory, not by their own bravery, but by the grace of God. And therefore I think that for a variety of causes are different worlds created, and the errors of those refuted who contend that worlds resemble each other." A fragment of the Greek original of the above is found in the epistle of Justinian to the patriarch of Constantinople. " If the things subject to Christ shall at the end be subjected also to God, all will lay aside their bodies; and then, I think, there will be a dissolution dux'hvaig) of the nature of bodies into non-existence (iig TO)? o'y), to come a second time into existence, if rational (beings) should again gradually come down (v7!-o t 3;)."

will undoubtedly again be attended by variety and diversity of bodies, by which the world is always adorned; nor will it ever be composed of anything save of variety and diversity, an effect which cannot be produced without a bodily matter.

4. And now I do not understand by what proofs they can maintain their position, who assert that worlds sometimes come into existence which are not dissimilar to each other, but in all respects equal. For if there is said to be a world similar in all respects to the present, then it will come to pass that Adam and Eve will do the same things which they did before: there will be a second time the same deluge, and the same Moses will again lead a nation numbering nearly six hundred thousand out of Egypt; Judas will also a second time betray the Lord; Paul will a second time keep the garments of those who stoned Stephen; and everything which has been done in this life will be said to be repeated, a state of things which I think cannot be established by any reasoning, if souls are actuated by freedom of will, and maintain either their advance or retrogression according to the power of their will. For souls are not driven on in a cycle which returns after many ages to the same round, so as either to do or desire this or that; but at whatever point the freedom of their own will aims, thither do they direct the course of their actions. For what these persons say is much the same as if one were to assert that if a medimnus of grain were to be poured out on the ground, the fall of the grain would be on the second occasion identically the same as on the first, so that every individual grain would lie for the second time close beside that grain where it had been thrown before, and so the medimnus would be scattered in the same order, and with the same marks as formerly; which certainly is an impossible result with the countless grains of a medimnus, even if they were to be poured out without ceasing for many ages. So therefore it seems to me impossible for a world to be restored for the second time, with the same order and with the same amount of births, and deaths, and actions; but that a diversity of worlds may exist with changes of no unimportant kind, so that the state of another world may be for some unmistakeable reasons better than this, and for others worse, and for others again intermediate. But what may be the number or measure of this I confess myself ignorant, although, if any one can tell it, I would gladly learn. 5. But this world, which is itself called an age, is said to be the conclusion of many ages. Now the holy apostle teaches that in that age which preceded this, Christ did not suffer, nor even in the age which preceded that again; and I know not that I am able to enumerate the number of anterior ages in which He did not suffer. I will show, however, from what statements of Paul I have arrived at this understanding. He says, "But now once in the consummation of ages. He was manifested to take away sin by the sacrifice of Himself." For he says that He was once made a victim, and in the consummation of ages was manifested to take away sin. Now that after this age, which is said to be formed for the consummation of other a es, there vill be other ao es ao; ain to follow, we have clearly learned from Paul himself, who says, "That in the ages to come He might show the exceeding riches of Plis grace in His kindness towards us."" He has not said, "in the age to come," nor "'in the two

ages to come," whence I infer that by his language many ages are indicated. Now if there is somethino; greater than ao-es, so that among created beings certain ages may be understood, but among other beings which exceed and surpass visible creatures, ages still greater (which perhaps will be the case at the restitution of all things, wdien the whole universe will come to a perfect termination), perhaps that period in which the consummation of all things will take place is to be understood as something more than an age. But here the authority of holy Scripture moves me, which says, "For an age and more." Now this word "more" undoubtedly means something greater than an age; and see if that expression of the Saviour, "I will that where I am, these also may be with me; and as I and Thou are one, these also may be one in us," may not 1 Heb. ix. 26. 2 gph. ii. 7.

3 In Eseculum et adhuc. Cf. John xvii. 24, 21, 22.

seem to convey something more than an age and ages, perhaps even more than ages of ages, that period, viz., when all things are now no longer in an age, but when God is in all.

6. Having discussed these points regarding the nature of the world to the best of our ability, it does not seem out of place to inquire what is the meaning of the term world, which in holy Scripture is shown frequently to have different significations. For what we call in Latin mundas is termed in Greek Koafio;, and Koo-fio; signifies not only a w orld, but also an ornament. Finally, in Isaiah, where the language of reproof is directed to the chief daughters of Sion, and where he says, "Instead of an ornament of a golden head, thou wilt have baldness on account of thy works," he emplo s the same term to denote ornament as to denote the world, viz. Koajiofi. For the plan of the world is said to be contained in the clothing of the high priest, as we find in the Wisdonr of Solomon, where he says, "For in the long garment was the whole world." That earth of ours, with its inhabitants, is also termed the world, as when Scripture says, "The whole world lieth in wickedness." Clement indeed, a disciple of the apostles, makes mention of those whom the Greeks called Avti'x Oove j and other parts of the earth, to which no one of our people can approach, nor can any one of those who are there cross over to us, which he also termed worlds, saying, "The ocean is impassable to men; and those are worlds which are on the other side of it, which are governed by these same arrangements of the ruling God." That universe which is bounded by heaven and earth is also called a world, as Paul declares: ' For the fashion of this world will pass aw ay." Oar Lord and Saviour also points out a certain other w orld besides this visible one, which it would indeed be difficult to describe and make known. He says,

Of. Isa. iii. 24. Origen here quotes the Septuagint, which differs both from the Hebrew and the Vulgate: x. a. i dvrl tov yjaccov tv;; y. z(pcc7. v g tov y pvslov (p(X."ha, x. pa ct, s sic Qio. rcc spy a.

2 Wisd. xviii. 24. Podcris, lit. "reaching to the feet."

"1 John V. 19. ' Clemens Rom. i. Ep. ad Cor. c. 20.

5 1 Cor. vii. 31.

' I am not of this world." For, as if He were of a certain other world, He says, "I am not of this world." Now, of this world we have said beforehand, that the explanation was difficult; and for this reason, that there might not be afforded to any an occasion of entertaining the supposition that we maintain the existence of certain imafjes which the Greeks call " ideas:" for it is certainly alien to our writers to speak of an incorporeal world existing in the imagination alone, or in the fleeting world of thoughts; and how they can assert either that the Saviour comes from thence, or that the saints w ill go thither, I do not see. There is no doubt, however, that something more illustrious and excellent than this present world is pointed out by the Saviour, at which He incites and encourages believers to aim. But whether that world to which He desires to allude be far separated and divided from this, either by situation, or nature, or glory; or whether it be superior in glory and quality, but confined within the limits of this world (which seems to me more probable), is nevertheless uncertain, and in my opinion an unsuitable subject for human thought. But from what Clement seems to indicate when he says, "The ocean is impassable to men, and those worlds which are behind it," speaking in the plural number of the worlds which are behind it, which he intimates are administered and governed by the same providence of the Most High God, he appears to throw out to us some germs of that view by which the whole universe of existing things, celestial and super-celestial, earthly and infernal, is generally called one perfect world, within which, or by which, other worlds, if any there are, must be supposed to be contained. For which reason he wished the globe of the sun or moon, and of the other bodies called planets, to be each termed worlds. Nay, even that pre-eminent globe itself which they call the non-wandering (atrxavrj), they nevertheless desire to have properly called world. Finally, they summon the book of Baruch the prophet to bear witness to this assertion, because in it the seven worlds or heavens are more clearly pointed out. Never- Jolm x ii. 16.

tlieless, above that sphere which they call non-wandering a7r avri)j they will have another sphere to exist, which they say, exactly as our heaven contains all things which are under it, comprehends by its immense size and indescribable extent the spaces of all the spheres together within its more magnificent circumference; so that all things are within it, as this earth of ours is under heaven. And this also is believed to be called in the holy Scriptures the good land, and the land of the living, having its own heaven, which is higher, and in which the names of the saints are said to be written, or to have been written, by the Saviour; by which heaven that earth is confined and shut in, which the Saviour in the Gospel promises to the meek and merciful. For they would have this earth of ours, which formerly was named " Dry," to have derived its appellation from the name of that earth, as this heaven also was named firmament from the title of that heaven. But we have treated at greater length of such opinions in the place where we had to inquire into the meaning of the declaration, that in the beginning " God made the heavens and the earth." For another heaven and another earth are shown to exist besides that " firmament" which is said to have been made after the second day, or that " dry land " which was afterwards called " earth." Certainly, what some say of this world, that it is corruptible because it was made, and yet is not corrupted, because the will of God, who made it and holds it together lest corruption should rule over it, is stronger and more powerful than corruption, may more correctly be supposed of that world which we have called above a " non-wandering " sphere, since by the will of God it is not at all subject to corruption, for the reason that it has not admitted any causes of corruption, seeing it is the world of the saints and of the thoroughly purified, and not of the wicked, like that w orld of ours. We must see, moreover, lest perhaps it is with reference to this that the apostle says, "While we look not at the things which are seen, but at the things which are not seen; for the things which are seen are temporal, but the things which are unseen are eternal. For we knov that if our earthly house of this tabernacle were dissolved, we have a building of God, an house not made with hands, eternal in the heavens." And when he says elsewhere, ' Because I shall see the heavens, the works of Thy fingers," and when God said, regarding all things visible, by the mouth of His prophet, "My hand has formed all these things," He declares that that eternal house in the heavens which He promises to His saints was not made with hands, pointing out, doubtless, the difference of creation in things which are seen and in those which are not seen. For the same thing is not to be understood by the expressions, "those things which are not seen," and " those things which are invisible." For those things which are invisible are not only not seen, but do not even possess the property of visibility, being what the Greeks call aa-wfiara i. e. incorporeal; whereas those of which Paul says, "They are not seen," possess indeed the property of being seen, but, as he explains, are not yet beheld by those to Yhom they are promised.

7. Having sketched, then, so far as we could understand, these three opinions regarding the end of all things, and the supreme blessedness, let each one of our readers determine for himself, with care and diligence, whether any one of them can be approved and adopted. For it has been said that we must suppose either that an incorporeal existence is possible, 1 2 Cor. iv. 18-v. 1. pg iii 3 3 ig. Lxvi. 2.

This passage is foimd in Jerome's letter to Avitus, and, literally-translated, is as follows: " A threefold suspicion, therefore, is suggested to us regarding the end, of which the reader may examine which is the true and the better one. For we shall either live without a body, when, being subject to Christ, we shall be subject to God, and God shall be all in all; or, as things subject to Christ will be subject along with Clu-ist Himself to God, and enclosed in one covenant, so all substance will be reduced to the best quality and dissolved into an ether, which is of a purer and simpler nature; or at least that sphere which we have called above Tr. otvij, and whatever is contained within its circumference (cir-culo), will be dissolved into nothing, but that one by which the anti-zone d'jtii cjyi) itself is held together and surrounded will be called a good land; and, moreover, another sphere which surrounds this very earth itself with its revolution, and is called heaven, will be preserved for a habitation of the saints."

after all things have become subject to Christ, and through Christ to God the Father, when God will be all and in all; or that when, notwithstanding all things have been made subject to Christ, and through Christ to God (with whom they formed also one spirit, in respect of spirits being rational natures), then the bodily substance itself also being united to most pure and excellent spirits, and being changed into an ethereal condition in proportion to the quality or merits of those who assume it (according to the apostle's w ords, "We also shall be changed"), will shine forth in splendour; or at least that when the fashion of those things which are seen passes away, and all corruption has been shaken off and cleansed away, and when the whole of the space occupied by this world, in which the spheres of the planets are said to be, has been left behind and beneath, then is reached the fixed abode of the pious and the good situated above that sphere, which is called non-wandering (atrxay??), as in a good land, in a land of the living, which will be inherited by the meek and gentle; to which land belongs that heaven (which, with its more magnificent extent, surrounds and contains that land itself) which is called truly and chiefly heaven, in which heaven and earth, the end and perfection of all things, may be safely and most confidently placed, where, viz., these, after their apprehension and their chastisement for the offences which they have undergone by way of purgation, may, after having fulfilled and discharged every obligation, deserve a habitation in that land; while those who have been obedient to the word of God, and have henceforth by their obedience shown themselves capable of wisdom, are said to deserve the kingdom of that heaven or heavens; and thus the prediction is more worthily fulfilled, ' Blessed are the meek, for they shall inherit the earth;" and, "Blessed are the poor in spirit, for they shall inherit the kingdom of heaven;" and the declaration in the Psalm, "Pie shall exalt thee, and thou shalt inherit the land."' For it is called a descent to this earth, but an 1 Omnique hoc mundi statu, in quo planetarum dicuutiir spli rse, snpergresso atqiie superato.

2 Matt. V. 5. 3 Matt. v. 3. ' Ps. xxxvii. 34.

exaltation to that which is on high. In this way, therefore, does a sort of road seem to be opened up by the departure of the saints from that earth to those heavens; so that they do not so much appear to abide in that Land, as to inhabit it with an intention, viz., to pass on to the inheritance of the kingdom of heaven, when they have reached that degree of perfection also.

CHAPTER IV.

THE GOD OF THE LAW AND THE PROPHETS, AND THE 1. Having now briefly arranged these points in order as we best could, it follows that, agreeably to our intention from the first, we refute those who think that the Father of our Lord Jesus Christ is a different God from Him who gave the; answers of the law to Moses, or commissioned the prophets, who is the God of our fathers, Abraham, Isaac, and Jacob. ' For in this article of faith, first of all, we must be firmly grounded. We have to consider, then, the expression of frequent recurrence in the Gospels, and subjoined to all the acts of our Lord and Saviour, " that it might be fulfilled which was spoken by this or that prophet," it being manifest that the prophets are the prophets of that God who made the world. From this therefore we draw the conclusion, that Pie wdio sent the prophets, Himself predicted what was to be foretold of Christ. And there is no doubt that the Father Himself, and not another different from Him, uttered these predictions. The practice, moreover, of the Saviour or His apostles, frequently quoting illustrations from the Old Testament, shows that they attribute authority to the ancients. The injunction also of the Saviour, when exhorting His disciples to the exercise of kindness, ' Be ye perfect, even as your Father wdio is in heaven is perfect; for He commands His sun to rise upon the evil and the good, and sendeth rain on the just and on the unjust," most evidently suggests even to 1 Matt. V. 48, 49.

a person of feeble understanding, that He is proposing to the imitation of His disciples no other God than the maker of heaven and the bestower of the rain. Again, what else does the expression, which ought to be used by those who pray, "Our Father who art in heaven," appear to indicate, save that God is to be sought in the better parts of the world, i. e. of His creation? Further, do not those admirable principles which He lays down respecting oaths, saying that we ought not to " swear either by heaven, because it is the throne of God; nor by the earth, because it is His footstool," harmonize most clearly with the words of the prophet, "Heaven is my throne, and the earth is my footstool?" And also when casting out of the temple those who sold sheep, and oxen, and doves, and pouring out the tables of the money-changers, and saying, "Take these things hence, and do not make my Father's house a house of merchandise," He undoubtedly called Him his Father, to whose name Solomon had raised a magnificent temple. The words, moreover, "Have ye not read what was spoken by God to Moses: I am the God of Abraham, and the God of Isaac, and the God of Jacob; He is not a God of the dead, but of the living," most clearly teach us, that He called the God of the patriarchs (because they were holy, and were alive) the God of the living, the same, viz., who had said in the prophets, "I am God, and besides me there is no God." For if the Saviour, knowing that He who is written in the law is the God of Abraham, and that it is the same who says, "I am God, and besides me there is no God," acknowledges that very one to be His Father who is ignorant of the existence of any other God above Himself, as the heretics suppose. He absurdly declares Him to be His Father who does not know of a greater God. But if it is not from ignorance, but from deceit, that He says there is no other God than Himself, then it is a much greater absurdity to confess that His Father is guilty of falsehood. From all which this conclusion is arrived at, that He knows 1 Matt. vi. 9. 2 Matt. v. 34, 35.

3 Isa. Ixvi. 1. John ii. IG.

Matt. xxii. 32; cf. Ex. iii. 6. Isa. xlv. 6.

of no other Father than God, the Founder and Creator of all things.

2. It would be tedious to collect out of all the passages in the Gospels the proofs by which the God of the law and or the Gospels is shown to be one and the same. Let us touclii briefly upon the Acts of the Apostles where Stephen and the other apostles address their prayers to that God who made heaven and earth, and who spoke by the mouth of His holy prophets, calling Him the " God of Abraham, of Isaac, and of Jacob;" the God who "brought forth His people out of the land of Egypt." Which expressions undoubtedly clearly direct our understandings to faith in the Creator, and implant an affection for Him in those who have learned piously and faithfully thus to think of Him; according to the words of the Saviour Himself, who, when He was asked which was the greatest commandment in the law, replied, "Thou shalt love the Lord thy God with all thy heart, and with all thy soul, and with all thy mind. And the second is like unto it, Thou shalt love thy neighbour as thyself." And to these J He added: " On these two commandments hang all the law and the prophets." How is it, then, that He commends to him whom He was instructing, and was leading to enter on the office of a disciple, this commandment above all others, by which undoubtedly love was to be kindled in him towards the God of that law, inasmuch as such had been declared by the law in these very words? But let it be granted, notwithstanding all these most evident proofs, that it is of some other unknown God that the Saviour says, "Thou shalt love the Lord thy God with all thy heart," etc. etc. How, in that case, if the law and the prophets are, as they say, from the Creator, i. e. from another God than He whom He calls good, shall that appear to be logically said which He subjoins, viz. that " on these two commandments hang the law and the prophets? " For how shall that which is strange and foreign to God depend upon Him? And when Paul says, "I

thank my God, whom I serve in my spirit from my forefathers with pure conscience," he clearly shows that he came not 1 Acts vii. 2 Matt. xxii. 37, 39, 40. 2 Tim. i. 3.

to some new God, but to Christ. For what other forefathers of Paul can be intended, except those of whom he says, "Are they Hebrews? so am I: are they Israelites? so am I." Nay, will not the very preface of his Epistle to the Romans clearly show the same thing to those who know how to understand the letters of Paul, viz. what God he preaches? For his words are: " Paul, the servant of Jesus Christ, called to be an apostle, set apart to the gospel of God, which He had promised afore by His prophets in the holy Scriptures concerning His Son, who was made of the seed of David according to the flesh, and who was declared to be the Son of God with power, according to the spirit of holiness, by the resurrection from the dead of Christ Jesus our Lord," etc. Moreover, also the following, "Thou shalt not muzzle the mouth of the ox that treadeth out the corn. Doth God take care for oxen? or saith he it altogether for our sakes? For our sakes, no doubt, this is written, that he that plougheth should plough in hope, and he that thresheth in hope of partaking of the fruits."" By which he manifestly shows that God, who gave the law on our account, i. e. on account of the apostles, says, "Thou shalt not muzzle the mouth of the ox that treadeth out the corn;" whose care was not for oxen, but for the apostles, who were preaching the gospel of Christ. In other passages also, Paul, embracing the promises of the law, says, ' Honour thy father and thy mother, which is the first commandment with promise; that it may be well with thee, and that thy days may be long upon the land, the good land, which the Lord thy God will give thee."' By which he undoubtedly makes known that the law, and the God of the law, and His promises, are pleasing to him.

3. But as those who uphold this heresy are sometimes accustomed to mislead the hearts of the simple by certain deceptive sophisms, I do not consider it improper to bring forward the assertions which they are in the habit of making, and to refute their deceit and falsehood. The following, then, are their declarations. It is written, that "no man 1 2 Cor. xi. 22. Rom. i. 1-4.

s 1 Cor. ix. 9,10; cf. Deut. xxv. 4. Eph. vi. 2, 3; cf. Ex. xx. 12.

hath seen God at anytime." But that God whom Moses preaches was both seen by Closes himself, and by his fathers before him; wdiereas He who is announced by the Saviour has never been seen at all by any one. Let us therefore ask them and ourselves whether they maintain that he whom they acknowledge to be God, and allege to be a different God from the Creator, is visible or invisible. And if they shall say that he is visible, besides being proved to go against the declaration of Scripture, wdiich says of the Saviour, "He is the image of the invisible God, the first-born of every creature,""" they will fall also into the absurdity of asserting that God is corporeal. For nothing can be seen except by help of form, and size, and colour, which are special properties of bodies. And if God is declared to be a body, then He will also be found to be material, since every body is composed of matter. But if He be composed of matter, and matter is undoubtedly corruptible, then, according to them, God is liable to corruption! We shall put to them a second question. Is matter made, or is it uncreated, i. e. not made? And if they shall answer that it is not made, i. e. uncreated, we shall ask them if one portion of matter is God, and the other part the world? But if they shall say of matter that it is made, it will undoubtedly follow that they confess Him w hom they declare to be God to have been made! a result which certainly neither their reason nor ours can admit. But they wall say, God is invisible. And what will you do? If you say that He is invisible by nature, then neither ought He to be visible to the Saviour. Whereas, on the contrary, God, the Father of Christ, is said to be seen, because "he wdio sees the Son," he says, " sees also the Father." This certainly would press us very hard, were the expression not understood by us more correctly of understanding, and not of seeing. For he wdio has understood the Son will understand the Father also. In this way, then, Moses too must be supposed to have seen God, not beholding Him with the bodily eye, but understanding Him with the vision of the heart and the perception of the mind, and that only in some 1 John i. 18. 2 coi i 15 3 jolm xiv. 9.

degree. For it is manifest that He, viz., who gave answers to Moses, said, ' You shall not see my face, but my hinder parts." These words are, of course, to be understood in that mystical sense which is befitting divine words, those old wives' fables being rejected and despised which are invented by ignorant persons respecting the anterior and posterior parts of God. Let no one indeed suppose that we have indulged any feeling of impiety in saying that even to the Saviour the Father is not visible. Let him consider the distinction which we employ in dealing with heretics. For we have explained that it is one thing to see and to be seen, and another to know and to be known, or to understand and to be understood. To see, then, and to be seen, is a property of bodies, which certainly will not be appropriately applied either to the Father, or to the Son, or to the Holy Spirit, in their mutual relations with one another. For tlie nature of the Trinity surpasses the measure of vision, granting to those who are in the body, i. e. to all other creatures, the property of vision in reference to one another. But to a nature that is incorporeal and for the i iost part intellectual, no other atttribute is appropriate save that of knowing or being known, as the Saviour Himself declares wdien He says, "No man knoweth the Son, save the Father; nor does any one know the Father, save the Son, and he to whom the Son will reveal Him." It is clear, then, that He has not said, "No one has seen the Father, save the Son;" but, "No one knoavetli the Father, save the Son."

4. And now, if, on account of those expressions which occur in the Old Testament, as when God is said to be angry or to repent, or when any other human affection or passion is described, our opponents think that they are furnished with grounds for refuting us, who maintain that God is altogether impassible, and is to be regarded as wholly free from all affections of that kind, we have to show them that similar 1 Ex. xxxiii. 20, cf. 23.

Aliud sit videre et videri, et aliud nosse et nosci, vel cognoscere atque cognosci. Matt. xi. 27.

statements are found even in the parables of the Gospel; as when it is said, that he who planted a vineyard, and let it out to husbandmen, who slew the servants that were sent to them, and at last put to death even the son, is said in anger to have taken away the vineyard from them, and to have delivered over the wicked husbandmen to destruction, and to have handed over the vineyard to others, who would yield liim the fruit in its season. And so also with regard to those citizens who, when the head of the household had set out to receive for himself a kingdom, sent messengers after him, saying, " We will not have this man to reign over us;" for the head of the household having obtained the kingdom, returned, and in anger commanded them to be put to death before him, and burned their city with fire. But when we read either in the Old Testament or in the New of the anger of God, we do not take such expressions literally, but seek in them a spiritual meaning, that we may think of God as He deserves to be thought of. And on these points, when expounding the verse in the second Psalm, ' Then shall He speak to them in His anger, and trouble them in His fury,"" we showed, to the best of our poor ability, how such an expression ought to be understood.

CHAPTER Y.

ON JUSTICE AND GOODNESS.

1. Now, since this consideration has weight with some, that the leaders of that heresy (of which we have been speaking) think they have established a kind of division, according to which they have declared that justice is one thing and goodness another, and have applied this division even to divine things, maintaining that the Father of our Lord Jesus Christ ' is indeed a good God, but not a just one, whereas the God jl of the law and the prophets is just, but not good; I think ') it necessary to return, with as much brevity as possible, an 1 Luke xix. 14. 2 pg,- i 5,

ORTG. G- answer to these statements. These persons, then, consider goodness to be some such affection as would have benefits conferred on all, although the recipient of them be unworthy and undeserving of any kindness; but here, in my opinion, they have not rightly applied their definition, inasmuch as they think that no benefit is conferred on him who is visited with any suffering or calamity. Justice, on the other hand, they view as that quality which rewards every one according to his deserts. But here, again, they do not rightly interpret the meaning of their own definition. For they think that it is just to send evils upon the wicked and benefits upon the, good; i. e. so that, according to their view, the just G. q4 does ; not appear to wish well to the bad, but to be animated by'a JJiind of hatred against them. And they gather togetlier instances of this, wherever they find a history in the Scriptures of the Old Testament, relating, e. g. the punishment of the deluge or the fate of those who are described as perishing in it, or the destruction of Sodom and Gomorrha by a shower of fire and brimstone, or the falling of all the people in the wilderness on account of their sins, so that none of those who had left Egypt were found to have entered the promised land, with the exception of Joshua and Caleb. Whereas from the New Testament they gather together words of compassion and piety, through which the disciples are trained by the Saviour, and by which it seems to be declared that no one is j: good save God the Father only; and by this means they i have ventured to style the Father of the Saviour Jesus Christ 1 a good God, but to say that the God of the world is a different one, whom they are pleased to term just, but not also good.

2. Now I think they must, in the first place, be required to show, if they can, agreeably to their own definition, that; the Creator is just in punishing according to their deserts, either those who perished at the time of the deluge, or the inhabitants of Sodom, or those who had quitted Egypt, seeing we sometimes behold committed crimes more wicked and detestable than those for which the above-mentioned persons were destroyed, while we do not yet see every sinner paying tlie penalty of his misdeeds. Will they say that He who at one time was just has been made good? Or will they rather be of opinion that He is even now just, but is patiently endurincr

human offences, while that then He was not even just, inasmuch as He exterminated innocent and sucking children along wdth cruel and ungodly giants? Now, such are their opinions, because they know not how to understand anything beyond the letter; otherwise they would show how it is literal justice for sins to be visited upon the heads of children to the third and fourth generation, and on children's children after them. By us, however, such things are not understood literally; but, as Ezekiel taught-wlien relating the parable, we inquire what is the inner meaning contained in the parable itself. Moreover, they ought to explain this also, how He is 'just, and rewards every one according to his merits, who punishes earthly-minded persons and the devil, seeing they have done nothing worthy of punishment. For they could not do any good if, according to them, they w ere of a wicked and ruined nature. For as they style Him a judge. He appears to be a judge not so much of actions as of natures; and if a bad nature cannot do good, neither can a good nature do evil. Then, in the next place, if He whom they call good is good to all. He is undoubtedly good also to those who are destined to perish. And why does He not save them? If He does not desire to do so. He will be no longer good; if He does desire it, and y cannot effect it, He will not be omnipotent. Why do they not rather hear the Father of our Lord Jesus Christ in the Gospels, preparing fire for the devil and his angels? And j how shall that proceeding, as penal as it is sad, appear to be, according to their view, the work of the good God? Even the Saviour Himself, the Son of the good God, protests in the Gospels, and declares that " if signs and wonders had been done in Tyre and Sidon, they would have repented long ago, sitting in sackcloth and ashes." And when He had come near to those very cities, and had entered their territory, why, pray, does He avoid entering those cities, and exhibiting Ezek. xviii. 3. ' Poenitentiam egissent.

to tliem abundance of signs and wonders, if it were certain that they would have repented, after they had been performed, in sackcloth and ashes? But as He does not do this, He undoubtedly abandons to destruction those whom the language of the Gospel shows not to have been of a wicked or ruined nature, inasmuch as it declares they were capable of re- pentance. Again, in a certain parable of the Gospel, where the king enters in to see the guests reclining at the banquet, he beheld a certain individual not clothed with wedding raiment, and said to him, "Friend, how earnest thou in hither, not having a wedding garment?" and then ordered his servants, " Bind him hand and foot, and cast him into outer darkness; there will be weeping and gnashing of teeth." Let them tell us who is that king who entered in to see the guests, and finding one amongst them with unclean garments, commanded him to be bound by his servants, and thrust out into outer darkness. Is he the same whom they call just , How then had he commanded good and bad alike to be invited, without directing their merits to be inquired into by his servants? By such procedure would be indicated, not the character of a just God who rewards according to men's deserts, as they assert, but of one who displays undiscriminating goodness towards all. Now, if this must necessarily be understood of the good God, i. e. either of Christ or of the. Father of Christ, what other objection can they bring against he justice of God's judgment? Nay, what else is there so unjust charged by them against the God of the law as to order him who had been invited by His servants, whom He had sent to call good and bad alike, to be bound hand and foot, and to be thrown into outer darkness, because he had on unclean garments?

3. And now, what we have drawn from the authorIt of Scripture ought to be sufficient to refute the arguments of the heretics. It will not, however, appear improper if we discuss the matter with them shortly, on the grounds of reason itself. We ask them, then, if they know what is regarded among men as the ground of virtue and wickedness, and if it 1 Matt. xxii. 12, 13.

appears to follow that we can speak of virtues in God, or, as they think, in these two Gods. Let them give an answer also to the question, whether they consider goodness to be a virtue; and as they will undoubtedly admit it to be so, what will they say of injustice? They will never certainly, in my opinion, be so foolish as to deny that justice is a virtue. Accordingly, if virtue is a blessing, and justice is a virtue, then without doubt justice is goodness. But if they say that justice is not a blessing, it must either be an evil or an indifferent thing. Now I think it folly to return any answer to those who say that justice is an evil, for I shall have the appearance of replying either to senseless words, or to men out of their minds. How can that appear an evil which is able to reward the good with blessings, as they themselves also admit? But if they say that it is a thing of indifference, it follows that since justice is so, sobriety also, and prudence, and all the other virtues, are things of indifference. And what answer shall we make to Paul, when he says, " If there be any virtue, and if there be any praise, think on these things, which ye have learned, and received, and heard, and seen in me?" Let them learn, therefore, by searching the holy Scriptures, what are the individual virtues, and not deceive themselves by saying that that God who rewards every one Ijn according to his merits, does, through hatred of evil, recompense the wicked with evil, and not because those wdio have sinned need to be treated with severer remedies, and because He applies to them those measures which, with the prospect of improvement, seem nevertheless, for the present, to produce a feeling of pain. They do not read what is written respecting the hope of those who were destroyed in the deluge; of which hope Peter himself thus speaks in his first epistle: ' That Christ, indeed, w as put to death in the flesh, but quickened by the Spirit, by which He went and preached to the spirits who were kept in prison, who once were unbelievers, when they awaited the long-suffering of God in the days of Noah, when the ark was preparing, in which a few, i. e. eight souls, were saved by water. Whereunto also baptism by a 1 Pliil. iv. 8, 9.

like figure now saves you." And witli regard to Sodom and Gomorrlia, let them tell us whether they believe the prophetic words to be those of the Creator God of Him, viz., who is related to have rained upon them a shower of fire and brimstone. What. does Ezeldel the prophet say of them " Sodom," he says, " shall be restored to her former condition." But why, in afflicting those who are deserving of punishment, does He not afflict them for their good? who also says to Chaldea, "Thou hast coals of fire, sit upon them; they will be a help to thee." And of those also who fell in the desert, let them hear what is related in the seventy-eighth Psalm, which bears the superscription of Asaph; for he says, "When He slew them, then they sought Him." He does not say that some sought Him after others had been slain, but he says that the destruction of those who were killed was of such a nature that, when put to death, they sought

God. By all which it is established, that the God of the law and the Gospels is one and the same, a just and good God, and that He confers benefits justly, and punishes with kindness; since neither goodness without justice, nor justice without goodness, can display the real dignity of the divine nature.

We shall add the following remarks, to which we are driven by their subtleties. If justice is a different thing from goodness, then, since evil is the opposite of good, and injustice of justice, injustice will doubtless be something else than an evil; and as, in your opinion, the just man is not good, so neither will the unjust man be wicked; and again, as the good man is not just, so the wicked man also will not be unjust. But wdio does not see the absurdity, that to a good God one should be opposed that is evil; while to a just God, whom they allege to be inferior to the good, no one should be opposed! For there is none who can be called unjust, as there is a Satan who is called wicked. What, then, are we to do? Let 1 1 Pet. iii. 18-21. gzek. xvi. 55, cf. 53.

s Isa. xlvii. 14, 15. The Septuagint here diiiers from the Hebrew: tycit? a, v6pcix, c(, g Trvpog, scadiax: etr ocvrovs, obroi iouvroii aoi (?07iiioi. Ps. Ixxviii. 34.

us give up the position which we defend, for tliey will not be able to maintain that a bad man is not also unjust, and an unjust man wicked. And if these qualities be indissolubly inherent in these opposites, viz. injustice in wickedness, or wickedness in injustice, then unquestionably the good man will be inseparable from the just man, and the just from the (good; so that, as we speak of one and the same wickedness I in malice and injustice, we may also hold the virtue of good-) I ness and justice to be one and the same, 4. They again recall us, however, to the words of Scripture, by bringing forw ard that celebrated question of theirs, affirming that it is written, "A bad tree cannot produce good fruits; for a tree is known by its fruit." What, then, is their position? What sort of tree the law is, is shown by its fruits, i. e. by the language of its precepts. For if the law-be found to be good, then undoubtedl ' He who gave it is believed to be a good God. But if it be just rather than good, then God also will be considered a just legislator. The Apostle Paul makes use of no circumlocution, when he says, "The law is good; and the commandmeiit is holy, and just, and good." From which it is clear that Paul had not learned the language of those who separate justice from goodness, but had been instructed by that God, and illuminated by His Spirit, who is at the same time both holy, and good, and just; and speaking by whose Spirit he declared that the commandment of the law was holy, and just, and good. And that he might show more clearly that goodness was in the commandment to a greater degree than justice and holiness, repeating his words, he used, instead of these three epithets, that of goodness alone, saying, "Was then that which is good made death unto me? God forbid."' As he knew that goodness was the gemis of the virtues, and that justice and holiness were species belonging to the genus, and having in the former verses named genus and species together, he fell back, when repeating his words, on the genus alone. But in those which follow he says, "Sin wtought death in me by that which is good,"' where he sums up generically what he had before- 1 Matt. vii. 18, cf. xii. 33.- Rom. vii. 12. j ojii. vii. 13.

hand explained specifically. And in this way also is to be nnderstood the declaration, "A good man, out of the good treasure of his heart, bringeth forth good things; and an evil man, out of the evil treasure, bringeth forth evil things." For here also he assumed that there was genus in good or evil, pointing out unquestionably that in a good man there were both justice, and temperance, and prudence, and piety, and everything that can be either called or understood to be good. In like manner also he said that a man was wicked who should w ithout any doubt be unjust, and impure, and unholy, and everything which singly makes a bad man. For as no one considers a man to be wicked without these marks of wickedness (nor indeed can he be so), so also it is certain that without these virtues no one will be deemed to be good. There still remains to them, however, that saying of the Lord in the Gosj)el, which they think is given them in a special manner as a shield, viz. " There is none good but one, God the Father."" This word they declare is peculiar to the Father of Christ, who, however, is different from the God who is Creator of all things, to which Creator he gave no appellation of goodness. Let us s-ee now if, in the Old Testament, the God of the prophets and the Creator and Legislator of the world is not called good. What are the expressions which occur in the Psalms? " How good is God to Israel, to the upright in heart! " and, " Let Israel now say that He is good, that His mercy endureth for ever;"" the language in the Lamentations of Jeremiah, ' The Lord is good to them that wait for Him, to the soul that seeketh Him." As therefore God is frequently called good in the Old Testament, so also the Father of our Lord Jesus Christ is styled just in the Gospels. Finally, in the Gospel according to John, our Lord Himself, when praying to the Father, says, "O just Father, the world hath not known Thee." And lest perhaps they should say that it was owinct to His havinoj assumed human flesh that He called the Creator of the world "Father," and styled Him "Just,"

1 Matt. xii. 35.- Matt. xix. 17. Ps. Ixxiii. 1.

Ps. cxviii. 2. Lam. iii. 25. John xvii. 25: Juste Pater.

they are excluded from such a refuge by the words that immediately follow, "The world hath not known Thee." But, according to them, the world is ignorant of the good God alone. For the world nnquestionably recognises its Creator, the Lord Himself saying that the world lovetli what is its own. Clearly, then, He whom they consider to be the good God, is called just in the Gospels. Any one may at leisure gather together a greater number of proofs, consisting of those passages, where in the New Testament the Father of our Lord Jesus Christ is called just, and in the Old also, where the Creator of heaven and earth is called good; so that the heretics, being convicted by numerous testimonies, may perhaps som. e time be put to the blush.

CHAPTEE YL

ON THE IXCAEXATIOX OF CHEIST.

1. It is now time, after this cursory notice of these points, to resume our investio-ation of the incarnation of our Lord and Saviour, viz. how or why He became man. Having therefore, to the best of our feeble ability, considered His divine nature from the contemplation of His own works rather than from our own feelings, and having nevertheless beheld (with the eye) His visible creation while the invisible creation is seen by faith, because human frailty can neither see all things with the bodily eye nor comprehend them by reason, seeing we men are weaker and frailer than any other rational beings (for those which are in heaven, or are supposed to exist above the heaven, are superior), it remains that we seek a beincp intermediate between all created thinfis and God, i. e. a Mediator, whom the Apostle Paul styles the " firstborn

of every creature." Seeing, moreover, those declarations regarding His majesty which are contained in holy Scripture, that He is called the " image of the invisible God, and the first-born of every creature," and that " in Him were all things created, visible and invisible, whether they be thrones, or dominions, or principalities, or powers, all things 1 Col. i. 15.

were created by Him, and in Him: and He is before all things, and by Ilim all things consist," who is the head of all things, alone having as head God the Father; for it is written, '- The head of Christ is God;" seeing clearly also that it is written, "No one knoweth the Father, save the Son, nor doth any one know the Son, save the Father" (for who can know what wisdom is, save He who called it into beinsc? Or who can understand clearlv what truth is, save the Father of truth? Who can investigate with certainty the universal nature of His Word, and of God Himself, which nature proceeds from God, except God alone, with whom the Word was), we ought to regard it as certain that this Word, or Eeason (if it is to be so termed), this Wisdom, this Trath, is known to no other than the Father only; and of Him it is written, that " I do not think that the world itself could contain the books which might be written," regarding, viz., the glory and majesty of the Son of God. For it is impossible to commit to writing all those particulars which belong to the glory of the Saviour. After the consideration of questions of such importance concerning the being of the Son of God, we are lost in the deepest amazement that such a nature, pre-eminent above all others, should have divested itself of its condition of majesty and become man, and tabernacled amongst men, as the grace that was poured upon His lips testifies, and as His heavenly Father bore Him witness, and as is confessed by the various signs and wonders and miracles that were performed by Him; who also, before that appearance of His which He manifested in the body, sent the prophets as His forerunners, and the messengers of His advent; and after His ascension into heaven, made His holy apostles, men ignorant and unlearned, taken from the ranks of tax-gatherers or fishermen, but who were filled with the power of His divinity, to itinerate throughout the world, that they might gather together out of every race and every nation a multitude of devout believers in Himself. 2. But of all the marvellous and mighty acts related of 1 Col. i. 16, 17. 2 1 Cor. xi. 3. Matt. xi. 27.

John xxi. 25. Virtutibus, probably for Iwafnaiu.

Him, this altogether surpasses human admiration, and is beyond the power of mortal frailness to understand or feel, how that mighty power of divine majesty, that very Word of the Father, and that very wisdom of God, in which were created all things, visible and invisible, can be believed to have existed within the limits of that man who appeared in Judea; nay, that the Wisdom of God can have entered the womb of a woman, and have been born an infant, and have uttered wailin s like the cries of little children! And that afterwards it should be related that He was greatly troubled in death, saying, as He Himself declared, "My soul is sorrowful, even unto death;" and that at the last He was brought to that death which is accounted the most shameful among men, although He rose again on the third day. Since, then, we see in Him some things so human that they appear to differ in no respect from the common frailty of mortals, and some things so divine that they can appropriately belong to nothing else than to the primal and ineffable nature of Deity, the narrowness of human understanding can find no outlet; but, overcome with the amazement of a mighty admiration, knows not whither to w ithdraw, or what to take hold of, or whither to turn. If it think of a God, it sees a mortal; if it think of a man, it beholds Him returning from the grave, after overthrowing the empire of death, laden with its spoils. And therefore the spectacle is to be contemplated with all fear and reverence, that the truth of both natures may be clearly sho-s ii to exist in one and the same Being; so that nothing unworthy or unbecoming may be perceived in that divine and ineffable substance, nor vet those thincrs which were done be supposed to be the illusions of imaginary appearances. To utter these things in human ears, and to explain them in words, far surpasses the powers either of our rank, or of our intellect and language. I think that it surpasses the power even of the holy apostles; nay, the explanation of that mystery may perhaps be beyond the grasp of the entire creation of celestial powers. Regarding Him, then, we shall state, in the fewest possible words, the contents of our creed rather 1 Matt. xxvi. 38.

than the assertions Yhich human reason is wont to advance; and this from no spirit of rashness, but as called for by the nature of our arrangement, laying before you rather what may be termed our suspicions than any clear affirmations.

3. The Only-begotten of God, therefore, through whom, as the previous course of the discussion has shown, all things were made, visible and invisible, accordhig to the view of Scripture, both made all things, and loves what He made. For since He is Himself the invisible image of the invisible God, He conveyed invisibly a share in Himself iqL all His rational creatures, so that each one obtained a part of Him exactly proportioned to the amount of affection with which he regarded Him. But since, agreeably to the faculty of freewill, variety and diversity characterized the individual souls, so that one was attached with a warmer love to the Author of its being, and another with a feebler and weaker regard, that soul (animd) regarding which Jesus said, "No one shall take my life (animam) from me," inhering, from the beginning of the creation, and afterwards, inseparably and indissolubly in Him, as being the Wisdom and Word of God, and the Trutli and the true Light, and receiving Him wholly, and passing into His light and splendour, was made with Him in a pre-eminent degree one spirit, according to the promise of the apostle to those who ought to imitate it, that " he who is joined in the Lord is one spirit."'" This substance of a soul, then, being intermediate between God and the flesh it being impossible for the nature of God to intermingle with a body without an intermediate instrument the God-man is born, as we have said, that substance being the intermediary to whose nature it was not contrary to assume a body. But neither, on the other hand, was it opposed to the nature of that soul, as a rational existence, to receive God, 1 Jolm X, 18. "No otlier soul wliich descended into a human body lias stamped on itself a pure and unstained resemblance of its former stamp, save that one of which the Saviour says, ' No one will take my soul from me, but I lay it down of myself." " Jerome, Epistle to Avitiis, p. 763.

2 Principaliter. 1 Cor. vi. 17.

into whom, as stated above, as into the Word, and the yisdom, and the Truth, it had ah'eady wholly entered. And there-f fore deservedly is it also called, along with the flesh which it had assumed, the Son of God, and the Power of God, the Christ, and the Wisdom of God, either because it was wholly in the Son of God, or because it received the Son of God wholly into itself. And again, the Son of God, through whom all things were created, is named Jesus Christ and the Son of man. For the Son of God also is said to have died in reference, viz., to that nature which could admit of death; and He is called the Son of man, who is announced as about to come in the glory of God the Father, with the holy angels. And for this reason, throughout the whole of Scripture, not only is the divine nature spoken of in human words, but the human nature is adorned by appellations of divine dignity. More truly indeed of this than of any other can the statement be affirmed, ' They shall both be in one flesh, and are no longer two, but one flesh." For the Word of God is to be considered as bein: more in one flesh w ith the soul than a man with his wife. But to whom is it more becoming to be also one spirit with God, than to this soul which has so joined itself to God by love as that it may justly be said to be one spirit with Him?

4. That the perfection of his love and the sincerity of his deserved affection formed for it this inseparable union with God, so that the assumption of that soul was not accidental, or the result of a personal preference, but was conferred as the reward of its virtues, listen to the prophet addressing it thus: " Thou hast loved righteousness, and hated wickedness: therefore God, thy God, hath anointed thee with the oil of gladness above thy fellows."" As a reward for its love, then, ' it is anointed with the oil of gladness; i. e. the soul of Christ alono; with the Word of God is made Christ. Because to be anointed ith the oil of irladness means nothiniij else than to be filled vith the Holy Spirit. And when it is said " above thy fellows," it is meant that the grace of the Spirit was not given to it as to the prophets, but that the essential fulness 1 Gen. ii. 2; cf. Mark x. 8.-' le iti afeectiis. pg. ly. 7.

of the Word of God Himself was in it, according to the saying of the apostle, "In whom dwelt all the fulness of the

Godhead bodily." Finally, on this account he has not only said, "Thou hast loved righteousness;" but he adds, " and

Thou hast hated wickedness." For to have hated wickedness is what the Scripture says of Him, that " He did no sin, neither was any guile found in His mouth," and that " He was tempted in all things like as we are, without sin." Nay, the Lord Himself also said, "Which of you will convince me of sin?" And again He says with reference to Himself,

"Behold, the prince of this world cometh, and findeth nothing

I in me." All which passages show that in Him there was ;, no sense of sin; and that the prophet might show more clearly that no sense of sin had ever entered into Him, he

I says, 'Before the boy could have knowledge to call upon father or mother. He turned away from wickedness."

5. Now, if our having shown above that Christ possessed a rational soul should cause a difficulty to any oncj seeing w e have frequently proved throughout all our discussions that the nature of souls is capable both of good and evil, the difficulty will be explained in the following way. That the nature, indeed, of His soul was the same as that of all others cannot be doubted, otherwise it could not be called a soul were it not truly one. But since the power of choosing good and evil is within the

reach of all, this soul which belonged to Christ elected to love righteousness, so that in proportion tojthe immensity of its love it clung to it unchangeably and inseparably, so that firmness of purpose, and immensity of affection, and an inextinguishable warmth of love, destroyed all susceptibility (sensum) for alteration and change; and that which formerly depended upon the will was changed by the power of long custom into nature; and so we must believe 1 Col. ii. 9. 2 isa. liii. 9. s H eb. iv. 15.

John viii. 46. Jolin xiv. 30.

This quotation is made up of two clifferent parts of Isaiah: chap, viii. 4, "Before the child shall have knowledge to cry, My lather and my mother; " and chap. vii. 16, "Before the child shall know' to refuse the evil, and choose the good.".

that there existed in Christ a human and rational soul, without supposing that it had any feeling or possibiuty of sin.

6. To explain the matter more fully, it will not appear absurd to make use of an illustration, although on a subject of so much difficulty it is not easy to obtain suitable illustrations. However, if we may speak without offence, the metal iron is capable of cold and heat. If, then, a mass of iron be kept constantly in the fire, receiving the heat through all its pores and veins, and the fire being continuous and the iron never removed from it, it become wholly converted into the latter; could we at all say of this, which is by nature a mass of iron, that wdien placed in the fire, and incessantly burning, it was at any time capable of admitting cold? On the contrary, because it is more consistent w-ith truth, do w e not rather say, wdiat we often see happening in furnaces, that it has become wholly fire, seeing nothing but fire is visible in it? And if any one were to attempt to touch or handle it, he would experience the action not of iron, but of fire. In this way, then, that soul which, like an iron in the fire, has been perpetually placed in the Word, and perpetually in the Wisdom, and perpetually in God,- is God in all that it does, feels, and understands, and therefore can be called neither convertible nor mutable, inasmuch as, being incessantly heated, it possessed immutabihty from its union with the Word of God. To all the saints, finally, some warmth from the Word of God must be supposed to have passed; and in this soul the divine fire itself must be believed to have rested, from which some warmth may have passed to others. Lastly, the expression, "God, thy God, anointed thee with the oil of gladness above thy fellows," " shows that that soul is anointed in one way with the oil of gladness, i. e. with the word of God and wisdom; and his fellows, i. e. the holy prophets and apostles, in another. For they are said to have " run in the odour of his ointments;" and that soul was the vessel which con-

Semper in verbo, semper in sapientia, semper in Deo. 2 Ps. xlv. 7.

Illi enim in odore imguentorum ejus circumire dicuntur; perhaps an allubion to Song of Sol. i. 3 or to Ps. xlv. 8.

tained that very ointment of whose fragrance all the worthy prophets and apostles were made partakers. As, then, the substance of an ointment is one thing and its odour another, so also Christ is one thing and His fellows another. And as the vessel itself, which contains the substance of the ointment, can by no means admit any foul smell; whereas it is possible that those who enjoy its odour may, if they remove a little way from its fragrance, receive any foul odour which comes upon them: so, in the same way, was it impossible that Christ, beina as it were the vessel itself, in which was the substance of the ointment, should receive an odour of an opposite kind, while they wdio are His " fellows" will be partakers and receivers of His odour, in proportion to their nearness to the vessel.

7. I think, indeed, that Jeremiah the prophet, also, understanding what was the nature of the wisdom of God in him which was the same also which he had assumed for the salvation of the world, said, "The breath of our countenance is Christ the Lord, to whom we said, that under His shadow we shall live among the nations." And inasmuch as the shadow of our body is inseparable from the body, and unavoidably performs and repeats its movements and gestures, I think that he, wishing to point out the work of Christ's soul, and the movements inseparably belonging to it, and which accomplished everything according to His movements and will, called this the shadow of Christ the Lord, under which shadow we were to live among the nations. For in the mystery of this assumption the nations live, who, imitating it through faith, come to salvation. David also, when saying, "Be mindful of my reproach, O Lord, with which they reproached me in exchange for Thy Christ," seems to me to indicate the same. And what else does Paul mean when he says, "Your Hfe is hid with Christ in God;"" and again in another passage, "Do you seek a proof of Christ, who speaketh in me?" And now he says that Christ was hid in God. The meaning of which expression, unless it be shown to be something such as we have pointed out above as intended by 1 Lam. iv. 20. 2 pg, j xxix. 50, 51. Col. iii. 3. 2 Cor. xiii. 3.

the prophet in the words " shadow of Christ," exceeds, perhaps, the apprehension of the human mind. But we see also very many other statements in holy Scripture respecting the meaninir of the word " shadow," as that well-known one in the Gospel according to Luke, where Gabriel says to Mary, "Tlie Spirit of the Lord shall come upon thee, and the power of the Highest shall overshadow thee." And the apostle says with reference to the law, that they who have circumcision in the flesh, " serve for the similitude and shadow of heavenly things."' And elsewhere, ' Is not our life upon the earth a shadow?" If, then, not only the law which is upon the earth is a shadow, but also all our life which is upon the earth is the same, and we live among the nations under the shadow of Christ, we must see whether the truth of all these shadows may not come to be known in that revelation, when no longer through a glass, and darkly, but face to face, all the saints shall deserve to behold the glory of God, and the causes and truth of things. And the pledge of this truth being already received through the Holy Spirit, the apostle said, "Yea, though we have known Christ after the flesh, yet now henceforth know we Him no more."

The above, meanwhile, are the thousihts which have occurred to US, when treating of subjects of such difficulty as the incarnation and deity of Christ. If there be any one, indeed, who can discover something better, and who can establish his assertions by clearer proofs from holy Scriptures, let his' opinion be received in preference to mine.

CHAPTER VIL

ON THE HOLY SPIRIT.

1. As, then, after those first discussions which, according to the requirements of the case, we held at the beginning regarding the Father, Son,- and Holy Spirit, it seemed right 1 Luke i. 35. 2 jjeb. viii. 5.

3 Job viii. 9. 9 Cor. v 16.

ORIG. H that we should retrace our steps, and show that the same God was the creator and founder of the world, and the Father of our Lord Jesus Christ, i. e. that the God of the law and of the prophets and of the gospel was one and the same; and that, in the next place, it ought to be shown, with respect to Christ, in what manner He who had formerly been demonstrated to be the Word and Wisdom of God became man; it remains that we now return with all possible brevity to the subject of the Holy Spirit.

It is time, then, that we say a few words to the best of our ability regarding the Holy Spirit, whom our Lord and Saviour in the Gospel according to John has named the Paraclete. For as it is the same God Plimself, and the same Christ, so also is it the same Holy Spirit who was in the prophets and apostles, i. e. either in those who believed in God before the advent of Christ, or in those who by means of Christ have sought refuge in God. We have heard, indeed, that certain heretics have dared to say that there are two Gods and two Christs, but we have never known of the doctrine of two Holy Spirits being preached by any one. For how could they maintain this out of Scripture, or what distinction could they lay down between Holy Spirit and Holy Spirit, if indeed any definition or description of Holy Spirit can be discovered? For although we should concede to Marcion or to Valentinus that it is possible to draw distinctions in the question of Deity, and to describe the nature of the good God as one, and that of the just God as another, vhat will he devise, or what will he discover, to enable him 'to introduce a distinction in the Holy Spirit? I consider, then, that they are able to discover nothing which may indicate a distinction of any kind whatever.

2. Now we are of opinion that every rational creature, without any distinction, receives a share of Him in the same 1 According to Pamphilus in his Apologij, Origen, in a note on Tit. iii. 10, has made a statement the opposite of this. His words are: "But there are some also who say, that it was one Holy Spirit who was in the prophets, and another who was in the apostles of om Lord Jesus Christ."

RUieUS.

way as of the Wisdom and of the Word of God. I observe, however, that the chief advent of the Holy Spirit is declared to men, after the ascension of Christ to heaven, rather than before His coming into the world. For, before that, it was upon the prophets alone, and upon a few individuals if there happened to be any among the people deserving of it that the gift of the Holy Spirit was conferred; but after the advent of the Saviour, it is written that the prediction of the prophet Joel was fulfilled, ' In the last days it shall come to pass, and I will pour out my Spirit upon all flesh, and they shall prophesy," which is similar to the well-known statement, All nations shall serve Him."' By the grace, then, of the Holy Spirit, along with numerous other results, this most glorious consequence is clearly demonstrated, that with regard to those things which were written in the prophets or in the law of Moses, it was only a few persons at that time, viz. the prophets themselves, and scarcely another individual out of the whole nation, who were able to look beyond the mere corporeal meaning and discover something greater, i. e. something spiritual, in the law or in the prophets; but now there are countless multitudes of believers Avho, although unable to unfold methodically and clearly the results of their spiritual understanding," are nevertheless most firmly persuaded that neither ought circumcision to be understood literally, nor the rest of the Sabbath, nor the pouring out of the blood of an animal, nor that answers were given by God to Moses on these;. points. And this method of apprehension is undoubtedly suggested to the minds of all by the power of the Holy Spirit.

3. And as there are many ways of apprehending Christ, who, although He is wisdom, does not act the part or possess the power of wisdom in all men, but only in those who give themselves to the study of wisdom in Him; and who, although called a physician, does not act as one towards all, but only towards those who understand their feeble and sickly condition, and flee to His compassion that they may obtain health; 1 Joelii. 28. 2 pg jxxii. 11.

Qui licet non omnes possint per ordinem atque ad liquidum spiritualis intelligentise explanare consequentiam.

so also I think Is it with the Holy Spirit, in whom is contained every kind of gifts. For on some is bestowed by the Spirit the word of wisdom, on others the word of knowledge, on others faith; and so to each individual of those who are capable of receiving Him, is the Spirit Himself made to be that quality, or understood to be that which is needed by the individual who has deserved to participate. These divisions and differences not being perceived by those who hear Him called Paraclete in the Gospel, and not duly considering in consequence of w hat work or act He is named the Paraclete, they have compared Him to some common spirits or other, and by this means have tried to disturb the churches of Christ, and so excite dissensions of no small extent among brethren; whereas the Gospel shows Him to be of such power and majesty, that it says the apostles could not yet receive those things which the Saviour wished to teach them until the advent of the Holy Spirit, who, pouring Him. self into their souls, might enlighten them regarding the nature and faith of the Trinity. But these persons, because of the ignorance of their understandings, are not only unable themselves logically to state the truth, but cannot even give their attention to what is advanced by us; and entertaining unworthy ideas of His divinity, have delivered themselves over to errors and deceits, being depraved by a spirit of error, rather than instructed by the teaching of the Holy Spirit, according to the declaration of the apostle, "Following the doctrine of devils, forbidding to marry, to the destruction and ruin of many, and to abstain from meats, that by an ostentatious exhibition of stricter observance they may seduce the souls of the innocent."

4. We must therefore know that the Paraclete is the Holy Spirit, who teaches truths which cannot be uttered in words, and which are, so to speak, unutterable, and " which it is not lawful for a man to utter, " i. e. which cannot be indicated

Ita per singulos, qui eum capere possunt, hoc efficitur, vel hoc intel-ligitur ipse Spiritus, quo indiget ille, qui eum participare meruerit. Schnitzer renders, "And so, in every one who is susceptible of them, the Spirit is exactly that which the receiver chiefly needs."

2 1 Tim. iv. 1-3. 2 2 Cor. xii. 4.

by human language. The phrase " it is not lawful" is, we think, used by the apostle instead of " it is not possible;" as also is the case in the passage where he says, "All things are lawful for me, but all things are not expedient: all things are lawful for me, but all things edify not." For those things which are in our power because we may hav e them, he says are lawful for us. But the Paraclete, who is calledj the Holy Spirit, is so called from His work of consolation, paraclesis being termed in Latin consolatio. For if any one) has deserved to participate in the Holy Spirit by the know"- ledge of His ineffable mysteries, he undoubtedly obtains f comfort and joy of heart. For since he comes by the i teaching of the Spirit to the knowledge of the reasons of all j things which happen liow or why they occur his soul can S in no respect be troubled, or admit any feeling of sorrow; nor is he alarmed by anything, since, clinging to the Word of 't God and His w isdom, he through the Holy Spirit calls Jesus Lord. And since we have made mention of the Paraclete, and have explained as v: e were able what sentiments ought j to be entertained regarding Him; and since our Saviour also is called the Paraclete in the Epistle of John, when he says, "If any of us sin, wc have a Paraclete with the Father, Jesus Christ the righteous, and He is the propitiation for our sins; " let us consider whether this term Paraclete should happen to have one meaning when applied to the Saviour, and anotlier w lien applied to the Holy Spirit. Now Paraclete, when spoken of the Saviour, seems to mean intercessor. For in Greek, Paraclete has both sicrnifications that of intercessor and comforter. On account, then, of the phrase which follows, when he says, "And He is the propitiation for our sins," the name Paraclete seems to be understood in the case of our Saviour as meaning intercessor; for He is said to intercede with the Father because of our sins. In the case of the Holy Spirit, the Paraclete must be) understood in the sense of comforter, inasmuch as He bestows v consolation upon the souls to whom He openly reveals the ' apprehension of spiritual knowledge.

1 1 Cor. X. 23.- 1 John ii. 1, 2.

ON THE SOUL (anIMA).

1. The order of our arrangement now requires us, after the discussion of the preceding subjects, to institute a general inquiry regarding the soul; and, beginning with points of inferior importance, to ascend to those that are of greater. Now, that there are souls in all living things, even in those which live in the waters, is, I suppose, doubted by no one. For the general opinion of all men maintains this; and confirmation from the authority of holy Scripture is added, when it is said that " God made great whales, and every living creature, that moveth which the waters brought forth after their kind."" It is confirmed also from the common intelligence of reason, by those who lay down in certain words a definition of soul. For soul is defined as follows: a substance (fiavrao-Tikrj and opitjr'. fcr, which may be rendered into Latin, although not so appropriately, sensibilis et mohilis This certainly may be said appropriately of all living beings, even of those which abide in the waters; and of winged creatures too, this same definition of anima may be shown to hold good. Scripture also has added its authority to a second opinion, when it says, "Ye shall not eat the blood, because the life of all flesh is its blood; and ye shall not eat the life with the flesh;"' in which it intimates most clearly that the blood of every animal is its life. And if any one now were to ask how it can be said with respect to bees, wasps, and ants, and those other things which are in the waters, oysters and cockles, and all others which are without blood, and are most

Anima.- Animse. " Animam animantiiim.

' Gen, i. 21: 'tzv. oocv-i vxvju uau, Sept.

Erasmus remarks, that (pxiruankV may be rendered imagimtiva, which, is the understanding: opy. yirizt, impulsa-a, which refers to tlie affections (Schnitzer).

6 Animam.

' Lev. xvii. 14:- vyj 'Trcitjr,; aapzcg c. uy. c avroli tw;, Sept.

clearly shown to be living things, that the " life of all flesh is the blood," we must answer, that In living things of that sort the force which is exerted in other animals by the power of red blood is exerted in them by that liquid which is within them, although it be of a different colour; for colour is a thing of no importance, provided the substance be endowed with llfe.- That beasts of burden or cattle of smaller size are endowed with souls, there is, by general assent, no doubt whatever. The opinion of holy Scripture, however, is manifest, when God says, "Let the earth bring forth the living creature after its kind, four-footed beasts, and creeping things, and beasts of the earth after their klnd."' And now Avith respect to man, although no one entertains any doubt, or needs to inquire, yet holy Scripture declares that " God breathed Into his countenance the breath of life, and man became a living soul." It remains that we inquire respecting the angelic order whether they also have souls, or are souls; and also respecting the other divine and celestial powers, as well as those of an opposite kind. We nowhere, indeed, find any authority in holy Scripture for asserting that either the angels, or any other divine spirits that are ministers of God, either possess souls or are called souls, and yet they are felt by very many persons to be endowed with life. But with regard to God, we find It written as follows: " And I will put my soul upon that soul which has eaten blood, and I will root him out from among his people;" and also in another passage,-Your new moons, and sabbaths, and great days, I will not accept; your fasts, and holidays, and festal days, my soul hateth." And in the t-wenty-second Psalm, regarding Christ for it is certain, as the Gospel bears witness, that this Psalm is spoken of Him the following words 1 Yitalis. Animantia.

Gen. i. 24, living creature, animam.

Gen. ii. 7, animam vlventem.

Lev. xvii. 10. It is clear that in the text which Origcn or his translator had before him he must have read pvx, yi instead of Trpoaoitzo-j: otherwise the quotation would be inappropriate (Schnitzer).

6 Isa. i. 13, 14.

occur: " O Lord, be not far from helping me; look to my defence: O God, deliver my soul from the sword, and my beloved one from the hand of the dog;" although there are also many other testimonies respecting the soul of Christ v hen He tabernacled in the flesh.

2. But the nature of the incarnation will render unnecessary any inquiry into the soul of Christ. For as He truly possessed flesh, so also He truly possessed a soul. It is difficult indeed both to feel and to state how that which is called in Scripture the soul of God is to be understood; for we acknowledge that nature to be simple, and without any intermixture or addition. In whatver way, however, it is to be understood, it seems, meanwhile, to be named the soul of God; whereas regarding Christ there is no doubt. And therefore there seems to me no absurdity in either understanding or asserting some such thing regarding the holy angels and the other heavenly powers, since that definition of soul appears applicable also to them. For Avho can rationally

deny that they are " sensible and moveable? " But if that definition appear to be correct, according to which a soul is said to be a substance rationally " sensible and moveable," the same definition would seem also to apply to angels. For what else is in them than rational feeling and motion? Now those beings who are comprehended under the same definition have undoubtedly the same substance. Paul indeed intimates that there is a kind of animal-man who, he says, cannot receive the things of the Spirit of God, but declares that the doctrine of the Holy Spirit seems to him foolish, and that he cannot understand what is to be spiritually discerned. In another passage he says it is sown an animal body, and arises a spiritual body, pointing out that in the resurrection of the just there will be nothing of an animal nature. And therefore we inquire whether there happen to be any substance which, in respect of its being anima, is imperfect. But whether it be imperfect because it falls away from perfection, or because it was so created by God, will form the subject of inquiry when each individual topic shall begin to be discussed 1 Ps. xxii. 20, 21, unicam meara, novce'jti y. ov. Animalem.

in order. For if the animal man receive not the things of the Spirit of God, and because he is animal, is nnable to admit the understanding of a better, i. e. of a divine nature, it is for this reason perhaps that Paul, wishing to teach us more plainly what that is by means of which we are able to comprehend those things which are of the Spirit, i. e. spiritual things, conjoins and associates with the Holy Spirit an understanding rather than a soul." For this, I think, he indicates when he says, "I will pray with the spirit, I will pray with the understanding also; I will sing with the spirit, I will sing with the understanding also."" And he does not say that "I will pray with the soul," but with the spirit and the understanding. Nor does he say, "I will sing with the soul," but with the spirit and the understanding.

3. But perhaps this question is asked. If it be the understanding which prays and sings with the spirit, and if it be the same which receives both perfection and salvation, how is it that Peter says, "Receiving the end of your faith, even the salvation of your souls? " If the soul neither prays nor sings with the spirit, how shall it hope for salvation? or when it attains to blessedness, shall it be no longer called a soul? Let us see if perhaps an answer may be given in this way, that as the Saviour came to save what was lost, that which formerly was said to be lost is not lost when it is saved; so also, perhaps, this which is saved is called a soul, and when it has been placed in a state of salvation will 1 Mens. 2 Anima.- 1 Cor. xiv. 15. 1 Pet. i. 9.

These words are found in Jerome's Epistle to Avitus, and, literally translated, are as follow: "Whence infinite caution is to be employed, lest perchance, after souls have obtained salvation and come to the blessed life, they should cease to be souls. For as our Lord and Saviour came to seek and to save what was lost, that it might cease to be lost; so the soul which was lost, and for whose salvation the Lord came, shall, when it has been saved, cease to be a soul. This point in like manner must be examined, whether, as that which has been lost was at one time not lost, and a time will come when it will be no longer lost; so also at some time a soul may not have been a soul, and a time may be when it will by no means continue to be a soul." A portion of the above is also found, in the original Greek, in the Emperor Justinian's letter to Menas, Patriarch of Constantinople.

receive a name from the Word tliat denotes its more perfect condition. But it appears to some that this also may be added, that as the thing which was lost undoubtedly existed before it was lost, at which time it was something else than destroyed, so also will be the case when it is no longer in a ruined condition. In like manner also, the soul which is said to have perished will appear to have been something at one time, when as yet it had not perished, and on that account would be termed soul, and being again freed from destruction, it may become a second time what it was before it perished, and be called a soul. But from the very signification of the name soul which the Greek word conveys, it has appeared to a few curious inquirers that a meaning Qf no small importance may be suggested. For in sacred language God is called a fire, as when Scripture says, "Our God is a consuming fire." Respecting the substance of the angels also it speaks as follows: " Who maketh His angels spirits, and His ministers a burning fire;" and in another place, "The angel of the Lord appeared in a flame of fire in the bush." We have, moreover, received a commandment to be " fervent in spirit;" by which expression undoubtedly the Word of God is shown to be hot and fiery. The prophet Jeremiah also hears from Him, who gave him his answers, "Behold, I have given my words into thy mouth a fire." As God, then, is a fire, and the angels a flame of fire, and all the saints are fervent in spirit, so, on the contrary, those who have fallen away from the love of God are undoubtedly said to have cooled in their affection for Him, and to have become cold. For the Lord also says, that, " because iniquity has abounded, the love of many will grow cold." N J? things, whatever they are, which in holy Scripture are compared with the hostile power, the devil is said to be perpetually finding cold; and what is found to be colder than he? In

Deut. iv. 24.- Ps, civ. 4; cf. Heb. i. 7.

3 Ex. iii. 2. 4 Kom. xii. 11.

Cf. Jer. i. 9. The word " fire " is found neither in the Hebrew nor in the Septnagint. c ratt. xxiv. 12.

the sea also the dragon is said to reign. For the prophet intimates that the serpent and dragon, which certainly is referred to one of the wicked spirits, is also in the sea. And elsewhere the prophet says, "I will draw out my holy sword npon the dragon the flying serpent, upon the dragon the crooked serpent, and will slay him."-' And again he says: " Even though they hide from my eyes, and descend into the depths of the sea, there will I command the serpent, and it shall bite them."' In the book of Job also, he is said to be the king of all things in the waters. The prophet'"' threatens that evils will be kindled by the north wind upon all who inhabit the earth. Now the north wind is described in holy Scripture as cold, according to the statement in the book of Wisdom, "That cold north wind;" which same thing also must undoubtedly be understood of the devil. If, then, those things which are holy are named fire, and light, and fervent, while those which are of an opposite nature are said to be cold; and if the love of many is said to w ax cold; we have to inquire whether perhaps the name soul, which in Greek is termed ' lrv r), be so termed from growing cold' out of a better and more divine condition, and be thence derived, because it seems to have cooled from that natural and divine warmth, and therefore has been placed in its present position, and called by its present name. Finally, see if you can easily find a place in holy Scripture where the soul is properly mentioned in terms of praise: it frequently occurs, on the contrary, accompanied with expressions of censure, as in the passage, "An evil soul ruins him who possesses it;" and, "The soul which sinneth, it shall die." For after it has been said, "All souls are mine; as the soul of the father, so also the soul of the son is mine," it seemed to follow that He would say, "The soul that doeth righteousness, it shall be saved,"' and " The soul which sinneth, it shall die." But 1 Cf. Ezek. xxxii. 2 seqq. igg,. xxvii. 1.

3 Amos ix. 3. Job xli. 34.

Jer. i. 14. Ecclus. xliii. 20.

'4 vx' from xjyjd ci. i. Ecclus. vi. 4.

Ezek. xviii. 4. cf. 20. " Ezek. xviii. 4, 19.

now we see that He has associated with the soul what is censurable, and has been silent as to that which was deserving of praise. We have therefore to see if, perchance, as we have said is declared by the name itself, it was called ' v' i, i. e. anima, because it has waxed cold from the fervour of just thincys,-'- and from participation in the divine fire, and yet has not lost the power of restoring itself to that condition of fervour in which it was at the beginning. Whence the prophet also appears to point out some such state of things by the words, "Return, O my soul, unto thy rest." From all which this appears to be made out, that the understanding, falling away from its status and dignity, was made or named soul; and that, if repaired and corrected, it returns to the condition of the understanding.

4. Now, if this be the case, it seems to me that this very decay and falling away of the understanding is not the same in all, but that this conversion into a soul is carried to a greater or less degree in different instances, and that certain understandings retain something even of their former vigour, and

"By falling away and. growing cold from a spiritual life, the soul has become what it now is, but is capable also of returning to what it was at the beginning, which I think is intimated by the prophet in the words, ' Return, 0 my soul, unto thy rest," so as to be wholly this." Epistle of Justinian to Patriarch of Constantinople.

2 Ps. cxvi. 7.

3 "The understanding (Noy;) somehow, then, has become a soul, and the soul, being restored, becomes an understanding. The understanding falling away, was made a soul, and the soul, again, when furnished with virtues, will become an understanding. For if we examine the case of Esau, we may find that he was condemned because of his ancient sins in a worse course of life. And respecting the heavenly bodies we must inquire, that not at the time when the world was created did the soul of Q sun, or whatever else it ought to be called, begin to exist, but before that it entered that shining and burning body. We may hold similar opinions regarding the moon and stars, that, for the foregoing reasons, they were compelled, unwillingly, to subject themselves to vanity on account of the rewards of the future; and to do, not their own will, but the will of their Creator, by whom they were arranged among their different offices."-Jerozie's Letter to Avitiis. From these, as well as other passages, it may be seen how widely Rufinus departed in his translation from the original.

others again either nothing or a very small amount. Whence some are found from the very commencement of their lives to be of more active intellect, others again of a slower habit of mincl, and some are born wholly obtuse, and altogether incapable of instruction. Our statement, however, that the understanding is converted into a soul, or whatever else seems to have such a meaning, the reader must carefully consider and settle for himself, as these views are not to be regarded as advanced by us in a dogmatic manner, but simply as opinions, treated in the style of investigation and discussion. Let the reader take this also into consideration, that it is observed with regard to the soul of the Saviour, that of those things which are written in the Gospel, some are ascribed to it under the name of soul, and others under that of spirit. For when it wishes to indicate any suffering or perturbation affecting Him, it indicates it under the name of soul; as when it says, "Now is my soul troubled;"- and, "My soul is sorrowful, even unto death;" and, "No man taketh my soup from me, but I lay it down of myself." Into the hands of His Father He commends not His soul, but His spirit; and when He says that the flesh is weak. He does not say that the soul is willing, but the spirit: whence it appears that the soul f is somethintt intermediate between the weak flesh and the ' willing spirit.

5. But perhaps some one may meet us with one of those objections which w e have ourselves warned you of in our statements, and say, "How then is there said to be also a soul of God?" To which we answer as follows: That as with respect to everything corporeal which is spoken of God, such as fingers, or hands, or arms, or eyes, or feet, or mouth, we say that these are not to be understood as human members, but that certain of his powers are indicated by these names of members of the body; so also we are to suppose that it is something else which is pointed out by this title soul of God. And if it is allowable for us to venture to say anything more on such a subject, the soul of God may perhaps be understood to mean the only-begotten Son of God. For as the 1 John xii. 27. Matt. xxvi. 38. Animam. Jolm x. 18.

soul, when implanted in the body, moves all things in it, and exerts its force over everything on which it operates; so also the only-begotten Son of God, who is His Word and Wisdom, stretches and extends to every power of God, being implanted in it; and perhaps to indicate this mystery is God either called or described in Scripture as a body. We must, indeed, take into consideration whether it is not perhaps on this account that the soul of God may be understood to mean His only-begotten Son, because He Himself came into this world of affliction, and descended into this valley of tears, and into this place of our humiliation; as He says in the Psalm, "Because Thou hast humihated us in the place of affliction." Finally, I am aware that certain critics, in explaining the words used in the Gospel by the Saviour, "My soul is sorrowful, even unto death," have interpreted them of the apostles, whom He termed His soul, as being better than the rest of His body. For as the multitude of believers is called His body, they say that the apostles, as being better than the rest of the body, ought to be understood to mean His soul.

We have brought forward as we best could these points regarding the rational soul, as topics of discussion for our readers, rather than as dogmatic and well-defined propositions. And with respect to the souls of animals and other dumb creatures, let that suffice which we have stated above in general terms.

CHAPTER IX.

ON THE WORLD AND THE MOVEMENTS OF RATIONAL CREATURES, WHETHER GOOD OR BAD; AND ON THE CAUSES or THEM.

1. But let us now return to the order of our proposed discussion, and behold the commencement of creation, so far as the understanding can behold the beginning of the creation of God. In that commencement, then, we are to suppose 1 Ps. xliv. 19.

2 The original of this passage is found in Justinian's Epistle to Menas, Patriarch of Constantinople, apud Jinem. " In that beginning which is tiiat God created so great a number of rational or intellectual creatures (or by whatever name they are to be called), which we have formerly termed understandings, as He foresaw would be sufficient. It is certain that lie made them according to some definite number, predetermined by Himself: for it is not to be imagined, as some would have it, that creatures have not a limit, because where there is no limit there can neither be any comprehension nor any limitation. Now if this were the case, then certainly created things could neither be restrained nor administered by God. For, naturally, whatever is infinite will also be incomprehensible. Moreover, as Scripture says, " God has arranged all things in number and measure; " and therefore number will be correctly applied to rational creatures or understandings, that they may be so numerous as to admit of being arranged, governed, and controlled by God. But measure will be appropriately applied to a material body; and this measure, we are to believe, was created by God such as He knew would be sufficient for the adorning of the world. These, then, are the things which we are to believe were created by God in the beginning, i. e. before all things. And this, we think, is indicated even in that beginning which Moses has introduced in terms somewhat ambiguous, when he says, "In the beginning God made the heaven and the earth."" For it is certain that the firmament is not spoken of, nor the dry land, but that heaven and earth from which this present heaven and earth which we now see afterwards borrowed their names.

cognisable by the imderstanding, God, by His own will, caused to exist as great a number of intelligent beings as was sufficient; for we must say that the power of God is finite, and not, under pretence of praising Plim, take away His limitation. For if the divine power be infinite, it must of necessity be unable to understand even itself, since that which is naturally illimitable is incapable of being comprehended. He made things therefore so great as to be able to apprehend and keep them under His power, and control them by His providence; so also He prepared matter of such a size (roauvrriv v? r,!) as He had the power to ornament."' 1 Wisd. xi, 20: " Thou hast ordered all things in measure, and number, and weight."

2 Gen. i. 1.

2. But since those rational natures, which we have said above were made in the beginning, were created when they did not previously exist, in consequence of this very fact of their non-existence and commencement of being, are they necessarily changeable and mutable; since whatever power was in their substance was not in it by nature, but was the result of the goodness of their Maker. What they are, therefore, is neither their own nor endures for ever, but is bestowed by God. For it did not always exist; and everything which is a gift may also be taken away, and disappear. And a reason for removal will consist in the movements of souls not being conducted according to right and propriety. For the Creator gave, as an indulgence to the understandings created by Him, the power of free and voluntary action, by which the good that was in them might become their own, being preserved by the exertion

of their own will; but sloth-fulness, and a dislike of labour in preserving what is good, and an aversion to and a neglect of better things, furnished the beginning of a departure from goodness. But to depart from good is nothing else than to be made bad. For it is certain that to want goodness is to be wicked. Whence it happens that, in proportion as one falls away from goodness, in the same proportion does he become involved in wickedness. In wdiich condition, according to its actions, each understanding, neglecting goodness either to a greater or more limited extent, was dragged into the opposite of good, which undoubtedly is evil. From which it appears that the Creator of all things admitted certain seeds and causes of variety and diversity, that He might create variety and diversity in proportion to the diversity of understandings, i. e. of rational creatures, which diversity they must be supposed to have conceived from that cause which we have mentioned above. And what we mean by variety and diversity is what we now wish to explain.

3. Now we term world everything which is above the heavens, or in the heavens, or upon the earth, or in those places which are called the lower regions, or all places whatever that anywhere exist, together with their inhabitants.

This whole, theu is called world. In which world certain beings are said to be super-celestial, i. e. placed in happier abodes, and clothed with heavenly and resplendent bodies; and among these many distinctions are shown to exist, the apostle, e. g., saying, "That one is the glory of the sun, another the glory of the moon, another the glory of the stars; for one star differeth from another star in glory." Certain beings are called earthly, and among them, i. e. among men, there is no small difference: for some of them are Barbarians, others Greeks; and of the Barbarians some are savage and fierce, and others of a milder disposition. And certain of them live under laws that have been thoroughly approved; others, again, under laws of a more common or severe kind;'" while some, again, possess customs of an inhuman and savage character, rather than laws. And certain of them, from the hour of their birth, are reduced to humiliation and subjection, and brought up as slaves, being placed under the dominion either of masters, or princes, or tyrants. Others, again, are brought up in a manner more consonant with freedom and reason: some w ith sound bodies, some with bodies diseased from their early years; some defective in vision, others in hearing and speech; some born in that condition, others deprived of the use of their senses immediately after birth, or at least undercroincp such misfortune on reachinc manhood. And why should I repeat and enumerate all the horrors of human misery, from wdiich some have been free, and in which others have been involved, when each one can wxigh and consider them for himself? There are also certain invisible powers to which earthty things have been entrusted for administration; and amongst them no small difference must be believed to exist, as is also found to be the case among men. The Apostle Paul indeed intimates that there are certain lower powers, and that among them, in like manner, must undoubtedly be sought a ground of diversity. Eegarding dumb animals, and birds, and those creatures which live in the waters, it seems superfluous to inquire; 1 Cor. XV. 41.- Vilioribiis et asperioribus.

Inferna. ORIG. I since it is certain that these ought to be regarded not as of primary, but of subordinate rank.

4. Seeing, then, that all things which have been created are said to have been made through Christ, and in Christ, as the Apostle Paul most clearly indicates, when he says, "For in Him and by Him were all things created, whether things in heaven or things on earth, visible and invisible, whether they be thrones, or powers, or principalities, or dominions; all things were created by Him, and in Him;"- and as in his Gospel John indicates the same thing, saying, "In the beginning was the Word, and the Word was with God, and the Word was God: the same was in the beginning with God: all things were made by Him; and without Him was not anything made;" and as in the Psalm also it is written, "In wisdom hast Thou made them all;" seeing, then, Christ is, as it were, the Word and Wisdom, and so also the Righteousness, it will undoubtedly follow that those things which were created in the Word and Wisdom are said to be created also in that righteousness which is Christ; that in created things there may appear to be nothing unrighteous or accidental, but that all things may be shown to be in conformity with the law of equity and righteousness. How, then, so great a variety of things, and so great a diversity, can be understood to be altogether just and righteous, I am sure no human power or language can explain, unless as prostrate suppliants we pray to the Word, and Wisdom, and Righteousness Himself, who is the only-begotten Son of God, and who, pouring Himself by His graces into our senses, may deign to illuminate what is dark, to lay open what is concealed, and to reveal what is secret; if, indeed, we should be found either to seek, or ask, or knock so worthily as to deserve to receive when we ask, or to find when we seek, or to have it opened to us when we knock. Not relying, then, on our own powers, but on the help of that Wisdom which made all things, and of that Righteousness which we believe to be in all His creatures, although we are in the meantime unable to declare it, yet, trusting in His mercy, we shall endeavour to examine 1 Col. i. 16. 3 John i. 1, 2. pg. civ. 24.

and inquire how that great variety and diversity in the world may appear to be consistent with all righteousness and reason. I mean, of course, merely reason in general; for it would be a mark of ignorance either to seek, or of folly to give, a special reason for each individual case.

5. Now, when we say that this world was established in the variety in which we have above explained that it was created by God, and when we say that this God is good, and righteous, and most just, there are numerous individuals, especially those who, coming from the school of Marcion, and Yalentinus, and Basilides, have heard that there are souls of different natures, who object to us, that it cannot consist with the justice of God in creating the world to assign to some of His creatures an abode in the heavens, and not only to give such a better habitation, but also to grant them a higher and more honourable position; to favour others with the grant of principalities; to bestow powers upon some, dominions on others; to confer upon some the most honourable seats in the celestial tribunals; to enable some to shine with more resplendent glory, and to glitter with a starry splendour; to give to some the glory of the sun, to others the glory of the moon, to others the glory of the stars; to cause one star to differ from another star in glory. And, to speak once for all, and briefly, if the Creator God wants neither the will to undertake nor the power to complete a good and perfect work, what reason can there be that, in the creation of rational natures, i. e. of beings of whose existence He Himself is the cause. He should make some of higher rank, and others of second,

or third, or of many lower and inferior degrees? In the next place, they object to us, with regard to terrestrial beings, that a happier lot by birth is the case with some rather than with others; as one man, e. g. is begotten of Abraham, and born of the promise; another, too, of Isaac and Eebekah, and who, while still in the womb, supplants his brother, and is said to be loved by God before he is born. Nay, this very circumstance, especially that one man is born among the Hebrews, with whom he finds instruction in the divine law; another among the Greeks, themselves also wise, and men of no small learning; and then another amongst the Ethiopians, who are accustomed to feed on human flesh; or amongst the Scythians, with whom parricide is an act sanctioned by law; or amongst the people of Taurus, where strangers are offered in sacrifice, is a ground of strong objection. Their argument accordingly is this: If there be this great diversity of circumstances, and this diverse and varying condition by birth, in which the faculty of free-will has no scope (for no one chooses for himself either where, or with whom, or in what condition he is born); if, then, this is not caused by the difference in the nature of souls, i. e. that a soul of an evil nature is destined for a wicked nation, and a good soul for a righteous nation, what other conclusion remains than that these things must be supposed to be regulated by accident and chance? And if that be admitted, then it will be no longer believed that the world was made by God, or administered by His providence; and as a consequence, a judgment of God upon the deeds of each individual will appear a thing not to be looked for. In which matter, indeed, what is clearly the truth of things is the privilege of Him alone to know who searches all things, even the deep things of God.

6. We, however, although but men, not to nourish the insolence of the heretics by our silence, will return to their objections such answers as occur to us, so far as our abilities enable us. We have frequently shown, by those declarations which we were able to produce from the holy Scriptures, that God, the Creator of all things, is good, and just, and all-powerful. When He in the beginning created those beings which He desired to create, i. e. rational natures, He had no other reason for creating them than on account of Himself, i. e. His own goodness. As He Himself, then, was the cause of the existence of those things which were to be created, in whom there was neither any variation nor change, nor want of power. He created all whom He made equal and alike, because there was in Himself no reason for producing "variety and diversity. But since those rational creatures themselves, as we have frequently shown, and will yet show in the proper place, were endowed with the power of free-will, this freedom of will incited each one either to progress ' by imitation of God, or reduced him to failure through negligence. And this, as we have already stated, is the cause of the diversity among rational creatures, deriving its origin not from the will or judgment of the Creator, but from the freedom of the individual will. Now God, who deemed it just to arrange His creatures according to their merit, brought down these different understandings into the harmony of one world, that He might adorn, as it were, one dwelling, in which there ought to be not only vessels of gold and silver, but also of wood and clay (and some indeed to honour, and others to dishonour), with those different vessels, or souls, or understandings. And these are the causes, in my opinion, why that world presents the aspect of diversity, Avhile Divine Providence continues to regulate each individual according to the variety of his movements, or

of his feelings and purpose. On which account the Creator will neither appear to be unjust in distributing (for the causes already mentioned) to every one according to his merits; nor will the happiness or unhappiness of each one's birth, or whatever be the condition that falls to his lot, be deemed accidental; nor will different creators, or souls of different natures, be believed to exist.

7. But even holy Scripture does not appear to me to be altogether silent on the nature of this secret, as when the Apostle Paul, in discussing the case of Jacob and Esau, says: " For the children beino; not vet born, neither havino done any good or evil, that the purpose of God according to election might stand, not of works, but of Him who calleth, it was said, The elder shall serve the younger, as it is written, Jacob have I loved, but Esau have I hated." And after that, he answers himself, and says, "What shall we say then? Is there unrio; hteousness with God?" And that he might furnish us with an opportunity of inquiring into these matters, and of ascertaining how these things do not happen without a reason, he answers himself, and says, ' God forbid." For the same question, as it seems to me, wliicli is raised concerning Jacob and Esau, may be raised regarding all celestial and terrestrial creatures, and even those of the lower world as well. And in like manner it seems to me, that as he tliere says, "The children being not yet born, neither having done any good or evil," so it might also be said of all other things, "When they were not yet" created, ' neither had yet done any good or evil, that the decree of God according to election may stand," that (as certain think) some things on the one hand were created heavenly, some on the other earthly, and others, again, beneath the earth, ' not of works" (as they think), " but of Him who calleth," what shall we say then, if these things are so? ' Is there unrighteousness with God? God forbid." As, therefore, when the Scriptures are carefully examined regarding Jacob and Esau, it is not found to be unrighteousness with God that it should be said, before they were born, or had done anything in this life, "the elder shall serve the younger;" and as it is found not to be unrighteousness that even in the womb Jacob supplanted his brother, if we feel that he was worthily beloved by God, according to the deserts of his previous life, so as to deserve to be preferred before his brother; so also is it with regard to heavenly creatures, if we notice that diversity was not the original condition of the creature, but that, owing to causes that have previously existed, a different office is prepared by the Creator for each one in proportion to the degree of liis merit, on this ground, indeed, that each one, in respect of having been created by God an understanding, or a rational spirit, has, according to the movements of his mind and the feelings of his soul, gained for himself a greater or less amount of merit, and has become either an object of love to God, or else one of dislike to Him; while, nevertheless, some of those who are possessed of greater merit are ordained to suffer with others for the adorning of the state of the world, and for the discharge of 1 The text runs, "Respondet sibi ipse, et ait," on wliicli Ruseus remarks tliat the sentence is incomplete, and that " absit" probably should be supphed. This conjecture has been adopted in the translation.

duty to creatures of a lower grade, in order that by this means they themselves may be participators in the endurance of the Creator, according to the words of the apostle: '- For the creature Avas made subject to vanity, not willingly, but by reason of him who hath subjected the same in hope." Keeping in view, then, the sentiment expressed by the apostle, when, speaking of the birth of Esau and Jacob, he says, "Is there unrighteousness wdth God? God forbid," I think it right that this same sentiment should be carefully applied to the case of all other creatures, because, as we formerly remarked, the righteousness of the Creator ought to appear in everything. And this, it appears to me, will be seen more clearly at last, if each one, whether of celestial or terrestrial or infernal beings, be said to have the causes of his diversity in himself, and antecedent to his bodily birth. For all things were created by the Word of God, and by His Wisdom, and w ere set in order by His Justice. And by the grace of His compassion He provides for all men, and encourages all to the use of whatever remedies may lead to their cure, and incites them to salvation.

8. As, then, there is no doubt that at the day of judgment the good will be separated from the bad, and the just from the unjust, and all by the sentence of God will be distributed according to their deserts throughout those places of wdiich they are w orthy, so I am of opinion some such state of things was formerly the case, as, God willing, we shall show in what follows. For God must be believed to do and order all things and at all times according to His judgment. For the words which the apostle uses wdien he says, " In a great house there are not only vessels of gold and silver, but also of w ood and of earth, and some to honour and some to dishonour;" and those which he adds, saying, "If a man purge himself, he will be a vessel unto honour, sanctified and meet for the jmaster's use, unto every good work," undoul3tedly point out this, that he who shall purge himself when he is in this life, will be prepared for every good work in that which is to come; while he who 1 Rom. viii. 20, 21. 2 2 Tim. ii. 20. 2 Tim. ii. 21.

does not purge himself will be, according to the amount of his impurity, a vessel unto dishonour, i. e. unworthy. It is therefore possible to understand that there have been also formerly rational vessels, whether purged or not, i. e. which either purged themselves or did not do so, and that consequently every vessel, according to the measure of its purity or impurity, received a place, or region, or condition by birth, or an office to discharge, in this world." All of which, down to the humblest, God providing for and distinguishing by the power of His wisdom, arranges all things by Plis controlling judgment, according to a most impartial retribution, so far as each one ought to be assisted or cared for in conformity with his deserts. In wdiich certainly every principle of equity is shown, while the inequality of circumstances preserves the justice of a retribution according to merit. But the grounds of the merits in each individual case are only recognised truly and clearly by God Himself, along with His only-begotten Word, and His Wisdom, and the Holy Spirit.

CHAPTER X.

ON THE RESUREECTION, AND THE JUDGMENT, THE FIPwe OF HELL, AND PUNISHMENTS.

1. But since the discourse has reminded us of the subjects of a future judgment and of retribution, and of the punishments of sinners, according to the threatenings of holy Scripture and the contents of the church's teaching-viz., that when the time of judgment comes, everlasting fire, and outer darkness, and a prison, and a furnace, and other punishments of like nature, have been prepared for sinners let us see what our opinions on these points ought to be. But that these subjects may be arrived at in proper

order, it seems to me that we ought first to consider the nature of the resurrection, that we may know what that body is which shall come either to punishment, or to rest, or to happiness; which question in other treatises which we have composed regarding the resurrection we have discussed at greater length, and have shown what our opinions were regarding it. But now, also, for the sake of logical order in our treatise, there will be no absurdity in re-stating a few points from such works, especially since some take offence at the creed of the church, as if our belief in the resurrection were foolish, and altogether devoid of sense; and these are principally heretics, who, I think, are to be answered in the following manner. If they also admit that there is a resurrection of the dead, let them answer us this, What is that which died? Was it not a body? It is of the body, then, that there will be a resurrection. Let them next tell us if they think that we are to make use of bodies or not. I think that when the Apostle Paul says, that " it is sown a natural body, it will arise a spiritual body," they cannot deny that it is a body which arises, or that in the resurrection we are to make use of bodies. What then? If it is certain that Ave are to make use of bodies, and if the bodies which have fallen are declared to rise again (for only that which before has fallen can be properly said to rise again), it can be a matter of doubt to no one that they rise again, in order that we may be clothed with them a second time at the resurrection. The one thing is closely connected with the other. For if bodies rise again, they undoubtedly rise to be coverings for us; and if it is necessary for us to be invested with bodies, as it is certainly necessary, we ought to be invested with no other than our own. But if it is true that these rise again, and that they arise "spiritual" bodies, there can be no doubt that they are said to rise from the dead, after casting away corruption and laying aside mortality; otherwise it will appear vain and superfluous for any one to arise from the dead in order to die a second time. And this, finally, may be more distinctly comprehended thus, if one carefully consider what are the qualities of an animal body, which, when sown into the earth, recovers the qualities of a spiritual body. For it is out of the animal body that the very power and grace of the resurrection educe the spiritual body, when it transmutes it from a condition of indignity to one of glory. 1 Cor. XV. 4:-i: natural, animale.

2. Since the heretics, howevei-j think themselves persons of great learning and wisdom, we shall ask them if every body-has a form of some kind, i. e. is fashioned according to some shape. And if they shall say that a body is that which is fashioned according to no shape, they will show themselves to be the most ignorant and foolish of mankind. For no one will deny this, save him who is altogether without any learning. But if, as a matter of course, they say that every body is certainly fashioned according to some definite shape, we shall ask them if they can point out and describe to us the shape of a spiritual body; a thing which they can by no means do. We shall ask them, moreover, about the differences of those who rise again. How will they show that statement to be true, that there is ' one flesh of birds, another of fishes; bodies celestial, and bodies terrestrial; that the glory of the celestial is one, and the glory of the terrestrial another; that one is the glory of the sun, another the glory of the moon, another the glory of the stars; that one star differeth from another star in glory, and that so is the resurrection of the dead?"- According to that gradation, then, which exists among heavenly bodies, let them show to us the differences in the glory of those who

rise again; and if they have endeavoured by any means to devise a principle that may be in accordance with the differences in heavenly bodies, we shall ask them to assign the differences in the resurrection by a comparison of earthly bodies. Our understanding of the passage indeed is, that the apostle, wishing to describe the great difference among those who rise again in glory, i. e. of the saints, borrowed a comparison from the heavenly bodies, saying, "One is the glory of the sun, another the glory of the moon, another the glory of the stars." And wishing again to teach us the differences among those who shall come to the resurrection, without having purged themselves in this life, i. e. sinners, he borrowed an illustration from earthly things, saying, ' There is one flesh of birds, another of fishes." For heavenly things are worthily compared to the saints, and earthly things to sinners. These statements are 1 1 Cor. XV. 39-42.

made in reply to those who deny the resurrection of the dead, i. e. the resurrection of bodies.

3. We now turn our attention to some of our own believers, who, either from feebleness of intellect or want of proper instruction, adopt a very low and abject view of the resurrection of the body. We ask these persons in what manner they understand that an animal body is to be changed by the grace of the resurrection, and to become a spiritual one; and how that which is sown in weakness will arise in power; how that which is planted in dishonour will arise in glory; and that which vras sown in corruption, will be changed to a state of incorruption. Because if they believe the apostle, that a body which arises in glory, and power, and incorruptibility, has already become spiritual, it appears absurd and contrary to his meaning to say that it can again be entangled with the passions of flesh and blood, seeing the apostle manifestly declares that "flesh and blood shall not inherit the kingdom of God, nor shall corruption inherit incorruption." But how do they understand the declaration of the apostle, "We shall all be changed?" This transformation certainly is to be looked for, according to the order which we have taught above; and in it, undoubtedly, it becomes us to hope for something vorthy of divine grace; and this we believe will take place in the order in which the apostle describes the sowing in the ground of a " bare grain of corn, or of any other fruit," to which " God gives a body as it pleases Him," as soon as the grain of corn is dead. For in the same way also our bodies are to be supposed to fall into the earth like a grain; and (that germ being implanted in them which contains the bodily substance) although the bodies die, and become corrupted, and are scattered abroad, yet by the word of God, that very germ which is always safe in the substance of the body, raises them from the earth, and restores and repairs them, as the power which is in the grain of wheat, after its corruption and death, repairs and restores the grain into a body having stalk and ear. And so also to those who shall deserve to obtain an inheritance in the kingdom of heaven, that germ of the body's restoration, which we have before mentioned, by God's command restores out of the earthly and animal body a spiritual one, capable of inhabiting the heavens; while to each one of those who may be of inferior merit, or of more abject condition, or even the lowest in the scale, and altogether thrust aside, there is yet given, in proportion to the dignity of his life and soul, a glory and dignity of body, nevertheless in such a way, that even the body which rises again of those who are to be destined to everlasting fire or to severe punishments, is by the very change of the resurrection so incorruptible, that it cannot

be corrupted and dissolved even by severe punishments. If, then, such be the qualities of that body which will arise from the dead, let us now see what is the meaning of the threatening of eternal fire.

4. We find in the prophet Isaiah, that the fire with which each one is punished is described as his own; for he says, "Walk in the light of your own fire, and in the flame which ye have kindled." By these words it seems to be indicated that every sinner kindles for himself the flame of his own fire, and is not plunged into some fire which has been already kindled by another, or was in existence before himself. Of this fire the fuel and food are our sins, which are called by the Apostle Paul wood, and hay, and stubble. And I think that, as abundance of food, and provisions of a contrary kind and amount, breed fevers in the body, and fevers, too, of different sorts and duration, according to the proportion in which the collected poison supplies material and fuel for disease (the quality of this material, gathered together from different poisons, proving the causes either of a more acute or more lingering disease); so, when the soul has gathered together a multitude of evil works, and an abundance of sins against itself, at a suitable time all that assembly of evils boils up to punishment, and is set on fire to chastisements; when the mind itself, or conscience, receiving by divine power into the memory all those things of which it had stamped on itself certain signs and forms at the moment of sinning, will see a kind of history, as it w ere, of all the foul, and shameful, and Isa. i. 11. 2 1 Qq jjj 12. 2 Intemperies.

unholy deeds which it has done, exposed before its eyes: then is the conscience itself harassed, and, pierced by its own loads, bccomes an accuser and a witness asjainst itself. And this, I think, was the opinion of the Apostle Paul himself, when he said, "Their thoughts mutually accusing or excusing them in the day when God will judge the secrets of men by Jesus Christ, according to my gospel." From which it is understood that around the substance of the soul certain tortures are produced by the hurtful affections of sins themselves.

5. And that the understanding of this matter may not appear very difficult, we may draw some considerations from the evil effects of those passions which are wont to befall some souls, as when a soul is consumed by the fire of love, or wasted away by zeal or env, or when the passion of anger is kindled, or one is consumed by the greatness of his madness or his sorrow; on which occasions some, finding the excess of these evils unbearable, have deemed it more tolerable to submit to death than to endure perpetually torture of such a kind. You will ask indeed whether, in the case of those who have been entangled in the evils arising from those, vices above enumerated, and who, while existing in this life, have been unable to procure any amelioration for themselves, and have in this condition departed from the world, it be sufficient in the way of punishment that they be tortured by the remaining in them of these hurtful affections, i. e. of the anger, or of the fury, or of the madness, or of the sorrow, whose fatal poison was in this life lessened by no healing medicine; or whether, these affections being changed, they will be subjected to the pains of a general punishment. Now I am of opinion that another species of punishment may be understood to exist; because, as we feel that when the limbs of the body are loosened and torn away from their mutual supports, there is produced pain of a most excruciating kind, so, when the soul shall be found to be beyond the order, and connection, and harmony in which

it was created by God for the purposes of good and useful action and observation, 1 Rom. ii. 13, 16.

and not to harmonize with itself in the connection of its rational movements, it must be deemed to bear the chastisement and torture of its own dissension, and to feel the punishments of its own disordered condition. And when this dissolution and rending asunder of soul shall have been tested by the application of fire, a solidification undoubtedly into a firmer structure will take place, and a restoration be effected.

6. There are also many other things which escape our notice, and are known to Him alone who is the physician of our souls. For if, on account of those bad effects which we bring upon ourselves by eating and drinking, w e deem it necessary for the health of the body to make use of some unpleasant and painful drug, sometimes even, if the nature of the disease demand, requiring the severe process of the amputating knife; and if the virulence of the disease shall transcend even these remedies, the evil has at last to be burned out by fire; how much more is it to be understood that God our Physician, desiring to remove the defects of our souls, which they had contracted from their different sins and crimes, should employ penal measures of this sort, and should apply even, in addition, the punishment of fire to those who have lost their soundness of mind! Pictures of this method of procedure are found also in the holy Scriptures. In the book of Deuteronomy, the divine word threatens sinners with the punishments of fevers, and colds, and jaundice, and with the pains of feebleness of vision, and alienation of mind, and paralysis, and blindness, and weakness of the reins. If any one, then, at his leisure gather together out of the whole of Scripture all the enumerations of diseases which in the threatenings addressed to sinners are called by the names of bodily maladies, he will find that either the vices of souls, or their punishments, are figuratively indicated by them. To understand now, that in the same way in which physicians apply remedies to the sick, in order that by careful treatment they may recover their health, God so deals towards those who have lapsed and fallen into sin, is proved by this, that Aurigine. Deut. xxviii.

the cup of God's fniy is ordered, through the agency of the prophet Jeremiah, to be offered to all nations, that they may drink it, and be in a state of madness, and vomit it forth. In doing which, He threatens them, saying, That if any one refuse to drink, he shall not be cleansed." By which certainly it is understood that the fury of God's vengeance is profitable for the purgation of souls. That the punishment, also, which is said to be applied by fire, is understood to be applied with the object of healing, is taught by Isaiah, who speaks thus of Israel: " The Lord will wash away the filth of the sons or daughters of Zion, and shall purge away the blood from the midst of them by the spirit of judgment, and the spirit of burning." Of the Chaldeans he thus speaks: " Thou hast the coals of fire; sit upon them: they will be to thee a help." " And in other passages he says, "The Lord will sanctify in a burning fire;" and in the prophecies of Malachi he says, "The Lord sitting will blow, and purify, and will pour forth the cleansed sons of Judah."

7. But that fate also which is mentioned in the Gospels as overtaking unfaithful stewards, who, it is said, are to be divided, and a portion of them placed along with unbelievers, as if that portion which is not their own were to be sent elsewhere, undoubtedly indicates some kind of punishment on those whose spirit, as it seems to

me, is shown to be separated from the soul. For if this Spirit is of divine nature, i. e. is understood to be a Holy Spirit, we shall understand this to be said of the gift of the Holy Spirit: that when, whether by baptism, or by the grace of the Spirit, the word of wisdom, or the word of knowledge, or of any other gift, has been bestowed upon a man, and not rightly administered, i. e. either buried in the earth or tied up in a napkin, the gift of the Spirit will certainly be withdrawn from his soul, and the other portion which remains, that is, the substance of the soul, will be assigned its place with unbelievers, being divided and separated from that Spirit with whom, by 1 Cf. Jer. XXV. 15, 16. " Cf. Jer. xxv. 28, 29.

Isa. iv. 4. Isa. xlvii. 14,15; vid. note, chap. v. 3.

Isa. X. 17, cf. Ixvi. 16. Cf. Mai. iii. 3.

joining itself to the Lord, it ought to have been one spirit. Now, if this is not to be understood of the Spirit of God, but of the nature of the soul itself, that will be called its better part which was made in the image and likeness of God; whereas the other part, that which afterw ards, through its fall by the exercise of free-will, was assumed contrary to the nature of its original condition of purity, this part, as being the friend and beloved of matter, is punished with the fate of unbelievers. There is also a third sense in which that separation may be understood, this viz., that as each believer, although the humblest in the church, is said to be attended by an angel, who is declared by the Saviour always to behold the face of God the Father, and as this angel was certainly one with the object of his guardianship; so, if the latter is rendered unworthy by his want of obedience, the angel of God is said to be taken from him, and then that part of him the part, viz., which belongs to his human nature being rent away from the divine part, is assigned a place along with unbelievers, because it has not faithfully observed the admonitions of the angel allotted it by God.

8. But the outer darkness, in my judgment, is to be understood not so much of some dark atmosphere without any light, as of those persons who, being plunged in the darkness of profound ignorance, have been placed beyond the reach of any light of the understanding. We must see, also, lest this perhaps should be the meaning of the expression, that as the saints will receive those bodies in which they have lived in holiness and purity in the habitations of this life, bright and glorious after the resurrection, so the wicked also, who in this life have loved the darkness of error and the night of ignorance, may be clothed with dark and black bodies after the resurrection, that the very mist of ignorance which had in this life taken possession of their minds within them, may appear in the future as the external covering of the body. Similar is the view to be entertained regarding the prison. Let these remarks, which have been made as brief as possible, that the order of our discourse in the meantime might be preserved, suffice for the present occasion.

1. Let us now briefly see what views we are to form regarding promises.

It is certain that there is no living thing which can be alto rether inactive and immoveable, but deli i; hts in motion of every kind, and in perpetual activity and volition; and this nature, I think it evident, is in all living things. Much more, then, must a rational animal, i. e. the nature of man, be in perpetual movement and activity. If, indeed, he is forgetful of himself, and ignorant of what becomes him, all his efforts are directed to serve the uses of the body, and in all his movements he is occupied with his own pleasures and bodily lusts; but if he be one who studies to care or provide for the general good, then, either by consulting for the benefit of the state or by obeying the magistrates, he exerts himself for that, whatever it is, which may seem certainly to promote the public advantage. And if now any one be of such a nature as to understand that there is something better than those things which seem to be corporeal, and so bestow his labour upon wisdom and science, then he will undoubtedly direct all his attention towards pursuits of that kind, that he may, by inquiring into the truth, ascertain the causes and reason of things. As therefore, in this life, one man deems it the highest good to enjoy bodily pleasures, another to consult for the benefit of the community, a third to devote attention to study and learning; so let us inquire whether in that life which is the true one (which is said to be hidden with Christ in God, Le. in that eternal life), there will be for us some such order and condition of existence.

2. Certain persons, then, refusing the labour of thinking, and adopting a superficial view of the letter of the law, and yielding rather in some measure to the indulgence of their own desires and lusts, being disciples of the letter alone, are

Eepromissionibus. OEIG. K of opinion that the fulfihnent of the promises of the future are to be looked for in bodily pleasure and luxury; and therefore they especially desire to have again, after the resurrection, such bodily structures as may never be without the power of eating, and drinking, and performing all the functions of flesh and blood, not following the opinion of the Apostle Paul regarding the resurrection of a spiritual body. And consequently they say, that after the resurrection there will be marriages, and the begetting of children, imagining to themselves that the earthly city of Jerusalem is to be rebuilt, its foundations laid in precious stones, and its vralls constructed of jasper, and its battlements of crystal; that it is to have a wall composed of many precious stones, as jasper, and sapphire, and chalcedony, and emerald, and sardonyx, and onyx, and chrysolite, and chrysoprase, and jacinth, and amethyst. Moreover, they think that the nativesr of other countries are to be given them as the ministers of their pleasures, whom they are to employ either as tillers of the field or builders of walls, and by whom their ruined and fallen city is again to be raised up; and they think that they are to receive the wealth of the nations to live on, and that they will have control over their riches; that even the camels of Midian and Kedar will come, and bring to them gold, and incense, and precious stones. And these views they think to establish on the authority of the prophets by those promises which are written regarding Jerusalem; and by those passages also where it is said, that they who serve the Lord shall eat and drink, but that sinners shall hunger and thirst; that the righteous shall be joyful, but that sorrow shall possess the wicked. And from the New Testament also they quote the saying of the Saviour, in which He makes a promise to His disciples concerning the joy of wine, saying, "Henceforth I shall not drink of this cup, until I drink it with you new in my Father's kingdom." They add, moreover, that declaration, in which the Saviour calls those blessed who now hunger and thirst,"' promising them that they shall be satisfied; and many other scriptural illustrations are adduced 1 Carnes. 2 att. xxvi. 29. Mtitt. v. 6.

by them, the meanii i: of which they do not perceive is to be taken figuratively. Then, again, agreeably to the form of thino-s in this life, and accordino; to the gradations of the dignities or ranks in this world, or the greatness of their powers, they think they are to be kings and princes, like those earthly monarchs wdio now exist; chiefly, as it appears, on account of that expression in the Gospel: " Have thou power over five cities." And to speak shortly, according to the manner of things in this life in all similar matters, do they desire the fulfilment of all things looked for in the promises, viz. that what now is should exist again. Such arc the views of those who, while believing in Christ, understand the divine Scriptures in a sort of Jewish sense, drawing from them nothing worthy of the divine promises.

3. Those, however, who receive the representations of Scripture according to the understanding of the apostles, entertain the hope that the saints will eat indeed, but that it will be the bread of life, which may nourish the soul with the food of truth and wisdom, and enlighten the mind, and cause it to drink from the cup of divine wisdom, according to the declaration of holy Scripture; " Wisdom has prepared her table, she has killed her beasts, she has mingled her vvine in her cup, and she cries with a loud voice, Come to me, eat the bread which I have prepared for you, and drink the wdne which I have mingled." By this food of wisdom, the understanding, being nourished to an entire and perfect condition like that in wdiich man was made at the beginning, is restored to the image and likeness of God; so that, although an individual may depart from this life less perfectly instructed, but W'ho has done works that are approved of, he will be capable of receiving instruction in that Jerusalem, the city of the saints, i. e. he will be educated and moulded, and made a living stone, a stone elect and precious, because he has undergone with firmness and constancy the struggles of life and the trials of piety; and will there come to a truer and clearer knowledo: e of that which here has been already 1 Cf. Luke xix. 19 and 17. 2 Cf. Prov. ix. 1-5.

Opera probabilia.

predicted, viz. that " man shall not live by bread alone, but by every word which proceedeth from the mouth of God." And they also are to be understood to be the princes and rulers who both govern those of lower rank, and instruct them, and teach them, and train them to divine things.

4. But if these views should not appear to fill the minds of those who hope for such results with a becoming desire, let us go back a little, and, irrespective of the natural and innate longing of the mind for the thing itself, let us make inquiry so that we may be able at last to describe, as it were, the very forms of the bread of life, and the quality of that wine, and the peculiar nature of the principalities, all in conformity with the spiritual view of things. Now, as in those arts which are usually performed by means of manual labour, the reason why a thing is done, or why it is of a special quality, or for a special purpose, is an object of investigation to the mind, while the actual work itself is unfolded to view by the agency of the hands; so, in those works of God which were created by Him, it is to be observed that the reason and understanding of those things which we see done by Him remains undisclosed. And as, when our eye beholds the products of an artist's labour, the mind, immediately on perceiving anything of unusual artistic excellence, burns to know of what nature it is, or how it was formed, or to what purposes it was fashioned; so, in a much greater degree, and in one that is beyond all comparison, does the mind burn with an inexpressible desire to know the reason of those things which we see done by God. This desire, this longing, we believe to be unquestionably implanted within us by God; and as the eye naturally

seeks the light and vision, and our body naturally desires food and drink, so our mind is possessed with a becoming and natural desire to become acquainted with the truth of God and the causes of things. Now we have received this desire from God, not in order that it should never

Deut. viii. 3.

2 The passage is somewhat obscure, but the rendering in the text seems to convey the meaning intended. Versatur in sensu.

be gratified or be capable of gratification; otherwise the love of truth would appear to have been implanted by God into our minds to no purpose, if it were never to have an opportunity of satisfaction. Whence also, even in this life, those who devote themselves with great labour to the pursuits of piety and religion, although obtaining only some small fragments from the numerous and immense treasures of divine knowledge, yet, by the very circumstance that their mind and soul is engaged in these pursuits, and that in the eagerness of their desire they outstrip themselves, do they derive much advantage; and, because their minds are directed to the study and love of the investigation of truth, are they made fitter for receiving the instruction that is to come; as if, when one would paint an image, he were first with a light pencil to trace out the outlines of the coming picture, and prepare marks for the reception of the features that are to be afterwards added, this preliminary sketch in outline is found to prepare the way for the laying on of the true colours of the painting; so, in a measure, an outline and sketch may be traced on the tablets of our heart by the pencil of our Lord Jesus Christ. And therefore perhaps is it said, "Unto every one that hath shall be given, and be added." By which it is established, that to those who possess in this life a kind of outline of truth and knowledge, shall be added the beauty of a perfect image in the future.

5. Some such desire, I apprehend, was indicated by him who said, "I am in a strait betwixt tw o, having a desire to depart, and to be with Christ, which is far better;" knowing that when he should have returned to Christ he would then know more clearly the reasons of all things which are done on earth, either respecting man, or the soul of man, or the mind; or regarding any other subject, such as, for instance, what is the Spirit that operates, what also is the vital spirit, or what is the grace of the Holy Spirit that is given to believers. Then also will he understand what Israel appears to be, or what is meant by the diversity of nations; what the twelve tribes of Israel mean, and wdiat the individual people of each tribe. ' Luko xix. 2G; cf. Mr. tt. xxv. 9. 2 'liw. i. 23.

Then, too, will he understand the reason of the priests and Levites, and of the different priestly orders, the type of which was in Moses, and also what is the true meaning of the jubilees, and of the weeks of years with God. He will see also the reasons for the festival days, and holy days, and for all the sacrifices and purifications. He will perceive also the reason of the purgation from leprosy, and what the different kinds of lejorosy are, and the reason of the purgation of those who lose their seed. He will come to know, moreover, what are the good influences,- and their greatness, and their qualities; and those too vdiich are of a contrary kind, and what the affection of the former, and what the strife-causing emulation of the latter is towards men. He will behold also the nature of the soul, and the diversity of animals (whether of those which live in the water, or of birds, or of wild beasts), and wdiy each of the genera is subdivided into so many species; and what intention of the Creator, or what purpose of His wisdom, is concealed in each individual thing. He will become acquainted, too, with the reason why certain properties are found associated with certain roots or herbs, and why, on the other hand, evil effects are averted by other herbs and roots. He will know, moreover, the nature of the apostate angels, and the reason why they have power to flatter in some things those who do not despise them w ith the whole power of faith, and why they exist for the purpose of deceiving and leading men astray. He will learn, too, the judgment of Divine Providence on each individual thing; and that, of those events which happen to men, none occur by accident or chance, but in accordance with a plan so carefully considered, and so stupendous, that it does not overlook even the number of the hairs of the heads, not merely of thfe saints, but perhaps of all human beings, and the plan of wdiich providential government extends even to caring for the sale of two sparrows for a denarius, whether sparrows there be understood figuratively or literally. Now indeed this providential government is still a subject of investigation, but then it will be fully manifested. Frouj all which we are to suppose, that mean- 1 Virtutes.

while not a little time may pass by until the reason of those things only which are upon the earth be pointed out to the worthy and deserving after their departure from life, that by the knowledge of all these things, and by the grace of full knowledge, they may enjoy an unspeakable joy. Then, if that atmosphere which is between heaven and earth is not devoid of inhabitants, and those of a rational kind, as the apostle says, ' Wherein in times past ye walked according to the course of this world, according to the prince of the power of the air, the spirit who now worketh in the children of disobedience." And again he says, "We shall be caught up in the clouds to meet Christ in the air, and so shall we ever be with the Lord."''

6. We are therefore to suppose that the saints will remain there until they recognise the twofold mode of o; oyernment in those things which are performed in the air. And when I say ' twofold mode," I mean this: When we were upon earth, we saw either animals or trees, and beheld the differences among them, and also the very great diversity among men; but although we saw these things, we did not understand the reason of them; and this only was suggested to us from the visible diversity, that we should examine and inquire upon what principle these things were either created or diversely arranged. And a zeal or desire for knowledge of this kind being conceived by us on earth, the full understanding and comprehension of it will be granted after death, if indeed the result should follow according to our expectations. When, therefore, we shall have fully comprehended its nature, v. e shall understand in a twofold manner what we saw on earth. Some such view, then, must we hold regarding this abode in the air. I think, therefore, that all the saints who depart from this life will remain in some place situated on the earth, which holy Scripture calls paradise, as in some place of instruction, and, so to speak, class-room or school of souls, in which they are to be instructed regarding all tlie 1 Eph. ii. 2. There is an evident omission of some Avords in the text, such as, "They vrill enter into it," etc.

2 1 Thess. iv. 17."

things which they had seen on earth, and are to receive also some information respecting things that are to follow in the future, as even wdien in this life they had obtained in some degree indications of future events, although "through v. glass darkly," all of which are revealed more clearly and distinctly to the saints in their proper time and place. If any one indeed be pure in heart, and holy in mind, and more practised in perception, he will, by making more rapid progress, quickly ascend to a place in the air, and reach the kingdom of heaven, through those mansions, so to speak, in the various places which the Greeks have termed spheres, i. e. globes, but which holy Scripture has called heavens; in each of which he will first see clearly what is done there, and in the second place, will discover the reason why things are so done: and thus he will in order pass through all gradations, following Him who hath passed into the heavens, Jesus the Son of God, vho said, "I will that where I am, these may be also." And of this diversity of places He speaks, when He says, "In my Father's house are many mansions." He Himself is everywhere, and passes swiftly through all things; nor are ve any longer to understand Him as existing in those narrow limits in which He v as once confined for our sakes, i. e. not in that circumscribed body which He occupied on earth, when dwelling among men, according to which He might be considered as enclosed in some one place.

7. When, then, the saints shall have reached the celestial abodes, they will clearly see the nature of the stars one by one, and will understand whether they are endued with life, or their condition, whatever it is. And they will comprehend also the other reasons for the works of God, which He Himself will reveal to them. For He will show to them, as to children, the causes of things and the power of His creation, and will explain why that star was placed in that particular quarter of the sky, and why it was separated from another by so great an intervening space; what,., would have been the consequence if it had been nearer or more remote; or if

Jolm xiv. 2.

2 Virtutem suie conditionis. Seine Scliopferkraft (Sclmitzer).

that star had been larger than this, how the totahty of things wouki not have remained the same, but all would have been transformed into a different condition of beino. And so, when they have finished all those matters which are connected with the stars, and with the heavenly revolutions, they will come to those which are not seen, or to those whose names only we have heard, and to things which are invisible, which the Apostle Paul has informed us are numerous, although what they are, or what difference may exist among them, we cannot even conjecture by our feeble intellect. And thus the rational nature, growing by each individual step, not as it grew in this life in flesh, and body, and soul, but enlarged in understanding and in power of perception, is raised as a mind already perfect to perfect knowledge, no longer at all impeded by those carnal senses, but increased in intellectual growth; and ever gazing purely, and, so to speak, face to face, on the causes of things, it attains perfection, firstly, viz. that by which it ascends to the truth, and secondly, that by which it abides in it, having problems and the understanding of things, and the causes of events, as the food on which it may feast. For as in this life our bodies grow physically to what they are, through a sufficiency of food in early life supplying the means of increase, but after the due height has been attained we use food no longer to grow, but to live, and to be preserved in life by it; so also I think that the mind, when it has attained perfection, eats and avails itself of suitable and appropriate food in such a degree, that nothing ought to be either deficient or superfluous. And in all things this food is to be understood as the contemplation and understanding of God, which is of a measure appropriate and suitable to this nature, wdiich was made and created; and this measure it is proper should be observed by every one of those who are beginning to see God, i. e. to understand Him through purity of heart.

1 In id: To that state of the soul in which it gazes purely ou the causes of things.

EADER, remember me in your prayers, that we too may deserve to be made emulators of the spirit. The two former books on TJie Principles I translated not only at your instance, but even under pressure from you during the days of Lent; but as you, my devout brother Macarius, were not only living near me during that time, but had more leisure at your command than now, so I also worked the harder; whereas I have been longer in explaining these two latter books, seeing you came less frequently from a distant extremity of the city to urge on my labour. Now if you remember what I warned you of in my former preface, that certain persons would be indignant, if they did not hear that we spoke some evil of Origen, that, I imagine, you have forthwith experienced, has come to pass. But if those demons who excite the tongues of men to slander were so infuriated by that work, in which he had not as yet fully unveiled their secret proceedings, what, think you, will be the case in this, in which he will expose all those dark and hidden ways, by which they creep into the hearts of men, and deceive weak and unstable souls? You will immediately see all things thrown into confusion, seditions stirred up, clamours raised throughout the whole city, and that individual summoned to receive sentence of condemnation Avho endeavoured to dispel the diabolical darkness of ignorance by means of the light of the gospel lamp. Let such things, however, be lightly 1 Diebus quadragesima).- Dtemoncs.

Evangelicse luceriice lumiiie diabolicas ignoranti e teiiebras.

esteemed by him who is desirous of being trained in divine learning, while retaining in its integrity the rule of the Catholic faitli.- I think it necessary, however, to remind you that the principle observed in the former books has been observed also in these, viz. not to translate what appeared contrary to Origen's other opinions, and to our own belief, but to pass by such passages as being interpolated and forged by others. But if he has appeared to give expression to any novelties regarding rational creatures (on which subject the essence of our faith does not depend), for the sake of discussion and of adding to our knowledge, when perhaps it was necessar ' for us to answer in such an order some heretical opinions, I have not omitted to mention these either in the present or preceding books, unless when he wished to repeat in the following books what he had already stated in the previous ones, when I have thought it convenient, for the sake of brevity, to curtail some of these repetitions. Should any one, however, peruse these passages from a desire to enlarge his knowledge, and not to raise captious objections, he will do better to have them expounded by persons of skill. For it is an absurdity to have the fictions of poetry and the ridiculous plays of comedy"" interpreted by grammarians, and to suppose that without a master and an interpreter any one is able to learn those things which are spoken either of God or of the heavenly virtues, and of the whole universe of things, in which some deplorable error either of pagan philosophers or of heretics is confuted; and the result of which is, that men would rather rashly and ignorantly condemn things that are difficult and obscure, than ascertain their meaning by diligence and study.

Salva fidei Catlolicse rcgula.- Coinoediarum ridiculas fabulas.

1. Some sucli opinions, we believe, ought to be entertained regarding the divine promises, when we direct our understanding to the contemplation of that eternal and infinite world, and gaze on its ineffable joy and blessedness. But as

The whole of this chapter has been preserved in the original Greek, which is literally translated in corresponding portions on each page, BO that the differences between Origen's own vords and the amplifications and alterations of the paraphrase of Rufinus may be at once patent to the reader.

TRANSLATION FROM THE GREEK.

CHAPTEE I.

WIT'K AN EXPLANATION AND INTERPRETATION OF THOSE STATE-MENTS OF SCRIPTURE WHICH APPEAR TO NULLIFY IT.

1. Since in the preaching of the church there is ioeluded the doctrine respecting a just judgment of God, which, when-believed to be true, incites those who hear it to live virtuously, and to shun sin by all means, inasmuch as they manifestly acknowledge that things worthy of praise and blame are ' 'TTipi rov a'jrs ovtxi'ov.

tlie preaching of the church inckides a behef in a future and just judgment of God, which behef incites and persuades men to a good and virtuous life, and to an avoidance of sin bv all possible means; and as by this it is undoubtedly indicated that it is within our own power to devote ourselves either to a life that is worthy of praise, or to one that is worthy of censure, I therefore deem it necessary to say a few words regarding the freedom of the will, seeing that this topic has been treated by very many writers in no mean style. And that we may ascertain more easily what is the freedom of the will, let us inquire into the nature of will and of desil'e.

2. Of all things which move, some have the cause of their motion within themselves, others receive it from without: and all those things only are moved from without which are without life, as stones, and pieces of wood, and whatever things are of such a nature as to be held together by the constitution of their matter alone, or of their bodily substance. That view must indeed be dismissed which would regard

Natura ipsius arbitrii voluntatisque.

2 Qu ecunqiie liujusmocli sunt, quae solo Iiabitu materise suae vel cor-pornm constant.

FROM THE GREEK.

within our own power, come and let us discuss by themselves a few points regarding the freedom of the will a question of all others most necessary. And that we may understand what the freedom of the will is, it is necessary to unfold the conception of it, that this being declared with precision, the subject may be placed before us.

2. Of things that move, some hav. e the cause of their motion within themselves; others, again, are moved only from without. Now only portable things are moved from without, such as pieces of wood, and stones, and all matter that is held together by their constitution alone. And let that view be removed from consideration which calls the flux of bodies the dissolatlon of bodies by corruption as motion, for it has

no bearing upon our present purpose. Others, again, have the cause of motion in themselves, as animals, or trees, and all things which are held together by natural life or soul; amonsj which some think ouc ht to be classed the veins of metals. Fire, also, is supposed to be the cause of its own motion, and perhaps also springs of water. And of those things which have the causes of their motion in, themselves, some are said to be moved out of themselves, others by themselves. And they so distinguish them, because those things are moved out of themselves which are auve indeed, but have no soul; whereas those things which hav a soul are moved by themselves, when a phantasy, i. e. a desire or incitement, is presented to them, which excites them to move towards something. Finally, in certain things endowed with a soul, there is such a phantasy, i. e. a will or feeling, as by a kind of natural instinct calls them forth, and arouses them to orderly and regular motion; as we see to be the case with spiders, which are stirred up in a most orderly manner by a phantasy, i. e. a sort of wish and desire for weaving, to undertake the production of a web, some natural movement undoubtedly calling forth the effort to work of this kind. Nor Xon tamen amma, ntia sunt. Phantasia. Voluntas vel sensiis.

FROM THE GREEK.

motion, since it is not needed for our present purpose. But animals and plants have the cause of their motion within themselves, and in general whatever is held together by nature and a soul, to which class of things they say that metals also belong. And besides these, fire too is self-moved, and perhaps also fountains of water. Now, of those things which have the cause of their movement within themselves, some, they say, are moved out of themselves, others from themselves: things without life, out of themselves; animate things, from themselves. For animate things are moved from themselves, a phantasy springing up in them which incites is tills very insect found to possess any other feeling than the natural desire of weaving; as in like manner bees also exhibit a desire to form honeycombs, and to collect, as they say, aerial lioney.

3. But since a rational animal not only has within itself these natural movements, but has moreover, to a greater extent than other animals, the power of reason, by which it can judge and determine regarding natural rhovements, and disapprove and reject some, while approving and adopting other?, so by the judgment of this reason may the movements of men be governed and directed towards a commendable life. And from this it follows that, since the nature of this reason whicli is in man has within itself the power of distinguishing between good and evil, and while distinguishing possesses the faculty of selecting what it has approved, it may justly be deemed worthy of praise in choosing what is good, and deserving of censure in following that whicli is base or wicked. This in-

Mella, lit aiimt, aeria congregandi. Rufinus seems to have read, iu tlie original, dipotT ugrffj instead of KYipo'TTT. uarilv an evidence that he followed in general the worst readings (Redepennuig).

FROM THE GREEK.

to effort. And again, in certain animals phantasies arc formed which call forth an effort, the nature of the phantasy stirring up the effort in an orderly manner, as in the spider is formed the phantasy of weaving; and the attempt to weave follows, the nature of its phantasy inciting the insect in an orderly manner to this alone. And besides its phantasial nature, nothing else is believed to belong to the insect. And in the bee there is formed the phantasy to produce wax.

3. The rational animal, however, has, in addition to its phantasial nature, also reason, whicli judges the phantasies, and disapproves of some and accepts others, in order that the animal may be led according to them. Therefore, since deed must by no means escape our notice, that in some dumb animals there is found a more regular movement than in others, as in hunting-dogs or war-horses, so that they may appear to some to be moved by a kind of rational sense. But we must believe this to be the result not so much of reason as of some natural instinct, largely bestowed for purposes of that kind. Now, as we had begun to remark, seeing that such is the nature of a rational animal, some things may happen to us human beings from without; and these, coming in contact with our sense of sight, or hearing, or any other of our senses, may incite and arouse us to good movements, or the contrary; and seeing they come to us from an external source, it is not within our own power to prevent their coming. But to determine and approve what use w e ought to make of those things wdiich thus happen, is the duty of no-other than of that reason within us, i. e. of our own judgment; by the decision of wdiich reason we use the incitement, Ordinatior quidem motus. Incentivo quodam et natural! motu.

FROM THE GREEK.

there are in the nature of reason aids towards the contemplation of virtue and vice, by following which, after beholding good and evil, we select the one and avoid the other, w e are deserving of praise when we give ourselves to the practice of virtue, and censurable when we do the reverse. We must not, however, be ignorant that the greater part of the nature assigned to all things is a varying quantity among animals, both in a greater and a less degree; so that the instinct in hunting-dogs and in war-horses approaches somehow, so to speak, to the faculty of reason. Now, to fall imder some one of those external causes which stir up within us this phantasy or that, is confessedly not one of those things that are dependent upon ourselves; but to determine that we shall use the occurrence in this way or differently, is the prerogative of nothing else than of the reason within us, wdiich, as occasion offers," arouses us towards efforts inciting to what is which comes to us from without for that purpose, which reason approves, our natural movements being determined by its authority either to good actions or the reverse.

4. If any one now were to say tliat those things wliich happen to us from an external cause, and call forth our movements, are of such a nature that it is impossible to resist them, whether they incite us to good or evil, let the holder of this opinion turn his attention for a little upon himself, and carefully inspect the movements of his own mind, unless he has discovered alreadj, that when an enticement to any desire arises, nothing is accomplished until the assent of tlie soul is gained, and the authority of the mind has granted indulgence to the wicked suggestion; so that a claim might seem to be made by two parties on certain probable grounds as to a judge residing within the tribunals of our heart, in order that, after the statement of reasons, the decree of execution may proceed from the judgment of reason. For, to take an illustration: if, to a man who has determined to live continently and chastely, and to keep himself free from all pollution with

Ita ut etiam verisimilibus quibusdam causis intra cordis nostri tri-bunalia velut judici resident! ex utfaque parte adhiberi videatur assertin, ut causis prius expositis gerendi sententia de rationis judicio proferatur.

FROM THE GREEK.

Virtuous and becoming, or turns us aside to Avhat is the reverse.

4. But if any one maintain that this very external cause is of such a nature that it is impossible to resist it when it comes in such a way, let him turn his attention to his own feelings and movements, and see whether there is not an approval, and assent, and inclination of the controlling principle towards some object on account of some specious arguments. For, to take an instance, a w oman who has appeared before a man that has determined to be chaste, and to refrain from carnal intercourse, and who has incited him to act contrary to his purpose, is not a perfect" cause of annulling his 056 TOig is rx: m ccv6ry; x;. xvtOTi.": g.

ORIG. L women, a woman should happen to present herself, inciting and alluring him to act contrary to his purpose, that woman is not a complete and absolute cause or necessity of his transgressing since it is in his power, by remembering his resolution, to bridle the incitements to lust, and by the stem admonitions of virtue to restrain the pleasure of the allurement that solicits him; so that, all feeling of indulgence being driven away, his determination may remain firm and enduring. Finally, if to any men of learning, strengthened by divine training, allurements of that kind present themselves, remembering forthwith what they are, and calling to mind what has long been the subject of their meditation and instruction, and fortifying themselves by the support of a holler doctrine, they reject and repel all incitement to pleasure, and drive away opposing lusts by the interposition of the reason implanted within them.

5. Seeing, then, that these positions are thus established by a sort of natural evidence, is it not superfluous to throw back the causes of our actions on those things which happen to us from without, and thus transfer the blame from our-

Causa ei perfecta et absoluta vel necessitas prsevaricandi.

FROM THE GREEK.

determination. For, being altogether pleased with the luxury and allurement of the pleasure, and not wishing to resist it, or to keep his purpose, he commits an act of licentiousness. Another man, again (when the same things have happened to him who has received more instruction, and has disciplined himself), encounters, indeed, allurements and enticements; but his reason, as being strengthened to a higher point, and carefully trained, and confirmed in its views towards a virtuous course, or being near to confirmation,- repels the incite-V ment, and extinguishes the desire. 0 5. Such being the case, to say that we are moved from js without, and to put away the blame from ourselves, by de- daring that we are like to pieces of wood and stones, which niykinx. Tt, " lyyvg ys rov (ii(lxia67 vui ybya ni ivos' selves, on whom it wholly lies? For this is to say that we are like pieces of wood, or stones, which have no motion in themselves, but receive the causes of their motion from without. Now such an assertion is neither true nor becoming, and is invented only that the freedom of the will may be denied; unless, indeed, we are to suppose that the freedom of the will consists in this, that nothing which happens to us from without can incite us to good or evil. And if any ont: were to refer the causes of our faults to the natural disorder of the body, such a theory is proved to be contrary to the reason of all teaching. For, as we see in very many individuals, that after living unchastely and intemperately, and after being the captives of luxury and lust, if they should happen to be aroused by the word of teaching and instruction to enter upon a better course of life, there takes place so great a change, that from being luxurious and wicked

Xaturalem corporis intemperiem; i'Ky."j rytv ccct(x, ax, iv u.

2 Contra rationem totius eruditionis. In the Greek, " contra ratio-nem" is expressed hy 'Trapa, ro hccpyi; san; and the words 'hoyou 'Tsrca-hvrikov (rendered by Rufinus " totius eruditionis," and connected with " contra rationem") belong to the following clause.

FROM THE GREEK.

are dragged about by those causes that act upon them from without, is neither true nor in conformity with reason, but is the statement of him who wishes to destroy the conception of free-will. For if we were to ask such an one what was freewill, he would say that it consisted in this, that when purposing to do some thing, no external cause came inciting to the reverse. But to blame, on the other hand, the mere constitution of the body, is absurd; for the disciplinr. ry reason, taking hold of those w ho are most intemperate and savage (if they will follow her exhortation), effects a transformation, so that the alteration and change for the better is most extensive, the most licentious men frequently becoming better than those who formerly did not seem to be such by nature; 'Trcipoc' xpkTTcd. ipi'h' i TTt'j KctruoyaV'iu, " "hoyov Trut' ivrikOV.

men, they are converted into those who are sober, and most chaste and gentle; so, again, we see in the case of those who are quiet and honest, that after associating with restless and shameless individuals, their good morals are corrupted by evil conversation, and they become like those whose wickedness is complete. And this is the case sometimes with men of mature age, so that such have lived more chastely in youth than when more advanced years have enabled them to indulge in a freer mode of life. The result of our reasoning, therefore, is to show that those things which happen to us from without are not in our own power; but that to make a good or bad use of those things which do so happen, by help of that reason which is within us, and which distinguishes and determines how these things ought to be used, is within ouiippwer.

6. And now, to confirm the deductions of reason by the authority of Scripture viz. that it is our own doing whether 1 Quibus nihil ad turpitudiiiem deest.

FROM THE GREEK.

and the most savage men passing into such a state of mildness, that those persons who never at any time were so savage as they were, appear savage in comparison, so great a degree of gentleness having been produced within them. And we see other men, most steady and respectable, driven from their state of respectability and steadiness by intercourse with evil customs, so as to fall into habits of licentiousness, often beginning their wickedness in middle age, and plunging into disorder after the period of youth has passed, which, so far as its nature is concerned, is unstable. Reason, therefore, demonstrates that external events do not depend on us, but that it is our own business to use them in this way or the opposite, having received reason as a judge and an investigator'- of the manner in which we ought to meet those events that come from without.

6. Now, that it is our business to live virtuously, and that we live rightly or not, and that we are not compelled, either by those causes which come to us from without, or, as some think, by the presence of fate we adduce the testimony of the prophet Micah, in these words: " If it has been announced to thee, O man, what is good, or what the Lord requires of thee, except that thou shouldst do justice, and love mercy, and be ready to walk with the Lord thy God." Moses also speaks as follows: " I have placed before thy face the way of life and the way of death: choose what is good, and walk in it."" Isaiah, moreover, makes this declaration: " If you are willing, and hear me, ye shall eat the good of the land. But if you be unwilling, and will not hear me, the sword shall consume you; for the mouth of the Lord has spoken this." In the psalm, too, it is written: " If my people had heard me, if Israel had walked in my ways, I would have humbled her enemies to nothing;"" by which he shows that it was in the power of the people to hear, and to walk in the ways of God. The Saviour also saying, "I say unto you, Resist not evil;" and, ' Whoever shall be angry with his brother, shall be in danger of the judg- 1 Mic. vi. 8. 2 Deut. xxx. 15. Isa. i. 19, 20.

Ps. lxxxi. 13, 14. 5 Matt. v. 39.

FROM THE GREEK.

God asks this of us, as not being dependent on Him nor on any other, nor, as some think, upon fate, but as being our own doing, the prophet Micah will prove when he says: ' If it has been announced to thee, O man, what is good, or what does the Lord require of thee, except to do justice and to love mercy?" Moses also: " I have placed before thy face the way of life, and the way of death; choose what is good, and walk in it." Isaiah too: ' If you are willing, and hear me, ye shall eat the good of the land; but if ye be unwilling, and will not hear me, the sword will consume you: for the mouth of the Lord hath spoken it." And in the Psalms: ' If my people had heard me, and Israel had walked in my Iic. vi. 8. 2 Qi Deut. xxx. 15, 16, cf. 19. jg. i. 19 20.

ment;" and, "Whosoever shall look upon a woman to Inst after her, hath already committed adultery with her in his heart;" and in issuing certain other commands, conveys no otlier meaning than this, that it is in our own power to observe what is commanded. And therefore we are rightly rendered liable to condemnation if we transgress those commandments which we are able to keep. And hence He Himself also declares: " Every one who hears my words, and doeth them, I will show to whom he is like: he is like a wise man who built his house upon a rock," etc." So also the declaration: " Whoso heareth these things, and doeth them not, is like a foolish man, who built his house upon the sand," etc." Even the words addressed to those who are on His right hand, "Come unto me, all ye blessed of my Father," etc.; " for I was an hungered, and ye gave me to eat; I was thirsty, and ye gave me drink," manifestly show 1 Matt. V. 22. 2 Matt. v. 28, 3 Matt. vii. 24.

4 Matt. vii. 26. Matt. xxv. 34 sq.

FROM THE GREEK.

ways, I would have humbled their enemies to nothing, and laid my hand upon those that afflicted them;" showing that it was in the power of His people to hear and to walk in the ways of God. And the Saviour also, when He commands, "But I say unto you, Kesist not evil;"" and, "Whosoever shall be angry with his brother, shall be in danger of the judgment;"' and, Whosoever shall look upon a woman to lust after her, hath already committed adultery with her in his heart;" and by any other commandment which He gives, declares that it lies with ourselves to keep what is enjoined, and that we shall reasonably be liable to condemnation if we transgress. And therefore He says in addition: " He that heareth my words, and doeth them, shall be likened to a prudent man, who built his house upon a rock," etc. etc.; " while he that heareth them, but doeth them not, is like a 1 Ps. Ixxx. 13, 14. 2 Matt. v. 89. Matt. v. 22

Matt. vii. 24. ivkoyas- that it depended upon themselves, that either these should be deserving of praise for doing what was commanded and receiving what was promised, or those deserving of censure who either heard or received the contrary, and to whom it was said, "Depart, ye cursed, into everlasting fire." Let us observe also, that the Apostle Paul addresses us as having power over our own will, and as possessing in ourselves the causes either of our salvation or of our ruin: " Dost thou despise the riches of His goodness, and of His patience, and of His long-suffering, not knowing that the goodness of God leadetli thee to repentance? But, according to thy hardness and impenitent heart, thou art treasuring up for thyself wrath on the day of judgment and of the revelation of the just judgment of God, who will render to every one according to his work: to those who by patient continuance in welldoing seek for glory and immortality, eternal life; while

The words in the text are: His qui secundum i atientiara boni operis, gloria et incorruptio, qui quserunt vitam eteruam.

FROM THE GREEK.

foolish man, who built his house upon the sand," etc. And when He says to those on His right hand, "Come, ye blessed of my Father," etc.; " for I was an hungered, and ye gave me to eat; I was athirst, and ye gave me to drink,"" it is exceedingly manifest that He gives the promises to these as being deserving of praise. But, on the contrary, to the others, as being censurable in comparison with them. He says, "Depart, ye cursed, into everlasting fire!" And let us observe how Paul also converses' with us as bavin aj free-dom of will, and as being ourselves the cause of ruin or salvation, when he says, "Dost thou despise the riches of His goodness, and of His patience, and of His long-suffering: not knowing that the goodness of God leadeth thee to repentance? But, according to thy hardness and impenitent heart, thou art treasuring up for thyself wrath on the day of wrath 1 Ci. Matt. vii. 26. ' Matt. xxv. 34.

3 Matt. XXV. 35. cix'hiyitoi. i.

to those who are contentious, and believe not the truth, but who beheve iniquity, anger, indignation, tribulation, and distress, on every soul of man that worketh evil, on the Jew first, and afterwards on the Greek; but glory, and honour, and peace to every one that doeth good, to the Jew first, and afterwards to the Greek." You will find also innumerable other passages in Holy Scripture, which manifestly show that we possess freedom of will. Otherwise there would be a contrariety in commandments being given us, by observing which we may be saved, or by transgressing which we may be condemned, if the power of keeping them w ere not implanted in us.

7. But, seeing there are found in the sacred Scriptures themselves certain expressions occurring in such a connection, that the oj posite of this may appear capable of being understood from them, let us bring them forth before us, and, discussing them according to the rule of piety, let us Rom. ii. 4-10.- Secundum pietatis regulam.

FROM THE GREEK.

and revelation of the righteous judgment of God; wdio will render to every one according to his works: to those who, by patient continuance in well-doing, seek for glory and immortality, eternal life; while to those who are contentious, and believe not the truth, but who believe iniquity, anger, wrath, tribulation, and distress, on every soul of man that w orketh evil; on the Jew first, and on the Greek: but glory, and honour, and peace to every one that worketh good; to the Jew first, and to the Greek."- There are, indeed, innumerable passages in the Scriptures wdiich establish with exceeding clearness the existence of freedom of w'lll.

7. But since certain declarations of the Old Testament and of the New lead to the opposite conclusion namely, that it does not depend on ourselves to keep the commandments and to be saved, or to transgress them and to be lost let us adduce them one by one, and see the explanations of them, 1 Rom. ii. 4-10.

furnish an explanation of them, in order that from those few passages which we now expound, the sokition of those others which resemble them, and by which any power over the will seems to be excluded, may become clear. Those expressions, accordingly, make an impression on very many, which are used by God in speaking of Pharaoh, as when He frequently says, "I will harden Pharaoh's heart." For if he is hardened by God, and commits sin in consequence of being so hardened, the cause of his sin is not himself. And if so, it will appear that Pharaoh docs not possess freedom of will; and it will be maintained, as a consequence, that, agreeably to this illustration, neither do others who perish owe the cause of their destruction to the freedom of their own will. That expression, also, in Ezekiel, when he says, "I will take away their stony hearts, and will give them hearts of flesh, that they may walk in my precepts, and keep my ways," may impress some, inasmuch as it seems to be a gift of God, 1 Ex. iv. 21, etc. 2 E22 j, i. 19, 20.

FROM THE GREEK.

in order that from those which we adduce, any one selecting in a similar way all the passages that seem to nullify freewill, may consider what is said about them by way of explanation. And now, the statements regarding Pharaoh have troubled many, respecting whom God declared several times, ' I will harden Pharaoh's heart." For if he is hardened by God, and commits sin in consequence of being hardened, he is not the cause of sin to himself; and if so, then neither does Pharaoh possess free-will. And some one will say that, in a similar way, they who perish have not free-will, and will not perish of themselves. The declaration also in Ezekiel, "I will take away their stony hearts, and will put in them hearts of flesh, that they may walk in my precepts, and keep my commandments," might lead one to think that it was God who gave the power to walk in His commandments, and to keep His precepts, by His withdrawing the hindrance the 1 Ex. iv. 21, cf. vii. 3. 2 Ezek. xi. 19, 20.

FiloM THE LATIN.

eitlier to walk in His ways or to keep His precepts,-' if He take away that stony heart which is an obstacle to the keeping of His commandments, and bestow and implant a better and more impressible heart, which is called now a heart of flesh. Consider also the nature of the answer given in the Gospel by our Lord and Saviour to those who inquired of Him why He spoke to the multitude in parables. His words are: " That seeing they may not see; and hearing they may hear, and not understand; lest they should be converted, and their sins be forgiven them." The words, moreover, used by the Apostle Paul, that " it is not of him that willeth, nor of him that runneth, but of God that showeth mercy;" in another passage also, " that to will and to do are of God;" and again, elsewhere, ' Therefore hath He mercy upon w hom He will, and whom He will He hardeneth. Thou wilt say then unto me, Why doth He yet find fault? For who shall resist His will? O man, who art thou that repliest against God? Shall the thing formed say to him who hath 1 Justiiicationes.

- The word " now " is added, as the term " flesh " is frequently used in the New Testament in a bad sense (Redepenning).

3 Mark iv. 12. jj ni. ix. 16. Phil. ii. 13.

FEOM THE GREEK.

stony heart, and implanting a better a heart of flesh. And let us look also at the passage in the Gospel the answer which the Saviour returns to those who inquired why He spake to the multitude in parables. His words are: '' That seeing they might not see; and hearing they may hear, and not understand; lest they should be converted, and their sins be forgiven them." The passage also in Paul: ' It is not of him that wdlleth, nor of him that runneth, but of God that showeth mercy." The declarations, too, in other places, that "both to will and to do are of God;" "that God hath mercy upon whom He will have mercy, and whom He will ' Cf. Matt. iv. 12 and Luke viii. 10.

2 Eom. ix. 16. 3 Cf. Phil. ii. 13.

formed it, Why liast thou made me thu? Hath not the potter power over the cliy, of the same lump to make one vessel unto honour, and another to dishonour?" these and similar declarations seem to have no small influence in preventing very many from believing that every one is to be considered as having freedom over his own will, and in making it appear to be a consequence of the will of God whether a man is either saved or lost.

8. Let us begin, then, with those words which were spoken to Pharaoh, who is said to have been hardened by God, in order that he might not let the people go; and, along with his case, the language of the apostle also will be considered, where he says, "Therefore Re hath mercy on whom He will, and whom He will He hardeneth." For it is on these passages chiefly that the heretics rely, asserting that salvii-tion is not in our own power, but that souls are of such a 1 Rom. ix. 18 sq. 2 j qq j. 18.

FROM THE GREEK.

He hardeneth. Thou wilt say then. Why doth He yet find fault? For who hath resisted His will?" "The persuasion is of Him that calleth, and not of us." " Nay, O man, who art thou that repliest against God? Shall the thing formed say to him that hath formed it, Why hast thou made me thus? Hath not the potter power over the clay, of the same lump to make one vessel unto honour, and another imto dishonour?" Now these passages are sufficient of themselves to trouble the multitude, as if man were not possessed of free-will, but as if it w ere God wdio saves and destroys whom He will.

8. Let us begin, then, with what is said about Pharaoh that he was hardened by God, that he might not send away the people; along with which will be examined also the statement of the apostle, "Therefore hatli He mercy on whom He will have mercy,

and whom He will He hardeneth." And certain of those who hold different opinions misuse these pas-, sages, themselves also almost destroying free-will by intro-j 1 Gal. V. 8. 2 2oi ix. 20, 21. Cf. Rom. ix. 18.

nature as must by all means be either lost or saved; and I that in no way can a soul which is of an evil nature become ' good, or one which is of a virtuous nature be made bad. And hence they maintain that Pharaoh, too, being of a ruined nature, was on that account hardened by God, who hardens those that are of an earthly nature, but has compassion on those who are of a spiritual nature. Let ns see, then, what is the meaning of their assertion; and let us, in the first place, request them to tell us whether they maintain that the soul of Pharaoh was of an earthly nature, such as thcy term lost. They will undoubtedly answer that it was of an earthly nature. If so, then to believe God, or to obey Him, when his nature opposed his so doing, was an impossibility. And if this were his condition by nature, what further need was there for his heart to be hardened, and this not once, but several times, unless indeed because it was possible for him to yield to persuasion? Nor could any one be said to be hardened by another, save him who of himself was not obdurate. And if he were not obdurate of himself, it follows that neither was he of an earthly nature, but such an one as might give way when overpowered by signs and wonders. But he was necessary for God's purpose, in order that, for the saving of the multitude. He might manifest in him His power by his offering resistance to numerous miracles, and struggling against the will of God, and his heart being by Obstupefactus.

FROM THE GREEK.

ducing ruined natures incapable of salvation, and others saved which It is impossible can be lost; and Pharaoh, they say, as being of a ruined nature, is therefore hardened by God, who has mercy upon the spiritual, but hardens the earthly. Let us see now what they mean. For we shall ask them if Pharaoh was of an earthy nature; and when they answer, we shall say that he who is of an earthy nature is altogether disobedient to God: but if disobedient, what need is there of his heart being hardened, and that not once, but frequently?

this means said to be hardened. Such are our answers, in the first place, to these persons; and by these their assertion may be overturned, according to which they think that Pharaoh was destroj ed in consequence of his evil nature. And with regard to the language of the Apostle Paul, we must answ er them in a similar way. For who are they whom God hardens, according to your view? Those, namely, whom you term of a ruined nature, and who, I am to suppose, would have done something else had they not been hardened. If, indeed, they come to destruction in consequence of being hardened, they no longer perish naturally, but in virtue of wdiat befalls them. Then, in the next place, upon whom does God show mercy? On those, namely, who are to be saved. And in what respect do those persons stand in need of a second compassion, who are to be saved I t.-LJ once by their nature, and so come naturally to blessedness, ' except that it is shown even from their case, that, because it Xaturaliter.

FROM THE GREEK.

Unless perhaps, since it was possible for him to obey (in which case he would certainly have obeyed, as not being earthy, when hard pressed by the signs and wonders), God needs him to be disobedient to a greater degree, in order that He may manifest His mighty deeds for the salvation of the multitude, and therefore hardens his heart. This will be our answer to them in the first place, in order to overturn (their supposition that Pharaoh was of a ruined nature. And the same reply must be given to them with respect to the statement of the apostle. For whom does God harden? Those who perish, as if they w ould obey unless they were hardened, or manifestly those who would be saved because they are not of a ruined nature. And on whom has He mercy? Is it on those who are to be saved? And how is there need of a second mercy for those who have been y prepared once for salvation, and who wdll by all means be- was possible for them to perish, they therefore obtain mercy, that so they may not perish, but come to salvation, and possess the kingdom of the good. And let this be our answer to those who devise and invent the fable of good or bad natures, i. e, of earthly or spiritual souls, in consequence of which, as they say, each one is either saved or lost.

9. And now we must return an answer also to those who would have the God of the law to be just only, and not also good; and let us ask such in what manner they consider the heart of Pharaoh to have been hardened by God by what acts or by what prospective arrangements. For we must observe the conception of a God who in our opinion is both just and good, but according to them only just. And let them show us how a God whom they also acknowledge to be just, can with justice cause the heart of a man to be har-

Commentitias fabulas introducunt. Quid faciente vel quid prospiciente.

Prospectus et intuitus Dei. Such is the rendering of 'iwoia, by Eufinus.

FEOM THE GREEK.

come blessed on account of their nature? Unless perhaps, since they are capable of incurring destruction, if they did not receive mercy, they will obtain mercy, in order that they may not incur that destruction of which they are capable, but may be in the condition of those who are saved. And this is our answer to such persons.

9. But to those who think they understand the term "hardened," we must address the inquiry. What do they mean by saying that God, by His working, hardens the heart, and with what purpose does He do this? For let them observe the conception of a God who is in reality just and good; but if they will not allow this, let it be conceded to them ior the present that He is just; and let them show how the good and just God, or the just God only, appears to be just, in hardening the heart of him who perishes because of

FRO r THE LATIN.

clened, that, in consequence of that very hardening, he may sin and be ruined. And how shall the justice of God be defended, if He Himself is the cause of the destruction of those whom, owing to their unbelief (through their being hardened), He has afterwards condemned by the authority of a judge? For why does He blame him, saying, "But since thou wilt not let my people go, lo, I will smite all the first-born in Egypt, even thy first-born," and whatever else was spoken through Moses by God to Pharaoh? For it behoves every one who maintains the truth of what is recorded in Scripture, and who desires to show that the God of the law and the prophets is just, to render a reason for all these things, and to show how there is in them nothing at all derogatory to the justice of God, since, although they deny His goodness, they admit that He is a just judge, and creator of the world. Different, however, is the method of our reply to those who l Ex. ix. 17, cf. xi. 5 and xii. 12.

FKOM THE GREEK.

his being hardened: and how the just God becomes the cause of destruction and disobedience, when men are chasrx tened by Him on account of their hardness and disobedience. And why does He find fault with him, saying, "Thou wilt not let my people go;" "Lo, I will smite all the firstborn in Egypt, even thy first-born;" and whatever else is recorded as spoken from God to Pharaoh through the intervention of Moses? For he who believes that the Scriptures are true, and that God is just, must necessarily endeavour, if he be honest, to show how God, in using such expressions, may be distinctly understood to be just. But if any one should stand, declaring with uncovered head that the Creator of the world vas inclined to wickedness, we should need other words to answer them.

l Cf. Ex. iv. 23 and ix. 17. " Cf. Ex. xii. 12.

ivyyaf Q'jyi. rpotvcjg.

d'Tioypot. pkfmios ri; yvy yji rri KS(pix,7 y) 'laiccro Tirpo; to ' royipou shat rou 'tnixiovpyo'j.

assert that the creator of this world is a malignant being, i. e. a devil.

10. But since we acknowledge the God who spoke bv Moses to be not only just, but also good, let us carefully inquire how it is in keeping with the character of a just and good Deity to have hardened the heart of Pharaoh. And let us see whether, following the example of the Apostle Paul, we are able to solve the difficulty by help of some parallel instances: if we can show, e. g., that by one and the same act God has pity upon one individual, but hardens another; not purposing or desiring that he who is hardened should be so, but because, in the manifestation of His goodness and patience, the heart of those who treat His kindness and forbearance with contempt and insolence is hardened by the punishment of their crimes being delayed; while those, on the other hand, who make His goodness and patience the occasion of their repentance and reformation, obtain compassion. To show more clearly, however, what we mean, let us take the illustration employed by the Apostle Paul in the Epistle to the Hebrews, where he says, "For the earth, which drinketh in the rain that cometli oft upon it, and bringeth forth herbs meet for them by whom

FROM THE GREEK.

10. But since they say that they regard Him as a jnst God, and w e as one who is at the same time good and just, let us consider how the good and just God could harden the heart of Pharaoh. See, then, wdiether, by an illustration used by the apostle in the Epistle to the Hebrews, we are able to prove that by one operation God has mercy upon one man while He hardens another, although not intending to harden; but, although having a good purpose, hardening follows as a result of the inherent principle of wickedness in such persons, and so He is said to harden him who is hardened. " The earth," he says, "which drinketh in the rain

Ivipyiicc.

Chap, l ORIGEN DE PPJNCIPIIS. llf)

FROM THE LATIN.

it is dressed, yi11 receive blessing from God; but that wliicli beareth thorns and briers is rejected, and is nigh unto curs-incr, whose end is to be burned." Now from those words of Paul which we have quoted, it is clearly shown that by one and the same act on the part of God that, viz. by which He sends rain upon the earth one portion of the ground, when carefully cultivated, brings forth good fruits; while another, neglected and uncared for, produces thorns and thistles. And if one, speaking as it were in the person of the rain,"" were to say, "It is I, the rain, that have made the good fruits, and it is I that have caused the thorns and thistles to grow," however hard the statement might appear, it would nevertheless be true; for unless the rain had fallen, neither fruits, nor thorns, nor thistles would have sprung up, whereas by the coming of the rain the earth gave birth to both. Now, although it is due to the beneficial action of the rain that the earth has produced herbs of both kinds, it is not to the rain that the diversity of the herbs is properly to be ascribed; but on those will justly rest the blame for the bad seed, who, although they might have turned up the ground by frequent ploughing, and have broken the clods by repeated harrowing, and have extirpated all useless and noxious Heb. vi. 7, 8. Ex persona iuibrium. Dm-e.

FROil THE GREEK.

that cometli oft upon it, and bringeth forth herbs meet for them for whom it is dressed, receiveth blessing from God; but that which beareth thorns and briers is rejected, and is nigh to cursing, whose end is to be burned."- As respects the rain, then, there is one operation; aiid there being one operation as regards the rain, the ground which is cultivated produces fruit, while that which is neglected and is barren produces thorns. Now, it might seem profane" for Him who rains to say, "I produced the fruits, and the thorns that are in the earth;" and yet, although profane, it is true. For, had rain not fallen, there would have been neither fruits 1 Heb. vi. 7, 8. 2 l.:, aq: Yiy. Qy.

weeds, and have cleared and prepared the fields for the coming showers by all the labour and toil which cultivation demands, have nevertheless neglected to do this, and who will accordingly reap briers and thorns, the most appropriate fruit of their sloth. And the consequence therefore is, that while the rain falls in kindness and impartiality equally upon the whole earth, yet, by one and the same operation of the rain, that soil which is cultivated yields with a blessing useful,. fruits to the diligent and careful cultivators, while that whicli has become hardened throucrh the nemect of the husband-man brings forth only thorns and thistles. Let us therefore view those signs and miracles which were done by God, as the showers furnished by Him from above; and the purpose and desires of men, as the cultivated and uncultivated soil, which is of one and the same nature indeed, as is every soil compared with another, but not in one and the same state of) ' cultivation. From which it follows that every one's will, if untrained, and fierce, and barbarous, is either- hardened by the miracles and wonders of God, growing more savage and thorny than ever, or it becomes more pliant, and yields itself up with the whole mind to obedience, if it be cleared from vice and subjected to training.

11. But, to establish the point more clearly, it will not be Bonitas et sequitas imbrium. Propositum.

FROM THE GREEK.

nor thorns; but, having fallen at the proper time and in moderation, both were produced. The ground, now, whicli drank in the rain which often fell upon it, and yet produced thorns and briers, is rejected and nigh to cursing. The blessing, then, of the rain descended even upon the inferior land; but it, being neglected and uncultivated, yielded thorns and thistles. In the same way, therefore, the wonderful works also done by God are, as it were, the rain; while the differing purposes are, as it were, the cultivated and neglected land being yet, like earth, of one nature.

11. And as if the sun, uttering a voice, were to say, "I superfluous to employ another illustration, as if, e. g., one were to say that it is the sun which hardens and hquefies, although liquefying" and hardening are things of an opposite nature. Now it is not incorrect to say that the sun, by one and the same power of its heat, melts w ax indeed, but dries up and hardens mud: not that its power operates one w ay upon mud, and in another way upon wax; but that the qualities of mud and wax are different, although according to nature they are one tiling, both being from the earth. In this way, then, one and the same working upon the part of God, which was administered by Moses in signs and wonders, made manifest the hardness of Pharaoh, wdiich he had conceived in the intensity of his wickedness, but exhibited the obedience of those other Egyptians wdio were intermingled with the Israelites, and wdio are recorded to have quitted Egypt at the same time with the Hebrews. With respect to the statement that the heart of Pharaoh was subdued by degrees, so that on one occasion he said, ' Go not far aw ay; ye shall go a three days' journey, but leave your wives, and your children, and your cattle,'" and as regards any other statements,

Limum. Cum utique secundum naturam unum sit.

3 Malitise su? e intentione conceperat. Cf. Ex. viii. 27-29.

FROM THE GREEK.

liquefy and dry up," liquefaction and drying up being opposite things, he would not speak falsely as regards the point in question- wax being melted and mud being dried by the same heat; so the same operation, which was performed through the instrumentality of Moses, proved the hardness of Pharaoh on the one hand, the result of his wickedness, and the yielding of the mixed Egyptian multitude who took their departure with the Hebrews. And the brief statement that the heart of Pharaoh was softened, as it w ere, wdien he said, "But ye shall not go far: ye will go a three days' journey, and leave your wives,"' and anything else which he said,

TTccpcc TO v'7rokSi usuou. K l TO KXTcic, TO (ipccy v OS civxysypx(pdcci.

3 Cf. Ex. viii. 28, 29.

according to wliicli he appears to yield gradually to the signs and wonders, what else is shown, save that the power of the signs and miracles was making some impression on him, but not so much as it ought to have done? For if the hardening were of such a nature as many take it to be, he would not indeed have given way even in a few instances. But I think there is no absurdity in explaining the tropical or jsgurative ' nature of that language employed in speaking of " hardening," according to common usage. For those masters who are remarkable for kindness to their slaves, are frequently accustomed to say to the latter, when, through much patience and indulgence on their part, they have become insolent and worthless: " It is I that have made you what you are; I have spoiled you; it is my endurance that has made you good for nothing: I am to blame for your perverse and wicked habits, because I do not have you immediately punished for every delinquency according to your deserts." For we must first attend to the tropical or figurative meaning of the language, and so come to see the force of the expression, and not find fault with the word, Tropum vel figuram sermonis.

FROM THE GREEK.

yielding little by little before the signs, proves that the wonders made some impression even upon him, but did not accomplish all that they might. Yet even this would not have happened, if that which is supposed by the many the hardening of Pharaoh's heart had been produced by God Himself. And it is not absurd to soften down such expressions agreeably to common usage: for good masters often say to their slaves, when spoiled by their kindness and forbearance, "I have made you bad, and I am to blame for offences of such enormity." For we must attend to the character and force of the phrase, and not argue sophistically,-disregarding the meaning of the expression. Paul accordingly, ovKo(pocvrfiu.

whose inner meaning we do not ascertain. Finally, the Apostle Paul, evidently treating of such, says to him who remained in his sins: " Despisest thou the riches of His goodness, and forbearance, and long-suffering; not knowing that the goodness of God leadeth thee to repentance? but, after thy hardness and impenitent heart, treasurest up unto thyself wrath on the day of wrath and revelation of the righteous judgment of God." Such are the words of the apostle to him who is in his sins. Let us apply these very expressions to Pharaoh, and see if they also are not spoken of him with propriety, since, according to his hardness and impenitent heart, he treasured and stored up for himself wrath on the day of wrath, inasmuch as his hardness could never have been declared and manifested, unless signs and wonders of such number and magnificence had been performed.

12. But if the proofs which we have adduced do not appear full enough, and the similitude of tlie apostle seem wanting 1 Rom, ii. 4, 5.

FROM THE GREEK.

having examined these points clearly, says to the sinner: " Or despisest thou the riches of His goodness, and forbearance, and lono–suffcrino;; not knowino; that the 2: oodnessof God leadeth thee to repentance? but, after thy hardness and impenitent heart, treasurest up unto thyself wrath against the day of V wrath and revelation of the righteous judgment of God." Now, let what the apostle says to the sinner be addressed to Pharaoh, and then the announcements made to him will be understood to have been made wdth peculiar fitness, as to one who, according to his hardness and unrepentant heart, was treasuring up to himself wrath; seeing that his hardness would not have been proved nor made manifest unless miracles had been performed, and miracles, too, of such magnitude and importance.

12. But since such narratives are slow to secure assent, and are considered to be forced," let us see from the prophetical Eom. ii. 4, 5. 2 ouatrudhg. 3 s o;.

in applicability,- let us add the voice of prophetic authority and see what the prophets declare regarding those who at first, indeed, leading a righteous life, have deserved to receive numerous proofs of the goodness of God, but afterwards, as being human beings, have fallen astray, with whom the prophet, making himself also one, says: ' Why, O Lord, hast Thou made us to err from Thy way? and hardened our heart, that we should not fear Thy name? Return, for Thy servants' sake, for the tribes of Thine inheritance, that we also for a little may obtain some inheritance from Thy holy hill." Jeremiah also employs similar language: " O Lord, Thou hast deceived us, and we were deceived; Thou hast held us, and Thou hast prevailed." The expression, then, "Why, O Lord, hast Thou hardened our heart, that we should not fear Thy name? " used by those who prayed for mercy, is to be taken In a figurative, moral acceptation, as if one were to say, "Why hast Thou spared us so long, and 1 Et apostolicee similitudiuis parum munimenti lial ere adhuc videtur assertio.

- Isa. Ixiii. 17, 18. Here the Septuagint differs from the Iasoretig text.

3 Jer. XX. 7. Morali utique tropo accipiendum.

FROM THE GREEK.

declarations also, what those persons say, who, although they have experienced the great kindness of God, have not lived virtuously, but have afterwards sinned. " Why, O Lord, hast Thou made us to err from Thy ways? Why hast Thou hardened our heart, so as not to fear Thy name? Return for Thy servants' sake, for the tribes of Thine inheritance, that we may inherit a small portion of Thy holy mountain." And In Jeremiah: " Thou hast deceived me, O Lord, and I was deceived; Thou wert strong, and Thou didst prevail." For the expression, "Why hast Thou hardened our heart, so as not to fear Thy name?" uttered by those who are begging to receive mercy, is In Its nature as follows: " Why Isa. Ixiii. 17, 18.- Jer. xx. 7.

didst not requite us when we sinned, but didst abandon us, tliat so our wickedness might increase, and our liberty of sinning be extended when punishment ceased? " In hke manner, unless a horse continually feel the spur- of his rider, and have his mouth abraded by a bit, he becomes hardened. And a boy also, unless constantly disciplined by chastisement, will grow up to be an insolent youth, and one ready to fall headlong into vice. God accordingly abandons and neglects those whom He has judged undeserving of chastisement: "For whom the Lord loveth He chasteneth, and scourgeth every son whom He receiveth." From which w e are to suppose that those are to be received into the rank and affection of sons, who have deserved to be scourged and chastened by the Lord, in order that they also, through endurance of trials and tribulations, may be able to say, " Who shall separate us from the love of God which is m Christ Jesus? shall tribulation, or anguish, or famine, or nakedness, or peril, or sword?" For by all these is each one's resolution manifested and displayed, and the firmness of his perseverance made known, not so much to God, who knows all things before they happen, as to the rational and heavenly virtues, who have obtained a part in the work of procuring human salvation, as being a sort of assistants and

Ferratum calcem. Frenis ferratis. Heb. xii. 6.

Rom. viii. 35. Rationabilibus coelestibiisque virtutibiis.

FROM THE GREEK.

hast Thou spared us so long, not visiting us because of our sins, but deserting us, until our transgressions come to a height?" Now He leaves the greater part of men unpunished, both in order that the habits of each one may be examined, so far as it depends upon ourselves, and that the virtuous may be made manifest in consequence of the test applied; while the others, not escaping notice from God for He knows all things before they exist but from the rational creation and themselves, may afterwards obtain the means of cure, seeing they w ould not have known the benefit ministers to God. Those, on the other hand, who do not yet offer themselves to God with such constancy and affection, and are not ready to come into His service, and to prepare their souls for trial, are said to be abandoned by God, i. e. not to be instructed, inasmuch as they are not prepared for instruction, their training or care being undoubtedly postponed to a later time. These certainly do not know what they will obtain from God, unless they first entertain the desire of being benefited; and this finally will be the case, if a man come first to a knowledge of himself, and feel what are his defects, and understand from whom he either ought or can seek the supply of his deficiencies. For he who does not know beforehand of his weakness or his sickness, cannot seek a physician; or at least, after recovering his health, that man will not be grateful to his physician who did not first recognise the dangerous nature of his ailment. And so, unless a man has first ascertained the defects of his life, and the evil nature of his sins, and made this known by confession from his own lips, he cannot be cleansed or acquitted, lest he should be ignorant that what he possesses has been bestowed on him by favour, but should consider as his own property what flows from the divine liberality, which idea undoubtedly generates arrogance of mind and pride, and finally becomes the cause of the individual's ruin. And this, v e must believe, was the

FROM THE GREEK.

had they not condemned themselves. It is of advantage to each one, that he perceive his own peculiar nature and the grace of God. For he who does not perceive his own weakness and the divine favour, although he receive a benefit, yet, not having made trial of himself, nor having condemned himself, will imagine that the benefit conferred upon him by the grace of Heaven is his own doing. And this imagination, producing also vanity, will be the cause of a dovv n-fall: which, w e conceive, was the case with the devil, who attributed to himself the priority which he possessed when in case with the devil, who viewed as his own, and not as given him by God, the primacy which he hekl at the time when he was unstained;' and thus was fulfilled in him the declaration, that "every one who exalteth himself shall be abased." From which it appears to me that the divine mysteries were concealed from the wise and prudent, according to the statement of Scripture, that " no flesh should glory before God," and revealed to children to those, namely, who, after they have become infants and little children, i. e. have returned to the humility and simplicity of children, then make progress; and on arriving at perfection, remember that they have obtained their state of happiness, not by their ow n merits, but by the grace and compassion of God.

13. It is therefore by the sentence of God that he is abandoned who deserves to be so, while over some sinners God exercises forbearance; not, how ever, without a definite principle of action.-J? the very fact that He is long-suffering coiiduces to the advantage of those very persons, since the

Primatus. Immaciilatus. Luke xviii. 14.

1 Cor. i. 29 Noil tarn en sine certa ratione.

FROM THE GREEK.

a state of sinlessness.- "' For every one that exalteth himself shall be abased," and " every one that humbleth himself shall be exalted." And observe, that for this reason divine things have been concealed from the w ise and prudent, in order, as says the apostle, that " no flesh should glory in the presence of God;" and they have been revealed to babes, to those who after childhood have come to better things, and I who remember that it is not so much from their own effort,. 7 i as by the unspeakable goodness of God, that they have. reached the greatest possible extent of blessedness.

13. It is not without reason, then, that he w ho is abandoned, is abandoned to the divine judgment, and that God is long-suffering wath certain sinners; but because it will be for their advantage, with respect to the immortality of 1 j. oj. 2 cf. L e xiv. 11. 3 Qi I Cor, 29.

soul over wlilcli He exercises this providential care is immortal; and, as being immortal and everlasting, it is not, although not immediately cared for, excluded from salvation, which is postponed to a more convenient time. For perhaps it is expedient for those who have been more deeply imbued with the poison of wickedness to obtain this salvation at a later period. For as medical men sometimes, although they could quickly cover over the scars of wounds, keep back and delay the cure for the present, in the expectation of a better and more perfect recovery, knowing that it is more salutary to retard the treatment in the cases of swellings caused by wounds, and to allow the malignant humours to flow off for a while, rather than to hasten a superficial cure, by shutting up in the veins the poison of a morbid humour, which, excluded from its customary outlets, will undoubtedly creep into the inner parts of the limbs, and penetrate to the very vitals of the viscera, producing no longer mere disease in the body, but causing destruction to life; so, in like manner, God also, who knows the secret things of the heart, and foreknows the future, in much forbearance allows certain events to happen, which, coming from without upon men, cause to

FR03I THE GREEK.

the soul and the unending world, that they be not quickly brought into a state of salvation, but be conducted to it more slowly, after having experienced many evils. For as physicians, who are able to cure a man quickly, when they suspect that a hidden poison exists in the body, do the reverse of healing, making this more certain through their very desire to heal, deeming it better for a considerable time to retain the patient under inflammation and sickness, in order that he may recover his health more surely, than to appear to produce a rapid recovery, and afterwards to cause a relapse, and thus that hasty cure last only for a time; in the same way, God also, who knows the secret things of the heart, and foresees future events, in His long-suffering, permits certain events rov oitTsipou oclcouoi. avvspytid voii.

come forth Into the light tlie passions and vices which are concealed within, that by their means those may be cleansed and cured who, through great negligence and carelessness, have admitted within themselves the roots and seeds of sins, so that, when driven outwards and brought to the surface, they may in a certain degree be cast forth and dispersed. And thus, although a man may appear to be afflicted with evils of a serious kind, suffering convulsions in all his limbs, he may nevertheless, at some future time, obtain relief and a cessation from his trouble; and, after enduring his afflictions to satiety, may, after many sufferings, be restored again to his proper condition. For God deals with souls not merely with a view to the short space of our present life, included within sixty years' or more, but with reference to a perpetual and never-ending period, exercising His providential care over souls that are immortal, even as He Himself is eternal and immortal. For He made the rational nature, which He formed in His own image and likeness, incorruptible; and therefore the soul, which is immortal, is not excluded by the 1 Digeri. The rendering " dispersed" seems to agree best with the meaning intended to be conveyed.

2 In the Greek the term is TrvjrrikCjrotiriscj.

fro:! the greek. to occur, and by means of those things which happen from without extracts the secret evil, in order to cleanse him who through carelessness has received the seeds of sin, that having vomited them forth when they come to the surface, although he may have been deeply involved in evils, he may afterwards obtain healing after his wickedness, and be renewed. For God governs souls not with reference, let me say, to the fifty"" years of the present life, but with reference to an illimitable"' age: for He made the thinking principle immortal in its 2 7rsury Kovrccericc'j. Riifinus has " scxaginta anuos." d'TTipocurov uiuiusc.

188 ORIGEN BE PRINCIPIIS. Book hi.

FROM THE LATIN.

shortness of the present life from the divine remedies and cures.

14. But let us take from the Gospels also the similitudes of those things which we have mentioned, in which is described a certain rock, having on it a little superficial earth, on which, when a seed falls, it is said quickly to spring up; but when sprung up, it withers as the sun ascends in the heavens, and dies away, because it did not cast its root deeply into the ground.- Now this rock undoubtedly represents the human soul, hardened on account of its own negligence, and converted into stone because of its wickedness. For God gave no one a stony heart b a creative act; but each individual's heart is said to become stony through his own wickedness and disobedience. As, therefore, if one were to blame a husbandman for not casting his seed more quickly- upon rocky ground, because seed cast upon other rocky soil was seen to spring up speedily, the husbandman would certainly say in reply: " I sow this soil more slowly, for this reason, that it may retain the seed which it has received; for 1 Of. Matt. xiii. 5, 6.

FROM THE GREEK.

nature, and kindred to Himself; and the rational soul is not, as in this life, excluded from cure.

14. Come now, and let us use the following image from the Gospel. There is a certain rock, with a little surface-soil, on which, if seeds fall, they quickly spring up; but when sprung up, as not having root, they are burned and withered when the sun has arisen. Now this rock is a human soul, hardened on account of its negligence, and converted to stone because of its wickedness; for no one receives from God a heart created of stone, but it becomes such in consequence of wickedness. If one, then, were to find fault with the husbandman for not sowing his seed sooner upon the rocky soil, when he saw other rocky ground which had received seed flourishing, the husbandman would reply, "I shall sow this from the latin. it suits this ground to be sown somewhat slowly, lest perhaps the crop, having sprouted too rapidly, and coming forth from the mere surface of a shallow soil, should be unable to withstand the rays of the sun." Would not he who formerly found fault acquiesce in the reasons and superior knowledge of the husbandman, and approve as done on rational grounds

what formerly appeared to him as founded on no reason? And in the same way, God, the thoroughly skilled husbandman of all His creation, undoubtedly conceals and delays to another time those things which we think ought to have obtained health sooner, in order that not the outside of things, rather than the inside, may be cured. But if any one now were to object to us that certain seeds do even fall upon rocky ground, i. e. on a hard and stony heart, we should answer that even this does not happen without the arrangement of Divine Providence; inasmuch as, but for this, it would not be known what condemnation was incurred by rashness in hearing and indifference in investigation," nor, certainly, what benefit was derived from being trained in an H83C.- Perscrutationis improbitas.

FROM THE GREEK, ground more slowly, casting in seeds that will be able to retain their hold, this slower method being better for the ground, and more secure than that which receives the seed in a more rapid manner, and more upon the surface." The person finding fault would yield his assent to the husbandman, as one who spoke with sound reason, and who acted with skill: so also the great Husbandman of all nature postpones that benefit which might be deemed premature, that it may not prove superficial. But it is probable that here some one may object to us with reference to this: " Why do some of the seeds fall upon the earth that has superficial soil, the soul being, as it were, a rock?" Now we must say, in answer to this, that it was better for this soul, which desired better things precipitately, and not by a way which led ra,-)CioV. 'Trpo'Tritsarspou, kxi ovy;) o6u Irr ocvroc ohivaotdvi.

orderly manner. And hence it happens that the soul comes to know its defects, and to cast the blame upon itself, and, consistently with this, to reserve and submit itself to training, i. e. in order that it may see that its faults must first be removed, and that then it must come to receive the instruction of wisdom. As, therefore, souls are innumerable, so also are their manners, and purposes, and movements, and ajdpetencies, and incitements different, the variety of which can by no means be grasped by the human mind; and therefore to God alone must be left the art, and the knowledge, and the power of an arrangement of this kind, as He alone can know both the remedies for each individual soul, and measure out the time of its cure. It is He alone then who, as we said, recognises the ways of individual men, and determines by what way He ought to lead Pharaoh, that through him His name might be named in all the earth, having previously chastised him by many blows, and finally drowning him in the sea. By this drowning, however, it is not to be supposed that God's providence as regards Pharaoh was terminated; for we must not imagine, because he w as drowned, that therefore he had fortlnvith completely- perished: " for in Substantiauter.

FROM THE GREEK.

to them, to obtain its desire, in order that, condemning itself on this account, it may, aft er a long time, endure to receive the husbandry wdiich is according to nature. For souls are, as one may say, innumerable; and their habits are innumerable, and their movements, and their purposes, and their assaults, and their efforts, of which there is only one admirable administrator, who knows both the seasons, and the fitting helps, and the avenues, and the ways, viz. the God and Father of all things, who knows how He conducts even Pharaoh by so great events, and by drowning in the sea, with which latter occurrence His superintendence of Pharaoh does not cease. For he was not annihilated when drowned: "For in the hand of God are both we and our words; all wisdom tlic hand of God are both ve and our words; all wisdom, also, and knowledge of workmanship," as Scripture declares. But these points we have discussed according to our ability, treating of that chapter" of Scripture in which it is said that God hardened the heart of Pharaoh, and agreeably to the statement, "He hath mercy on whom He will have mercy, and whom He will He hardeneth."

15. Let us now look at those passages of Ezekiel where he says, ' I will take away from them their stony heart, and I will put in them a heart of flesh, that they may walk in my statutes, and keep mine ordinances." For if God, when He pleases, takes away a heart of stone and bestows a heart of flesh, that His ordinances may be observed and His commandments may be obeyed, it will then appear that it is not in our power to put away wickedness. For the taking away of a stony heart seems to be nothing else than the removal of the wickedness by which one is hardened, from whomsoever God pleases to remove it. Nor is the bestowal of a heart of

"Wiisd. vii. 16.- Capitulum.

3 Rom. ix.-18. 4 Ezek. xi. 19, 20.

FROM THE GREEK.

also, and knowledge of workmanship." And such is a moderate defence with regard to the statements that " Pharaoh's heart was hardened," and that " God hath mercy upon whom He will have mercy, and whom He will He hardeneth."

15. Let us look also at the declaration in Ezekiel, which says, "I shall take away their stony hearts, and will put in them hearts of flesh, that they may walk in my statutes and keep my precepts."" For if God, when He wills, takes away the stony hearts, and implants hearts of flesh, so that His precepts are obeyed and His commandments are observed, it is not in our power to put away wickedness. For the taking away of the stony hearts is nothing else than the taking away of the wickedness, according to which one is hardened, from him from whom God wills to take it; and the implant-1

Cf. Wisd. vii. 16. Ezek. xi. 19, 20.

ilesh, that the precepts of God may be observed and His commandments obeyed, any other thing than a man becoming obedient, and no longer resisting the truth, but performing works of virtue. If, then, God promises to do this, and if, before He takes away the stony heart, we are unable to remove it from ourselves, it follows that it is not in our power, but in God's only, to cast away wickedness. And again, if it is not our doing to form within us a heart of flesh, but the work of God alone, it will not be in our power to live virtuously, but it will in everything appear to be a work of divine grace. Such are the assertions of those who wish to prove from the authority of Holy Scripture that nothing lies in our own power. Now to these we answer, that these passages are not to be so understood, but in the following manner. Take the case of one who was ignorant and untaught, and who, feeling the disgrace of his ignorance, should, driven either by an exhortation from some person, or incited by a desire to emulate other wise men, hand himself over to

FROM THE GREEK.

ing of a heart of flesh, so that a man may walk in the precepts of God and keep His commandments, what else is it than to become somewhat yielding and unresistent to the truth, and to be capable of practising virtues? And if God promises to do this, and if, before He takes away the stony hearts, we do not lay them aside, it is manifest that it does not depend upon ourselves to put away wickedness; and if it is not we who do anything towards the production within us of the heart of flesh, but if it is God's doing, it will not be our own act to live agreeably to virtue, but altogether the result of divine grace. Such will be the statements of him who, from the mere words of Scripture, annihilates freewill." But we shall answer, saying, that we ought to understand these passages thus: That as a man, e. g. who happened to be ignorant and uneducated, on perceiving his own defects, either in consequence of an exhortation from his teacher, or

"dtTo roj'j ' li'hojv pviruv to lp' (mv duxipcov.

one by whom he is assured that he will be carefully trained and competently instructed. If he, then, who had formerly hardened himself in ignorance, yield himself, as we have said, with full purpose of mind to a master, and promise to obey him in all things, the master, on seeing clearly the resolute nature of his determination, will appropriately promise to take away all ignorance, and to implant knowledge w ithin his mind; not that he undertakes to do this if the disciple refuse or resist his efforts, but only on his offering and binding himself to obedience in all things. So also the word of God promises to those who draw near to Him, that He will take away their stony heart, not indeed from those who do not listen to His word, but from those who receive the precepts of His teaching; as in the Gospels we find the sick approaching the Saviour, asking to receive health, and thus at last be cured. And in order that the blind might be healed and regain their sight, their part consisted in making supplication to the Saviour, and in believing that their cure could be effected by Him; while Plis part,

FROM THE GREEK.

in some other way, should spontaneously give himself up to him wdiom he considers able to introduce him to education and virtue; and, on his yielding himself up, his instractor promises that he will take away his ignorance, and implant instruction, not as if it contributed nothing to his training, and to the avoiding of ignorance, that he brought himself to be healed, but because the instructor promised to improve him who desired improvement; so, in the same way, the word of God promises to take away wickedness, which it calls a stony heart, from those who come to it, not if they are unwilling, but only if they submit themselves to the Physician of the sick, as in the Gospels the sick are found coming to the Saviour, and asking to obtain healing, and so are cured. And, let me say, the recovery of sight by the blind is, so far as their request goes, the act of those who yjtpo(, yuy, Gitu. ORIG. N on the other hand, lay in restoring to them the power of vision. And in this way also does the Word of God promise to bestow instruction by taking away the stony heart, i. e. by the removal of wickedness, that so men may be able to walk in the divine precepts, and observe the commandments of the law.

16. There is next brought before us that declaration uttered by the Saviour in the Gospel: "That seeing they may see, and not perceive; and hearing they may hear, and not understand; lest they should happen to be converted, and their sins be forgiven them." On which our opponent will remark: " If those who shall hear more distinctly are by all means to be corrected and converted, and converted in such a manner as to be worthy of receiving the remission of sins, and if it be not in their own power to

hear the word distinctly, but if it depend on the Instructor to teach more openly and distinctly, while he declares that he does not proclaim 1 Mark iv. 12.

FROM THE GREEK.

believe that they are capable of being healed; but as respects the restoration of sight, it is the work of our Saviour. Thus, then, does the word of God promise to implant knowledge in those who come to it, by taking away the stony and hard heart, which is wickedness, in order that one may walk in the divine commandments, and keep the divine injunctions.

16. There was after this the passage from the Gospel, where the Saviour said, that for this reason did He speak to those without in parables, that " seeing they may not see, and hearing they may not understand; lest they should be converted, and their sins be forgiven them."- Now, our opponent will say, "If some persons are assuredly converted on hearing words of greater clearness, so that they become worthy of the remission of sins, and if it does not depend upon themselves to hear these words of greater clearness, but upon him 1 Mark iv. 12.

to them the word with clearness, lest they should perhaps hear and understand, and be converted, and be saved, it will follow, certainly, that their salvation is not dependent upon themselves. And if this be so, then we have no free-will either as regards salvation or destruction." Now were it not for the words that are added, "Lest perhaps they should be converted, and their sins be forgiven them," we might be more inclined to return the answer, that the Saviour was unwilling that those individuals whom He foresaw would not become good, should understand the mysteries of the kingdom of heaven, and that therefore He spoke to them in parables; but as that addition follows, "Lest perhaps they should be converted, and their sins be forgiven them," the explanation is rendered more difficult. And, in the first place, we have to notice what defence this passage furnishes against those heretics who are accustomed to hunt out of the Old Testament any expressions which seem, according to their view, to predicate severity and cruelty of God the Creator, as when

Filoil THE GREEK.

who teaches, and he for this reason does not announce them to them more distinctly, lest they should see and understand, it is not within the power of such to be saved; and if so, we are not possessed of free-will as regards salvation and destruction." Effectual, indeed, would be the reply to such arguments, were it not for the addition, "Lest they should be converted, and their sins be forgiven them," namely, that the Saviour did not wish those who were not to become 2; ood and virtuous to understand the more mystical parts of His teaching, and for this reason spake to them in parables; but now, on account of the words, '- Lest they should be converted, and their sins be forgiven them," the defence is more difficult. In the first place, then, we must notice the passage in its bearing on the heretics, who hunt out those portions from the Old Testament where is exhibited, as they themselves daringly assert, the cruelty of the Creator of the world- in

He is described as being affected with the feeling of vengeance or punishment, or by any of those emotions, however named, from which they deny the existence of goodness in the Creator; for they do not judge of the Gospels with the same mind and feelings, and do not observe whether any such statements are found in them as they condemn and censure in the Old Testament. For manifestly, in the passage referred to, the Saviour is shown, as they themselves admit, not to speak distinctly, for this very reason, that men may not be converted, and when converted, receive the remission of sins. Now, if the words be understood according to the letter merely, nothing less, certainly, will be contained in them than in those j assages which they find fault with in the Old Testament. And if they are of opinion that any expressions occurring in such a connection in the New Testament stand in need of explanation, it will necessarily follow that those also occurring in the Old Testament, which are the

FROM THE GREEK.

His purpose of avenging and punishing the wicked, or by whatever other name they wish to designate such a quality, so speaking only that they may say that goodness does not exist in the Creator; and who do not deal with the New Testament in a similar manner, nor in a spirit of candour, but pass by places similar to those which they consider censurable in the Old Testament. For manifestly, and according to the Gospel, is the Saviour shown, as they assert, by His former words, not to speak distinctly for this reason, that men might not be converted, and, being converted, might become deservino; of the remission of sins: which statement of itself is nothing inferior to those passages from the Old Testament which are objected to. And if they seek to defend the Gospel, we must ask them whether they are not acting in a blameworthy manner in dealing differently with the same questions; and, while not stumbling against the New Testa- subject of censure, may be freed from aspersion by an explanation of a similar kind, so that by such means the passages found in both Testaments may be shown to proceed from one and the same God. But let us return, as we best may, to the question proposed.

17. We said formerly, when discussing the case of Pharaoh, that sometimes it does not lead to good results for a man to be cured too quickly, especially if the disease, being shut up within the inner parts of the body, rage with greater fierceness. YV hence God, who is acquainted with secret things, and knows all things before they happen, in His great goodness delays the cure of such, and postpones their recovery to a remoter period, and, so to speak, cures them by not curing them, lest a too favourable state of health should render them incurable. It is therefore possible that, in the case of those to whom, as being '-' without," the words of our Lord and Saviour were addressed. He, seeing from His scrutiny of the hearts and reins that Prospera sanitas.

FROM THE GREEK.

ment, but seeking to defend it, they nevertheless bring a charge against the Old regarding similar points, whereas they ought to offer a defence in the same way of the passages from the New. And therefore we shall force them, on account of the resemblances, to regard all as the writings of one God. Come, then, and let us, to the best of our ability, furnish an answer to the question submitted to us.

17. We asserted also, when investigating the subject of Pharaoh, that sometimes a rapid cure is not for the advantage of those who are healed, if, after being seized by troublesome diseases, they should easily get rid of those by which they had been entangled. For, despising the evil as one that is easy of cure, and not being on their guard a second time against falling into it, they will be involved in it again. Wherefore, in the case of such persons, the everlasting God, the Knower of secrets, who knows

all things before they exist, in conformity with His goodness, delays sending them tliey were not yet able to receive teaching of a clearer type, veiled by the covering of language the meaning of the pro-founder mysteries, lest perhaps, being rapidly converted and healed, i. e. having quickly obtained the remission of their sins, they should again easily slide back into the same disease which they had found could be healed without any difficulty. For if this be the case, no one can doubt that the punishment is doubled, and the amount of wickedness increased; since not only are the sins which had appeared to be forgiven repeated, but the court- of virtue also is desecrated when trodden by deceitful and polluted beings,- filled within with hidden wickedness. And what remedy can there ever be for those who, after eating the impure and filthy food of wickedness, have tasted the pleasantness of virtue, and received its sweetness into their mouths, and yet have again, betaken themselves to the deadly and poisonous provision of 1 Aula. 2 Mentes.

FROM THE GREEK.

more rapid assistance, and, so to speak, in helping them does not help, the latter course being to their advantage. It is probable, then, that those " without," of w hom we are speaking, having been foreseen by the Saviour, according to our supposition, as not likely to prove steady in their conversion, if they should hear more clearly the words that were spoken, were so treated by the Saviour as not to hear distinctly the deeper things of His teaching, lest, after a rapid conversion, and after being healed by obtaining remission of sins, they should despise the wounds of their wickedness, as being slight and easy of healing, and should again speedily relapse into them. And perhaps also, suffering punishment for their former transgressions against virtue, which they had committed when they had forsaken her, they had not yet filled up the full time; in order that, being abandoned by the divine superintendence, and being filled" to so ptziciuovg f)v (iilbcc'iqvg 'iasadoit iv rri iiiriarpocpyi.

sin? And who doubts that it is better for delay and a teniporarv abandonment to occur, in order that if, at some future time, they should happen to be satiated with wickedness, and the filth with which they are now delighted should become loathsome, the word of God may at last be appropriately made clear to them, and that which is holy be not given to the dogs, nor pearls be cast before swine, which will trample them under foot, and turn, moreover, and rend and assault those who have proclaimed to them the word of God? These, then, are they who are said to be ' without," undoubtedly by way of contrast with those who are said to be "'within," and to hear the word of God with greater clearness. And yet those who are ' without" do hear the word, although it is covered by parables, and overshadowed by proverbs. There are others, also, besides those who are without, who are called Tyrians, and who do not hear at all, respecting whom the Saviour knew that they would have repented long ago, sitting in sackcloth and ashes, if the miracles performed among others had been done amongst them, and yet these do not hear those things which are heard

FROM THE GREEK.

a greater degree by their own evils which they had sown, they may afterwards be called to a more stable repentance; so as not to be quickly entangled again in those evils in which they had formerly been involved when they treated with insolence the requirements of virtue, and devoted themselves to worse things. Those, then, who are said to be " without" (manifestly by comparison with those " within"), not being very far from those "within," while those "within" hear clearly, do themselves hear indistinctly, because they are addressed in parables; but nevertheless they do hear. Others, again, of those " without," who are called Tyrians, although it was foreknown that they would have repented long ago, sitting in sackcloth and ashes, had the Saviour come near their borders, do not hear even those words which are heard by those " without" (being, as is probable, very far even by those who are "without:" and I believe, for this reason, that the rank of such in wickedness w as far lower and w orse than that of those who are said to be "without," Le. Avho are not far from those who are within, and who have deserved to hear the w ord, although in parables; and because, perhaps, their cure was delayed to that time when it will be more tolerable for them on the day of judgment, than for those before whom those miracles wdiich are recorded were performed, that so at last, being then relieved from the weight of their sins, they may enter Avith more ease and power of endurance vipon the way of safety. And this is a point which I wish impressed upon those who peruse these pages, that with respect to topics of such difficulty and obscurity we use our utmost endeavour, not so much to ascertain clearly the solutions of the questions (for every one will do this as the Spirit gives him utterance), as to maintain the rule of faith in the most unmistakeable manner, by striving to show that the providence of God, wdiicli equitably administers all things, governs also immortal souls on thejustest principles, conferring rewards according to the merits and motives of each individual; the present economy of things not being con- 1 Evidentissima assertione pietatis regulam teneamus.

2 Dispensatio liumana.

FEOM THE GREEK.

inferior in merit to those " without"), in order that at another season, after it has been more tolerable for them than for those who did not receive the w ord (among wdiom he mentioned also the Tyrians), they may, on hearing the word at a more appropriate time, obtain a more lasting repentance. But observe whether, besides our desire to investigate the truth, we do not rather strive to maintain an attitude of piety in everything regarding God and His Christ, seeing we endeavour by every means to prove that, in matters so

"ug sikog fioit y ou vroppa oursg rtjg d iccg tuv 'i a.

"d jt4)j ctaAoy hf dg Trpog ru s erxatikU kcci to svasf5sg yroiuTYi ciyaut- 6jxi oe, Tripuv TTipi 0 oy, etc.

from the latin. fined within the life of this world, but the pre-existing state of merit always furnishing the ground for the state that is to follow and thus by an eternal and immutable law of equity, and by the controlling influence of Divine Providence, the immortal soul is brought to the summit of perfection. If one, however, were to object to our statement, that the word of preaching was purposely put aside by certain men of wicked and worthless character, and were to inquire why the word was preached to those over whom the Tyrians, who were certainly despised, are preferred in comparison (by which proceeding, certainly, their wickedness was increased, and their condemnation rendered more severe, that they should hear the word who were not to believe it), they must be answered in the following manner: God, who is the Creator of the minds of all men, foreseeing complaints against His providence, especially on the part of those who say, "How could we believe when we neither beheld those thino; s which others saw, nor heard those words which were preached to others? in so far is the blame removed from us, since they to whom the word was announced, and the signs manifested, 1 Futuri status causam prajstat semper anterior meritorum status.

FEOM THE GREEK.

great and so peculiar regarding the varied providence of God, He takes an oversight of the immortal soul. If, indeed, one were to inquire regarding those things that are objected to, why those who saw wonders and who heard divine words are not benefited, while the T a'ians would have repented if such had been performed and spoken amongst them; and should ask, and say. Why did the Saviour proclaim such to these persons, to their own hurt, that their sin might be reckoned to them as heavier? we must say, in answer to such an one, that He who understands the dispositions of all those who find fault with His providence alleging that it is owing to it that they have not believed, because it did not permit them to see what it enabled others to behold, and did made no delay whatever, but became believers, overpowered by the very force of the miracles;" wishing to destroy the grounds for complaints of this kind, and to show that it was no concealment of Divine Providence, but the determination of the human mind which was the cause of their ruin, bestowed the grace of His benefits even upon the unworthy and the unbelieving, that every mouth might indeed be shut, and that the mind of man might know that all the deficiency was on its own part, and none on that of God; and that it may, at the same time, be understood and recognised that he receives a heavier sentence of condemnation who has despised the divine benefits conferred upon him than he who has not deserved to obtain or hear them, and that it is a peculiarity of divine compassion, and a mark of the extreme justice of its administration, that it sometimes conceals from certain individuals the opportunity of either seeing or hearing the mysteries of divine power, lest, after beholding the power of the miracles, and recognising and hearing the mysteries of its wisdom, they should, on treating them with contempt and indifference, be punished with greater severity for their impiety.

FKOM THE GREEK.

not arrange for them to hear those words by which others, on hearing them, were benefited wishing to prove that their defence is not founded on reason. He grants those advantages which those who blame His administration asked; in order that, after obtaining them, they may notwithstanding be convicted of the greatest impiety in not having even then yielded themselves to be benefited, and may cease from such audacity; and having been made free in respect to this very point, may learn that God occasionally, in conferring benefits upon certain persons, delays and procrastinates, not conferring the favour of seeing and hearing those things which, when seen and heard, would render the sin of those who did not believe, after acts so great and peculiar, heavier and more serious.

18. Let US now look to the expression, "It is not of him thatwilleth, nor of him that runneth, but of God that showeth mercy." For our opponents assert, that if it does not depend upon him that willeth, nor on him that runneth, but on God that showeth mercy, that a man be saved, our salvation is not in our own power. For our nature is such as to admit of our either being saved or not, or else our salvation rests solely on

the will of Him who, if He wills it, shows mercy, and confers salvation. Now let us inquire, in the first place, of such persons, whether to desire blessings be a good or evil act; and whether to hasten after good as a final aim"' be w orthy of praise. If they were to answer that such a procedure was deserving of censure, they would evidently be mad; for all holy men both desire blessings and run after them, and certainly are not blameworthy. How, then, is it that he who is not saved, if he be of an evil nature, desires blessings, and runs after them, but does not find them? For Eom. ix. 16. Ad finem boni.

FROM THE GREEK.

18. Let US look next at the passage: " So, then, it is not of him that willeth, nor of him that runneth, but of God that showeth mercy." For they who find fault say: If "it is not of him that willeth, nor of him that runneth, but of God that showeth mercy," salvation does not depend upon ourselves, but upon the arrangement made by Him who has formed us such as we are, or on the purpose of Him who showeth mercy when He pleases. Now we must ask these persons the following questions: Whether to desire what is good is virtuous or vicious; and whether the desire to run in order to reach the goal in the pursuit of what is good be worthy of praise or censure? And if they shall say that it is worthy of censure, they will return an absurd answer; since the saints desire and run, and manifestly in so acting do nothing that is blameworthy. But if they shall say that it is vir-

Rom. ix. 16. KocrocaycivTii;. KccruakivuscivTog.

they say that a bad tree does not bring forth good fruits, whereas it is a good fruit to desire blessings. And how is the fruit of a bad tree good? And if they assert that to desire blessings, and to run after them, is an act of indifference,- Le. neither good nor bad, we shall reply, that if it be an indifferent act to desire blessings, and to run after them, then the opposite of that will also be an indifferent act, viz. to desire evils, and to run after them; whereas it is certain that it is not an indifferent act to desire evils, and to run after them, but one that is manifestly wicked. It is established, then, that to desire and follow after blessings is not an indifferent, but a virtuous proceeding.

Having now repelled these objections by the answer which we have given, let us hasten on to the discussion of the subject itself, in which it is said, "It is not of him that willeth, nor of him that runneth, but of God that showeth mercy." In the book of Psalms In the songs of Degrees, Medium est velle bona. Rq j. 16.

FROM THE GREEK.

tuous to desire what is good, and to run after what is good, we shall ask them how a perishing nature desires better things; ' for it is like an evil tree producing good fruit, since it is a virtuous act to desire better things. They will give perhaps a third answer, that to desire and run after what Is good is one of those things that are indifferent, and neither beautiful nor wicked. Now to this we must say, that if to desire and to run after what is good be a thing of indifference, then the opposite also is a thing of indifference, viz. to desire what is evil, and to run after it. But it is not a thing of indifference to desire what is evil, and to run after It. And therefore also, to desire what is good, and to run after It, is not a thing of indifference. Such, then, is the defence which I think we can offer to the statement, that "it is not of him that willeth, nor of him that runneth, but of God that showeth mercy." Solomon

Tu, KpittTO'Jcc.- rcov f idcJ! larl. darslou. Rom. ix. 16.

wliich are ascribed to Solomon the following statement occurs: ' Except the Lord build the house, they labour in vain that build it; except the Lord keep the city, the watchman waketh but in vain." By which words he does not indeed indicate that we should cease from building or watching over the safe keeping of that city which is within us; but what he points out is this, that whatever is built without God, and whatever is guarded without Him, is built in vain, and guarded to no purpose. For in all things that are well built and well protected, the Lord is held to be the cause either of the building or of its protection. As if, e. g., we were to behold some magnificent structure and mass of splendid building reared with beauteous architectural skill, would we not justly and deservedly say that such was built not by human power, but by divine help and might? And yet from such a statement it will not be meant that the labour and industry of human effort were inactive, and effected Ps. cxxvi. 1.

FROM THE GREEK.

says in the book of Psalms (for the song of Degrees- is his, from which we shall quote the words): " Unless the Lord build the house, they labour in vain that build it; except the Lord keep the city, the watchman waketh in vain:"" not dissuading us from building, nor teaching us not to keep watch in order to guard the city in our soul, but showing that what is built without God, and does not receive a guard from Him, is built in vain and watched to no purpose, because God might reasonably be entitled the Lord of the building; and the Governor of all things, the Euler of the guard of the city. As, then, if we were to say that such a building is not the work of the builder, but of God, and that it was not owing to the successful effort of the watcher, but of the God who is over all, that such a city suffered no injury from its enemies, we should not be wrong, it being understood that something also had been done by human means, but the uh'i ru'j duxiiccdi ojy. Ps. CXXvi. 1. ovk oiu Trrccioi iv.

206 ORIGEN BE PRINCIPIIS. Book hi.

FROM THE LATIN.

nothing at all. Or again, if we were to see some city surrounded by a severe blockade of the enemy, in which threatening engines were brought against the walls, and the place hard pressed by a vallum, and weapons, and fire, and all the instruments of war, by which destruction is prepared, would we not rightly and deservedly say, if the enemy were repelled and put to flight, that the deliverance had been wrought for the liberated city by God? And yet we would not mean, by so speaking, that either the vigilance of the sentinels, or the alertness of the young men, or the protection of the guards, had been w anting. And the apostle also must be understood in a similar manner, because the human will alone is not sufficient to obtain salvation; nor is any mortal running able to win the heavenly rewards, and to obtain the prize of our high calling of God in Christ Jesus, unless this very good will of ours, and ready purpose, and whatever that diligence within us may be, be aided or furnished with divine help. And therefore most logically did the apostle say, that "it is not of him that willeth, nor of him that runneth, but of God that showeth mercy;" in the same manner as if we were to say of agriculture what is actually written: " I planted, Apollos watered; but God gave the 1 Procinctum juvenum. gupernse vocationis.

2 Valde consequenter.

FROM THE GREEK.

' benefit being gratefully referred to God who brought it to pass; so, seeing that the mere human desire is not sufficient to attain the end, and that the running of those who are, as it were, athletes, does not enable them to gain the prize of the high calling of God in Clmst Jesus for these things are accomplished with the assistance of God it is well said that " it is not of him that willeth, nor of him that runneth, but of God that showeth mercy." As if also it were said with regard to husbandry what also is actually recorded: " I planted, Apollos watered; and God gave the increase. So then neither is he that planteth anything, neither he that increase. So then neither is he that planteth anything, neither he that watereth; but God that giveth the increase." As, therefore, when a field has brought good and rich crops to perfect maturity, no one would piously and logically assert that the husbandman had made those fruits, but would acknowledge that they had been produced by God; so also is our own perfection brought about, not indeed by our remaining inactive and idle, but by some activity on our part: and yet the consummation of it will not be ascribed to us, but to God, who is the first and chief cause of the work. So, when a ship has overcome the dangers of the sea, although the result be accomplished by great labour on the part of the sailors, and by the aid of all the art of navigation, and by the zeal and carefulness of the pilot, and by the favouring influence of the breezes, and the careful obser- 1 1 Cor. iii. 6, 7.

2 "Nostra perfectio non quidem nobis cessantibus et otiosis efficitur." There is an ellipsis of some sucli-words as, " but by activity on our part."

FROM THE GREEK.

watereth; but God that giveth the increase." Now we could not piously assert that the production of full crops was the work of the husbandman, or of him that watered, but the work of God. So also our own perfection is brought about, not as if we ourselves did nothing; for it is not completed" y by us, but God produces th e greater p art of it. And that this assertion may be more clearly believed, we shall take an illustration from the art of navigation. For in comparison with the effect of the winds," and the mildness of the air,"' and the light of the stars, all co-operating in the preservation of the crew, what proportion could the art of navigation be said to bear in the bringing of the ship into harbour? since even the sailors themselves, from piety, do not venture to assert 1 1 Cor. iii. 6, 7.

7 7 fieri pet Tit iicfjdtg ov l fvyioSu 7 fSi: j Trpcc xvtUu yhstXi.

cctrapril srcci. ttvovju.

iuKpocalccv. ciptfio'j.

208 ORIGEN BE PRINCIPIIS. Book hi.

FROM THE LATIN.

vation of the signs of the stars, no one in his sound senses would ascribe the safety of the vessel, when, after being tossed by the waves, and wearied by the billows, it has at last reached the harbour in safety, to anything else than to tlie mercy of God. Not even the sailors or pilot venture to say, " I have saved the ship," but they refer all to the mercy of God; not that they feel that the have contributed no skill or labour to save the ship, but because they know that while they contributed the labour, the safety of the vessel was ensured by God. So also in the race of our life we ourselves must expend labour, and bring diligence and zeal to bear; but it is from God that salvation is to be hoped for as the fruit of our labour. Otherwise, if God demand none of our labour, His commandments will appear to be superfluous. In vain, also, does Paul blame some for having fallen from the truth, and praise others for abiding in the faith; and to no purpose does he deliver certain precepts

FROM THE GREEK.

often that they had saved the ship, but refer all to God; not as if they had done nothing, but because what had been done by Providence was infinitely greater than what had been effected by their art. And in the matter of our salvation, what is done by God is infinitely greater than what is done by ourselves; and therefore, I think, is it said that " it is not of him that willeth, nor of him that runneth, but of God that showeth mercy." For if in the manner which they imagine we must explain the statement, that " it is not of him that willeth, nor of him that runnetii, but of God that showeth mercy," the commandments are superfluous; and it is in vain that Paul himself blames some for having fallen away, and approves of others as having remained upright, and enacts laws for the churches: it is in vain also that we give ourselves up to desire better things, and in vain also to attempt to run. But it is not in vain that Paul gives such advice, censuring some and approving of others; nor in vain fkom the latin. and institutions to the churches: in vain, also, do we ourselves either desire or run after what is goed. But it is certain that these things are not done in vain; and it is certain that neither do the apostles give instructions in vain, nor the Lord enact laws without a reason. It follows, therefore, that we declare it to be in vain, rather, for the heretics to speak evil of these good declarations.

19. After this there followed this point, that " to will and to do are of God." Our opponents maintain that if to will be of God, and if to do be of Him, or if, whether we act or desire well or ill, it be of God, then in that case we are not possessed of free-will. Now to this we have to answer, that the words of the apostle do not say that to will evil is of God, or that to will good is of Him; nor that to do good or evil is of God; but his statement is a general one, that to will and to do are of God. For as we have from God this very quality, that we are men," that we breathe, that we move; so also we

Cf. Phil. ii. 13. 2 Hoc ipsum, quod liomines sumiis.

fro: m the greek. that we give ourselves up to the desire of better things, and to the chase after things that are pre-eminent. They have accordingly not well explained the meaning of the passage.-"- 19. Besides these, there is the passage, "Both to will and to do are of God." And some assert that, if to will be of God, and to do be of God, and if, whether we will evil or do evil, these movements come to us from God, then, if so, we are not possessed of free-will. But again, on the other hand, when we will better things, and do things that are more excellent, seeing that willing and doing are from God, it is not we who have done the more excellent things, but we only appeared to perform them, while it vras God that bestowed them; so that even in this respect we do not possess free- 2 Cf. Phil. ii. 13. 2 liuqjioo'JTU.

OPJG. O have from God the facuuy by which we will, as if we were to say that our power of motion is from God or that the performing of these duties by the individual members, and their movements, are from God. From which, certainly, I do not understand this, that because the hand moves, e. g. to punish unjustly, or to commit an act of theft, the act is of God, but only that the power of motion is from God; while it is our duty to turn those movements, the power of executing which we have from God, either to purposes of good or evil. And so what the apostle says is, that we receive indeed the power of volition, but that we misuse the wall either to good or evil desires. In a similar way, also, we must judge of results.

1 Sicut dicamus, quod movemur. ex Deo est. " Hoc ipsum, quod movetur.

FROJI THE GREEK.

will. Now to this we have to ansaver, that the language of the apostle does not assert that to will evil is of God, or to will good is of Him (and similarly with respect to doing better and worse); but that to will in a general w ay, and to run in a general way, are from Him. For as we have from God the property of being living things and human beings, so also have we that of willing generally, and, so to speak, of motion in general. And as, possessing the property of life and of motion, and of moving, e. g. these members, the hands or the feet, we could not rightly say that we had from God this species of motion, whereby we moved to strike, or destroy, or take away another's goods, but that we had received from Him simply the generic power of motion, which we employed to better of worse purposes; so we have obtained from God the power of acting, in respect of our being living things, and the power to will from the Creator, while we employ the power of will, as well as that of action, for the noblest objects, or the opposite.

TO x. cx. do'hov 6i7. iiu. 2 iv'hoyus, to dlijcoi role.

TO (. iv yiviicou TO Kiviiadoıt. n xiovpyov.

from the latin. 20. But with respect to the declaration of the apostle, "Therefore hath He mercy on whom He will have mercy, and whom He will He hardeneth. Thou wilt say then unto me, Why doth He yet find fault? For who hath resisted His will? Nay but, O man, who art thou that repliest against God? Shall the thing formed say to him that formed it, Why hast thou made me thus? Hath not the potter power over the clay, of the same lump to make one vessel unto honour, and another unto dishonour? " Some one will perhaps say, that as the potter out of the same lump makes some vessels to honour, and others to dishonour, so God creates some men for perdition, and others for salvation; and that it is not therefore in our own power either to be saved or to perish; by which reasoning we appear not to be possessed of free-will. We must answer those wdio are of this opinion with the question, Whether it is possible for the apostle to contradict himself? And if this cannot be imagined of 1 Rom. ix. 18-21.

FROM THE GREEK.

20. Still the declaration of the apostle will appear to drag us to the conclusion that we are not possessed of freedom of will, in which, objecting against himself, he says, "Therefore hath He mercy on whom He will have mercy, and whom He will He hardeneth. Thou wilt say then unto me. Why doth He yet find fault? For who hath resisted His will? Nay but, O man, who art thou that repliest against God? Shall the thing formed say to him that formed it. Why hast thou made me thus? Hath not the potter power over the clay, of the same lump to make one vessel unto honour, and another unto dishonour? " For it will be said: If the potter of the same lump make some vessels to honour and others to dishonour, and God thus form some men for salvation and others for ruin, then salvation or ruin does not depend upon ourselves,

nor are we possessed of free-will. Now we must ask him who deals so with these passages, whether it is pos-1 Rom. ix. 18-21.

an apostle, how shall he appear, according to them, to be just in blaming those who committed fornication in Corinth, or those who sinned, and did not repent of their unchas-tity, and fornication, and uncleanness, which they had committed? How, also, does he greatly praise those who acted rightly, like the house of Onesiphorus, saying, "The Lord give mercy to the house of Onesiphorus; for he oft refreshed me, and was not ashamed of my chain: but, when he had come to Rome, he sought me out very diligently, and found me. The Lord grant unto him that he may find mercy of the Lord in that day." Now it is not consistent with apostolic gravity to blame him who is worthy of blame, Le. who has sinned, and greatly to praise him who is deserving of praise for liis good works; and again, as if it were in no one's power to do any good or evil, to say that it was the Creator's doing that every one should act virtuously 1 2 Tim. i. 16-18.

FROM THE GREEK.

sible to conceive of the apostle as contradicting himself. I presume, however, that no one will venture to say so. If, then, the apostle does not utter contradictions, how can he, according to him who so understands him, reasonably find fault, censuring the individual at Corinth who had committed fornication, or those who had fallen away, and had not repented of the licentiousness and impurity of which they had been guilty? And how can he bless those whom he praises as having done well, as he does the house of Onesiphorus in these words: " The Lord give mercy to the house of Onesiphorus; for he oft refreshed me, and was not ashamed of my chain: but, when he was in Rome, he sought me out very diligently, and found me. The Lord grant to him that he may find mercy of the Lord in that day." It is not consistent for the same apostle to blame the sinner as worthy of censure, and to praise him who had done well as deserving of approval; and again, on the other hand, to say, 1 2 Tim. i. lg-18. ov y. ctnx. rou cx-vritv ovi d7r6uro7s.6i iari.

or Tvickedly, seeing He makes one vessel to honour, and another to dishonour. And how can he add that statement, "We must all stand before the judgment-seat of Christ, that every one of us may receive in his body, according to what he hath done, whether it be good or bad?"' For what reward of good will be conferred on him who could not commit evil, being formed by the Creator to that very end? or what punishment will deservedly be inflicted on him who was unable to do good in consequence of the creative act of his Maker? Then, again, how is not this opposed to that other declaration elsewhere, that "in a great house there are not only vessels of gold and silver, but also of wood and of earth, and some to honour, and some to dishonour. If a man therefore purge himself from these, he shall be a vessel unto honour, sanctified, and meet for the Master's use, prepared unto every good work." He, accordingly, who 2 Cor. V. 10.- Ex ipsa conditoris creatione. 2 Tim, ii. 20, 21.

FROM THE GREEK.

as if nothing depended on ourselves, that the cause Tvas in the Creator why the one vessel was formed to honour, and the other to dishonour. And how is this statement correct r "For w e must all appear before the judgment-seat of Christ; that every one may receive the things done in his body, according to that he hath done, whether it be good or bad," since they who have done evil have advanced to this pitch of wickedness' because they were created vessels unto dishonour, while they that have lived virtuously have done good because they were created from the beginning for this purpose, and became vessels unto honour? And again, how-does not the statement made elsewhere conflict wdth the view which these persons draw from the words which we have quoted (that it is the fault of the Creator that one vessel is in honour and another in dishonour), viz. "' that in a great house there are not only vessels of gold and silver, but also z'ct. pa. TYiu otlriccu rou OYiy-iovpyoy. " yih' 2 2 Cor. V. 10. etzl rovtO 'Trpx sa;.

purges himself, is made a vessel unto honour, while he who has disdained to cleanse himself from his impurity is made a vessel unto dishonour. From such declarations, in my opinion, the cause of our actions can in no degree be referred to the Creator. For God the Creator makes a certain vessel unto honour, and other vessels to dishonour; but that vessel which has cleansed itself from all impurity He makes a vessel unto honour, while that which has stained itself with the filth of vice He makes a vessel unto dishonour. The conclusion from which, accordingly, is this, that the cause of each one's actions is a pre-existing one; and then every one, according to his deserts, is made by God either a vessel unto honour or dishonour. Therefore every individual vessel has furnished to its Creator out of itself the causes and occasions of its being formed by Him to be either a vessel unto honour or one unto dishonour. And if the assertion appear correct, as it certainly is, and in harmony with all piety, that it is due to previous causes that every vessel be prepared by God

FROM THE GREEK, of wood and of earth; and some to honour, and some to dishonour. If a man therefore purge himself, he shall be a vessel unto honour, sanctified, and meet for the Master's use, and prepared unto every good work;" for if he who purges himself becomes a vessel unto honour, and he who allows himself to remain unpurged becomes a vessel unto dishonour, then, so far as these words are concerned, the Creator is not at all to blame. For the Creator makes vessels of honour and vessels of dishonour, not from the bea-innin; accordino-to His foreknowledge," since He does not condemn or justify beforehand according to it; but He makes those into vessels of honour who purged themselves, and those into vessels of dishonour who allowed themselves to remain unpurged: so that it results from older causes which operated in the forma- 2 Tim. ii. 20, 21.- dtnpiy. ocdotprov sscvrou Trspi'inau.

Tfpoyvoiatv. TrpokOiroix-phii vj 'Trpolikoctol.

kx, Trpiffivripuv cclriau.

eitlicr to honour or to dishonour, it does not appear absurd that, in discussing remoter causes in the same order, and in the same method, we sliould come to the same conclusion respecting the nature of souls, and believe that this was the reason why Jacob was beloved before he was born into this world, and Esau hated, while he still was contained in the womb of his mother.

21. Nay, that very declaration, that from the same lump a vessel is formed both to honour and to dishonour, will not push us hard; for we assert that the nature of all rational souls is the same, as one lump of clay is described as being under the treatment of the potter. Seeing, then, the nature of rational creatures is one, God, according to

the previous grounds of merit, created and formed out of it, as the potter out of the one lump, some persons to honour and Secundum preecedentes meritorum causas.

FEOM THE GREEK.

tion of the vessels unto honour and dishonour, that one was created for the former condition, and another for the latter. But if we once admit that there were certain older causes at work in the forming of a vessel unto honour, and of one unto dishonour, what absurdity is there in going back to the subject of the soul, and in supposing that a more ancient cause for Jacob being loved and for Esau being hated existed wuth respect to Jacob before his assumption of a body, and with regard to Esau before he was conceived in the womb of Rebecca?

21. And at the same time, it is clearly shown that, as far as regards the underlying nature, as there is one piece of clay which is under the hands of the potter, from which piece vessels are formed unto honour and dishonour; so the one nature of every soul being in the hands of God, and, 50 to speak, there being only one lump of reasonable beings, certain causes of more ancient date led to some being created

OGOV 771 TV7 V7T0X. itl, Vjri (pvCSl.

others to dishonour. Now, as regards the language of the apostle, which he utters as if in a tone of censure, "Nay but, 0 man, who art thou that repliest against God?" he means, 1 think, to point out that such a censure does not refer to any believer who lives rightly and justly, and who has confidence in God, i. e. to such an one as Moses was, of whom Scripture says that "Moses spake, and God answered him by a voice;" and as God answered Moses, so also does every saint answer God. But he who is an unbeliever, and loses confidence in answering before God owing to the unworthi-ness of his life and conversation, and who, in relation to these matters, does not seek to learn and make progress, but to oppose and resist, and who, to speak more plainly, is such an one as to be able to say those words which the apostle indicates, when he says, "Why, then, does He yet find fault? for who w ill resist His will?" to such an one may the censure of the apostle rightly be directed, "Nay but, O man, who art thou that repliest against God?" This censure accordingly 1 Ex. xix. 19.

FROM THE GREEK.

vessels unto honour, and others vessels unto dishonour. But if the language of the apostle convey a censure when he says, "Nay but, O man, who art thou that repliest against God?" it teaches us that he who has confidence before God, and is faithful, and has lived virtuously, would not hear the words, "Who art thou that repliest against God?" Such an one, e. g., as Moses was, "For Moses spake, and God answered him with a voice; " and as God answers Moses, so does a saint also answer God. But he who does not possess this confidence, manifestly, either because he has lost it, or because he investigates these matters not from a love of knowledge, but from a desire to find fault," and who therefore says, "Why does He yet find fault? for who hath resisted His will? " would merit the language of censure, which says, "Nay but, O man, who art thou that repliest against God? " Now to Cf. Ex. xix. 19. Kcctoi (pit ouiiciocv.

applies not to believers and saints, but to unbelievers and wicked men.

Now, to those who introduce souls of different natures, and who turn this declaration of the apostle to the support of their own opinion, we have to reply as follows: If even they are agreed as to what the apostle says, that out of the one lump are formed both those who are made to honour and those who are made to dishonour, whom they term of a nature that is to be saved and destroyed, there will then be no longer souls of different natures, but one nature for all. And if they admit that one and the same potter may undoubtedly denote one Creator, there will not be different creators either of those who are saved, or of those who perish. Now, truly, let them choose whether they will have a good Creator to be intended who creates bad and ruined men, or one who is not good, who creates good men and those who are prepared to honour. For the necessity of returning an answer will extort from them one of these two alternatives. But according to our declaration, whereby we say that it is owing to preceding causes that God makes vessels either to honour or to dishonour, the approval of God's justice is in no respect limited. For it is possible that this vessel, which 1 Diversas auimarum naturas.

FROM THE GREEK.

those who introduce different natures, and who make use of the declaration of the apostle to support their view, the following must be our answer. If they maintain that those who perish and those who are saved are formed of one lump, and that the Creator of those who are saved is the Creator also of them who are lost, and if He is good who creates not only spiritual but also earthy natures (for this follows from their view), it is nevertheless possible that he who, in consequence of certain former acts of righteousness," had now been made a vessel of honour, but who had not afterwards acted in a similar manner, nor done thino; s befittino; a vessel of owing to previous causes was made in this world to honour, may, if it behave neghgently, be converted in another world, according to the deserts of its conduct, into a vessel unto dishonour: as again, if any one, owing to preceding causes, was formed by his Creator in this life a vessel unto dishonour, and shall mend his ways and cleanse himself from all filth and vice, he may, in the new world, be made a vessel to honour, sanctified and useful, and prepared unto every good work. Finally, those who were formed by God in this world to be Israelites, and who have lived a life unworthy of the nobility of their race, and have fallen away from the grandeur of their descent, will, in the world to come, in a certain degree be converted, on account of their unbelief, from vessels of honour into vessels of dishonour; while, on the other hand, many who in this life were reckoned among Egyptian or Idumean vessels, having adopted the faith and practice of Israelites, when they shall have done the works of Israelites, and shall have entered the church of the Lord, will exist as vessels of honour in the revelation of the sons of God. From which it is more agreeable to the rule of piety to believe that every rational being, according to his purpose and manner of life, is converted, sometimes from bad to good, and falls away sometimes from good to bad: that some Quodammodo.

FROM THE GREEK.

honour, was converted in another vv orld into a vessel of dishonour; as, on the other hand, it is possible that he who, owing to causes more ancient than the present life, was here a vessel of dishonour, may after reformation become in the new creation "a vessel of honour, sanctified and meet for the Master's use, prepared unto every good work." And perhaps those who are now Israeutes, not having lived worthily of their descent, will be deprived of their rank, being changed, as it were, from vessels of honour into those of dishonour; and many of the present Egyptians and Idumeans who came near to Israel, when they shall have borne fruit to a larger abide in good, and otliers advance to a better condition, and always ascend to higher things, until they reach the highest grade of all; while others, again, remain in evil, or, if the wickedness within them begin to spread itself further, they descend to a worse condition, and sink into the lowest depth of wickedness. Whence also we must suppose that it is possible there may be some who began at first indeed with small offences, but who have poured out wickedness to such a degree, and attained such proficiency in evil, that in the measure of their wickedness they are equal even to the opposing powers: and again, if, by means of many severe administrations of punishment, they are able at some future time to recover their senses, and gradually attempt to find healing for their wounds, they may, on ceasing from their wickedness, be restored to a state of goodness. Whence we are of opinion that, seeing the soul, as we have frequently said, is immortal and eternal, it is possible that, in the many and endless periods of duration in the immeasurable and different worlds, it may descend from the highest good to the lowest evil, or be restored from the lowest evil to the highest good.

22. But since the words of the apostle, in what he says regarding vessels of honour or dishonour, that if a man therefore purge himself, he will be a vessel unto honour, sanc-

FEOM THE GREEK.

extent, shall enter into the church of the Lord, being no longer accounted Egyptians and Idumeans, but becoming Israelites: so that, according to this view, it is owing to their varying purposes that some advance from a worse to a better condition, and others fall from better to worse; while others, again, are preserved in a virtuous course, or ascend from good to better; and others, on the contrary, remain in a course of evil, or from bad become worse, as their wickedness flows on. 22. But since the apostle in one place does not pretend that the becoming of a vessel unto honour or dishonour depends upon God, but refers back the whole to ourselves, saying, "If, then, a man purge himself, he will be a vessel tified and meet for the Master's service, and prepared unto every good work," appear to place nothing in the power of God, but all in ourselves; while in those in which he declares that "the potter hath power over the clay, to make of the same lump one vessel to honour, another to dishonour," he seems to refer the whole to God, it is not to be understood that those statements are contradictory, but the two meanings are to be reduced to agreement, and one signification must be drawn from both, viz. that we are not to suppose either that those things which are in our own power can be done without the help of God, or that those which are in God's hand can be brought to completion without the intervention of our acts, and desires, and intention; because we have it not in our own power so to will or do anything, as not to know that this very faculty, by which we are able to will or to do, was bestowed on us by God, according to the distinction which we indicated above. Or again, when God forms vessels, some to honour and others to dishonour, we are to

FROM THE GREEK.

unto honour, sanctified, meet for the Master's use, and prepared unto every good work;" and elsewhere does not even pretend that it is dependent upon ourselves, but appears to attribute the whole to God, saying, "The potter hath power over the clay, of the same lump to make one vessel unto honour and another to dishonour;" and as his statements are not contradictory, we must reconcile them, and extract one complete statement from both. Neither does our own power, apart from the knowledge of God, compel us to make progress; nor does the knowledge of God do so, unless we ourselves also contribute something to the good result; nor does our own power, apart from the knowledge of God, and the use of the power that worthily belongs to us, make a man ' TO l(p' Vi(Ah.

itTiarvifiyi; probably in the sense of 'Trpoyuojaic.

TTis x. dtuxp'Af tag rov , a, r duuv rov i(p' vifa lv. " Nec sine usu liberi nostri arbitrii, quod peculiare nobis et meriti nostri est" (Redepenning).

suppose that He does not regard either our wills, or our purposes, or our deserts, to be the causes of the honour or dishonour, as if they were a sort of matter from which He may form the vessel of each one of us either to honour or to dishonour; wdiereas the very movement of the soul itself, or the purpose of the understanding, may of itself suggest to him, who is not unaware of his heart and the thoughts of his mind, whether his vessel ought to be formed to honour or to dishonour. But let these points suffice, which w e have discussed as we best could, regarding the questions connected with the freedom of the will.

FROM THE GREEK.

become a vessel unto honour or dishonour; nor does the will of God alone form a man to honour or dishonour, unless He hold our will to be a kind of matter that admits of variation, and that inclines to a better or worse course of conduct. And these observations are sufficient to have been made by us on the subject of free-will.

ovtS rov kirl tu Qss ad'jov. vx y riuoi 0 cc(popocg.

1. We have now to notice, agreeably to the statements of Scripture, how the opposing powers, or the devil himself, contends with the human race, inciting and instigating men to sin. And in the first place, in the book of Genesis, the serpent is described as having seduced Eve; regarding whom, in the work entitled The Ascension of Hoses' (a little treatise, of which the Apostle Jude makes mention in his epistle), the archangel Michael, when disputing with the devil regarding the body of Moses, says that the serpent, being inspired by the devil, was the cause of Adam and Eve's transgression. This also is made a subject of inquiry by some, viz. who the angel was that, speaking from heaven to Abraham, said, "Now I know that thou f earest God, and on my account hast not spared thy beloved son, whom thou lovedst." For he is manifestly described as an angel who said that he knew then that Abraham feared God, and had not spared his beloved son, as the Scripture declares, although he did not say that it was on account of God that Abraham had done this, but on his, that is, the speaker's account. We must also ascertain who that is of whom it is stated in the book of Exodus that he wished to slay Moses, because he was taking his departure for Egypt; and after-

Gen. iii.

2 This apocryphal work, entitled in Hebrew nti jtTidS, and in Greek dvut Yi- ig, or duxfiaaig Muvasojg, is mentioned by several ancient writers; e. g. by Athanasius, in his Synopsis Sacrae Scripturx; Nicephorus Con-stantinopolitanus in his Stichometria,

appended to the Chronicon of Eusebius (where he says the 'A;; ocayj ? contained 1400 verses), in the Acts of the Council of Nice, etc. etc. (Ruseus).

Gen. xxii. 12. The reading in the text is according to the Septuagint and Vulgate, with the exception of the words " quern dilexisti," which are an insertion.

4 Cf. Ex. iv. 24-26.

wards, also, who he is that is called the destroying angel, as well as he who in the book of Leviticus is called Apopom-pa3us, i. e. Averter, regarding whom Scripture says, "One lot for the Lord, and one lot for Apopompgeus, z. e. the Averter."'" In the first book of Kings, also, an evil spirit is said to strangle Saul; and in the third book, Micaiah the prophet says, "I saw the Lord of Israel sitting on His throne, and all the host of heaven standing by Him, on His right hand and on His left. And the Lord said, Who will deceive Achab king of Israel, that he may go up and fall at Ramoth-gilead? And one said on this manner, and another said on that manner. And there came forth a spirit, and stood before the Lord, and said, I will deceive him. And the Lord said to him, Wherewith? And he said, I will go forth, and I will be a lying spirit in the mouth of all his prophets. And he said, Thou shalt deceive him, and prevail also: go forth, and do so quickly. And now therefore the Lord hath put a lying spirit in the mouth of all thy prophets: the Lord hath spoken evil concerning thee." Now by this last quotation it is clearly shown that a certain spirit, from his own free will and choice, elected to deceive Achab, and to work a lie, in order that the Lord miorht mislead the kino; to his death, for he deserved to suffer. In the first book of Chronicles also it is said, "The devil, Satan, stood up against Israel, and provoked David to number the people." In the Psalms, moreover, an evil angel is said to harass certain persons. In the book of Ecclesiastes, too, Solomon says, "If the spirit of the ruler rise up against thee, leave not thy place; for soundness will restrain many transgressions." In 1 Ex. xii. 23, exterminator. Peraissor, Yulgate; ot ohsvau, Sept.

- Lev. xvi. 8. 'ATrotrofctrxjo; is the reading of the Sept., "Caper emissarius" of the Vulgate, hl of the Masoretic text. Cf. Fiirst and. y-.

Gesenius s. v. Rufinus translates Apopompjeiis by " transmissor." 1 Sam. xviii. 10, effocare. Septuagint has 'itrsffs; Vulgate, ' in- vasit;" the Masoretic text nbv1, fell on.

1 Kings xxii. 19-23. i Chron. i. 1. Atterere.

" Eccles. x. 4, "For yielding pacifieth great offences." The words in the text are, "Quoniam sanitas compescet multa peccata." The

Zechariali- we read that the devil stood on the right hand of Joshua, and resisted him. Isaiah saj s that the sword of the Lord arises against the dragon, the crooked serpent. And what shall I say of Ezekiel, who in his second vision prophesies most unmistakeably to the prince of Tyre regarding an opposing power, and who says also that the dragon dwells in the rivers of Egypt? " Nay, with what else are the contents of the whole work which is written regarding Job occupied, save with the doings of the devil, who asks that power may be given him over all that Job possesses, and over his sons, and even over his person? And yet the devil is defeated through the patience of Job. In that book the Lord has by His answers imparted much information regarding the power of that dragon which opposes us. Such, meanwhile, are the statements made in the Old Testament, so far as we can at present recall them, on the subject of hostile powers being either named in Scripture, or being said to oppose the human race, and to be afterwards subjected to punishment.

Let us now look also to the New Testament, where Satan approaches the Saviour, and tempts Him: wherein also it is stated that evil spirits and unclean demons, which had taken possession of very many, were expelled by the Saviour from the bodies of the sufferers, who are said also to be made free by Him. Even Judas, too, when the devil had already put it in his heart to betray Christ, afterwards received Satan wholly into him; for it is Avritten, that after the sop " Satan entered into him." And the Apostle Paul teaches us that we ought not to give place to the devil; but "put on," he says, "the armour of God, that ye may be able to resist the wiles of the devil:" pointing out that the saints have to " wrestle not against flesh and blood, but against principalities, against powers, against the rulers of the darkness of this world, against spiritual wickedness in high

Vulgate has, "Curatio faciet cessare peccata maxima." The Septuagint reads, "Isc. wa KCitcctrc vai oi . ex, ptia, g (.!, iya."Kug while the Masoretic text has 5and (curatio).

1 Zecii. iii. 1. 2 Perversum. Isa. xxvii. 1.

4 Ezek. xxviii. 12 sq. Cf. John xiii. 27. Eph. vi. 13.

places. ' Nay, he says that the Saviour even was crucified by the princes of this world, who shall come to nought," whose wisdom also, he says, he docs not speak. By all this, therefore, holy Scripture teaches us that there are certain invisible enemies that fight against us, and against whom it commands us to arm ourselves. Whence, also, the more simple among the believers in the Lord Christ are of opinion, that all the sins which men have committed are caused by the persistent efforts of these opposing powers exerted upon the minds of sinners, because in that invisible strufrme these powers are found to be superior to man. For if, for example, there were no devil, no single human being would FO astrav.

2. AYe, however, who see the reason of the thing more clearly, do not hold this opinion, taking into account those sins which manifestly originate as a necessary consequence of our bodily constitution." Must we indeed suppose that the devil is the cause of our feeling hunger or thirst? Nobody, I think, will venture to maintain that. If, then, he is not the cause of our feelinij hunfier and thirst, wherein lies the difference when each individual has attained the acre of puberty, and that period has called forth the incentives of the natural heat? It will undoubtedly follow, that as the devil is not the cause of our feeling hunger and thirst, so neither is he the cause of that appetency which naturally arises at the time of maturity, viz. the desire of sexual intercourse. Now it is certain that this cause is not always so set in motion by the devil that we should be obliged to suppose that bodies would not possess a desire for intercourse of that kind if the devil did not exist. Let us consider, in the next place, if, as we have ali'eady shown, food is desired by human beings, not from a suggestion of the devil, but by a kind of natural instinct, whether, if there were no devil, it were possible for human experience to exhibit such restraint in partaking of food as never to exceed the proper limits; i. e. that no one would either take otherwise than the case 1 Eph. Ti. 12. 2 cf. 1 Cor. ii. G.

Nemo hominum omnino. Ex corporal! necessitate descendunt.

ORIG. P required, or more than reason would allow; and so it would result that men, observing due measure and moderation in the matter of eating, would never go wrong. I do not think, indeed, that so great moderation could be observed by men (even if there were no instigation by the devil inciting thereto), as that no individual, in partaking of food, would go beyond due limits and restraint, until he had learned to do so from long usage and experience. What, then, is the state of the case? In the matter of eatino; and drinkino; it was possible for us to go wrong, even without any incitement from the devil, if we should happen to be either less temperate or less careful than we ought; and are we to suppose, then, in our appetite for sexual intercourse, or in the restraint of our natural desires, our condition is not something similar? I am of opinion, indeed, that the same course of reasoning must be understood to apply to other natural movements, as those of covetousness, or of anger, or of sorrow, or of all those generally which through the vice of intemperance exceed the natural bounds of moderation. There are therefore manifest reasons for holding the opinion, that as in good things the human wilf is of itself weak to accomplish any good (for it is by divine help that it is brought to perfection in everything); so also, in things of an opposite nature we receive certain initial elements, and, as it were, seeds of sins, from those things which we use agreeably to nature; but when we have indulged them beyond what is proper, and have not resisted the first movements to intemperance, then the hostile power, seizing the occasion of this first transgression, incites and presses us hard in every vray, seeking to extend our sins over a wider field, and furnishing us human beings with occasions and beginnings of sins, which these hostile powers spread far and wide, and, if possible, beyond all limits. Thus, when men at first for a little desire money, covetousness begins to grow as the passion increases, and finally the fall into avarice takes place. And after this, vhen blindness of mind has succeeded passion, and the hostile

Quod non simile aliqiiid pateremur? Propopitum,

Qufe in usu iiaturaliter habentiir.

powers, by their suggestions, liurry on the mind, money is now no longer desired, but stolen, and acquired by force, or even by shedding human blood. Finally, a con-firmatory evidence of the fact that vices of such enormity proceed from demons, may be easily seen in this, that those individuals who are oppressed either by immoderate love, or incontrollable an O'er, or excessive sorrow, do not suffer less than those who are bodily vexed by devils. For it is recorded in certain histories, that some have fallen into madness from a state of love, others from a state of anger, not a qw from a state of sorrow, and even from one of excessive joy; which results, I think, from this, that those opposing powers, i. e those denions, having gained a lodgment in their minds which has been already laid open to them by intemperance, have taken complete possession of their sensitive nature,- especially wdien no feeling of the glory of virtue has aroused them to resistance.

3. That there are certain sins, however, which do not proceed from the opposing powers, but take their beginnings from the natural movements of the body, is manifestly declared by the Apostle Paul in the passage: " The flesh lusteth against the Spirit, and the Spirit against the flesh: and these are contrary the one to the other; so that ye cannot do the things that ye would." If, then, the flesh lust against thc Spirit, and the

Spirit against the flesh, we have occasionally to wrestle against flesh and blood, i. e. as being men, and walking according to the flesh, and not capable of being tempted by greater than human temptations; since it is said of us, "There hath no temptation taken you, but such as is common to man: but God is faithful, who will not suffer you to be tempted above that ye are able." For as the presidents of the public games do not allow the competitors to enter the lists indiscriminately or fortuitously, but after a careful examination, pairing in a most impartial consideration either of size or age, this individual with that boys, e. g., with boys, men with men, who are nearly related to each other either in age or strength; so also must we understand

Sensum eoriim penitiis possederint.- Gal. v. 17. 1 Cor. x. 13.

the procedure of divine providence, which arranges on most impartial principles all who descend into the struggles of this human life, according to the nature of each individual's power, which is known only to Him who alone beholds the hearts of men: so that one individual fights against one temptation of the flesh another against a second; one is exposed to its influence for so long a period of time, another only for so long; one is tempted by the flesh to this or that indulgence, another to one of a different kind; one has to resist this or that hostile power, another has to combat two or three at the same time; or at one time this hostile influence, at another that; at some particular date having to resist one enemy, and at another a different one; being, after the performance of certain acts, exposed to one set of enemies, after others to a second. And observe whether some such state of things be not indicated by the language of the apostle: " God is faithful, who will not suffer you to be tempted above what ye are able,". e. each one is tempted in proportion to the amount of his strength or power of resistance. Now, although we have said that it is by the just judgment of God that every one is tempted according to the amount of his strength, we are not therefore to suppose that he who is tempted ought by all means to prove victorious in the struggle; in like manner as he who contends in the lists, although paired with his adversary on a just principle of arrangement, will nevertheless not necessarily prove conqueror. But unless the powers of the combatants are equal, the prize of the victor will not be justly won; nor will blame justly attach to the vanquished, because He allows us indeed to be tempted, but not " beyond what we are able:" for it is in proportion to our strength that we are tempted; and it is not written that, in temptation, He will make also a way to escape so as that we should bear it, but a way to escape so as that we should be able to bear it. But it depends upon ourselves to use either with 1 Carnem talem. 1 Cor. x. 13.

Pro virtutis suse quantitate, vel possibilitate.

Nee tamen scriptum est, quia faciei in tentatione etiam exitum sus-tinendi, sed exitum ut sustinere possimus.

energy or feebleness tliis power wliicli He has given us. For there is no doubt that under every temptation we have a power of endurance, if we employ properly the strength that is granted us. But it is not the same thing to possess the jyower of conquering and to be victorious, as the apostle himself has shown in very cautious language, saying, ' God will make a way to escape, that you may be ahle to bear it," not that you icill bear it. For many do not sustain temptation, but are overcome by it. Now God enables us not to sustain temptation, otherwise there would appear to be no struggle, but to have the i ower of sustaining it." But this power which is given us to enable us to conquer may be used, according to our faculty of free-will, either in a diligent manner, and then we prove victorious, or in a slothful manner, and then we are defeated. For if such a power were wholly given us as that we must by all means prove victorious, and never be defeated, what further reason for a struggle could remain to him who cannot be overcome? Or what merit is there in a victory, where the power of successful resistance is taken away? But if the possibility of conquering be equally conferred on us all, and if it be in our own power how to use this possibility, i. e. either diligently or slothfully, then Avill the vanquished be justly censured, and the victor be deservedly lauded. Now from these points which we have discussed to the best of our power, it is, I think, clearly evident that there are certain transgressions which we by no means commit under the pressure of malignant powers; while there are others, again, to which we are incited by instigation on their part to excessive and immoderate indulgence. Whence it follows that we have to inquire how those opposing powers produce these incitements within us.

4. With respect to the thoughts which proceed from our heart, or the recollection of things which we have done, or the contemplation of any things or causes whatever, we find that they sometimes proceed from ourselves, and sometimes are originated by the opposing powers; not seldom also are 1 Cor. X. 13. Ut sustinere possimus.

Repiignandi vincendique.

they suggested by God, or by the holy angels. Now such a statement will perhaps appear incredible,- unless it be confirmed by the testimony of holy Scripture. That, then, thoughts arise within ourselves, David testifies in the Psalms, saying, "The thought of a man will make confession to Thee, and the rest of the thought shall observe to Thee a festival day." That this, however, is also brought about by the opposing powers, is shown by Solomon in the book of Eccle-siastes in the following manner: " If the spirit of the ruler rise up against thee, leave not thy place; for soundness restrains great offences." The Apostle Paul also will bear testimony to the same point in the words: " Casting down imaginations, and every high thing that exalteth itself against the knowledge of Christ." That it is an effect due to God, nevertheless, is declared by David, when he says in the Psalms, "Blessed is the man wdiose help is in Thee, O Lord,-Thy ascents (are) in his heart." And the apostle says that " God put it into the heart of Titus." That certain thoughts are suggested to men's hearts either by good or evil angels, is shown both by the angel that accompanied Tobias, and by the language of the prophet, where he says, "And the angel who spoke in me answered." The book of the Shepherd declares the same, saying that each individual is attended by two angels; that whenever good thoughts arise in our hearts,

Fabulosum.

Ps. Ixxvi. 10. Such is the reading of the Vulgate and of the Sep-tuagint. The authorized version follows the Masoretic text.

3 Eccles. X. 4; cf. note 7, p. 223. 2 Cor. x. 5.

Ps. Ixxxiv. 5. The words in the text are: Beatus vir, cujus est susceptio apud te, Domine, adscensus in corde ejus. The Vulgate reads: Beatus vir, cujus est auxilium abs te: ascensiones in corde suo disposuit. The Septuagint the same. The Masoretic text has D DD ("festival march or procession:" Finest). Probably thc Septuagint and

Vulgate had rii? i?0 before them, the similarity between Samech and Ayin accounting for the error in transcription.

c 2 Cor. viii. 16.

Zech. i. 14. The Vulgate, Septuagint, and Masoretic text all have ' in me," although the authorized version reads "with me."

Shepjierd of Hennas, Command, vi. 2. See Ante-Nicene Library, vol Apostolic Fathers, p. 359.

they are suggested bj the good angel; but when of a contrary kind, they are the mstigation of the evil angel. The same is declared by Barnabas in his epistle where he says there are two ways, one of light and one of darkness, over which lie asserts that certain angels are placed, the angels of God over the way of light, the angels of Satan over the way of darkness. We are not, however, to imagine that any other result follows from what is suggested to our heart, whether good or bad, save a mental commotion only, and an incitement instigating us either to good or evil. For it is quite within our reach, when a malignant power has begun to incite us to evil, to cast away from us the wicked suggestions, and to resist the vile inducements, and to do nothing that is at all deserving of blame. And, on the other hand, it is possible, when a divine power calls us to better things, not to obey the call; our freedom of will being preserved to us in either case. We said, indeed, in the foregoing pages, that (ertain recollections of good or evil actions were suggested to us either by the act of divine providence or by the opposing powers, as is shown in the book of Esther, when Artaxerxes had not remembered the services of that just man Mordecai, but, when wearied out with his nightly vigils, had it put into his mind by God to require that the annals of his great deeds should be read to him; whereon, being reminded of the benefits received from Mordecai, he ordered his enemy Haman to be hanged, but splendid honours to be conferred on him, and impunity from the threatened danger to be granted to the whole of the holy nation. On the other hand, however, we must suppose that it was through the hostile influence of the devil that the suggestion was introduced into the minds of the high priests and the scribes which they made to Pilate, when they came and said, "Sir, we remember that that deceiver said, while he was yet alive. After three days I will rise again." The design of Judas, also, respecting the betrayal of our Lord and Saviour, did not originate in the

Epistle of Barnahas, Aute-Nlcene Library, vol. Apostolic Fathers p. 131, etc.

2 Iatt. xxvii. 63.

wickedness of liis mind alone. For Scripture testifies that the "devil had already put it into liis heart to betray Him."- And therefore Solomon rightly commanded, saying, "Keep thy heart with all diligence." And the Apostle Paul warns us: "Therefore we ought to give the more earnest heed to the things which we have heard, lest perhaps we should let them shp." And when he says, "Neither give place to the devil," he shows by that injunction that it is through certain acts, or a kind of mental slothfulness, that room is made for the devil, so that, if he once enter our heart, he will either gain possession of us, or at least will pollute the soul, if he has not obtained the entire mastery over it, by casting on us his fiery darts; and by these we are sometimes deeply wounded, and sometimes only set on fire. Seldom indeed, and only in a few instances, are these fiery darts quenched, so as not to find a place where they may wound, i. e.

when one is covered by the strong and mighty shield of faith. The declaration, indeed, in the Ej)istle to the Ephesians, "We wrestle not against flesh and blood, but against principalities, against powers, against the rulers of the darkness of this world, against spiritual wickedness in high places," must be so understood as if " w e " meant, "I Paul, and you Ephesians, and all who have not to wrestle against flesh and blood:" for such have to struggle against principalities and powers, against the rulers of the darkness of this world, not like the Corinthians, whose strufi2: le was as yet ac ainst flesh and blood, and who had been overtaken by no temptation but such as is common to man.

5. We are not, however, to suppose that each individual has to contend against all these adversaries. For it is impossible for any man, although he were a saint, to carry on a contest against all of them at the same time. If that indeed were by any means to be the case, as it is certainly impossible it should be so, human nature could not possibly bear it without undergoing entire destruction. But as, for example, if 1 John xiii. 2. 2 Proy. iv. 23.

3 Heb. ii. 1. 4 Eph. iv. 27.

Eph. vi. 12. 6 gijie maxima subversione sui.

fifty soldiers were to say tlint they were about to engage witli fifty others, they would not be understood to mean that one of them had to contend airainst the whole fiftv, but each one would rightly say that "our battle was against fifty," all against all; so also this is to be understood as the apostle's meaninir, that all the athletes and soldiers of Christ have to wrestle and struirixle aojainst all the adversaries enumerated, the struggle having, indeed, to be maintained against all, but by single individuals either with individual powers, or at least in such manner as shall be determined by God, who is the just president of the struggle. For I am of opinion that there is a certain limit to the powers of human nature, although there may be a Paul, of whom it is said, "He is a chosen vessel unto me;" or a Peter, against whom the gates of hell do not prevail; or a Moses, the friend of God: yet not one of them could sustain, without destruction to himself, the whole simultaneous assault of these opposing powers, unless indeed the might of Him alone were to work in him, who said, "Be of orood cheer, I have overcome the world."'" And therefore Paul exclaims with confidence, " I can do all things through Christ, who strengtheneth me; "' and again, "I laboured more abundantly than they all; yet not I, but the grace of God which was with me." On account, then, of this power, which certainly is not of human origin, operating and speaking in him, Paul could say, "For I am persuaded that neither death, nor life, nor angels, nor principalities, nor powers, nor things present, nor things to come, nor height, nor depth, nor power, nor any other creature, shall be able to separate us from the love of God, which is in Christ Jesus our Lord." For I do not think that human nature can alone of itself maintain a contest with angels, and with the powers of the height and of the abyss, and with any other creature; but when it

Acts ix. 15.- Sine aliqua pernicie sui. John xvi. 33.

Phil. iv. 13. 1 Cor. xv. 10.

Rom. viii. 38, 39. The word "virtus," ovvuf. i; occurrmg in the text, is not found in the text, recept. Tischendorf reads vvx nc in loco (edit. 7). So also Codex Sinaiticus.

Excelsa et profunda.

feels the presence of the Lord dwelling within it, confidence in the divine help will lead it to say, "The Lord is my light, and my salvation; whom 'shall I fear? The Lord is the protector of my life; of whom shall I be afraid? When the enemies draw near to me, to eat my flesh, my enemies who trouble me, they stumbled and fell. Though an host encamp against me, my heart shall not fear; though w ar should rise against me, in Him shall I be confident." From which I infer that a man perhaps w ould never be able of himself to vanquish an opposing power, unless he had the benefit of divine assistance. Hence, also, the angel is said to have wrestled with Jacob. Here, however, I understand the writer to mean, that it was not the same thing for the angel to have wrestled with Jacob, and to have wrestled against him; but the angel that wrestles with him is he who was present with him in order to secure his safety, wdio, after knowing also his moral progress, gave him in addition the name of Israel, i. e. he is luith him in the struggle, and assists him in the contest; seeing there was undoubtedly another angel against whom he contended, and against whom he had to carry on a contest. Finally, Paul has not said that we wrestle loitli princes, or with powers, but against principalities and powers. And hence, although Jacob wrestled, it was unquestionably against some one of those powers which, Paul declares, resist and contend with the human race, and especially with the saints. And therefore at last the Scripture says of him that " he wrestled with the angel, and had power with God," so that the struggle is supported by help of the angel, but the prize of success conducts the conqueror to God.

6. Nor are we, indeed, to suppose that struggles of this kind are carried on by the exercise of bodily strength, and of the arts of the wrestling school; but spirit contends with spirit, according to the declaration of Paul, that our struggle is against principalities, and powers, and the rulers of the darkness of this w orld. Nay, the following is to be understood as the nature of the straggles; when, e. g., losses and Ps. xxvii. 1-3. 2 Palsestricse artis exercitiis.

dangers befall us, or calumnies and false accusations are brought against us, it not being the object of the hostile powers that we should suffer these trials only, but that by-means of them we should be driven either to excess of anger or sorrow, or to the last pitch of despair; or at least, which is a greater sin, should be forced, when fatigued and overcome by any annoyances, to make complaints against God, as one who does not administer human life justly and equitably; the consequence of which is, that our faith may be weakened, or our hopes disappointed, or we may be compelled to give up the truth of our opinions, or be led to entertain irreligious sentiments regarding God. For some such things are written regarding Job, after the devil had requested God that power should be given him over his goods. By which also we are taught, that it is not by any accidental attacks that we are assailed, whenever we are visited with any such loss of property, nor that it is owing to chance w hen one of us is taken prisoner, or when the dwellings in wdiich those who are dear to us are crushed to death, fall in ruins; for, with respect to all these occurrences, every believer ought to say, "Thou couldst have no power at all against me, except it were given thee from above." For observe that the house of Job did not fall upon his sons until the devil had first received power against them; nor would the horsemen have made an irruption in three bands, to carry away his camels or his oxen, and other cattle, unless they had been instigated by that spirit to whom they had delivered themselves up as the servants of his will. Nor vould that fire, as it seemed to be, or thunderbolt, as it has been considered, have fallen upon the sheep of the patriarch, until the devil had said to God, "Hast Thou not made a hedge about all that is without and within his house, and around all the rest of his property? But now put forth Thy hand, and touch all that he hath, and see if he do not renounce Thee to Thy face."

7. The result of all the foregoing remarks is to show, that

John xix. 11.- Tribus ordiiiibus.

2 Cf. Job i. 10, 11. " Nisi in faciein benedixerit tibi." The Hebrew all the occurrences in tlie world wliicli are considered to be of an intermediate kind, whether they be mournful or otherwise, are brought about, not indeed by God, and yet not without Him; while He not only does not prevent those wicked and opposing powers that are desirous to bring about these things from accomplishing their purpose, but even permits them to do so, although only on certain occasions and to certain individuals, as is said with respect to Job himself, that for a certain time he was made to fall under the power of others, and to have his house plundered by unjust persons. And therefore holy Scripture teaches us to receive all that happens as sent by God, knowing that without Him no event occurs. For how can we doubt that such is the case, viz. that nothing comes to man without the will of God, when our Lord and Saviour declares, "Are not two sparrows sold for a farthing? and one of them shall not fall on the ground without your Father who is in heaven." But the necessity of the case has drawn us away in a lengthened digression on the subject of the struggle waged by the hostile powers against men, and of those sadder events which happen to human life, i. e. its temptations according to the declaration of Job, "Is not the whole life of man upon the earth a temptation?" in order that the manner of their occurrence, and the spirit in which we should regard them, might be clearly shown. Let us notice next, how men fall away into the sin of false knowledge, or with what object the opposing powers are wont to stir up conflict with us regarding such things.

verb "ij"!! has the double signification of "blessing" and "cursing." Cf. Davidson's Commentary on Job, p. 7. Septuag. ivt oyvjan.

1 Matt. X. 29.

2 Cf. Job vii. 1. The Septuagint reads, ttotspov ovx) Trsipar'jpiov, etc.; the Vulgate, "militia;" the Masoretic text has j nv- Cf. Davidson's

Commentary on Job, in loc.

1. The holy apostle, wishing to teach us some great and hidden truth respecting science and wisdom, says, in the first Epistle to the Corinthians: " We speak wisdom among them that are perfect; yet not the wisdom of this world, nor of the princes of the world, that come to nought: but we speak the wisdom of God in a mystery, even the hidden wisdom, which God ordained before the world unto our glory: which none of the princes of the world knew: for had they known it, they would not have crucified the Lord of glory." In this passage, wishing to describe the different kinds of wisdom, he points out that there is a wisdom of this world, and a wisdom of the princes of this world, and another wisdom of God. But when he uses the expression " wisdom of the princes of this world," I do not tliink that he means a wisdom common to all the princes of this world, but one rather that is peculiar to certain individuals

among them. And again, when he says, "We speak the wisdom of God in a mystery, even the hidden wisdom, which God ordained before the world unto our glory," we must inquire whether his meaning be, that this is the same wisdom of God which was hidden from other times and generations, and was not made known to the sons of men, as it has now been revealed to His holy apostles and j)rophets, and which was also that wisdom of God before the advent of the Saviour, by means of which Solomon obtained his wisdom, and in reference to which the language of the Saviour Himself declared, that what He taught was greater than Solomon, in these words, "Behold, a greater than Solomon is here," words which show, that those who were instructed by the Saviour were instructed in something higher than the knowledge of Solomon. For if one were to assert that the Saviour did indeed Himself possess greater knowledge, but did not communicate 1 1 Cor. ii. 6-8. 2 i c r. ii. 7. 3 Matt. xii. 42.

more to others than Solomon did, how will that am-ee with the statement which follows: " The queen of the south shall rise up in the judgment, and condemn the men of this generation, because she came from the ends of the earth to hear the wisdom of Solomon; and, behold, a greater than Solomon is here?" There is therefore a wisdom of this world, and also probably a wisdom belonging to each individual prince of this world. But with respect to the wisdom of God alone, we perceive that this is indicated, that it operated to a less degree in ancient and former times, and was afterwards more fully revealed and manifested through Christ. We shall inquire, however, regarding the wisdom of God in the proper place.

2. But now, since we are treating of the manner in which the opposing powers stir up those contests, by means of which false knowdedge is introduced into the minds of men, and human souls led astray, while they imagine that they have discovered wisdom, I think it necessary to name and distinguish the wisdom of this world, and of the princes of this world, that by so doing w e may discover who are the fathers of this wisdom, nay, even of these kinds of wisdom." I am of opinion, therefore, as I have stated above, that there is another wisdom of this world besides those different kinds of wisdom wdiich belong to the princes of this world, by which wisdom those things seem to be understood and comprehended which belong to this world. This wisdom, however, possesses in itself no fitness for forming any opinion either respecting divine things, or the plan of the world's government, or any other subjects of importance, or regarding the training for a good or happy life; but is such as deals wholly with the art of poetry, e. g. or that of grammar, or rhetoric, or geometry, or music, with which also, perhaps, medicine should be classed. In all these subjects we are to suppose that the wisdom of this world is included. The wisdom of the princes of this world, on the other hand, we understand to be such as the secret and occult philo-

Matt. xii. 42. 2 Sapientiarum liariim.

' Sa'pientias illas. De divinitate.

sopliy, as they call it, of the Egyptians, and the astrology of the Chaldeans and Indians, who make profession of the knowledge of high things, and also that manifold variety of opinion which prevails among the Greeks regarding divine tilings. Accordingly, in the holy Scriptures we find that there are princes over individual nations; as in Daniel' we read that there was a prince of the kingdom of Persia, and another prince of the kingdom of Gra cia, who are clearly shown, by the nature of the passage, to be not human beings, but certain powers. In the prophecies of Ezekiel, also, the prince of Tyre is unmistakeably shown to be a kind of spiritual power. When these, then, and others of the same kind, possessing each his own wisdom, and building up his own opinions and sentiments, beheld our Lord and Saviour professing and declaring that He had for this purpose come into the world, that all the opinions of science, falsely so called, might be destroyed, not knowing what was concealed within Him, they forthwith laid a snare for Him: for "the kings of the earth set themselves, and the rulers assembled together, ao; ainst the Lord and His Christ." But their snares bein discovered, and the plans which they had attempted to carry out being made manifest when they crucified the Lord of glory, therefore the apostle says, "We speak wisdom among them that are perfect, but not the wisdom of this world, nor of the princes of this world, who are brought to nought, which none of the princes of this world knew: for had they known it, they would not have crucified the Lord of glory."

3. We must, indeed, endeavour to ascertain whether that wisdom of the princes of this world, with which they endeavour to imbue men, is introduced into their minds by the opposing powers, with the purpose of ensnaring and injuring them, or only for the purpose of deceiving them, i. e. not with the object of doing any hurt to man; but, as these princes of this world esteem such opinions to be true, they desire to impart to others what they themselves believe to be the truth:

De scientia excelsi pollicentium.- Cf. Dan. x.

3 Cf. Ezek. xxvi. Ps. ii. 2.

1 Cor. ii. 6-8. Istse sapientise.

and tills is the view which I am inclined to adopt. For as, to take an illustration, certain Greek authors, or the leaders of some heretical sect, after having imbibed an error in doctrine instead of the truth, and having come to the conclusion in their own minds, that such is the truth, proceed, in the next place, to endeavour to persuade others of the correctness of their opinions; so, in Hke manner, are we to suppose is the procedure of the princes of this world, in which to certain spiritual powers has been assigned the rule over certain nations, and wdio are termed on that account the princes of this world. There are besides, in addition to these princes, certain special energies of this world, i. e. spiritual powers, which bring about certain effects, which they have themselves, in virtue of their freedom of will, chosen to produce, and to these belong those princes who practise the wisdom of this world: there being, for example, a peculiar energy and. power, which is the inspirer of poetry; another, of geometry; and so a separate power, to remind us of each of the arts and professions of this kind. Lastly, many Greek writers have been of opinion that the art of poetry cannot exist without madness; whence also it is several times related in their histories, that those whom they call poets were suddenly filled with a kind of spirit of madness. And what are we to say also of those whom they call diviners, from whom, by the working of those demons who have the mastery over them, answers are given in carefully constructed verses? Those persons, too, whom they term Magi or Malevolent, frequently, by invoking demons over boys of tender years, have made them repeat poetical compositions which were the admiration and amazement of all. Now these effects we are to suppose are brought about in the following manner: As holy and immaculate souls, after devoting themselves to God with all affection and purity, and after preserving themselves free from all contagion of evil spirits, and after being purified by lengthened abstinence, and imbued with holy and religious training, assume by this means a portion 1 Energise. Insania. Vates.

Divinos. Magi vel malefici. Dsemonum.

of divinity, and earn tlie grace of prophecy, and other divine gifts; so also are we to suppose that those who place themselves in the way of the opposing powers, i. e. who purposely admire and adopt their manner of life and habits, receive their inspiration, and become partakers of their wisdom and doctrine. And the result of this is, that they are filled with the working of those spirits to whose service they have subjected themselves.

4. With respect to those, indeed, who teach differently regarding Christ from what the rule of Scripture allows, it is no idle task to ascertain whether it is from a treacherous purpose that these opposing powers, in their struggles to prevent a belief in Christ, have devised certain fabulous and impious doctrines; or whether, on hearing the word of Christ, and not being able to cast it forth from the secrecy of their conscience, nor yet to retain it pure and holy, they have, by means of vessels that were convenient to their use, and, so to speak, through their prophets, introduced various errors contrary to the rule of Christian truth. Now we are to suppose rather that apostate and refugee powers, which have departed from God out of the very wickedness of their mind and will, or from envy of those for whom there is prepared (on their becoming acquainted with the truth) an ascent to the same rank, whence they themselves had fallen, did, in order to prevent any progress of that kind, invent these errors and delusions of false doctrine. It is then clearly established, by many proofs, that while the soul of man exists in this body, it may admit different energies, i. e. operations, from a diversity of good and evil spirits. Now, of wicked spirits there is a twofold mode of operation: i. e. when they either take complete and entire possession of the mind, so as to allow their captives the power neither of understanding nor feeling; as, for instance, is the case with those commonly called possessed," whom we see to be deprived of reason, and insane

Id est, industria vita, vel studio amico illis et accepto.

2 Per vasa opportuna sibi. Apostatae et refngse virtutes.

Propositi. Penitus ex iiitegro.

Eos quos obsederint. Energumenos.

ORIG. Q (sucli as those were wlio are related in the Gospel to have been cured by the Saviour); or when by their wicked suggestions they deprave a sentient and intelh'gent soul with thoughts of various kinds, persuading it to evil, of which Judas is an illustration, who was induced at the suggestion of the devil to commit the crime of treason, according to the declaration of Scripture, that ' the devil had already put it into the heart of Judas Iscariot to betray Him."

But a man receives the energy, i. e. the working, of a good spirit, when he is stirred and incited to good, and is inspired to heavenly or divine things; as the holy angels and God Himself wrought in the prophets, arousing and exhorting them by their holy suggestions to a better course of life, yet so, indeed, that it remained within the will and judgment of the individual, either to be willinsj or unwillinoj to follow the call to divine and heavenly things. And from this manifest distinction, it is seen how the soul is moved by the presence of a better spirit, i. e. if it encounter no perturbation or alienation of mind whatever from the impending inspiration, nor lose the free control of its will; as, for instance, is the case with all, whether prophets or apostles, who ministered to the divine responses without any perturbation of mind. Now, that by the suggestions of a good spirit the memory of man is aroused to the recollection of better things, we have already shown by previous instances, when we mentioned the cases of Iordecai and Artaxerxes.

5. This too, I think, should next be inquired into, viz. what are the reasons why a human soul is acted on at one time by good spirits, and at another by bad: the grounds of which I suspect to be older than the bodily birth of the individual, as John the Baptist showed by his leaping and exulting in his mother's womb, when the voice of the salutation of Mary reached the ears of his mother Elisabeth; and as Jeremiah the prophet declares, who was known to God before he was formed in his mother's womb, and before he was born was sanctified by Him, and while yet a boy received the grace of prophecy." And again, on the other hand, it Jolm xix. 2. 2 jer. i. 5 6.

is shown beyond a doubt, that some have been possessed by hostile spirits from the very beginning of their lives: i. e. some Yere born with an evil spirit; and others, according to credible histories, have practised divination from childhood. Others have been under the influence of the demon called Python, i. e. the ventriloquial spirit, from the commencement of their existence. To all which instances, those who maintain that everything in the world is under the administration of divine providence (as is also our own belief), can, as it appears to me, give no other answer, so as to show that no shadow of injustice rests upon the divine government, than by holding that there were certain causes of prior existence, in consequence of which the souls, before their birth in the body, contracted a certain amount of guilt in their sensitive nature, or in their movements, on account of which they have been judged worthy by Divine Providence of being placed in this condition. For a soul is always in possession of free-will, as w ell when it is in the body as when it is without it; and freedom of will is always directed either to good or evil. Nor can any rational and sentient being, i. e. a mind or soul, exist w ithout some movement either good or bad. And it is probable that these movements furnish grounds for merit even before they do anything in this world; so that on account of these merits or grounds they are, immediately on their birth, and even before it, so to speak, assorted by Divine Providence for the endurance either of good or evil.

Let such, then, be our views respecting those events which appear to befall men, either immediately after birth, or even before they enter upon the light. But as regards the suggestions wdiich are made to the soul, i. e. to the faculty of human thought, by different spirits, and which arouse men to good actions or the contrary, even in such a case we must suppose that there sometimes existed certain causes anterior to bodily birth. For occasionally the mind, when watchful, and casting away from it what is evil, calls to itself the aid of the good; or if it be, on the contrary, negligent and slothful, i Divinasse.

it makes room througli insufficient caution for these spirits, which, lying in wait secretly like robbers, contrive to rush into the minds of men when they see a lodgment made for them by sloth; as the Apostle Peter says, "that our adversary the devil goes about like a roaring lion, seeking whom he may devour." On which account our heart must be kept with all carefulness both by day and night, and no place be given to the devil; but every effort must be used that the ministers of God those spirits, viz., who were sent to minister to them who are called to be heirs of salvation may find a place within us, and be delighted to enter into the guest-chamber of our soul, and dwelling within us may guide us by their counsels; if, indeed, they shall find the habitation of our heart adorned by the practice of virtue and holiness. But let that be sufficient which we have said, as we best could, regarding those powers which are hostile to the human race.

CHAPTER IV.

ox HUMAN TEMPTATIONS.

1. And now the subject of human temptations must not, in my opinion, be passed over in silence, which take their rise sometimes from flesh and blood, or from the wisdom of flesh and blood, which is said to be hostile to God. And whether the statement be true which certain allege, viz. that each individual has as it were two souls, we shall determine after we have explained the nature of those temptations, which are said to be more powerful than any of human origin, i. e. which we sustain from principalities and powers, and from the rulers of the darkness of this world, and from spiritual wickedness in high places, or to which we are subjected from wicked spirits and unclean demons. Now, in the investigation of this subject, we must, I think, inquire according to a logical method whether there be in us human beings, who are composed of soul and body and vital spirit, some other element, ' 1 Pet. v. 8. "" Heb. i. 14. Hospitium.

possessing an incitement of its own, and evoking a movement towards evil. For a question of this kind is wont to be discussed by some in this way: whether, viz., as two souls are said to co-exist within us, the one is more divine and heavenly and the other inferior; or whether, from the very fact that we inhere in bodily structures which according to their own proper nature are dead, and altogether devoid of life (seeing it is from us, i. e. from our souls, that the material body derives its life, it being contrary and hostile to the spirit), we are drawn on and enticed to the practice of those evils which are agreeable to the body; or whether, thirdly (which was the opinion of some of the Greek philosophers), although our soul is one in substance, it nevertheless consists of several elements, and one portion of it is called rational and another irrational, and that which is termed the irrational part is again separated into two affections those of covetousness and passion. These three opinions, then, regarding the soul, which we have stated above, we have found to be entertained by some, but that one of them, which we have mentioned as being adopted by certain Grecian philosophers, viz. that the soul is tripartite, I do not observe to be greatly confirmed by the authority of holy Scripture; while with respect to the remaining two-there is found a considerable number of passages in the holy Scriptures which seem capable of application to them.

2. Now, of these opinions, let us first discuss that which is maintained by some, that there is in us a good and heavenly soul, and another earthly and inferior; and that the better soul is implanted within us from heaven, such as was that which, while Jacob was still in the womb, gave him the prize of victory in supplanting his brother Esan,

and which in the case of Jeremiah was sanctified from his birth, and in that of John was filled by the Holy Spirit from the womb. Now, that which they term the inferior soul is produced, they allege, along with the body itself out of the seed of the body, whence they say it cannot live or subsist beyond the body, on which account also they say it is frequently termed flesh. For the expression, "The flesh lusteth against the spirit,"

1 Gal. V. 17.

they take to be applicable not to the flesh, but to this soul, which is properly the soul of the flesh. From these words, moreover, they endeavour notwithstanding to make good the declaration in Leviticus: " The life of all flesh is the blood thereof." For, from the circumstance that it is the diffusion of the blood throughout the whole flesh which produces life in the flesh, they assert that this soul, which is said to be the life of all flesh, is contained in the blood. This statement, moreover, that the flesh struggles against the spirit, and the spirit against the flesh; and the further statement, that " the life of all flesh is the blood thereof," is, according to these writers, simply calling the wisdom of the flesh by another name, because it Is a kind of material spirit, which is not subject to the law of God, nor can be so, because It has earthly washes and bodily desires. And It Is with respect to this that they think the apostle uttered the words: " I see another law in my members, warring against the law of my mind, and bringing me Into captivity to the law of sin which is In my members." And if one were to object to them that these words were spoken of the nature of the body, which Indeed, agreeably to the peculiarity of its nature, is dead, but is said to have sensibility, or wisdom, which is hostile to God, or which struggles against the spirit; or If one were to say that, in a certain degree, the flesh itself was possessed of a voice, which should cry out against the endurance of hunger, or thirst, or cold, or of any discomfort arising either from abundance or poverty, they would endeavour to weaken and impair the force of such arguments, by showing that there were many other mental perturbations' which derive their origin In no respect from the flesh, and yet against which the spirit struggles, such as ambition, avarice, emulation, envy, pride, and others like these; and seeing that with these the human mind or spirit wages a kind of contest, they lay down as the cause of all these evils, nothing else than this corporal soul, as It were, of which we have spoken above, and which Is generated from the seed by a process of traducianism.

1 Lev. xvii. 14. 2 Ro, y i 23.

Sensum vel sapientiam. " Passiones animas.

They are accustomed also to adduce, in support of tlieir assertion, the declaration of the apostle, "Now the works of the flesh are manifest, which are these, fornication, uncleanness, lasciviousness, idolatry, poisonings, hatred, contentions, emulations, wrath, quarrelling, dissensions, heresies, sects, envyings, drunkenness, revellings, and the like;" asserting that all these do not derive their origin from the habits or pleasures of the flesh, so that all such movements are to be regarded as inherent in that substance which has not a soul, i. e. the flesh. The declaration, moreover, "For ye see your calling, brethren, how that not many wise men among you according to the flesh are called,"" would seem to require to be understood as if there were one kind of wisdom, carnal and material, and another according to the spirit, the former of which cannot indeed be called wisdom, unless there be a soul of the flesh, which is wise in respect of wdiat is called carnal wisdom. And in addition to these passages they adduce the following: "Since the flesh lusteth against the spirit, and the spirit against the flesh, so that we cannot do the things that we would." What are these things now respecting which he says, " that we cannot do the things that we would?" It is certain, they reply, that the spirit cannot be intended; for the will of the spirit suffers no hindrance. But neither can the flesh be meant, because if it has not a soul of its own, neither can it assuredly possess a will. It remains, then, that the will of this soul be intended which is capable of having a will of its own, and which certainly is opposed to the will of the spirit. And if this be the case, it is established that the will of the soul is something intermediate between the flesh and the spirit, undoubtedly obeying and serving that one of the two which it has elected to obey. And if it yield itself up to the pleasures of the flesh, it renders men carnal; but when it unites itself with the spirit, it produces men of the spirit, and who on that account are termed spiritual. And this seems to be the meaning of the apostle in the words, "But ye are not in the flesh, but in the spirit."

Veneficia. ioipy. ccksici. " Witchcraft," autli. version, 2 Gal. V. 19-21. 2 1 Cor. i. 26. Gal. v. 17. Rom. viii. 9.

We have accordingly to ascertain what is this very will intermediate between flesh and spirit, besides that will which is said to belong to the flesh or the spirit. For it is held as certain, that everything which is said to be a work of the spirit is a product of the will of the spirit, and everything that is called a work of the flesh proceeds from the will of the flesh. What else then, besides these, is that will of the soul which receives a separate name, and which will, the apostle being opposed to our executing, says: " Ye cannot do the things that ye would?" By this it would seem to be intended, that it ought to adhere to neither of these two, i. e. to neither flesh nor spirit. But some one will say, that as it is better for the soul to execute its own will than that of the flesh; so, on the other hand, it is better to do the will of the spirit than its own will. How, then, does the apostle say, "that ye cannot do the things that ye would?" Because in that contest which is wa ed between flesh and spirit, the spirit is by no means certain of victory, it being manifest that in very many individuals the flesh has the mastery.

But since the subject of discussion on which we have entered is one of great profundity, which it is necessary to consider in all its bearings, let us see whether some such point as this may not be determined: that as it is better for the soul to follow the spirit when the latter has overcome the flesh, so also, if it seem to be a worse course for the former to follow the flesh in its struggles against the spirit,

The text here is very obscure, and has given some trouble to commentators. The words are: " Quae ergo ista est prseter hsec voluntas animse quae extrinsecus nominatur," etc. Eedepenning understands " extrinsecus" as meaning " seorsim," " insuper," and refers to a note of Origen upon the Epistle to the Romans (tom. i. p. 466): "Et idcirco extrinsecus eam (animam, corporis et spiritus mentione facta, Rom. i. 3, 4) apostolus non nominat, sed carnem tantum vel spiritum," etc. Schnitzer supposes that in the Greek the words were, Tijs s'io) Koct ovf surig, where T a is to be taken in the sense of x, ara so that the expression would mean " anima inferior."

2 In qua necesse est ex singulis quibusque partibus qu 2 possiint moveri discutere.

vlien the latter would recall the soul to its influence, it may nevertheless appear a more advantageous procedure for the soul to be under the mastery of the flesh than to remain under the power of its own will. For, since it is said to be neither hot nor cold, but to continue in a sort of tepid condition, it will find conversion a slow and somewhat difficult undertaking. If indeed it clung to the flesh, then, satiated at length, and filled with those very evils which it suffers from the vices of the flesh, and wearied as it were by the lieavy burdens of luxury and lust, it may sometimes be converted with greater ease and rapidity from the filthiness of matter to a desire for heavenly things, and to a taste for spiritual graces. And the apostle must be supposed to have said, that "the spirit contends against the flesh, and the flesh against the spirit, so that w e cannot do the things that we would" (those things, undoubtedly, which are designated as being beyond the will of the spirit, and the wall of the flesh), meaning (as if we vere to express it in other words) that it is better for a man to be either in a state of virtue or in one of wickedness, than in neither of these; but that the soul, before its conversion to the spirit, and its union with it, appears durinor its adherence to the bodv, and its meditation of carnal things, to be neither in a good condition nor in a manifestly bad one, but resembles, so to speak, an animal. It is better, however, for it, if possible, to be rendered spiritual through adherence to the spirit; but if that cannot be done, it is more expedient for it to follow even the wickedness of the flesh, than, placed under the influence of its own will, to retain the position of an irrational animal.

These points we have now discussed, in our desire to consider each individual opinion, at greater length than we intended, that those views might not be supposed to have escaped our notice wdiich are generally brought forward by those who inquire whether tliere is within us any other soul than this heavenly and rational one, which is naturally opposed to the latter, and is called either the flesh, or the wisdom of the flesh, or the soul of the flesh.

' Priui=qiiain imum efficiatur cum eo.

4. Let us o y see what answer is usually returned to these statements by those who maintain that there is in us one movement, and one life, proceeding from one and the same soul, both the salvation and the destruction of which are ascribed to itself as a result of its own actions. And, in the first place, let us notice of what nature those commotions of the soul are which we suffer, when we feel ourselves inwardly drawn in different directions; when there arises a kind of contest of thoughts in our hearts, and certain probabilities are suggested us, agreeably to which we lean now to this side, now to that, and by which we are sometimes convicted of error, and sometimes approve of our acts. It is nothing remarkable, however, to say of wicked spirits, that they have a varying and conflicting judgment, and one out of harmony with itself, since such is found to be the case in all men, wdienever, in deliberating upon an uncertain event, counsel is taken, and men consider and consult what is to be chosen as the better and more useful course. It is not therefore surprising that, if two probabilities meet, and suggest opposite views, they should drag the mind in contrary directions. For example, if a man be led by reflection to believe and to fear God, it cannot then be said that the flesh contends against the spirit; but, amidst the uncertainty of what may be true and advantageous, the mind is drawn in opposite directions. So, also, when it is supposed that the flesh provokes to the indulgence of lust, but better counsels

oppose allurements of that kind, we are not to suppose that it is one life which is resisting another, but that it is the tendency of the nature of the body, wdiich is eager to empty out and cleanse the places filled with seminal moisture; as, in like manner, it is not to be supposed that it is any opposing power, or the life of another soul, which excites within us the appetite of thirst, and impels us to drink, or which causes us to feel hunger, and drives us to satisfy it. But as it is by the natural movements of the body that food and

Passiones.

Quibus nunc quidem arguimur, nunc vero nosmet ipsos amplec-timur.

drink are either desired or rejected so also the natural seed, collected together in course of time in the various vessels, has an eager desire to be expelled and thrown away, and is so far from never being removed, save by the impulse of some exciting cause, that it is even sometimes spontaneously emitted. When, therefore, it is said that " the flesh struggles against the spirit," these persons understand the expression to mean that habit or necessity, or the delights of the flesh, arouse a man, and withdraw him from divine and spiritual things. For, owing to the necessity of the body being drawn away, w e are not allowed to have leisure for divine things, which are to be eternally advantageous. So again, the soul, devoting itself to divine and spiritual pursuits, and being united to the spirit, is said to fight against the flesh, by not permitting it to be relaxed by indulgence, and to become unsteady through the influence of those pleasures for wdiicli it feels a natural delight. In this w ay, also, they claim to understand the words, "The wisdom of thc flesh is hostile to God," not that the flesh really has a soul, or a w isdom of its own. But as we are accustomed to say, by an abuse of language, that the earth is thirsty, and wishes to drink in w ater, this use of the word "wishes" is not proper, but catachrestic, as if we were to say again, that this house wants to be rebuilt," and many other similar expressions; so also is the wisdom of the flesh to be understood, or the expression, that " the flesh lusteth against the spirit." They generally connect wdth these the expression, "The voice of thy brother's blood crieth unto me from the ground." For what cries unto the Lord is not properly the blood which was shed; but the blood is said improperly to cry out, vengeance being demanded upon him who had shed it. The declaration also of the apostle, "I see another law in my members, warring against the law of my mind," they so understand as if he had said, That he who wishes to devote himself to the word of God is, on account of his bodily necessities and habits, which like a sort of law are ingrained in the body, distracted, and divided, 1 Evacuautur.- Cf. Rom. viii. 2. Abusive.

4 Recomponi vult. Gen. iv. 10. c j om. vii. 23.

and impeded, lest, by devoting himself vigorously to the study of wisdom, he should be enabled to behold the divine mysteries.

5. With respect, however, to the following being ranked among the works of the flesh, viz. heresies, and envyings, and contentions, or other vices, they so understand the passage, that the mind, being rendered grosser in feeling, from its yielding itself to the passions of the body, and being oppressed by the mass of its vices, and having no refined or spiritual feelings, is said to be made flesh, and derives its name from that in which it exhibits more vigour and force of will. They also make this further inquiry,

"Who will be found, or who will be said to be, the creator of this evil sense, called the sense of the flesh?" Because they defend the opinion that there is no other creator of soul and flesh than God. And if we w ere to assert that the good God created anything in His own creation that was hostile to Himself, it would appear to be a manifest absurdity. If, then, it is written, that " carnal wisdom is enmity against God," and if this be declared to be a result of creation, God Himself wall appear to have formed a nature hostile to Himself, vhich cannot be subject to Him nor to His law, as if it were supposed to be an animal of which such qualities are predicated. And if this view be admitted, in what respect will it appear to differ from that of those who maintain that souls of different natures are created, w hich, according to their natures," are destined either to be lost or saved? But this is an opinion of the heretics alone, who, not being able to maintain the justice of God on grounds of piety, compose impious inventions of this kind. And now we have brought forward to the best of our ability, in the person of each of the parties, what might be advanced by way of argument regarding the several views, and let the reader choose out of them for himself that which he thinks ought to be preferred. 1 Plus studii vel propositi. Rom. viii. 7. Naturaliter.

1. And now, since there is one of the articles of the church which is held principally in consequence of our belief in the truth of our sacred history, viz. that this world vras created and took its beginning at a certain time, and, in conformity to the cycle of time decreed to all things, is to be destroyed on account of its corruption, there seems no absurdity in re-discussing a few points connected with this subject. And so far, indeed, as the credibility of Scripture is concerned, the declarations on such a matter seem easy of proof. Even the heretics, although widely opposed on many other things, yet on this appear to be at one, yielding to the authority of Scripture.

Concerning, then, the creation of the world, what portion of Scripture can give us more information regarding it, than the account which Moses has transmitted respecting its origin? And although it comprehends matters of pro-founder significance than the mere historical narrative appears to indicate, and contains very many things that are to be spiritually understood, and employs the letter, as a hind of veil, in treating of profound and mystical subjects; nevertheless the language of the narrator shows that all visible things were created at a certain time. But with regard to the consummation of the world, Jacob is the first who gives any information, in addressing his children in the words: " Gather yourselves together unto me, ye sons of Jacob, that I may tell you what shall be in the last days," or "after the last days." If, then, there be "last days," or a period " succeeding the last days," the days which had a beginning must necessarily come to an end. David, too,

De ecclesiasticis definitionibus nnum. 2 Consummationem sseciili.

Gen. xlix. 1. The Vulgate has, "In diebiis novissimis;" the Septuag. 'Er igyjira'j ruu 7 y. spuv " the Masoretic text, n "inn2.

declares: " The heavens shall perish, but Thou shalt endure; yea, all of thein shall wax old as doth a garment: as a vesture shalt Thou change them, and they shall be changed: but Thou art the same, and Thy years shall have no end." Our Lord and Saviour, mdeed, in the words, "He who made them at the beginning, made them male and female,"" Himself bears witness that the world was created; and again, when He says, "Heaven and earth shall pass away, but my words shall not pass away," He points out that they are perishable, and must come to an end. The apostle, moreover, in declaring that " the creature was made subject to vanity, not willingly, but by reason of him who hath subjected the same in hope, because the creature itself also shall be delivered from the bondage of corruption into the glorious liberty of the children of God," manifestly announces the end of the world; as he does also when he again says, "The fashion of this world passeth away." Now, by the expression which he employs, " that the creature was made subject to vanity," he shows that there was a beginning to this world: for if the creature were made subject to vanity on account of some hope, it was certainly made subject from a cause; and seeing it was from a cause, it must necessarily have had a beginning: for, without some beginning, the creature could not be subject to vanity, nor could that creature hope to be freed from the bondage of corruption, which had not begun to serve. But any one who chooses to search at his leisure, will find numerous other passages in holy Scripture in which the world is both said to have a beginning and to hope for an end.

2. Now, if there be any one who would here oppose either the authority or credibility of our Scriptures, we would ask of him whether he asserts that God can, or cannot, comprehend all things? To assert that He cannot, would manifestly be an act of impiety. If then he answer, as he must, that God comprehends all things, it follows from the very 1 Ps. cii. 26, 27. Matt. xix. 4. Matt. xxiv. 35.

4 Rom. viii. 20, 21. 1 Cor. vii. 31.

Auctoritate Scripturae nostras, vel fidei.

fact of tlieir being capable of comprehension, tliat they are understood to have a beghming and an end, seeing that which is altogether Avithout any beginning cannot be at all comprehended. For however far understanding may extend, so far is the faculty of comprehending illimitably withdrawn and removed when there is held to be no befiinnino;.

3. But this is the objection which they generally raise: they say, "If the world had its beginning in time, what was God doing before the world began? For it is at once impious and absurd to say that the nature of God is inactive and immoveable, or to suppose that goodness at one time did not do good, and omnipotence at one time did not exercise its power." Such is the objection Avhich they are accustomed to make to our statement that this world had its beo'innino; at a certain time, and that, agreeably to our belief in Scripture, we can calculate the years of its past duration. To these propositions I consider that none of the heretics can easily return an answer that will be in conformity with the nature of their opinions. But we can give a logical answer in accordance with the standard of religion, when we say that not then for the first time did God begin to work w hen He made this visible world; but as, after its destruction, there will be another w orld, so also we believe that others existed before the present came into being. And both of these positions will be confirmed by the authority of holy Scripture. For that there will be another w orld after this, is taught by Isaiah, who says, " There will be a new heavens, and a new earth, which I shall make to abide in my sight, saitli the Lord;" and that before this world others also existed is shown by Ecclesiastes, in the words: " What is that which hath been? Even that which shall be. And what is that which has been created? Even this which is to be created: and

there is nothing altogether new under the sun. Who shall speak and declare, Lo, this is new? It hath already been in the ao; es which have been before us."' Bv these
Regulam pietatis.- Cf. Isa. lxvi. 22.
"Cf. Eccles. i. 9. The text is in conformity with the Septuag.: T to yiyov6g Avro to yiunoof vjov. 'Keel ri to 'zstroiriyjuow Airo to Trofidiao- testimonies it is established both that there were ages before our own, and that there will be others after it. It is not, however to be supposed that several worlds existed at once, but that, after the end of this present world, others will take their beginning; respecting which it is unnecessary to repeat each particular statement, seeing we have already done so in the preceding pages.

4. This point, indeed, is not to be idly passed by, that the holy Scriptures have called the creation of the world by a new and peculiar name, terming it fcaraSoxr, which has been very improperly translated into Latin by "constitutio;" for in Greek Katajsoxy signifies rather " dejicere," i. e. to cast downwards, a word which has been, as we have already remarked, improperly translated into Latin by the phrase "constitutio mundi," as in the Gospel according to John, where the Saviour says, "And there will be tribulation in those days, such as was not since the beginning of the world;" in which passage KaraSoxfj is rendered by beginning (con-stitutio)y which is to be understood as above explained. The apostle also, in the Epistle to the Ephesians, has employed the same language, saying, "Who hath chosen us before the foundation of the world;"'" and this foundation he calls cara-fiokt, to be understood in the same sense as before. It seems worth while, then, to inquire what is meant by this new term; and I am, indeed, of opinion that, as the end and consum- suoy. Kcsi ovx, sariv 'tco. v '7rp6apoi. rou vtto rou 'Xor. "O? 7. cihviaii koii Ipu' "I'hs rovro Ktzivou kanv, yj ykyottv Iv roig uloxriu rolg ' ivof, dvoi; d'Tro 1 Ssecula. 2 tt. xxiv. 21. s ph. i. 4.

The following is Jerome's version of this passage (Epistle to Avitus): " A divine habitation, and a true rest above (apud superos), I think is to be understood, where rational creatures dwelt, and where, before their descent to a lower position, and removal from invisible to visible worlds, and fall to earth, and need of gross bodies, they enjoyed a former blessedness. Whence God the Creator made for them bodies suitable to their humble position, and created this visible world, and sent into the world ministers for the salvation and correction of those who had fallen: of whom some were to obtain certain localities, and be subject to the necessities of the world; others were to discharge with care and attention the duties enjoined upon them at all times, and which raatlon of the saints will be in those ages which are not seen, and are eternal, we must conclude (as frequently pointed out in the preceding pages), from a contemplation of that very end, that rational creatures had also a similar beginning. And if they had a beginning such as the end for which they hope, they existed undoubtedly from the very beginning in those ages which are not seen, and are eternal. And if this is so, then there has been a descent from a higher to a low'er condition, on the part not only of those souls who have deserved the change by the variety of their movements, but also on that of those who, in order to serve the whole world, were brought down from those higher and invisible spheres to these lower and visible ones, although against their will ' Because the creature was subjected to vanity, not willingly, were known to God, the Arranger of all things. And of these, the sun, moon, and stars, which are called

' creature' by the apostle, received the more elevated places of the world. "Which ' creature' was made subject to vanity, in that it was clothed with gross bodies, and was open to view; and yet was subject to vanity, not voluntarily, but because of the will of Him who subjected the same in hope." And again: " AYhile others, whom we believe to be angels, at different places and times, which the Arranger alone knows, serve the government of the world." And a little further on: " Which order of things is regulated by the providential government of the whole world; some powers falling down from a loftier position, others gradually sinking to earth: some falling voluntarily, others being cast down against their will: some undertaking, of their own accord, the service of stretching out the hand to those who fall; others being compelled to i erseuere for so long a time in the duty which they have undertaken." And again: "Whence it follows that, on account of the various movements, various worlds also are created; and after this world which we now inhabit, there will be another greatly dissimilar. But no other being save God alone, the Creator of all things, can arrange the deserts of all, both to the time to come and to that which preceded, suitably to the differing lapses and advances of individuals, and to the rewards of virtues or the punishment of vices, both in the present and in the future, and in all times, and to conduct them all again to one end: for He knows the causes why He allows some to enjoy their own will, and to fall from a higher rank to the lowest condition; and why He begins to visit others, and bring them back gradually, as if by giving them His hand, to their pristine state, and placing them in a lofty position" (Ruseus).

ORIG. E but because of liim who subjected the same in hope;" so that both sun, and moon, and stars, and angels might discharge their duty to the world, and to those souls which, on account of their excessive mental defects, stood in need of bodies of a grosser and more solid nature; and for the sake of those for whom this arrangement was necessary, this visible world was also called into being. From this it follows, that by the use of the word cara Boxij, a descent from a higher to a lower condition, shared by all in common, would seem to be pointed out. The hope indeed of freedom is entertained by the whole of creation of being liberated from the corruption of slavery when the sons of God, who either fell away or vv ere scattered abroad, shall be gathered together into one, or when they shall have fulfilled their other duties in this world, which are knovm to God alone, the Disposer of all things. We are, indeed, to suppose that the world vvas created of such quality and capacity as to contain not only all those souls which it was determined should be trained in this world, but also all those powers which were prepared to attend, and serve, and assist them. For it is established by many declarations that all rational creatures are of one nature: on which ground alone could the justice of God in all His dealings with them be defended, seeing every one has the reason in himself, why he has been placed in this or that rank in life.

5. This arrangement of things, then, which God afterwards appointed (for He had, from the very origin of the world, clearly perceived the reasons and causes affecting those who, either owing to mental deficiencies, deserved to enter into bodies, or those who were carried away by their desire for visible things, and those also who, either willingly or unwillingly, were compelled, by Him v ho subjected the same in hope, to perform certain services to such as had fallen into that condition), not being understood

by some, who failed to perceive that it was owing to preceding causes, originating in free-will, that this variety of arrangement had been instituted by God, they have concluded that all things 2 Dispersi.

in ting world are directed either by fortuitous movements or by a necessary fate, and that nothing is within the power of our own will. And, therefore, also they w ere unable to show that the providence of God was beyond the reach of censure. 6. But as we have said that all the souls who lived in this world' stood in need of many ministers, or rulers, or assistants; so, in the last times, when the end of the world is already imminent and near, and the whole human race is verging upon the last destruction, and when not only those wdio were governed by others have been reduced to weakness, but those also to w hom had been committed the cares of government, it was no longer such help nor such defenders that were needed, but the help of the Author and Creator Himself was required to restore to the one the discipline of obedience, wdiich had been corrupted and profaned, and to the other the discipline of rule. And hence the only-begotten Son of God, wdio was the Word and the Wisdom of the Father, when He w as in the possession of that glory with the Father, which He had before the world was, divested Plimself "" of it, and, taking the form of a servant, was made obedient unto death, that He might teach obedience to those who could not otherwise than by obedience obtain salvation. He restored also the laws of rule and government vhich had been corrupted, by subduing all enemies under His feet, that by this means (for it was necessary that He should reign until He had put all enemies under Plis feet, and destroyed the last enemy death) He might teach rulers themselves moderation in their government. As He had come, then, to restore the discipline, not only of government, but of obedience, as we have said, accomplishing in Himself first what He desired to be accomplished by others. He became obedient to the Father, not only to the death of the cross, but also, in the end of the world, embracing in Himself all whom He subjects to the Father, and who by Him come to salvation. He Himself, along with them, and in them, is said also to be subject to the Father; all things subsisting in Him, and He Himself being the Head of all things, and in Him being the 1 Exinanivit semet ipsum. 2 Regendi regnandique.

salvation and the fulness of those who obtain salvation. And this consequently is what the apostle says of Him: " And when all things shall be subjected to Him, then shall the Son also Himself be subject to Him that put all things under Him, that God may be all in all."

7. I know not, indeed, how the heretics, not understanding the meaning of the apostle in these words, consider the term " subjection " degrading as applied to the Son; for if the propriety of the title be called in question, it may easily be ascertained from making a contrary supposition. Because if it be not good to be in subjection, it follows that the opposite will be good, viz. not to be in subjection. Now the language of the apostle, according to their view, appears to indicate by these words, "And when all things shall be subdued unto Him, then shall the Son also Himself be subject unto Him that put all things under Him," that He, who is not now in subjection to the Father, will become subject to Him wdien the Father shall have first subdued all thinn; s unto Him. But I am astonished how it can be conceived to be the meaning, that He who, while all things are not yet subdued to Him, is not Himself In subjection, should at a

time when all things have been subdued to Him, and when He has become King of all men, and holds sway over all things be supposed then to be made subject, seeing He was not formerly in subjection; for such do not understand that the subjection of Christ to the Father indicates that our happiness has attained to perfection, and that the work undertaken by Him has been brought to a victorious termination, seeing He has not only purified the power of supreme government over the whole of creation, but presents to the Father the principles of the obedience and subjection of the human race in a corrected and Improved condition. If, then, that subjection be held to be good and salutary by which the Son is said to be subject to the Father, It is an extremely rational and logical inference 1 1 Cor. XV. 28.

2 Cum non solum regeudi ac regnandi summam, quam in universam emendaverit creaturam, verum etiam obedientise et subjectioue correcta reparataque liumani generis Patri offerat iustituta.

to decluce tliat the subjection also of enemies, which is said to be made to the Son of God, should be understood as being also salutary and useful; as if, when the Son is said to be subject to the Father, the perfect restoration of the whole of creation is signified, so also, when enemies are said to be subjected to the Son of God, the salvation of the conquered and the restoration of the lost is in that understood to consist. 8. This subjection, however, will be accomplished in certain ways, and after certain training, and at certain times; for it is not to be imagined that the subjection is to be brought about by the pressure of necessity (lest the whole w orld should then appear to be subdued to God by force), but by word, reason, and doctrine; by a Cc U to a better course of things, by the best systems of training, by the employment also of suitable and appropriate threatenings, which will justly impend over those who despise any care or attention to their salvation and usefulness. In a word, w e men also, in training either our slaves or children, restrain them by threats and fear while they are, by reason of their tender age, incapable of using their reason; but when they have begun to understand what is good, and useful, and honourable, the fear of the lash being over, they acquiesce through the suasion of words and reason in all that is good. But how, consistently with the preservation of freedom of will in all rational creatures, each one ought to be regulated, i. e. who they are whom the word of God finds and trains, as if they were already prepared and capable of it; who they are whom it puts off to a later time; who these are from whom it is altogether concealed, and who are so situated as to be far from hearing it; who those, again, are who despise the word of God when made known and preached to them, and who are driven by a kind of correction and chastisement to salvation, and whose conversion is in a certain degree demanded and extorted; who those are to whom certain opportunities of salvation are afforded, so tliat sometimes, their faith being proved by an answ er alone, they have unquestionably obtained salvation; from what

By a profession of faith in baptism.- Indubitatam ceperit salutem.

causes or on wliat occasions these results take place, or wl at the divine wisdom sees within them, or what movements of their will leads God so to arrange all these things, is known to Him alone, and to His only-begotten Son, through whom all things were created and restored, and to the Holy Spirit, throuo-h whom all things are sanctified, who proceedeth from the Father, to whom be glory for ever and ever. Amen.

CHAPTEE YI.
ON THE END OF THE W OELD.

1. Now, respecting the end of the world and the consummation of all things, we have stated in the preceding pages, to the best of our ability, so far as the authority of Holy Scripture enabled us, what we deem sufficient for purposes of instruction; and we shall here only add a few admonitory remarks, since the order of investigation has brought us back to the subject. The highest good, then, after the attainment of which the whole of rational nature is seeking, wdiich is also called the end of all blessings," is defined by many philosophers as follows: The highest good, they say, is to become as hke to God as possible. But this definition I regard not so much as a discovery of theirs, as a view derived from holy Scripture. For this is pointed out by Moses, before all other philosophers, when he describes the first creation of man in these words; ' And God said. Let us make man in our own image, and after our likeness;" and then he adds the words: '- So God created man in His own image: in the imase of God created He him; male and female created He 1 It was not until the third Synod of Toledo, a. d. 589, that the " Filioque" clause was added to the Creed of Constantinople, this difference forming, as is well known, one of the dogmatic grounds for the disunion between the Western and Eastern Churches down to the present day, the latter church denying that the Spirit proceedeth from the Father and the Son.

- Finis omnium: "bonormn" understood. Gqji.2Q.

them, and He blessed them' Now the expression, "In the image of God created He him," without any mention of the word "likeness,"'" conveys no other meaning than this, that man received the dio-nity of God's imacje at his first creation; but that the perfection of his likeness has been reserved for the consummation, namely, that he might acquire it f(n-himself by the exercise of his own diligence in the imitation of God, the possibility of attaining to perfection being granted him at the beginning through the dignity of the divine image, and the perfect realization of the divine likeness being reached in the end by the fulfilment of the necessary works. Now, that such is the case, the Apostle John points out more clearly and unmistakeably, when he makes this declaration: " Little children, we do not yet know what we shall be; but if a revelation be made to us from the Saviour, ye will say, without any doubt, we shall be like Him." By which expression he points out with the utmost certainty, that not only was the end of all things to be hoped for, which he says was still unknown to him, but also the likeness to God, which will be conferred, in proportion to the completeness of our deserts. The Lord Himself, in the Gospel, not only declares that these same results are future, but that they are to be brought about by His own intercession, He Himself deigning to obtain them from the Father for His disciples, saying, "Father, I will that where I am, these also m ay be with me; and as Thou and I are one, they also may be one in us."' In which the divine likeness itself already appears to advance, if we may so express ourselves, and from being merely similar, to become the same, because undoubtedly in the consummation or end God is "all and in all." And with reference to this, it is made a question by some'

1 Gen. i. 27, 28.- Imago. gimilitudo. Cf. 1 Jolin iii. 2.

Cf. John xvii. 24, cf. 21. Ex simili unnm licri.

" Jerome, in bis Epistle to Avitus, No. 94, has the j assage thus: " Since, as we have already frequently observed, the beginning is generated again from the end, it is a question whether then also there will be bodies, or whether existence will be maintained at some time without them when they shall have been annihilated, and thus the life of incorporeal beings must be believed to be iucorporeal, as we know is whether the nature of bodily matter, although cleansed and purified, and rendered altogether spiritual, does not seem either to offer an obstruction towards attaining the dignity of the divine likeness, or to the property of unity, because neither can a corporeal nature appear capable of any resemblance to a divine nature, which is certainly incorporeal; nor can it be truly and deservedly designated one with it, especially since we are taught by the truths of our religion that that which alone is one, viz. the Son with the Father, must be referred to a peculiarity of the divine nature.

2. Since, then, it is promised that in the end God will be tlie case with God. And there is no doubt that if all the bodies which are termed visible by the apostle, belong to that sensible world, the life of incorporeal beings will be incorporeal." And a little after: " That expression, also, used by the apostle, ' The whole creation will be freed from the bondage of corruption into the glorious liberty of the children of God' (Rom. viii. 21), we so understand, that we say it was the first creation of rational and incorporeal beings which is not subject to corruption, because it was not clothed with bodies 5 for wherever bodies are, corruption immediately follows. But afterwards it will he freed from the bondage of corruption, when they shall have received the glory of the sons of God, and God shall be all in all." And in the same place: 'That we must believe the end of all things to be incorporeal, the language of the Saviour Himself leads us to think, when He says, ' As I and Thou are one, so may they also be one in us' (John xvii. 21). For we ought to know what God is, and what the Saviour will be in the end, and how the hkeness of the Father and the Son has been promised to the saints; for as they are one in Him, so they also are one in them. For we must adopt the view, either that the God of all things is clothed with a body, and as we are enveloped with flesh, so He also with some material covering, that the likeness of the life of God may be in the end produced also in the samts; or if this hypothesis is unbecoming, especially in the judgment of those who desire, even in the smallest degree, to feel the majesty of God, and to look upon the glory of His uncreated and all-surpassing nature, we are forced to adopt the other alternative, and despair either of attaining any likeness to God, if we are to inhabit for ever the same bodies, or if the blessedness of the same life with God is promised to us, we must live in the same state as that in which God lives." All these points have been omitted by Rufinus as erroneous, and statements of a different kind here and there inserted instead (Ruseus).

1 Ad unitatis proprietatem.

all and in all, we are not, as is fitting, to suppose that animals, eitlier sheep or other cattle, come to that end, lest it should be implied that God dwelt even in animals, wdiether sheep or other cattle; and so, too, with pieces of wood or stones, lest it should be said that God is in these also. So, again, nothing that is wicked must be supposed to attain to that end, lest, while God is said to be in all things. He may also be said to be in a vessel of wickedness. For if we now assert that God is everywhere and in all things, on the ground that nothing can be empty of God, we nevertheless do not say that He is now " all things " in those in whom He is. And hence we must look more carefully as to what that is which denotes the perfection of blessedness and the end of things, which is not only said to be God in all things, but also " all in all." Let us then inquire what all those things are which God is to become in all.

3. I am of opinion that the expression, by w hicli God is said to be "all in all," means that He is "all" in each individual person. Now He will be "all" in each individual in this way: when all which any rational understanding, cleansed from the dregs of every sort of vice, and w itli every cloud of wickedness completely swept away, can either feel, or understand, or think, will be w holly God; and when it will no longer behold or retain anything else than God, but when God will be the measure and standard of all its movements; and thus God will be " all," for there wdll no longer be any distinction of good and evil, seeing evil nowhere exists; for God is all things, and to Him no evil is near: nor will there be any longer a desire to eat from the tree of the knowledge of good and evil, on the part of him who is always in the possession of good, and to wdiom God is all. So then, when. the end has been restored to the beginning, and the termination of things compared with their commencement, that condition of things will be re-established in which rational nature was placed, when it had no need to eat of the tree of the knowledge of o; ood and evil; so that when all feelino- of wickedness has been removed, and the individual has been purified and cleansed, He who alone is the one good God becomes to him " all," and that not in the case of a few individuals, or of a considerable number, but He Himself is " all in all." And when death shall no longer anywhere exist, nor the sting of death, nor any evil at all, then verily God will be " all in all." But some are of opinion that that perfection and blessedness of rational creatures, or natures, can only remain in that same condition of which we have spoken above, i. e. that all things should possess God, and God should be to them all things, if they are in no degree prevented by their union with a bodily nature. Otherwise they think that the glory of the highest blessedness is impeded by the intermixture of any material substance. But this subject we have discussed at greater length, as may be seen in the preceding pages.

4. And now, as we find the apostle making mention of a spiritual body, let us inquire, to the best of our ability, what idea we are to form of such a thing. So far, then, as our understanding can grasp it, we consider a spiritual body to be of such a nature as ought to be inhabited not only by all holy and perfect souls, but also by all those creatures which will be liberated from the slavery of corruption. Respecting the body also, the apostle has said, ' We have a house not 1 " Here the honesty of Rufinus iii his translation seems very suspicious; for Origen's well-known opinion regarding the sins and lapses of blessed spirits he here attributes to others. Nay, even the opinion-which he introduces Origen as ascribing to others, he exliiibits him as refuting a little further on, sec. 6, in these words: 'And in this condition of blessedness we are to believe tha, t, by the will of the Creator, it will abide for ever without any change," etc. I suspect, therefore, that all this is due to Eufinus himself, and that he has inserted it, instead of what is found in the beginning of the chapter, sec. 1, and which in Jerome's Epistle to Avitus stands as follows: ' Nor is there any doubt that, after certain intervals of time, matter will again exist, and bodies be formed, and a diversity be estabhshed in the world, on account of the varying Yills

of rational creatures, who, after enjoying perfect blessedness down to the end of all things, have gradually fallen away to a lower condition, and received into them so much vickedness, that they are converted into an opposite condition, by their unvilhngness to retain their original state, and to preserve their blessedness uncor-rupted. Nor is this point to be suppressed, that many rational creatures made with hands, eternal in the lieavens," i, c. in the mansions of the blessed. And from this statement we may form a conjecture, how pure, how refined, and how glorious are the qualities of that body, if w e compare it with those which, altliough they are celestial bodies, and of most brilhant splendour, were nevertheless made with hands, and are visible to our siixht. But of that bodv it is said, that it is a house not made with hands, but eternal in the heavens. Since, then, tliose things " which are seen are temporal, but those things which arc not seen arc eternal,"" all those bodies which we see either on earth or in heaven, and which are capable of being seen, and have been made with hands, but are not eternal, are far excelled in glory by that which is not visible, nor made with hands, but is eternal. From which comparison it may be conceived how great are the comeliness, and splendour, and brilliancy of a spiritual body; and how true it is, that ' eye hath not seen, nor ear heard, nor hath it entered into the heart of man to conceive, what God hath prepared for them that love Him." We ought not, however, to doubt that the nature of this present body of ours may, by the will of God, who made it wdiat it is, be raised to those qualities of refinement, and purity, and splendour which characterize the body referred to, according as the condition of things requires, and the deserts of our rational nature shall demand. Finally, when the world required variety and retain their first condition (princijumii) even to the second and third and fourth worlds, and allow no room for any change within them; while others, again, will lose so little of then- pristine state, that they will appear to have lost almost nothing, and some are to be precipitated with great destruction into the lowest pit. And God, the disposer of all things, when creating His worlds, knows how to treat each individual agreeably to his merits, and He is acquainted with the occasions and causes by which the government (guhernacla) of the world is sustained and commenced; so that he who surpassed all others in wickedness, and brought himsek completely down to the earth, is made in another world, which is af terwr. rds to be formed, a devil, the beginning of the creation of the Lord (Job xl. 19), to be mocked by the angels who have lost the virtue of their original condition' exordii virtiitem)."''

RUieUS.

1 1 Cor. V. 1. 2 2 Cor. iv. 18. i Cor. ii. 9; cf. Isa. lxiv. 4.

diversity, matter yielded itself with all docility tlirougliout the diverse appearances and species of things to the Creator, as to its Lord and Maker, that He might educe from it the various forms of celestial and terrestrial beino; s. But when things have begun to hasten to that consummation that all may be one, as the Father is one with the Son, it may be understood as a rational inference, that where all are one, there will no longer be any diversity.

5. The last enemy, moreover, who is called death, is said on this account to be destroyed, that there may not be anything left of a mournful kind when death does not exist, nor anything that is adverse when there is no enemy. The destruction of the last enemy, indeed, is to be understood, not as if its substance, which was formed by

God, is to perish, but because its mind and hostile will, which came not from God, but from itself, are to be destroyed. Its destruction, therefore, will not be its non-existence, but its ceasing to be an enemy, and to be death. For nothing is impossible to the Omnipotent, nor is anything incapable of restoration to its Creator; for He made all things that they might exist, and those things which were made for existence cannot cease to be. For this reason also will they admit of change and variety, so as to be placed, according to their merits, either in a better or worse position; but no destruction of substance can befall those things which were created by God for the purpose of permanent existence. For those things which agreeably to the common opinion are believed to perish, the nature either of our faith or of the truth will not permit us to suppose to be destroyed. Finally, our flesh is supposed by ignorant men and unbelievers to be destroyed after death, in such a degree that it retains no relic at all of its former substance. We, however, who believe in its resurrection, understand that a change only has been produced by death, but that its substance certainly remains; and that by the will of its Creator, and at the time appointed, it will be restored to life; and that a second time a change will take place in it, so that what at first was flesh formed out of 1 lusanabile.- Ut essent et pcrmanerent.

earthly soil, and was afterwards dissolved by death, and again reduced to dust and ashes ("For dust thou art," it is said, " and to dust shalt thou return"), will be again raised from the earth, and shall after this, according to the merits of the indwelling soul, advance to the glory of a spiritual body.

6. Into this condition, then, we are to suppose that all this bodily substance of ours will be brought, when all things shall be re-established in a state of unity, and when God shall be all in all. And this result must be understood as being brought about, not suddenly, but slowly and gradually, seeing that the process of amendment and correction will take place imperceptibly in the individual instances during the lapse of countless and unmeasured ages, some outstripping others, and tending by a swifter course towards perfection, while others again follow close at hand, and some again a long way behind; and thus, through the numerous and uncounted orders of progressive beings who are being reconciled to God from a state of enmity, the last enemy is finally reached, who is called death, so that he also may be destroyed, and no longer be an enemy. When, therefore, all rational souls shall have been restored to a condition of this kind, then the nature of this body of ours wdll undergo a change into the glory of a spiritual body. For as we see it not to be the case with rational natures, that some of them have lived in a condition of degradation owing to their sins, while others have been called to a state of happiness on account of their merits; but as we see those same souls who had formerly been sinful, assisted, after their conversion and reconciliation to God, to a state of happiness; so also are we to consider, wdth respect to the nature of the body, that the one which we now make use of in a state of meanness, and corruption, and weakness, is not a different body from that which we shall possess in incorruption, and in power, and in glory; but that the same body, when it has cast away the infirmities in which it is now entangled, shall be transmuted into a condition of glory, being rendered spiritual, Gen. iii. 19. 2 j suinma.

so that what was a vessel of dishononr may, when cleansed, become a vessel unto honour, and an abode of blessedness. And in this condition, also, we are to believe, that by the will of the Creator it will abide for ever without any change, as is confirmed by the declartition of the apostle, when he says, "We have a house, not made with hands, eternal in the heavens." For the faith of the church does not admit the view of certain Grecian philosophers, that there is besides the body, composed of four elements, another fifth body, which is different in all its parts, and diverse from this our present body; since neither out of sacred Scripture can any produce the slightest suspicion of evidence for sncli an opinion, nor can any rational inference from things allow the reception of it, especially when the holy apostle manifestly declares, that it is not new bodies wdiich are given to those wdio rise from the dead, but that they receive those identical ones which they had possessed when living, transformed from an inferior into a better condition. For his words are: " It is sown an animal body, it will rise a spiritual body: it is sown in corruption, it will arise in incorraption: it is sown in weakness, it will arise in power: it is sown in dishonour, it will arise in glory." As, therefore, there is a kind of advance in man, so that from being first an animal being, and not understanding what belongs to the Spirit of God, he reaches by means of instruction the stage of being-made a spiritual being, and of judging all things, while he himself is judged by no one; so also, with respect to the state of the body, we are to hold that this very body which now, on account of its service to the soul, is styled an animal body, will, by means of a certain progress, when the soul, united to God, shall have been made one spirit with Him (the body even' then ministering, as it were, to the spirit), attain to a spiritual condition and quality, especially since, as we have often pointed out, bodily nature was so formed by the Creator, as to pass easily into whatever condition He should wish, or the nature of the case demand.

7. The wdiole of this reasoning, then, amounts to this: 1 1 Cor. XV. 23.

that God created two general natures, a visible, i. e. a corporeal nature; and an invisible nature, which is incorporeal. Now these two natures admit of two different permutations. That invisible and rational nature changes in mind and purpose, because it is endowed with freedom of will, and is on this account found sometimes to be engaged in the practice of good, and sometimes in that of the opposite. But this corporeal nature admits of a change in substance; whence also God, i Q arranger of all things, has the service of this matter at His command in the moulding, or fabrication, or re-touching of wdiatever He wishes, so that corporeal nature may be transmuted, and transformed into any forms or species whatever, according as the deserts of things may demand; wdiich tlie prophet evidently has in view when he says, "It is God who makes and transforms all things."

8. And now the point for investigation is, wdiether, when God shall be all in all, the wdiole of bodily nature will, in the consummation of all things, consist of one species, and the sole quality of body be that which shall shine in the indescribable glory w hich is to be regarded as the future possession of the spiritual body. For if we rightly understand the matter, this is the statement of Moses in the beginning of his book, when he says, "In the beginning God created the heavens and the earth."' For this is the bemnninr of all creation: to this beginning the end and consummation of all things must be recalled, i. e. in order that that heaven and that earth may be the habitation and resting-place of the pious; so that all the holy ones, and the meek, may first obtain an inheritance in that land, since this is the teaching of the law, and

of the prophets, and of the gospel. In which land I believe there exist the true and living forms of that worship which Moses handed down under the shadow of the law; of which it is said, that " they serve unto the example and shadow of heavenly things" those, viz., wdio were in subjection in the law. To Moses himself also was the in- 1
Cf. Ps. cii. 25, 2Q.

2 Gen. i. 1.

"Heb. viii. 5.

junction given, "Look that thou make them after the form and pattern which were showed thee on the mount." From which it appears to me, that as on this earth the law was a sort of schoolmaster to those who by it were to be conducted to Christ, in order that, being instructed and trained by it, they might more easily, after the training of the law, receive the more perfect principles of Christ; so also another earth, which receives into it all the saints, may first imbue and mould them by the institutions of the true and everlasting law, that they may more easily gain possession of those perfect institutions of heaven, to which nothing can be added; in which there will be, of a truth, that gospel which is called everlasting, and that Testament, ever new, which shall never grow old.

9. In this way, accordingly, v-e are to suppose that at the consummation and restoration of all things, those who make a gradual advance, and who ascend in the scale of improvement, will arrive in due measure and order at that land, and at that training which is contained in it, where they may be prepared for those better institutions to which no addition can be made. For, after His agents and servants, the Lord Christ, who is King of all, will Himself assume the kingdom; i. e. after instruction in the holy virtues. He will Himself instruct those wdio are capable of receiving Him in respect of His being wisdom, reigning in them until He has subjected them to the Father, who has subdued all things to Himself, i. e. that wdien they shall have been made capable of receiving God, God may be to them all in all. Then accordingly, as a necessary consequence, bodily nature will obtain that hifrhest condition to which nothing more can be added.

1 Ex. XXV. 40.

2 Jerome (Epistle to Avitus, No. 94) says that Origen, "after a most lengthened discussion, in which he asserts that all bodily nature is to be changed into attenuated and spiritual bodies, and that all substance is to be converted into one body of perfect purity, and more brilhant than any splendour mundisslmum et omni splendore imrius) and such as the human mind cannot now conceive," adds at the last, "And God will be ' all in all," so that the whole of bodily nature may be reduced into that substance which is better than all others, into the divine, viz.,

Havino- discussed, up to this point, the quauty of bodily nature? or of spiritual body, Ye leave it to the choice of the reader to determine what he shall consider best. And here we may bring the third book to a conclusion.

thr-n v liicli none is better." From which, since it seems to follow that God possesses a body, although of extreme tenuity (licet tenuissmum), Kufinus has either suppressed this view, or altered the meanmg of Origen's words (Ruseus).

OPJG.

BOOK ly.

TRANSLATED FEOM THE LATIN OF RUFINUS.

CHAPTER I.

THAT THE SCRIPTURES ARE DIVINELY INSPIRED.

1. But as it is not sufficient, in the discussion of matters of such importance, to entrust the decision to the human senses and to the human understanding, and to pronounce on tilings invisible as if they were seen by us,- we must, in order to ' Yisibiliter de invisibilibus pronunciare.

TRANSLATION FROM THE GREEK.

CHAPTER I.

ON THE INSPIRATION OF HOLY SCRIPTURE, AND HOW THE SAME IS TO BE READ AND UNDERSTOOD, AND WHAT IS THE REASON OF THE UNCERTAINTY IN IT; AND OF THE IMPOSSIBILITY OR IRRATIONALITY OF CERTAIN

The translation from the Greek is designedly literal, that the difference between the original and the jjaraphrase of Rufinus may be more clearly seen, 1. Since, in our investigation of matters of such Importance, not satisfied with the common opinions, and with the clear evidence of visible things,- we take in addition, for the proof of our statements, testimonies from what are believed rfi svoipyeicf, rav SAg'ro gy y.

establish the positions which we have laid down, adduce the testimony of Holy Scripture. And that this testimony may produce a sure and unh sitatiug belief, either with regard to what we have still to advc 'ice, or to what has been already stated, it seems necessary to s o jii the first place, that the Scriptures themselves are divij'i? i. e. were inspired by the Spirit of God. We shall therefore i 'ith all possible brevity draw forth from the Holy Script cs themselves, such evidence on this point as may nrorl-tce upon us a suitable impression, making our quotatiov ' from Moses, the first legislator of the Hebrew nation, from the words of Jesus Christ, the Author and Chief the Christian religious system. For although there have been numerous legislators among the Greeks and Bar-barif "S, and also countless teachers and philosophers wdio pi Qiessed to declare the truth, we do not remember any legislator who was able to produce in the minds of foreign nations a i affection and a zeal for him such as led them either yoluntarily to adopt his laws, or to defend them with all the Principis Christianonim rehgionis et dogmatis.

FEOM THE GEEEK.

by us to be divine writings, viz. from that wmich is called the Old Testament, and that which is styled the New, and endeavour by reason to confirm our faith; and as we have not yet spoken of the Scriptures as divine, come and let us, as if by way of an epitome, treat of a few points respecting them, laying down those reasons Avhich lead us to regard them as divine writino; s. And before makin"; use of the words of the writings themselves, and of the thin!; s which are exhibited in them, we must make the following statement regarding Moses and Jesus Christ, the lawgiver of the Plebrews, and the Introducer of the savincj doctrines accord-ing to Christianity. For, although there have been very many legislators among the. Greeks and Barbarians, and teachers who announced opinions which professed to be the truth, we have heard of no legislator who was able to imbue other nations with a zeal for the reception of his w ords;

FROil THE LATI efforts of their mind. No one, then, has been able to introduce and make known what seemed to, himself the truth among, I do not say many foreign nationjg but even amongst the individuals of one single nation, in s xch a manner that a knowledge and belief of the same should extend to all. And yet there can be no doubt that it was t j e wish of the len-is-lators that their laws should be observed by all men if possible; and of the teachers, that what apjpeared to themselves to be truth, should become known to all. n- i knowing that they could by no means succeed in producing. ij such mighty power within them as would lead foreign nat. 'ons to obey their laws, or have regard to their statements, they not venture even to essay the attempt, lest the failure (-) tbe undertaking should stamp their conduct wdth the mai. f imprudence. And yet there are throughout the whole Wv j; (- throughout all Greece, and all foreign countries coui-it-less individuals who have abandoned the laws of theji. country, and those whom they had believed to be gods, aurj have yielded themselves up to the obedience of the law of

FROM THE GREEK.

and although those who professed to philosophize about truth brought forward a great apparatus of apparent logical demonstration, no one has been able to impress what was deemed by him the truth upon other nations, or even on any number of persons worth mentioning in a single nation. And yet not only would the legislators have liked to enforce those laws which appeared to be good, if possible, upon the whole human race, but the teachers also" to have spread what they imagined to be truth everywhere throughout the w orld. But as they were unable to call men of other languages and from many nations to observe their laws, and accept their teaching, they did not at all attempt to do this, considering not unwisely the impossibility of such a result happening to them. Whereas all Greece, and the barbarous part of our world, contains innumerable zealots, wlio have deserted the laws of their fathers and the established gods, for the observance of the

Moses, and to the discipleship aud worship of Christ; and have done this, not without exciting against themselves the intense hatred of the worshippers of images, so as frequently to be exposed to cruel tortures from the latter, and sometimes even to be put- to death. And yet they embrace, and with all affection preserve, the words and teaching of Christ.

2. And we may see, moreover, how that religion itself grew up in a short time, making progress by the punishment and death of its worshippers, by the plundering of their goods, and by the tortures of every kind which they endured; and this result is the more surprising, that even the teachers of it themselves neither were men of skill, nor very numerous; and yet these words are preached throughout the whole world, so that Greeks and Barbarians, wise and foolish, adopt the doctrines of the Christian religion. From which it is no doubtful inference, that it is not by human power or might that the words of Jesus Christ come to prevail with all faith and power over the understandings and souls of all men. For, that these results were both predicted by Him, and Satis idonei. 2 Reljo-ionem Cliristianae doctrine.

FROM THE GREEK, laws of J loses and the discipleship of the words of Jesus Christ; although those who clave to the law of Moses were hated by the worshippers of images, and those wdio accepted the words of Jesus Christ were exposed, in addition, to the danger of death.

2. And if we observe how powerful the vrord has become in a very few years, notwithstanding that against those who acknowledged Christianity conspiracies were formed, and some of them on its account put to death, and others of them lost their property, and that, notwithstanding the small number of its teachers, it was preached everywhere throughout the world, so that Greeks and Barbarians, wise and foohsh, gave themselves up to the worship that is through Jesus, we have no difficulty in saying that the result is beyond established by divine answers proceeding from Him, is clear from His own words: " Ye sliall be brought before governors and kings for my sake, for a testimony against them and the Gentiles." And again: " This gospel of the kingdom shall be preached among all nations." And again: 'Many shall say to me in that day, Lord, Lord, havt!" re not eaten and drunk in Thy name, and in Thy name cast out devils? And I will say unto them. Depart from me, ye workers of iniquity, I never knew you." If these sayings, indeed, had been so uttered by Him, and yet if these predictions had not been fulfilled, they might perhaps appear to be untrue, and not to possess any authority. But now, when His declarations do pass into fulfilment, seeing they were predicted with such power and authority, it is most clearly shown to be true that He, when He w as made man, delivered to men the precepts of salvation.

3. What, then, are we to say of this, which the prophets 1 Matt. X. 18. 2 cf. Matt. xxiv. 14.- Cf. Matt. vii. 22, 23J

Fortasse minus vera esse viderentur. Salutaria prsecepta.

FROM THE GREEK.

any human power,- Jesus having taught with all authority and persuasiveness that His w ord should not be overcome; so that we may rightly regard as oracular responses those utterances of His, such as, "Ye shall be brought before governors and kings for my sake, for a testimony against them and the Gentiles;" ' and, "Many shall say unto me in that day. Lord, Lord, have we not eaten in Thy name, and drunk in Thy name, and in Thy name cast out devils? And I shall say unto them, Depart from me, ye workers of iniquity, I never knew you."" Now it was perhaps once probable that, in uttering these words. He spoke them in vain, so that they w'ere not true; but when that which was delivered with so much authority has come to pass, it shows that God, having really become man, delivered to men the doctrines of salvation. 3. And what need is there to mention also that it vas f sl ov '?" KcitCi clvqpoitrov TO 'itpu. yy cc il'vai.

s Matt. X. 18. ' Cf. Matt. vii. 22, 23.

had beforehand foretold of Him, that princes would not cease from Judah, nor leaders from between his thighs, until lie should come for Avliom it has been reserved (viz. the kingdom), and until the expectation of the Gentiles should cop-ie? For it is most distinctly evident from tlie history itself, from wucio is clearly seen at the present day, that from the times of Christ onwards there were no kinscs amcngst the Jews. Nay, even all those objects of Jewish priae, of which they vaunted so much, and in which they exulted, whether regarding the beauty of the temple or the ornaments of the altar, and all those sacerdotal fillets and robes of the high priests, were all destroyed together. For the prophecy was fulfilled which had declared, "For the children of Israel shall abide many days without king and prince: there shall be no victim, nor altar, nor priesthood, nor answers."[1] These testimonies, accordingly, we employ 1 Illse omnes ambitiones Judaicai.- Cf. Hos. iii. 4.

FROM THE GREEK.

predicted of Christ that then would the rulers fail from Judah, and the leaders from his thighs," wdien He came for whom it is reserved (the kingdom, namely); and that the expectation of the Gentiles should dwell in the land?"'[2] For it is clearly manifest from the history, and from what is seen at the present day, that from the times of Jesus there were no longer any wdio were called kings of the Jews;" all those Jewish institutions on which they prided themselves I mean those arrangements relating to the temple and the altar, and the offering of the service, and the robes of the high priest having been destroyed. For the prophecy was fulfilled which said, ' The children of Israel shall sit many days, there being no king, nor ruler, nor sacrifice, nor altar, nor priesthood, nor responses." '"" And these predictions wc employ to answer those who, in their perplexity as to the words spoken

Trpoi Yitivsri 6 XpigTo;. sk rai y Yiouu.

It: ihfiy. r, a ovk 'in fiotai'hii; ' Jovocciccu i' p'iiixTicoiv.

Cf. Hos. iii. 4. Quoted from the Septuagint.

against those who seem to assert that what is spoher. in Genesis by Jacob refers to Judah; and who say tha: there still remains a prince of the race of Judah he, vi'L., who is the prince of. their nation, whom they style Pati'iarch and that there cannot fail a ruler of his seed, who will remain until the advent of that Christ whom they picture tu themselves. But if the prophet's words be true, when he says, "The children of Israel shall abide many days without king, without prince; and there shall be no victim, nor altar, nor priesthood;" and if, certainly, since the overthrow of the temple, victims are neither offered, nor any altar found, nor any priesthood exists, it is most certain that, as it is written, princes have departed from Judah, and a leader from between his thifi hs, until the cominc of him for whom it has been reserved. It is established, then, that he is come for whom it has been reserved, and in whom is the expectation of the Gentiles. And this manifestly seems to be fulfilled in the 1 On the Patriarch of the Jews, cf. Milman's History of the Jeios vol. ii. p. 399 sq., and vol. iii. p. 7 sq.

2 Dent, xxxii.

FROM THE GREEK.

in Genesis by Jacob to Judah, assert that the Ethnarch, being of the race of Judah, is the ruler of the people, and that there will not fail some of his seed, until the advent of that Christ whom they figure to their imagination. But if " the children of Israel are to sit many days without a king, or ruler, or altar, or priesthood, or responses;" and if, since the temple was destroyed, there exists no longer sacrifice, nor altar, nor priesthood, it is manifest that the ruler has failed out of Judah, and the leader from between his thighs. And since the prediction declares that " the ruler shall not fail from Judah, and the leader from between his thighs, until what is reserved for him shall come," it is manifest that He is come to whom belongs what is reserved the expectation of the Gentiles. And this is clear from the multitude 1 Termed by Rufinus " Patriarch."

Chap, 1 ORIGEK DE PPJNCIPIIS.281 fkom the latix. multitude of those who have beheved on God through Christ oui- of the different nations.

4. In the song of Deuteronomy also, it is proplietically declared that, on account of the sins of the former people, there was to be an election of a foolish nation, no other, certainly, than that which was brought about by Christ; for thus the words run: " They have moved me to anger with their images, and I will stir them up to jealousy; I will arouse them to anger against a foolish nation." We may therefore evidently see how the Hebrews, who are said to have excited God's anger by means of those idols, which are no gods, and to have aroused His wrath by their images, were themselves also excited to jealousy by means of a foolish nation, which God liath chosen by the advent of Jesus Christ and His disciples. For the following is the language of the apostle: " For ye see your calling, brethren, how that not 1 Dcut. xxxii.- Deut. xxxii. 21.

FROM THE GREEK.

of the heathen who have believed ou God through Jesus Christ.

4. And in the song in Deuteronomy, also, it is prophetically made known that, on account of the sins of the former people, there was to be an election of foolish nations, which has been brought to pass by no other than by Jesus. " For they," He says, " moved me to jealousy with that which is not God, they have provoked me to anger with their idols; and I will move them to jealousy with those which are not a people, and will provoke them to anger with a foolish nation." Now it is possible to understand with all clearness how the Hebrews, who are said to have moved God to jealousy by that which is not God, and to have provoked Him to anger by their idols, were themselves aroused to jealousy by that which was not a people the foolish nation, namely, which God chose by the advent of Jesus Christ and His disciples. We see, inaeed, " our callini, that not many Deut. xxxii.- rov Trporepov T xov. " Deut. xxxii. 21.

many wise men among you after the flesh, not many mighty, not many noble (are called): but God has chosen the foolish things of the world, and the things which are not, to destroy the things which formerly existed." Carnal Israel, therefore, should not boast; for such is the term used by the apostle: " No flesh, I say, should glory in the presence of God."- 5. What are we to say, moreover, regarding those prophecies of Christ contained in the Psalms, especially the one with the superscription, "A song for the Beloved;" in which it is stated that " His tongue is the pen of a ready waiter; fairer than the children of men;" that " grace is poured into His lips?" Now", the indication that grace has been poured upon His lips is this, that, after a short period had elapsed for He taught only during a year and some months the whole world, nevertheless, became filled with His doctrine, 1 1 Cor. i. 26-28. Quae erant prius.

2 1 Cor. i. 29. 3 Ps. liv. 2, 3.

FROM THE GREEK.

wise men after the flesh, not many mighty, not many noble (are called); but God hath chosen the foolish things of the world to confound the wise; and base things, and things that are despised, hath God chosen, and things that are not, to bring to nought the tilings which formerly existed;" and let not the Israel according to the flesh, which is called by the apostle ' flesh," boast in the presence of God.

5. And what are we to say regarding the prophecies of Christ in the Psalms, there being a certain ode with the superscription "For the Beloved," whose "tongue" is said to be the " pen of a ready writer, wlio is fairer than the sons of men," since "grace was poured on His lips V For a proof that grace was j oured on His lips is this, that although tlie period of His teaching was short for He taught some-

Cf. 1 Cor. i. 26-28. " The things which formerly existed, roi-Trpo-2 Ps. xlv. 42.

and with faith in His reh'gion. There arose, tlien, "in His days righteous men, and abundance of peace," abiding even to the end, which end is entitled "the taking away of the moon:" and "His dominion sliall extend from sea to sea, and from the river to the ends of the earth."" There was a sign also given to the house of David. For a virgin conceived, and bare Emmanuel, which, when interpreted, signifies, "God with us: know it, O nations, and be overcome."' For we are conquered and overcome, who are of the Gentiles, and remain as a kind of spoils of His victory, who have subjected our necks to His grace. Even the place of His birth was predicted in the prophecies of licah, who said, "And thou, Bethlehem, land of Judah, art by no means small among the leaders of Judah: for out of thee shall come forth a Leader, who shall rule my people Israel."" The 1 Cf. Ps. Ixxii. 7.- Ps. Ixxii. 8.

3 Cf. Isa. viii. 8, 9. Quoted from tlie Septuagint.

4 Cf. Mic. V. 2 and Matt. ii. G.

FROM THE GREEK.

where about a year and a few months the world has been filled with His teaching, and with the worship of God established through Him. For there arose " in His days righteousness and abundance of peace," which abides until the consummation, which has been called the takino; awav of the moon; and He continues " ruling from sea to sea, and from the rivers to the ends of the earth."- And to the house of David has been given a sign: for the Virgin bore, and was pregnant, and brought forth a son, and His name is Emmanuel, which is, "God with us;" and as the same prophet says, the prediction has been fulfilled. " God is with us; know it, O nations, and be overcome; ye who are strong, be vanquished:" for we of the heathen have been overcome and vanquished, we who have been taken by the grace of His 1 Ps. Ixxii. 7.-' Ps. Ixxii. 8.

Quoted from the Septuagint.

weeks of years, also, which the prophet Daniel had predicted, extending to the leadership of Christ, have been fulfilled. Moreover, He is at hand, who in the book of Job is said to be about to destroy the huge beast, who also gave power to His own disciples to tread on serpents and scorpions, and on all the power of the enemy, without being injured by him. But if any one will consider the journeys of Christ's apostles throughout the different places, in which as His messengers the preached the gospel, he will find that both what they ventured to undertake is beyond the power of man, and what they were enabled to accomplish is from God alone. If we consider how men, on hearing that a new doctrine was introduced by these, were able to receive them; or rather, when desiring often to destroy them, they were prevented by 1 Cf. Dan. ix. 4. Ad ducem Christum; "To Messiah the Prince," anth. vers.

2 The allusion is perhaps to Job xli. 1.

FROM THE GREEK.

teaching. The place also of His birth has been foretold in the prophecies of Micah: " For thou, Bethlehem," he says, " land of Judah, art by no means the least among the rulers of Judah; for out of thee shall come forth a Ruler, who shall rule my people Israel." And according to Daniel, seventy Aveeks were fulfilled until the coming of Christ the Ruler. And He came, who, according to Job, has subdued the great fish, and has given power to His true disciples to tread upon serpents and scorpions, and all the power of the enemy, without sustaining any injury from them. And let one notice also the universal advent of the apostles sent by Jesus to announce the gospel, and he will see both that the undertaking was beyond human power, and that the commandment came from God. And if we examine how men, on hearing new doctrines, and strange words, yielded themselves up to these teachers, being overcome, amid the very desire to plot 1 Cf. Mic. V. 2 with Matt. ii. 6. 2 cf. Dan. ix. 24.

2 Cf. Job xl. and xli. to tycoctiro, Cf. Luke x. 19.

from the latin. a divine power whicli was in them, we shall find that in this nothing w as effected by human strength, but that the whole was the result of the divine power and providence, signs and wonders, manifest beyond all doubt, bearing testimony to their word and doctrine.

6. These points now being briefly established, viz. regarding the deity of Christ, and the fulfilment of all that w as prophesied respecting Him, I think that this position also has been made good, viz. that the Scriptures themselves, which contained these predictions, were divinely inspired, those, namely, which had either foretold His advent, or the power of His doctrine, or the bringing over of all nations to His obedience. To which this remark must be added, that the divinity and inspiration both of the predictions of the prophets and of the law of Moses have been clearly revealed and confirmed, especially since the advent of Christ into the world. For before the fulfilment of those events which were predicted by them, they could not, although

FKOM THE GEEEK.

against them, hy a divine power that watched over these teachers, we shall not be incredulous as to whether they also-wrought miracles, God bearing witness to their words both by signs, and wonders, and divers miracles.

6. And while ve thus briefly demonstrate the deity of Christ, and in so doing make use of the prophetic declarations regarding Him, w e demonstrate at the same time that the writings which prophesied of Him were divinely inspired; and that those documents which announced His coming and His doctrine were given forth with all power and authority, and that on this account they obtained the election from the Gentiles. We must say, also, that the divinity of the pro- j) etic declarations, and the spiritual nature of the law of t., j Mioses, shone forth after the advent of Christ. For before ' the "idvent of Christ it was not altogether possible to exhibit r mani st proofs of the divine inspiration of the ancient f-Script ' s; whereas His coming led those who might suspect 1 sj" lu l itoy. fi.- ix rovtO r j xtto tuu ksvu'j iky. oyijg KSKpurrtkorcc.

true and inspired by God, be shown to be so, because they were as yet unfulfilled. But the coming of Christ was a declaration that their statements were true and divinely inspired, although it was certainly doubtful before that whether there would be an accomplishment of those things which had been foretold.

If any one, moreover, consider the words of the prophets Avith all the zeal and reverence which they deserve, it is certain that, in the perusal and careful examination thus given them, he will feel his mind and senses touched by a divine breath, and will acknowledge that the words which he reads were no human utterances, but the language of God; and from his own emotions he will feel that these books were the composition of no human skill, nor of any mortal eloquence, but, so to speak, of a style that is divine. The splendour of Christ's advent, therefore, illuminating the law of Moses by the light of truth, has taken away that veil which had been placed over the letter of the law, and has unsealed, for every one who believes upon Him, all the blessino-s which were concealed by the coverincj of the word.

7. It is, however, a matter attended with considerable Divino, ut ita dixerim, cotliurno.

FROM TPIE GREEK.

the law and the prophets not to be divine, to the clear conviction that they were composed by the aid of heavenly grace. And he who reads the words of the prophets with care and attention, feeling by the very perusal the traces of the divinity- that is in them, will be led by his own emotions to believe that those words which have been deemed to be the words of God are not the compositions of men. The light, moreover, wdiich was contained in the law of Mose? but which had been concealed by a veil, shone forth at t e advent of Jesus, the veil being taken away, and those bh. ss-ings, the shadow of which was contained in the letter, coining forth gradually to the knowledge of men.

7. It would be tedious now to enumerate the most "ancient labour, to point out, in every instance, liow and when the predictions of the prophets were fulfilled, so as to appear to confirm those who are in doubt, seeing it is possible for every one who wishes to become more thoroughly acquainted with these things, to gather abundant proofs from the records of the truth themselves. But if the sense of the letter, which is beyond man, does not appear to present itself at once, on the first glance, to those wdio are less versed in divine discipline, it is not at all to be wondered at, because divine things are brought down somewhat slowdy to the comprehension of men, and elude the view in proportion as one is either sceptical or unw orth3 For although it is certain that all things which exist in this world, or take place in it, are ordered by the providence of God, and certain events indeed do appear with sufficient clearness to be under the disposal of His providential government, yet others again unfold themselves so mysteriously and incomprehensibly, that the plan of Divine

FROM THE GREEK.

prophecies respecting each future event, in order that the doubter, being impressed by their divinity, may lay aside all hesitation and distraction, and devote himself with his whole soul to the words of God. But if in every part of the Scriptures the superhuman element of thought does not seem to present itself to the uninstructed, that is not at all A onderful; for, with respect to the works of that providence which embraces the wdiole world, some show with the utmost clearness that they are works of providence, while others are so concealed as to seem to furnish ground for unbelief with respect to that God who orders all things w ith unspeakable skill and power. For the artistic plan" of a providential Ruler is not so evident in those matters belono-ino;

to the earth, as in the case of the sun, and moon, and stars; and not so clear in what relates to human occurrences, as it is in the souls and bodies of animals, the object and reason of the impulses, and phantasies and natr. res of animals, and the structure of their bodies, being carefully ascertained by those who attend to

Providence with regard to them is completely concealed; so that it is occasionally helieved by some that particular occurrences do not belong to the plan of Providence, because the principle eludes their grasp, according to which the works of Divine Providence are administered with indescribable skill; which principle of administration, however, is not equally concealed from all. For even among men themselves, one individual devotes less consideration to it, another more; while by every man, He who is on earth, whoever is the inhabitant of heaven, is more acknowledged.-' And the 1 " Nam et inter ipsos homines ab alio minus, ab alio amplius conside-ratur: plus vero ab omni liomine, qui in terris est, quis-qviis ille est coeli habitator, agnoscitur." The translation of Rufinus, as Eedepenning remarks, seems very confused. Probably also the text is corrupt. The Greek without doubt gives the genuine thought of Origen. By omitting the cib we approximate to the Greek, and get: " but he, whoever he be, who is inhabitant of heaven, is better known than any man who is on the earth;" or according to the punctuation in the old editions, "but he who is inhabitant of heaven is better known than any man on earth, whoever he be."

FROM THE GREEK.

these things. But as the doctrine of providence is not at ill weakened (on account of those things which are not

"understood) in the eyes of those who have once honestly ac- cepted it, so neither is the divinity of Scripture, which extends f to the whole of it, lost on account of the inability of our j weakness to discover in every expression the hidden splen-

Idour of the doctrines veiled in common and unattractive phraseology. For we have the treasure in earthen vessels, that the excellency of the power of God may shine forth, and that it may not be deemed to proceed from us who are but human beings. For if the hackneyed methods of demon-

"Stration common among men, contained in the books of

Scpo'B ot Toij 'Tvpog riy. cil hszc. r'iuog svpiakOfiiuov rolg rovtau l gao wlvof, TTtpl rcx, g opfi g, x, ci. i rag Cpoe, vrcx. Gioigj x, oc, i (pvastg ruu aav,-. cd roig tcoi. roi. ayaVxg ray acof ccrau.

XpsokOTrehxi.

h ihn'hfi Kccl svkotra povvirqi T i it. (. a.67i oi svy, iv(Zi.

frO: M THE LATIN.

nature of bodies is clear to us in one way, that of trees in another, that of animals in a tliird; the nature of souls, again, is concealed in a different way; and the manner in which the diverse movements of rational understandino; s are ordered by Providence, eludes the view of men in a greater degree, and even, in my opinion, in no small degree that of the angels also. But as the existence of divine providence is not refuted by those especially who are certain of its existence, but who do not comprehend its workings or arrangements by the powers of the human mind; so neither will the divine inspiration of holy Scripture, which extends throughout its body, be believed to be non-existent, because the weakness of our understandino; is unable to trace out the hidden and secret meaning in each individual word, the treasure of divine wisdom beins: hid in the vul jar and un-polished vessels of words, as the apostle also points out vvhen he says, "We have this treasure in earthen vessels," ' that the virtue of the divine power may shine out the more brightly, no colouring of human elequence being intermingled with the truth of the doctrines. For if our books induced men to believe because they were composed either by rhetorical arts or by the wisdom of philosophy, then undoubtedly our faith would be considered to be based on the art of words, and on human wisdom, and not upon the power of God; whereas it is now known to all that the word of this preaching has 1 In vilioribus et incomptis verborum vasculis. Cf, 2 Cor. iv. 7.

FKOM THE GREEK.

the Bible, had been successful in producing conviction, then our faith would rightly have been supposed to rest on the wisdom of men, and not on the power of God; but now it is manifest to every one who lifts up his eyes, that the word and preaching have not prevailed among the multitude 'by persuasive words of wisdom, but by demonstration of the Spirit and of power." Wherefore, since a celestial or even a super-celestial power compels us to worship the only 12 Cor. ii. 4. ORIG. T been so accepted by numbers thronghont almost the whole world, because they understood their belief to rest not on the persuasive words of human wisdom, but on the manifestation of the Spirit and of power. On which account, being led by a heavenly, nay, by a more than heavenly power, to faith and acceptance, that we m. ay worship the sole Creator of all things as our God, let us also do our utmost endeavour, by abandoning the language of the elements of Christ, which are but the first beginnings of wisdom, to go on to perfection, in order that that wisdom which is given to them who are perfect, may be given to us also. For such is the promise of him to whom was entrusted the preaching of this wisdom, in the words: ' Howbeit we speak wisdom among them that are perfect; yet not the wisdom of this world, nor of the princes of this world, who will be brought to nought;"" by which he shows that this wisdom of ours has nothing in common, so far as regards the beauty of language, with the wisdom of this world. This wisdom, then, will be inscribed more clearly and perfectly on our hearts, if it be made known to us according to the revelation of the mystery v hich has been hid from eternity, but now is manifest through the Scriptures of prophecy, and the advent of our Lord and Saviour Jesus Christ, to whom be glory for ever. Amen. Ad fidem credulitatemque. 1 Cor. ii. 6. Temporibus eternis.

FROM THE GREEK.

Creator, let us leave the doctrine of the beginning of Christy i. e. the elements,- and endeavour to go on to perfection, in order that the wisdom spoken to the perfect may be spoken to us also. For he who possesses it promises to speak wisdom among them that are perfect, but another wisdom than that of this world, and of the rulers of this world, which is brouf ht to nouixht. And this wisdom will be distinctly. stamped upon us, and will produce a revelation of the 'mystery that was kept silent in the eternal ages, but now has been manifested through the prophetic Scriptures, and

Many, not understanding tlie Scriptures in a spiritual sense, but incorrectly have fallen into lieresies.

8. These particulars, then, being briefly stated regarding the inspiration of the sacred Scriptures by the Holy Spirit, it seems necessary to explain this point also, viz. how certain persons, not reading them correctly, have given themselves over to erroneous opinions, inasmuch as the procedure to be followed, in order to attain an understanding' of the holy writings, is unknown to many. The Jews, in fine, owing to the hardness of their heart, and from a desire to appear wise in their own eyes, have not believed in our Lord and Saviour, judging that those statements which were uttered respecting Him ought to be understood literally, i. e. that He ought in a sensible and visible manner to preach deliverance to the captives, and first build a city which they truly deem the city of God, and cut off at the same time the chariots of Ephraim," and the horse from Jerusalem: that He ought also to eat butter and honey, in order to 1 Male. 2 cf. Zech. ix. 10. qi ig. vii. 15.

FROM THE GREEK.

the appearance of our Lord and Saviour Jesus Christ, to whom be glory for ever and ever. Amen.

8. Having spoken thus briefly on the subject of the; divine inspiration of the holy Scriptures, it is necessary to proceed to the consideration of the manner in which they are to be read and understood, seeing numerous errors have been committed in consequence of the method in which the holy documents" ought to be examined, not having been discovered by the multitude. For both the hardened in heart, and the ignorant persons belonging to the circumcision, have not believed on our Saviour, thinking that they I are following the language of the prophecies respecting Him, I and not perceiving in a manner palpable to their senses that He had proclaimed liberty to the captives, nor that He had clioose the good before He sliould come to know how to bring forth evil. They think, also, that it has been predicted that the wolf that four-footed animal is, at the coming of Christ, to feed with the lambs, and the leopard to lie down with kids, and the calf and the bull to pasture with lions, and that they are to be led by a little child to the pasture; that the ox and the bear are to lie down together in the green fields, and that their young ones are to be fed together; that lions also will frequent stalls with the oxen, and feed on straw. And seeing that, according to history, there was no accomplishment of any of those things predicted of Him, in which they believed the signs of Christ's advent were especially to be observed, they refused to acknowledge the presence of our Lord Jesus Christ; nay, contrary to all the principles of human and divine law, i. e. contrary to the faith of prophecy, they crucified Him for assuming to Himself the name of Christ. Thereupon the heretics, reading that it is written in the law, "A fire has been kindled in mine anger;" and that " I the Lord am a jealous God, visiting the sins

Ut priusquam cognosceret proferre malum, eligeret boniira. Contra jus fasque. " Cf. Jer. xv. 14.

FROM THE GREEK built up what they truly consider the city of God, nor cut off " the chariots of Ephraim, and the horse from Jerusalem," nor eaten butter and honey, and, before knowing or preferring the evil, had selected the good. And thinking, moreover, that it was prophesied that the wolf the four-footed animal was to feed with the lamb, and the leopard to lie down with the kid, and the calf and bull and lion to feed together, being led by a little child, and that the ox and bear were to pasture together, their young ones growing up together, and that the lion was to eat straw like the ox: seeing none of these things visibly accomplished during the advent of Him who is believed by us to be Christ, they did not accept our Lord Jesus; but, as having called Himself 1 Cf. Zech. ix. 10. 2 Cf. Isa. vii. 15. Cf. Isa. xi. 6, 7.

of the fatliers upon tlie cliilclren unto tlie third and fourth generation;" and that "it repenteth me that I anointed Saul to be king;"""' and, "I am the Lord, who make peace and create evil;" and again, "There is not evil in a city Avhich the Lord hath not done;"" and, "Evils came down from the Lord upon the gates of Jerusalem;" " and, "An evil spirit from the Lord plagued Saul;" and reading many otlier passages similar to these, whicli are found in Scripture, they did not venture to assert that these were not the Scriptures of God, but they considered them to be the words of that creator God whom the Jews worshipped, and who, they judged, ought to be regarded as just only, and not also as good; but that the Saviour had come to announce to us a more perfect God, who, they allege, is not the creator of the world, tliere being different and discordant opinions among them even on this very point, because, when they 1 Cf. Ex. XXV. 5. 2 cf. 1 Sam. xv. 11. cf. Isa. xlv. 7.

Cf. Amos iii. IG. cf. Mic. i. 12. Cf. 1 Sam. xviii. 10.

rr. OM THE GREEK.

Christ improperl ', they crucified Him. And those belonging to heretical sects reading this statement, "A fire has been kindled in mine anger;" and this, "I am a jealous God, visiting the iniquities of the fathers upon the children unto the third and fourth generation;" ' and this, "I re-)ent of having anointed Saul to be king;" and this, "I am a God that Jniiketli peace, and createth eyil;" and, among others, this, "There is not wickedness in the city 1 which the Lord hath not done;" and again this, "Evils I came down from the Lord upon the gates of Jerusalem;" and, "An evil spirit from the Lord plagued Saul;" and countless otlier passages like these they have not ventured-to disbelieve these as the Scriptures of God; but believing! tliem to be the words of the Demiurge, whom the Jews 1 'Trapx, TO Qiov. Cf. Jor. xv. 14. " Cf. Ex. xxv. 5.

4 Cf. 1 Sam. xv. 11. '"' Cf Iga xlv. 7. 6 Qf. Amos iii. 6.

7 Cf. Mic. i. 12. Cf. 1 Sam. xvi. 15.

once depart from a belief in God the Creator, who is Lord of all, they have given themselves over to various inventions and fables, devising certain fictions, and asserting that some things were visible, and made by one God, and that certain other things were invisible, and were created by another, according to the vain and fanciful suggestions of their own minds. But not a few also of the more simple of those, who appear to be restrained within the faith of the church, are of opinion that there is no greater God than the Creator, holding in this a correct and sound opinion: and yet they entertain reojardlnoj Him such views as would not be enter-tained regarding the most unjust and cruel of men.

9. Now the reason of the erroneous apprehension of all these points on the part of those whom we have mentioned above, is no other than this, that holy Scripture is not understood by them according to its spiritual, but according to its

FROM THE GREEK.

worship, they thought that as the Demiurge was an imperfect land unbenevolent God, the Saviour had come to announce a more perfect Deity, who, they say, is not the Demiurge, being of different opinions regarding Him; and having once departed from the Demiurge, who is the only uncreated God, they have given themselves up to fictions, inventing to themselves hypotheses, according to wdiich they imagine that there are some things which are visible, and certain other things which are not visible, all which are the fancies of their own minds. And yet, indeed, the more simple among those who profess to belong to the church have supposed that there is no deity greater than the Demiurge, being right in so thinking, while they imagine regarding Him such things as would not be believed of the most savage and unjust of mankind. ' 9. Now the cause, in all the points previously enumerated, of the false opinions, and of the impious statements or ignorant assertions about God, appears to be nothing else than the not understanding the Scripture according to its from the latin. literal meaning. And therefore we shall endeavour, so far as our moderate capacity will permit, to point out to those who believe the holy Scriptures to be no human compositions, but to be written by inspiration of the Holy Spirit, and to be transmitted and entrusted to us by the will of God tlie Father, through His only-begotten Son Jesus Christ, what appears to us, who observe things by a right way of understanding, to be the standard and discipline delivered to the apostles by Jesus Christ, and which they handed down in succession to their posterity, the teachers of the holy church. Now, that there are certain mystical economies indicated in holy Scripture, is admitted by all, I think, even the simplest of believers. But what these are, or of what kind they are, 1 The text, as it stands, is probably corrupt: " Propter quod cona-bimur pro mediocritate sensus nostri his, qui credunt Scripturas sanctas lion humana verba ahqua esse composita, sed sancti Spiritus inspiratione conscripta, et voluntate Dei patris per unigenitum fihum suum Jesum Christum nobis quoque esse tradita et commissa, quse nobis videntur, recta via intelligentise observantibiis, demonstrare illam regiilam et dis-ciphnam, quam ab Jesu Christo traditam sibi apostoh per successionem posteris quoque suis, sanctam ecclesiam docentibus, tradideruut."

2 Dispensationcs.

FH05I THE GREEK.

spiritual meaning, but the interpretation of it agreeably to the mere letter. And therefore, to those who believe that the sacred books are not the compositions of men, but that they were composed by inspiration of the Holy Spirit,; agreeably to the will of the Father of all things through A

Jesus Christ, and that they have come down to us, we must', v oint out the ways of interpreting them which appear KP v Jorrect to us, who cling to the standard" of the heavenly TV rjL nurcli of Jesus Christ according to the sue cess ion of. tlie Tit)ostles. Now, that there are certain mystical economies ' ade known by the holy Scriptures, all even the most I. ni)le of those who adhere to the word-have believed: but oil- , at these are, candid and modest individuals confess that

"6-7: 177'JOlag. " Kccvovog, lie who is rightly minded, and not overcome with the vice of boasting, will scrupulously acknowdedge himself to be ignorant. For if any one, e. g., were to adduce the case of tlie dau2; hters of Lot, who seem, contrary to the law of God,"" to have had intercourse with their father, or that of the two wives of Abraham, or of the two sisters who were married to Jacob, or of the two handmaids who increased the number of his sons, wdiat other answer could be returned than that these were certain mysteries, and forms of spiritual things, but that we are ignorant of wdiat nature they are? Nay, even when we read of the construction of the tabernacle, we deem it certain that the written descriptions are the figures of certain hidden things; but to adapt these to their appropriate standards, and to open up and discuss every individual point, I consider to be exceedingly difficult, not to say impossible. That that description, however, is, as I have said, full of mysteries, does not escape even the common understanding. But all the narrative portion, relating either to the marriages, or to the begetting of the children, or to Religiosius. Contra fas. Sacramenta qusedam.

FROM THE GREEK.

, they know not. If, then, one were to be perplexed about ' the intercourse of Lot with his daughters, and about the two wives of Abraham, and the two sisters married to Jacob, and the two handmaids who bore him children, they can return, no other answer than this, that these are mysteries not under- lv stood by us. Nay, also, wdien the description of the fitting out of the tabernacle is read, believing that wdiat is written i? a type, they seek to adapt wdiat they can to each particubj, related about the tabernacle, not beino" wronc so far as re gards their belief that the tabernacle is a type of soinetjiing, h erring sometimes in adapting the description of that of whicj the tabernacle is a type, to some special thing in a maiin worthy of Scripture. And all the history that is consider to tell of marriao; es, or the beo-ettino; of children, or of wr battles of different kinds, or to any other histories whatever, Avliat else can they be supposed to be, save the forms and figures of hidden and sacred things? As men, however, make little effort to exercise their intellect, or imagine that they possess knowledge before they really learn, the consequence is that they never begin to have knowledge; or if there be no want of a desire, at least, nor of an instructor, and if divine knowledge be sought after, as it ought to be, in a religious and holy spirit, and in the hope that many points will be opened up by the revelation of God since to human sense they are exceedingly difficult and obscure then, perhaps, ho who seeks in such a manner will find what it is lawful to discover.

10. But lest this difficulty perhaps should be supposed to exist only in the language of the prophets, seeing the prophetic style is allowed by all to abound in figures and enigmas, what do we find when we come to the Gospels'? Is there not hidden there also an inner, namely a divine sense, wdiicli is revealed by that grace alone which he had received who said, "But we have the mind of Christ, that 1 Fas.

FROM THE GREEK.

or any histories whatever that are in circulation among the multitude, they declare to be types; but of what in each individual instance, partly owing to their habits not being thoroughly exercised partly, too, owing to their precipitation sometimes, even when an individual does happen to be well trained and clear-sighted, owing to the excessive difficulty of discovering things on the part of men, the nature of each particular regarding these types is not clearly ascertained.

10. And what need is there to speak of the prophecies, which we all know to be filled with enigmas and dark savings? And if we come to the Gospels, the exact understanding of these also, as being the mind of Christ, requires the grace that was given to him who said, "But we have the mind of Christ, that we might know the things freely we miglit know the things freely given to us by God. Which thinors

also we speak, not in the words which man's wisdom teaches, but which the Spirit teacheth?" ' And if one now were to read the revelations which were made to John, how amazed would he not be that there should be contained within them so great an amount of Indden, ineffable mysteries, in which it is clearly understood, even by those who cannot comprehend idiat is concealed, that something certainly is concealed. And yet are not the epistles of the apostles, which seem to some to be plainer, filled with meanings so profound, that by means of them, as by some small receptacle, the clearness of incalculable light appears to be poured into those who are capable of understanding the meaning of divine wisdom? And therefore, because this is the case, and because there are many who go wrong in this life, I do not consider that it is easy to pronounce, without danger, that any one knows or understands those things, which, in order to be opened up, need the key of knowledge; 1 Cf. 1 Cor. ii. "16 and 12, 11.

2 Tantam occultationem ineffabiliiini sacramentorum.

Per breve quoddam receptaculum. Immeusge lucis claritas.

FROM THE GREEK.

given to us by God. Which things also we speak, not in the words which man's wisdom teacheth, but which the Spirit teacheth." And who, on reading the revelations made to John, would not be amazed at the unspeakable mysteries therein concealed, and which are evident even to him who does not comprehend what is written? And to what person, skilful in investigating words, would the epistles of the apostles seem to be clear and easy of understanding, since even in them there are countless numbers of most profound ideas, which, issuing forth as by an aperture, admit of no rapid comprehension? And therefore, since these things 1 1 Cor. ii. 12, 13, and 16 ad fin. I5pux, ihiv cipop r, u '7rcnpsx, o'jrcuv.

which key, the Saviour declared, lay with those who were skilled in the law. And here, although it is a digression, I think we should inquire of those who assert that before the advent of the Saviour there was no truth among those who were engaged in the study of the law, how it could be said by our Lord Jesus Christ that the keys of knowledge were with them, who had the books of the prophets and of the law in their hands. For thus did He speak: " Woe unto you, ye teachers of the law, who have taken away the key of knowledge: ye entered not in yourselves, and them who wished to enter in ye hindered."

11. But, as we had begun to observe, the way which seems to us the correct one for the understandinor of the

Scriptures, and for the investigation of their meaning, we consider to be of the following kind: for we are instructed by Scripture itself in regard to the ideas which we ought to form of it. In the Proverbs of Solomon we find some such 1 Luke xi. 52.

FROM THE GREEK.

are so, and since innumerable individuals fall into mistakes, it is not safe in reading the Scriptures to declare that one easily understands what needs the key of knowledge, which the Saviour declares is with the lawyers. And let those answer who will not allow that the truth was with these before the advent of Cln'ist, how the key of knowledge is said by our Lord Jesus Christ to be with those who, as they allege, had not the books which contain the secrets- of knowledge, and perfect mysteries. For His words run thus: " Woe unto you, ye lawyers! for ye have taken away the key of knowledge: ye have not entered in yourselves, and them that were entering in ye hindered."

11. The way, then, as it appears to us, in which we ought to deal with the Scriptures, and extract from them their meaning, is the following, which has been ascertained from the Scriptures themselves. By Solomon in the Proverbs ectToppyitcc, Trx'jrst vj y. vat7: pix. 3 Luke xi. 52.

Book iv.

FEOM THE LATIN.

rule as the following laid down, respecting the consideration of holy Scripture: " And do thou," he says, " describe these things to thyself in a threefold manner, in counsel and knowledge, and that thou mayest answer the words of truth to those who have proposed them to thee." Each one, then, ouo; ht to describe in his own mind, in a threefold manner, the understanding of the divine letters, that is, in order that all the more simple individuals may be edified, so to speak, by the very body of Scripture; for such we term that common and historical sense: while, if some have commenced to make considerable progress, and are able to see something more than that, they may be edified by the very soul of Scripture. Those, again, who are perfect, and who resemble those of whom the apostle says, ' We speak 1 Cf. Prov. xxii. 20, 21. The Masoretic text reads, T T 2T '2 hn

D DX n"'L b ridj j np; t c ' v Srh: nj;'i'i ni ybn(D" f', T eri) uszh

FEOM THE GREEK.

we find some such rule as this enjoined respecting the divine doctrines of Scripture: " And do thou portray them in a threefold manner, in counsel and knowledge, to answer words of truth to them who propose them to thee." The individual ought, then, to portray the ideas of holy Scripture in a threefold manner upon his own soul; in order that the simple man may be edified by the " flesh," as it were, of the, Y"i; Scripture, for so we name the obvious sense; while he who- has ascended a certain way may be edified by the " soul," as it were. The perfect man, again, and he who resembles

The Septuagint: K; av Bg dtroypx pon a, vroi o-eotvra rpiaaz; slg (iavt Ytv y. otl yvoiuiu ttrl ro 'Trt tx. rog rr g tcxpciccg aov oiqcx.(7x, co cvv as Ayj ij 'koyov X. XI yvcoaiu oct r, ' vtrockOvsiu, rou ci'Trokpi'isadce. i as T oyovg dt rihlotg Tolg Trpo a-hy. ofisvoig aoi. The Vulgate reads: Ecce, descripsi earn tibi tripliciter in cogitationibus et scientia, ut ostenderem tibi firmitatem et eloquia veritatis, respondere ex his illis, qui miseruut te.

Cf. note 1, ut supra.

wisdom among them that are perfect, but not the YIsclom of this yorlcl, nor of the princes of this world, who will he brought to nought; but we speak the wisdom of God, hidden in a mystery, which God hath decreed before the ages unto our glory;" all such as these may be edified by the spiritual law itself (which has a shadow of good things to come), as if by the Spirit. For as man is said to consist of body, and soul, and spirit, so also does sacred Scripture, which has been granted by the divine bounty for the salvation of man; which we see pointed out, moreover, in the little book of TJie Shepherd, which seems to be despised by some, where Hermas is commanded to write two little books, and afterwards to announce to the presbyters of the church what he learned from the Spirit. For these are the words that are written: " And you will write," he says, " two books; and you will give the one to Clement, and the other to Grapte." And let Grapte admonish the widows and orphans, 1 Cor. ii. 6, 7. Largitione.

Cf. Ante-Xicene Library, vol. containieg " Apostolic Fathers," p. o31 and note.

FROM THE GREEK.

those spoken of by the apostle, when he says, We speak wisdom among them that are perfect, but not the wisdom of the world, nor of the rulers of this world, who come to nought; but we speak the wisdom of God in a mystery, the hidden wisdom, which God hath ordained before the ages, unto our glory," n'J y receive edification from the spiritual law, which has a shadow of good things to come. For (is man consists of body, and soul, and spirit, so in the san e way does Scripture, which has been arranged to be given by God for the salvation of men. And therefore we deduce this also from a book which is despised by some Th Shepherd in respect of the command given to Hennas to write two books, and after so doing to announce to the presbyters of the church what he had learned from the 1 1 Cor. ii. 6, 7.

and let Clement send through all the cities which ai abroad, while you will announce to the presbyters of the church." Grapte, accordingly, who is commanded to admonish the orphans and widows, is the pure understanding of the letter itself; by which those youthful minds are admonished, who have not yet deserved to have God as their Father, and are on that account styled orphans. They, again, are the widows, who have withdrawn themselves from the unjust man, to whom they had been united contrary to law; but who have remained widows, because they have not yet advanced to the stage of being joined to a heavenly Bridegroom. Clement, moreover, is ordered to send into those cities which are abroad what is written to those individuals who already are withdrawing from the letter, as if the meaning were to those souls who, being built up by this means, have begun to rise above the cares of the body and the desires of the flesh; wdile he himself, who had learned from the Holy Spirit, is commanded to announce, not by letter nor by book, but by

FROM THE GREEK.

Spirit. The words are as follow: " You will write two books, and give one to Clement, and one to Grapte. And Grapte shall admonish the widows and the orphans, and Clement will send to the cities abroad, while you will announce to the presbyters of the church." Now Grapte, wdio admonishes the widows and the orphans, is the mere letter of Scripture, which admonishes those who are yet children in soul, and not able to call God their Father, and who are on that account styled orphans, admonishing, moreover, those who no longer have an unlawful bridegroom, but who remain widows, because they have not yet become worthy of the heavenly Bridegroom; while Clement, who is already beyond the letter, is said to send what is written to the cities abroad, as if we were to call these the " souls," who are above the influence of bodily affections and C. Ante-Nicene Library, vol. "Apostolic Fathers," p. 331 and note.

the living voice, to the presbyters of the churcli of Christ, i. e. to those who possess a mature faculty of wisdom, capable of receiving spiritual teaching.

12. This point, indeed, is not to be passed by without notice, viz. that there are certain passages of Scripture wliere this " body," as we termed it, i. e. this inferential historical sense, is not always found, as we shall prove to be the case in the following pages, but where that wliich we termed ' sonl" or 'spirit" can only be understood. And

tliis, I think, is indicated in the Gospels, wliere there are said to be placed, according to the manner of purification among the Jews, six water-vessels, containing two or three firkins a-piece; by which, as I have said, the language of the Gospel seems to indicate, with respect to those who are secretly called by the apostle " Jews," that they are purified by the word of Scripture, receiving indeed sometimes two firkins, i. e. the understanding of the soul" or " spirit," Codsequentia histoiialis intelligentise. Metretes.

FROM THE GREEK.

degraded ideas, the disciple of the Spirit himself being enjoined to make know-n, no longer by letters, but by living words, to the presbyters of the whole church of God, who have become grey through wisdom.

12. But as there are certain passages of Scripture which do not at all contain the ' corporeal" sense, as we shall show in the following paragraphs, there are also places where we must seek only for the " soul," as it were, and ' spirit" of Scripture. And perhaps on this account the w ater-vessels containing two or three firkins a-piece are said to lie for the purification of the Jews, as we read in tlie Gospel according to John: the expression darkly intimating, wutli respect to those who are called by the apostle " Jews " secretly, that they are purified by the word of Scripture, receiving sometimes two firkins, i. e., so to speak, the " psycdii-cal" and " spiritual " sense; and sometimes three firkins, ': T '7ro7. ic,)Uiuoi;.

according to our statement as above; sometimes t, ven three firkins, when in the reading of Scripture the " bodily ' sense, which is the " historical," may be preserved for the edification of the people. Now six w ater-vessels are appropriately spoken of, with regard to those persons who are purified by being placed in the world; for we read that in six days wdiich is the perfect number this world and all things in it were finished. How great, then, is the utility of this first " historical " sense wdiich w e have mentioned, is attested by the multitude of all believers, who believe with adequate faith and simplicity, and does not need much argument, because it is openly manifest to all; whereas of that sense which we have called above the ' soul," as it were, of Scripture, the Apostle Paul has given us numerous examples in the first Epistle to the Corinthians. For w e find the ex)ression, " Thou shalt not muzzle the mouth of the ox that treadeth out the corn." And afterwards, when explaining wdiat precept ought to be understood by this, he adds the w ords: " Doth God take care for oxen'? or saith He it altogether for our sakes? For our sakes, no doubt, this is written; 1 Cf. 1 Cor. ix, 9 and Deut. xxv. 4.

FROM THE GREEK.

since some have, in addition to those already mentioned, also the ' corporeal" sense, which is capable of producing edification. And six water-vessels are reasonably appropriate to those who are purified in the world, which was made in six days the perfect number. That the first " sense," then, is profitable in this respect, that it is capable of imparting edification, is testified by the multitudes of genuine and simple believers; wdiile of that interpretation which is referred back to the " soul," there is an illustration in Paul's first Epistle to the Corinthians. The expression is, "Thou shalt not muzzle the mouth of the ox that treadeth out the corn; " to which he adds, ' Doth

God take care of oxen? or saith He it altogether for our sakes? For our sakes, no 1 Cf. 1 Cor. ix. 9 and Deut. xxv. 4.

that lie who plongheth should plough in hope, and he that thresheth, in hope of partaking." Very many other passages also of this nature, whicli are in this way explained of the law, contribute extensive information to the hearers.

13. Now a " spiritual" interpretation is of this nature: when one is able to point out what are the heavenly things of which these serve as the patterns and shadow, who are Jews ' according to the flesh," and of what things future the law contains a shadow, and any other expressions of this kind that may be found in holy Scripture; or when it is a subject of inquiry, what is that wisdom hidden in a mystery which ' God ordained before the world for our glory, which none of the princes of this world knew;" or the meaning of the apostle's language, when, employing certain illustrations from Exodus or Numbers, he says; " These things happened to them in a figure, and they are WTitten on our account, on 1 Cf. 1 Cor. ix. 9, 10. 2 f 1 Qq ii, 7 3 In figiu-a. Greek text, recept tvttoi. Lachmann reads rvtrikug.

FROM THE GREEK.

doubt, this was written: that he that plougheth should plough in hope, and that he who thresheth, in hope of partaking." And there are numerous interpretations adapted to the multitude which are in circulation, and which edify those who are unable to understand profounder meanings, and which have somewhat the same character.

13. But the interpretation is " spiritual," when one is able to show of what heavenly things the Jews 'according to the flesh" served as an example and a shadow, and of wliat future blessings the law contains a shadow. And, generally, we must investigate, according to the apostolic promise, ' the wisdom in a mystery, the hidden wisdom which God ordained before the world for the glory" of the just, which " none of the princes of this world knew." And the same apostle says somewhere, after referring to certain events mentioned as occurring in Exodus and Numbers, " that these things 1 1 Cor. ix. 9, 10. 2 Cf. 1 Cor. ii. G, 7, 8.

ORIG. U whom tlie ends of the ages have come." Now, an opportunity is afforded iis of understanding of what those things which happened to them were figures, when he adds: ' And they drank of that spiritual rock which followed them, and that rock was Christ."" In another epistle also, when re-ferrinp" to the tabernacle, he mentions the direction which was given to Moses: "Thou shalt make all things according to the pattern which was showed thee in the mount." And writing to the Galatlans, and upbraiding certain individuals who seem to themselves to read the law, and yet without understanding It, because of their Ignorance of the fact that an allegorical meaning underlies what is written, he says to them In a certain tone of rebuke: " Tell me, ye who desire to be under the law, do ye not hear the law? For It Is written that Abraham had two sons; the one by a bond maid, the other by a free woman. But he who was of the bond 1 1 Cor. X. 11. 2 1 Cor. x. 4.

3 cf. Ex. XXV. 40 and Heb. viii. 5.

FROM THE GREEK.

happened to tjiem figuratively, but that they were written on our account, on whom the ends of the world are come." And he gives an opportunity for ascertaining of what things these were patterns, when he says: ' For they drank of the spiritual rock that followed them, and that rock v as Christ." And In another epistle, when sketching the various matters relating to the tabernacle, he used the words: " Thou shalt make everything according to the pattern showed thee In the mount." Moreover, In the Epistle to the Galatlans, as if upbraiding those wdio think that they read the law, and yet do not understand It, judging that those do not understand It who do not reflect that alleiiories are contained under what is written, he says: ' Tell me, ye that desire to be under the law, do ye not hear the law? For It Is written, Abraham liad two sons; the one by the bond maid, the other by the 1 1 Cor. X. 11. 2 1 Cor. x. 4.

3 Cf. Ex. xxy. 40 and Heb. viii. 5.

woman was born according to the flesh; but he of the free Avoman was by promise. Wliich things are an allegory: for these are the two covenants." And here this point is to be attended to, viz. the caution witli which the apostle employs the expression, "Ye who are under the law, do ye not hear tlielaw?" Do ye not heai', i. e. do ye not understand and know? In the Epistle to the Colossians, again, briefly summing up and condensing the meaning of the whole law, he says: " Let no man therefore judge you in meat, or in drink, or in respect of holy days, or of the new moon, or of the Sabbath, which are a shadow of things to come." Writing to the Hebrews also, and treating of those who belong to the circumcision, he says: " Those who serve to the example and shadow of heavenly things." Now perhaps, through these illustrations, no doubt will be entertained regarding the five books of Closes, by those who hold the 1 Gal. iv. 21-24. 2 q i- lo. Heb. viii. 5.

FROM THE GREEK.

free woman. But he who was by the bond maid was born according to the flesh; but he of the free woman was by jc promise. Which things are an allegory: for these are the two covenants," and so on. Now we must carefully observe each word employed by him. He says: "Ye who desire to be. under the law," not " Ye that are under the law;" and, "Do ye not hecu' the law?" " hearing" being understood to mean " comprejiending' and " hnoicing' And in the Epistle to tlie Colossians, briefly abrido-inc: the meanino; of the whole leiiis-lation, he says: "Let no man therefore judge you in meat, and in drink, or in respect of a festival, or of a new moon, or of Sabbaths, which are a shadow of things to conie." Iore-over, in the Epistle to the Hebrews, discoursing of those who belong to the circumcision, he writes: " who serve for an ensample and shadow of heavenly things."' Now it is probable that, from these illustrations, those will entertain no doubt with respect to the five books of! Moses, who have once d'htKT. yopovy. vjcc. Col. ii. IG. Ileb. viii. 5.

writings of the apostle, as divinely in spired. And if tliey require, with respect to the rest of the history, that those events which are contained in it should be consiciered as having happened for an ensample to those of whom they are written, we have observed that this also has been stjited in the Epistle to the Romans, where the apostle adduces an instance from the third book of Kings, saying, "I have left me seven thousand men who have not bowed the knee to Baal;" which expression Paul understood as figuratively spoken of those who are called Israelites according to the election, in order to show that the advent of Christ had not only now been of advantage to the Gentiles, but that very many even of the race of Israel had been called to salvation. 14. This being the state of the case, we shall sketch out, as if by way of illustration and pattern, what may occur to us with regard to the manner in which Holy Scripture is to be understood on these several points, repeating in the first Rom. xi. 4; cf, 1 Kings xix. 18.

FEOM THE GREEK.

given in their adhesion to the apostle, as divinely inspired; but do you wish to know, with regard to the rest of the history, if it also happened as a pattern? We must note, then, the expression in the Epistle to the Eomans, "I have left to myself seven thousand men, who have not bowed the knee to Baal," quoted from the third book of Kings, which Paul has understood as equivalent in meaning to those who are Israelites according to election, because not only were the Gentiles benefited by the advent of Christ, but also certain of the race of God.

14. This being the state of the case, we have to sketch what seem to us to be the marks of the true understanding of Scriptures. And, in the first place, this must be pointed out, that the object of the Spirit, which by the providence of 2 Rom. xi. 4; cf. 1 Kings xix. 18.

Tivecs dtTo rov iiov-yivovg, i. e. Israelites.

instance, and pointing out tlis fact, that the Holy Spirit, by the providence and will of God, through the power of His only-begotten Word, who was in the beginning God with God, enlightened tlie ministers of truth, the prophets and apostles, to understand the mysteries of those things or causes which take place among men, or with respect to men. And by " men," I now mean souls that are placed in bodies, who, relating those mysteries that are known to them, and revealed through Christ, as if they were a kind of human transactions, or handino; down certain leo: al observances and injunctions, described them figuratively;" not that anyone who pleased might view these expositions as deserving to be trampled under foot, but that he who should devote himself with all chastity, and sobriety, and watchfulness, to studies of this kind, might be able by this means to trace out the meaning of the Spirit of God, which is perhaps lying profoundly buried, and tlie context, which may be pointing again in another direction than the ordinary usage of speech would 1 Quse inter homines, vel de hominibus geruntur.

2 Fisfiu-aliter describebant.

FROM THE GREEK.

God, throuo; h the Word who was in the beo; inninop with God, illuminated the ministers of truth, the prophets and apostles, was especially the communication of ineffable mysteries regarding the affairs of men (now by men I mean those souls that make use of bodies), in order that he who is capable of instruction may by investigation, and by devoting himself to the study of the profundities of meaning contained in the words, become a participator of all the doctrines of his counsel. And among those matters which relate to souls (wdio cannot otherwise obtain perfection apart from the rich and wise truth of God), the doctrines belonging to God and His only-begotten Son are necessarily laid down as primary, viz. of what nature He is, and in what manner He is the Son of God, and what are the causes of His descending even to the assumption of human flesh, and of complete indicate. And In this way he might become a sharer In the knowled e of the Spirit, and a partaker in the divine counsel, because the soul cannot come to th. e perfection of knowledge otherwise than by inspiration of the truth of the divine wisdom. Accordingly, it is of God, i. e. of the Father, and of the Son, and of the Holy Spirit, that these men, filled with the Divine Spirit, chiefly treat; then the mysteries relating to the Son of God how the Word became flesh, and why He descended even to the assumption of the form of a servant are the subject, as I have said, of explanation by those persons who are filled with the Divine Spirit. It next followed, necessarily, that they should instruct mortals by divine teaching, regarding rational creatures, both those of heaven and tlie happier ones of earth; and also should explain the differences among souls, and the origin of these differences; and then should tell what this w orld is, and why it was created; whence also sprung the great and terrible w ickedness which extends over the earth. And whether that wickedness is found on this earth only, or in other places, is a point which it w as necessary for us to learn from divine teaching. Since, then, it was the intention of the Holy Spirit

FEOM THE GREEK.

humanity; and wdiat, also, is the operation of this Son, and upon whom and when exercised. And it was necessary also that the subject of kindred beings, and other rational creatures, both those who are divine and those who have fallen from blessedness, together with the reasons of their fall, should be contained in the divine teaching; and also that of the diversities of souls, and of the origin of these diversities, and of the nature of the world, and the cause of its existence. We must learn also the origin of the great and terrible wickedness which overspreads the earth, and whether it is confined to this earth only, or prevails elsewhere. Now, while these and similar objects were present to the Spirit, who enlightened the souls of the holy ministers of the truth, there was a second object, for the sake of those to enllf liten witli respect to tliese and similar subjects, those holy souls who had devoted themselves to the service of the truth, this object was kept iu view, in the second place, viz. for the sake of those who either could not or would not give themselves to this labour and toil by which they might deserve to be instructed in or to recoo nise thincjs of such value and importance, to wrap up and conceal, as we said before, in ordinary language, under the covering of some history and narrative of visible things, hidden mysteries. There is therefore introduced the narrative of the visible creation, and the creation and formation of the first man; then the offspring which followed from him in succession, and some of the actions wdiich were done by the good among his posterity,, are related, and occasionally certain crimes also, which are stated to have been committed by them as being human; and afterwards certain unchaste or wicked deeds also are narrated as being the acts of the wicked. The description of battles, moreover, is given in a wonderful manner, md the alternations of victors and vanquished, by which certain ineffable mysteries are made known to those who know how to investigate statements of that kind. By an admirable

FP. OM THE GREEK.

who were unable to endure the fatio ue of investln-atino; matters so important, viz. to conceal the doctrine relating to the previously mentioned subjects, in expressions containing a narrative which conveyed an announcement regarding the things of the visible creation, the creation of man, and the successive descendants of the first men until they became numerous; and other histories relating the acts of just men, and the sins occasionally committed by these same men as beino; human beino; s, and the wicked deeds, both of unchastitv and vice, committed by sinful and ungodly men. And what is most remarkable, by the history of wars, and of the victors, and the vanquished, certain mysteries are indicated to those who are able to test these statements. And more w onderful discipline of wisdom, too, the law of truth, even of the prophets, is implanted in the Scriptures of the law, each of which is woven by a divine art of wisdom, as a kind of covering and veil of spiritual truths; and this is what we have called the " body" of Scripture, so that also, in this way, what we have called the covering of the letter, w oven by the art of wisdom, might be capable of edifying and profiting many, when others would derive no benefit.

15. But as if, in all the instances of this covering (i. e. of this history), the logical connection and order of the law had been preserved, we would not certainly believe, when thus possessing the meaning of Scripture in a continuous series, that anything else was contained in it save what was indicated on the surface; so for that reason divine wisdom took care that certain stumbling-blocks, or interruptions, to the historical meaning should take place, by the introduction into Intercapedines.

FROM THE GREEK.

still, the laws of truth are predicted by the written legislation; all these being described in a connected series, with a power which is truly in keeping with the wisdom of God. For it was intended that the covering also of the spiritual truths I mean the " bodily" part of Scripture should not be without profit in many cases, but should be capable of improving the multitude, according to their capacity.

15. But since, if the usefulness of the legislation, and the sequence and beauty of the history, were universally evident of itself, we should not believe that any other thing could be understood in the Scriptures save what was obvious, the word of God has arranged that certain stumbling-blocks, as it were, and offences,. and impossibilities, should be introduced into the midst of the law and the history, in order that we may not, through being drawn away in all directions by the merely attractive nature of the language, either altogether fall away y'Kxcpvpou. " tzvrodiv.

VTTo rvis X gac s'Kx. ofaSvoi to dyayov ax, pci(, rov ixovang.

FnoM THE LATIN.

the midst of the narrative of certain impossibilities and incongruities; that in this way the very interruption of the narrative might, as by the interposition of a bolt, present an obstacle to the reader, Yhereby he might refuse to acknowledge the way Avhich conducts to the ordinary meaning; and being thus excluded and debarred from it, we might be recalled to the bcojinnino; of another way, in order that, bv entering upon a narrow path, and passing to a loftier and more sublime road, he might lay open the immense breadth of divine wisdom. This, however, must not be unnoted by us, that as the chief object of the Holy Spirit is to preserve the coherence of the spiritual meaning, either in those things which ought to be done or which have been already performed, if He anywhere finds that those events which, according to the history, took place, can be adapted to a spiritual meaning, He composed a texture of both kinds in one style of narration, always concealing the hidden meaning more deeply; but where the historical narrative could not be made appropriate to the spiritual coherence of the occurrences. He

Ut ita celsioris cujusdam et emmentioris tramitis per angusti callis icgressum inunensam divmas scientise latitudinem pandat.

FROM THE GREEK.

from the true doctrines, as learning nothing worthy of God, or, by not departing from the letter, come to the knowledge of nothing more divine. And this also we must know, that the principal aim being to announce the spiritual" connection in those thinojs that are done, and that ouoht to be done, where the Word found that things done according to the history could be adapted to these mystical senses, He made use of them, concealing from the multitude the deeper meaning; but where, in the narrative of the development of sn)er-sensual things,- there did not follow the performance of those certain events, which was already indicated by the m-stical meaning, the Scripture interwove in the history the account of some event that did not take place, sometimes what could iv TYi Oriyy'jsi zvig Treol ruv vor, aj oiko'hovdiccg.

inserted sometimes certain thino-s which either did not take place or could not take place; sometimes also what might happen, but what did not: and He does this at one time in a few words, whicli, taken in their " bodily " meaning, seem incapable of containing truth, and at another by the insertion of many. And this we find frequently to be the case in the legislative portions, where there are many things manifestly useful among the " bodily " precepts, but a very great number also in which no principle of utility is at all discernible, and sometimes even things which are judged to be impossibilities. Now all this, as we have remarked, was done by the Holy Spirit in order that, seeing those events whicli lie on the surface can be neither true nor useful, we may be led to the investigation of that truth which is more deeply concealed, and to the ascertaining of a meaning worthy of God in those Scriptures which w e believe to be inspired by Him.

16. Nor was it only with regard to those Scriptures which were composed down to the advent of Christ that the Holy

FROM THE GREEK.

not have happened; sometimes what could, but did not. And I sometimes a few words are interpolated which are not true in their literal acceptation, and sometimes a larger number. ' And a similar practice also is to be noticed with regard to the legislation, in which is often to be found what is useful in itself, and appropriate to the times of the legislation; and sometimes also what does not appear to be of utility; and at other times impossibilities are recorded for the sake of the more skilful and inquisitive, in order that they may give themselves to the toil of investigating what is WTitten, and thus attain to a becomino; conviction of the manner in which a meaning worthy of God must be sought out in such subjects.

16. It was not only, however, with the Scriptures composed before the advent of Christ that the Spirit thus

Kocrai to auf. a,.

Spirit thus dealt; but ns being one and tlie same Spirit, and proceeding from one God, lie dealt in tlie same way with the evangelists and apostles. For even those narratives which He inspired them to write were not composed without the aid of that wisdom of Ilis, tlie nature of wliich we have above explained. Whence also in them were intermingled not a few things by which, the historical order of the narrative being interrupted and broken up, the attention of the reader might be recalled, by the impossibility of the case, to an examination of the inner meanino. But, that our meaninn-may be ascertained by the facts themselves, let ns examine the passages of Scripture. Now who is there, pray, possessed of understanding, that will rec ard the statement as appropriate, that the first day, and the second, and the third, in which also both evening and morning are mentioned, existed without sun, and moon, and stars the first day even without a sky? And who is found so ignorant as to suppose Consequeuter, alii " convenientcr."

FKOM THE GREEK.

dealt; but as being the same Spirit, and proceeding from the one God, He did the same thing both with the evangelists and the apostles, as even these do not contain throughout a pure history of events, which are interwoven indeed according to the letter, but which did not actually occur. Nor even do the law and the commandments wdiolly convey what is agreeable to reason. For who that has understanding will suppose that the first, and second, and tliird day, and the evening and the morning, existed without a sun, and moon, and stars? and that the first day was, as it were, also without a sky? And wlio is so foolish as to suppose that God, after the manner of a husbandman, planted a paradise in

Ovoi TOVTOrj TTi. 'TYj UKpuTOV TViv IfftOpixV TU'J 'TTpoffv Xdliii'JCOy KCtt TO

TTU'JTug TO ivmyov ly. 'uivo'jtu. One MS. reads yiyiunyayriv referring to iaropixu, on which one-editor remarks, "Hie ct in sequentibus imploro tidem cod-icum!"

316 OEIGEiw DE PRINCIPIIS. Book iv.

FROM THE LATIN.

that God, as if He had been a husbandman, planted trees in paradise, in Eden towards the east, and a tree of life in it, i. e. a visible and palpable tree of wood, so that any one eating of it with bodily teeth should obtain life, and, eating again of another tree, should come to the knowdedge of good and evil? No one, I think, can doubt that the statement that God walked in the afternoon in paradise, and that Adam lay hid under a tree, is related figuratively in Scripture, that some mystical meaning may be indicated by it. The departure of Cain from the presence of the Lord will manifestly cause a careful reader to inquire what is the presence of God, and how any one can go out from it. But not to extend the task which we have before us beyond its due limits, it is very easy for any one who pleases to gather out of holy Scripture what is recorded indeed as having been done, but wdiat nevertheless cannot be believed as having reasonably and appropriately occurred according to the historical account.

Lifi-num.

FROM THE GREEK.

Eden, tow ards the east, and placed in it a tree of life, visible and palpable, so that one tasting of the fruit by the bodily teeth obtained life? and again, that one was a partaker of good and evil by masticating what was taken from the tree? And if God is said to w alk in the paradise in the evening, and Adam to hide himself under a tree, I do not suppose that any one doubts that these things figuratively indicate certain mj steries, the history having taken place in appearance, and not literally.- Cain also, when going forth from the presence of God, certainly appears to thoughtful men as likely to lead the reader to inquire wdiat is the presence of God, and what is the meaning of going out from Him. And what need is there to say more, since those who are not altogether blind can collect countless insta' ces of a similar kind recorded as having occurred, but wdiica did not literally secret ir v T i iu.

FROM THE LATrx.

The same stj'-le of scriptural narrative occurs abundantly in the Gospels, as when the devil is said to have placed Jesus on a lofty mountain, that he might show Him from thence all the kingdoms of the world, and the glory of them. How could it literally come to pass, either that Jesus should be led up by the devil into a high mountain, or that the latter should show Him all the kingdoms of the world (as if they were lying beneath his bodily eyes, and adjacent to one mountain), i. e. the kingdom of the Persians, and Scythians, and Indians? or how could he show in what manner the kings of these kingdoms are glorified by men? And many other instances similar to this will be found in the Gospels by any one who will read them with attention, and will observe that in those narratives which appear to be literally recorded, there are inserted and interwoven things which cannot be admitted historically, but which may be accepted in a spiritual signification.

17. In the passages containing the commandments also, similar things are found. For in the law Moses is com-

FEOM THE GREEK, take place? Nay, the Gospels themselves are filled with the same kind of narratives; e. g. the devil leading Jesus up into a high mountain, in order to show Him from thence the kingdoms of the whole world, and the glory of them. For who is there amonoj those who do not read such accounts care-lessly, that would not condemn those who think that with the eye of the body which requires a lofty height in order that the parts lying immediately under and adjacent may be seen the kingdoms of the Persians, and Scythians, and Indians, and Parthians, were beheld, and the manner in which their princes are glorified among men? And the attentive reader may notice in the Gospels innumerable other passages like these, so that he will be convinced that in the histories that are literally recorded, circumstances that did not occur are inserted.

17. And if we come to the legislation of Moses, many of niandecl to destroy every male that is not circumcised on the eighth day, which is exceedingly incongruous," since it would be necessary, if it were related that the law was executed according to the history, to command those parents to be punished who did not circumcise their children, and also those who were the nurses of little children. The declaration of Scripture now is, "The uncircurncised male, i. e. who shall not have been circumcised, shall be cut off from his people." And if we are to inquire regarding the impossibilities of the law, we find an animal called the goat-stag," which cannot possibly exist, but which, as being in the number of clean beasts, Moses commands to be eaten; and a griffin," which no one ever remembers or heard of as yielding to human power, but which the legislator forbids to be used for

Inconsequens. " Cf. Gen. xvii. 14.

Tragelaphus; " wild goat," auth. vers. Deut. xiv. 5; Heb. S'p' 0.7:01 'hty.

Gryplms; " ossifrage," autli. vers. Lev. xi. 13; Heb. D"i3-

FROM THE GREEK.

the laws manifest the irrationality, and others the impossibility, of their literal observance. The irrationality in this, that the people are forbidden to eat vultures, although no one even in the direst famines was ever driven by want to have recourse to this bird; and that children eight days old, which are uncircumcised, are ordered to be exterminated from among tlieir people, it being necessary, if the law were to be carried out at all literally with regard to these, that their fathers, or those with whom they are brought up, should be commanded to be put to death. Now the Scripture says: ' Every male that is uncircumcised, who shall not be circumcised on the eighth day, shall be cut off from among his people." And if you wish to see impossibilities contained in the legislation, let us observe that the goat-stag is one of those animals that cannot exist, and yet Moses commands us to offer it as being a clean beast; whereas a griffin, which is Vo itTi ru Kxl)' kavtOvg TYipsladxt. Gen. xvii. 14.

fo cl. Ecspecting tlie celebrated observance of the Sabbath ah. o he thus speaks: ' Ye shall sit, every one in your dwellings; no one shall move from his place on the Sabbath-day."'' Which precept it is impossible to observe literally; for no man can sit a whole day so as not to move from the place where he sat down. With respect to each one of these points now, those who belong to the circumcision, and all who would have no more meaning to be found in sacred Scripture than what is indicated by the letter, consider that there should be no investio-ation reo-ardlncj the i; oat-stao:, and the o-riffin. and the vulture; and they invent some empty and trifling tales about the Sabbath, drawn from some traditional sources or other, alleging that every one's place is computed to him within two thousand cubits. Others, again, among whom is Dositheus the Samaritan, censure indeed expositions of this kind, but themselves lay down something more ridiculous, viz. that each one must remain until the evenlncp in the Opinatissima.- Cf. Ex. xvi. 29. Ulnas.

FROM THE GREEK.

not recorded ever to have been subdued by man, the lawgiver forbids to be eaten. Nay, he who carefully considers the famous injunction relating to the Sabbath, "Ye shall sit each one in your dwellings; let no one go out from his place on the seventh day," will deem it impossible to be literally observed: for no living being is able to sit throughout a, whole day, and remain without moving from a sitting position. And therefore those who belong to the circumcision, and all who desire that no meaniniv should be exhibited, save the literal one, do not investigate at all such subjects as those of the goat-stag and griffin and vulture, but indulge in foolish talk on certain points, multiplying words and adducing tasteless traditions; as, for example, with retjard to the Sabbath, savins; that two thousand cubits is each one's limit. Others, again, among whom is Dositheus ' Ex. xvi. 29. 2-ip'jxpy-S TTctpciloasi;.

posture, place, or position In which he found himself on the Sabbath-clay; i. e. if found sitting, he is to sit the whole d: ij, or If reclining, he is to recline the wdiole day. Moreover, the Injunction which runs, "Bear no burden on the Sabbai. h-day," seems to me an impossibility. For the Jewish doctors, in consequence of these prescriptions, have betaken themselves, as the holy apostle says, to innumerable fables, saying that it is not accounted a burden if a man w ear shoes without nails, but that it is a burden if shoes with nails be worn; and that if it be carried on one shoulder, they consider it a burden; but if on both, they declare it to be none.

18. And now, if we institute a similar examination wdth regard to the Gospels, how shall it appear otherwise than absurd to take the injunction literally, "Salute no man by the way? " And yet there are simple individuals, who think that our Saviour gave this command to His apostles! How, also, can it appear possible for such an order as this to be Jer. xvii. 21. Luke x. 4.

FROM THE GREEK.

the Samaritan, condemning such an interpretation, think that in the position in which a man is found on the Sabbath-day, he is to remain until evening. Moreover, the not carrying of a burden on the Sabbath-day is an impossibility; and therefore the Jewish teachers have fallen into countless ab-surdlties,- saying that a shoe of such a kind was a burden, but not one of another kind; and that a sandal which had nails was a burden, but not one that was without them; and in like manner what was borne on one shoulder was a load, but not that which was carried on both.

18. And if we go to the Gospel and institute a similar examination, what would be more irrational than to take literally the injunction, "Salute no man by the way,"" which simple persons think the Saviour enjoined on the apostles? The command, moreover, that the right cheek should be smitten, is most incredible, since every one who

EV dtrspctvroaoyiocv it n'hvdccat. Liike x. 4.

from the latix. observed, especially in those countries where there is a rigorous winter, attended by frost and ice, viz. that one should possess 'neither two coats, nor shoes?" And this, that when one is smitten on the right cheek, he is ordered to present tlie left also, since every one who strikes with the right hand smites tlie left cheek? This precept also in the Gospels must be accounted among impossibihties, viz. that if the right eye " offend " thee, it is to be plucked out; for even if we were to suppose that bodily eyes were spoken of, how shall it appear appropriate, that when both eyes have the property of sight, tlie responsibility of the 'offence"' should be transferred to one eye, and that the right one? Or who shall be considered free of a crime of the greatest enormity, that lays hands upon himself? But perhaps the epistles of the Apostle Paul will appear to be beyond this. For wdiat is his meaning, when he says, ' Is any man called, being circumcised? Let him not become uncircumcised."""' This expression indeed, in the first place, does not on careful consideration seem to be spoken 1 Luke X. 4.- 1 Cor. vii. 18.

I'RO. M THE GlleEK.

strikes, unless he happen to liave some bodily defect, smites the left cheek with his oiglit hand. And it is impossible to take literally, the statement in the Gospel about the "offending" of the right eye. For, to grant the possibility of one being " offended " by the sense of sight, how, when there are two eyes that see, should the blame be laid upon the right eye? And who is there that, condemning himself for having looked upon a woman to lust after her, would rationally transfer the blame to the right eye alone, and throw it away? The apostle, moreover, lays down the law, saying, "Is any man called, being circumcised? Let him not become uncir-cumcised." "' In the first place, any one will see that he does not utter these words in connection with the subject before him.

For, wdien laying down precepts on marriage and purity, how will it not appear that he has introduced these words at si f4, vi olpoi TTitroydug ri Trxpcc. (pcai'j Tvyy, u, uoi. 1 Cor. vii. 18.

ORIG. X with reference to the subject of which he was treating at the time, for this discourse consisted of injunctions relating to marriage and to chastity; and these words, therefore, will have the appearance of an unnecessary addition to such a subject. In the second place, however, what objection would there be, if, for the sake of avoiding that unseemliness which is caused by circumcision, a man were able to become un-circumcised? And, in the third place, that is altogether impossible.

The object of all these statements on our part, is to show that it was the design of the Holy Spirit, who deigned to bestow upon us the sacred Scriptures, to show that we were not to be edified by the letter alone, or by everything in it, a thing which we see to be frequently impossible and inconsistent; for in that way not only absurdities, but impossibilities, would be the result; but that we are to understand that certain occurrences were interwoven in this " visible " history, which, when considered nd understood in their inner meaning, give forth a law which is advantageous to men and worthy of God.

Secundo vero, quid obesset, si obscoenitatis vitandse causa ejus, quse ex circum-cisione est, posset aliquis revocare prseputium?

FROM THE GREEK.

random? But, in the second place, who will say that a man does wrong who endeavours to become uncircumcised, if that be possible, on account of the disgrace that is considered by the multitude to attach to circumcision?

All these statements have been made by us, in order to show that the design of that divine power which gave us the sacred Scriptures is, that we should not receive what is presented by the letter alone (such things being sometimes not true in their literal acceptation, but absurd and impossible), but that certain things have been introduced into the actual history and into the legislation that are useful in their literal sense.

slx,. 2 y Kccroi TO pnrov xp ai(, av voy. odiaix.

19. Let no one, however, entertain the suspicion that we do not believe any history in Scripture to be real, because we suspect certain events related in it not to have taken place; or that no precepts of the law are to be taken literally, because we consider certain of them, in which either the nature or possibility of the case so requires, incapable of being observed; or that we do not believe those predictions which were written of the Saviour to have been fulfilled in a manner palpable to the senses; or that His commandments are not to be literally obeyed. We have therefore to state in answer, since we are manifestly so of opinion, that the truth of the history may and ought to be preserved in the majority of instances. For who can deny that Abraham was buried in the double cave at Hebron, as well as Isaac and Jacob, and each of their wives? Or who doubts tliat Shechem was given as a portion to Joseph? or that Jerusalem is the metropolis of Judea, on which the temple of God was built by Solomon? and countless other statements. For the passages which hold

Duplici spelunca. 2 q Qqtl. xlviii. 22 and Josh. xxiv. 32.

FROM THE GREEK.

19. But that no one may suj)pose that we assert respecting the whole that no history is real because a certain one is not; and that no law is to be literally observed, because a certain one, understood according to the letter, is absurd or impossible; or that the statements regarding the Saviour are not true in a manner perceptible to the senses; or that no commandment and precept of his ought to be obeyed; we have to answer that, with regard to certain things, it is perfectly clear to us that the historical account is true; as that Abraham was buried in the double cave at Hebron, as also Isaac and Jacob, and the wives of each of them; and that Shechem was given as a portion to Joseph; and that Jerusalem is the metropolis of Judea, in which the temple of God was built by Solomon; and innumerable other state-

Cf. Gen. xlviii. 22 and Josh. xxiv. 32.

good in tlieir liistorical acceptation are much more numerous than those which contain a purely spiritual meaning. Then, again, who would not maintain that the command to "honour thy father and thy mother, that it may be well with thee," is sufficient of itself without any spiritual meaning, and necessary for those wdio observe it? especially when Paul also has confirmed the command by repeating it in the same words. And what need is there to speak of the prohibitions, "Thou shalt not commit adultery," ' Thou shalt not steal," " Thou shalt not bear false witness," and others of the same kind? And with respect td the precepts enjoined in the Gospels, no doubt can be entertained that very many of these are to be literally observed, as e. g. when our Lord says, "But I say unto you. Swear not at all; " and when He says, ' Whosoever looketh upon a woman to lust after her, hath committed adultery with 1

Cf. Ex. XX. 12 and Eph. vi. 2, 3.

2 Cf. Ex. XX. 13. 3 Cf. Matt. v. 22.

FROM THE GREEK.

ments. For the passages that are true in their historical meaning are much more numerous than those which are interspersed with a purely spiritual signification. And again, who would not say that the com. mand which enjoins to "honour thy father and thy mother, that it may be well with thee," is useful, apart from all allegorical meaning," and ought to be observed, the Apostle Paul also having employed these very same words And what need is there to speak of the prohibitions, "Thou shalt not commit adultery," "Thou shalt not kill," "Thou shalt not steal," " Thou shalt not bear false witness? " And again, there are commandments contained in the Gospel which admit of no doubt whether they are to be observed according to the letter or not; e. g. that which says, "But I say unto you, Whoever is angry with his brother," and so on. And again, 1 Ex. XX. 12 and Epli. vi. 2, 3. xapu 'Traavig dvuyojytig.

3 Cf. Ex. XX. 12 and Eph. vi. 2, 3. Cf. Ex. xx. 13.

her already in his heart;" the admonitions also which are found in the writings of the Apostle Paul, "Warn them that are unruly, comfort the feeble-minded, support the weak, be patient towards all men," and very many others. And yet I have no doubt that an attentive reader will, in numerous instances, hesitate whether this or that history can be considered to be literally true or not; or whether this or that precept ought to be observed according to the letter or no. And therefore great pains and labour are to be employed, until every reader reverentially understand that he is dealing with divine and not human words inserted in the sacred books. 20. The understanding, therefore, of holy Scripture which 1 Matt. V. 28. 2 1 xhess. v. 14.

1-ROM THE GREEK.

"But I say unto you, Swear not at all." And in the writings of the apostle the literal sense is to be retained: " Warn them that are unruly, comfort the feeble-minded, support the weak, be patient towards all men;" although it is possible for those ambitious of a deeper meaning to retain the profundities of the wisdom of God, without setting aside the commandment in its literal meaning. The careful reader, however, will be in doubt as to certain points, being unable to show without long investigation whether this history so deemed literally occurred or not, and whether the literal meaning of this law is to be observed or not. And therefore the exact reader must, in obedience to the Saviour's injunction to "search the Scriptures," carefully ascertain in how far the literal meaning is true, and in how far impossible; and so far as he can, trace out, by means of similar statements, the meaning everywhere scattered through Scripture of that which cannot be understood in a literal signification. 20. Since, therefore, as will be clear to those who read, the 1 Matt. v. 22. 2 I Tiiess 14

E Kctl 'TTupoi roig (pit orifioTSpoi; ovuocrcn al) siu 'ikoiatOu ocv-uu y. itcc Toy j dsitilaqcit T' u kcctoc to prrrov iuTOA'ii, fia,6yt Qiov aocpiccg. '7rspie7: KVG-, Gitcct. John V. o9.

we consider ought to be deservedly and consistently maintained, is of the following kind. A certain nation is declared by holy Scripture to have been chosen by God upon the earth, which nation has received several names: for sometimes the whole of it is termed Israel, and sometimes Jacob; and it was divided by Jeroboam son of Nebat into two portions; and the ten tribes which were formed under him w ere called Israel, while tiie two remaining ones (with which were united the tribe of Levi, and that which was descended from the royal race of David) was named Judah. Now the whole of the country possessed by that nation, which it had received from God, was called Judea, in which was situated the metropolis, Jerusalem; and it is called metropolis, being as it were the mother of many cities, the names of which you

FROM THE GREEK.

connection taken literally is impossible, while the sense preferred " is not impossible, but even the true one, it must be our object to grasp the whole meaning, which connects the account of what is literally impossible in an intelligible manner with what is not only not impossible, but also historically true, and which is allegorically understood, in respect of its not having literally occurred. For, with respect to holy Scripture, our opinion is that the whole of it has a " spiritual," but not the whole a " bodily" meaning, because the bodily meaning is in many places proved to be impossible. And therefore great attention must be bestowed by the cautious reader on the divine books, as being divine writings; the manner of understanding which appears to us to be as follows: The Scriptures relate that God chose a certain nation upon the earth, which they call by several names. For the whole of this nation is termed Israel, and also Jacob. And when it

KXroi TVi'j 7 es, iu dovvarau 'hoyou vofixzic. rolg ov y ovov oiix, dowtkrotg dxhu. Koil d'htfiqiai Koitoi, T')iu iatOpi'oiv, avvoi. Khyiyopovta, iuoig roig oaov stti t5 "hi st, yyi ysysuyif svoig.

will frequently find mentioned here and there in the other books of Scripture, but which are collected together into one catalogue in the book of Joshua the son of Nun.

21. This, then, being the state of the case, the holy apostle desiring to elevate in some degree, and to raise our understanding above the earth, says in a certain place, "Behold Israel after the flesh; " by which he certainly means that In libro Jesu Xauc.- 1 Cor. x. 18.

FROM THE GREEK.

was divided in the times of Jeroboam the son of Nebat, the ten tribes related as being subject to him were called Israel; and the remaining two, along with the tribe of Levi, being ruled over by the descendants of David, were named Judah. And the whole of the territory which the people of this nation inhabited, being given them by God, receives the name of Judah, the metropolis of which is Jerusalem, a metropolis, namely, of numerous cities, the names of which lie scattered about in many other passages of Scripture, but are enumerated too; ether in the book of Joshua the son of Nun.-"-21. Such, then, being the state of the case, the apostle, elevating our power of discernment above the letter, says somewhere, "Behold Israel after the flesh," as if there were an Israel " according to the Spirit." And in another place he says, For they who are the children of the flesh are not the children of God; " nor are " they all Israel who are of Israel; " nor is " he a Jew who is one outwardly, nor is that circumcision' which is outward in the flesh: but he is a Jew who is one ' inwardly;' and circumcision is that of the heart, in the spirit, and not in the letter." For if the judgment respecting the "Jew inwardly" be adopted, we must understand that, as there is a " bodily " race of Jews, so also is there a race of " Jews inwardly," the soul having acquired this nobility for certain mysterious reasons. Moreover, there are many prophecies which predict regarding

S'j ' r, aou ra roy ccvvj. " 1 Cor. x. 18.

3 Rom. ix. 6 8. "" Rom. ii. 28.

there is anotlier Israel which is not according to the flesh, but according to the Spirit. And again in another passage, "For they are not all Israelites who are of Israel."- 22. Being taught, then, by him that there is one Israel Rom. ix. 6.

FROM THE GREEK,

Israel and Judah what is about to befall them. And do not such promises as are written concerning them, in respect of their being mean in expression, and manifesting no elevation of thought, nor anything worthy of the promise of God, need a mystical interpretation? And if the " spiritual " promises are announced by visible signs, then they to whom the promises are made are not " corporeal." And not to linger over the point of the Jew who is a Jew " inwardly," nor over that of the Israelite accordino; to the " inner man" these statements being sufficient for those who are not devoid of understanding we return to our subject, and say that Jacob is the father of the twelve patriarchs, and they of the rulers of the people; and these, again, of the other Israelites. Do not, then, the " corporeal" Israelites refer their descent to the rulers of the people, and the rulers of the people to the patriarchs, and the patriarchs to Jacob, and those still higher up; while are not the "spiritual" Israelites, of whom the "corporeal" Israelites were the type, sprung from the families, and the families from the tribes, and the tribes from some one individual whose descent is not of a " corporeal" but of a better kind, he, too, being born of Isaac, and he of Abraham, all going back to Adam, whom the apostle declares to be Christ? For every beginning of those families which have relation to God as to the Father of all, took its commencement lower down with Christ, who is next to the God and Father of all, being thus the Father of every soul, as Adam is the father of all men. And if Eve also is intended by the apostle to refer to the church, it is not surprising that Cain, who was born of Eve, and all after him, whose descent goes

Uxacc yccp upx'h "Tvot rpiuu rau ag Trpog tov ruv o'huv Qsou, Kocrurtpa citto rov 'Xp: atOv 'Jip ocro rov ros rou rau o'huv Qsou kxi 'Tzocrtpoi.

from the latin. according to the flesh, and another according to the Spirit, when the Saviour says, ' I am not sent but to the lost sheep of the house of Israel," we do not understand these words as those do who savour of earthly things, i. e. the Ebionites, who derive the appellation of " poor" from their very name (for " Ebion" means " poor" in Hebrew'); but we understand that there exists a race of souls which is termed " Israel," as is indicated by the interpretation of the name itself: for Israel is interpreted to mean a " mind," or " man seeing God." The apostle, again, makes a similar revelation respecting Jerusalem, saying, "The Jerusalem which is above is free, which is the mother of us all." And in another of his epistles he says: "But ye are come unto mount Zion, and to the city of the living God, and to the heavenly Jerusalem, and to an innumerable company of angels, and to the 1 Matt. XV. 24.

2 Ebion, Heb. V3X, (from n3S, to desire), lit. " wishing," " desii'- 2 Gal. iv. 26.

FROM THE GREEK.

back to Eve, should be types of the church, inasmuch as in a pre-eminent sense they are all descended from the church. 22. Now, if the statements made to us regarding Israe, and its tribes and its families, are calculated to impress us, when the Saviour says, ' I was not sent but to the lost sheep of the house of Israel," we do not understand the ex-, pression as the Ebionites do, wdio are poor in understanding! (deriving their name from the poverty of their intellect! Ebion signifying " poor " in Hebrew), so as to suppose that the Saviour came specially to the " carnal" Israelites; for " they who are the children of the flesh are not the children of God." ' Again, the apostle teaches regarding Jerusalem as follows: " The Jerusalem which is above is free, which is the mother of us all." "' And in another epistle: " But ye are come unto mount Zion, and to the city of the living God, to the heavenly Jerusalem, and to an innumerable company 1 Matt. XV. 24.- Rom. ix. 8. 1. iv. 26.

church of the first-born which is written in heaven." If, then, there are certain souls in this world who are called Israel, and a city in heaven which is called Jerusalem, it follows that those cities which are said to belong to the nation of Israel have the heavenly Jerusalem as their metropolis; and that, agreeably to this, we understand as referring to the whole of Judah (of which also we are of opinion that the prophets have spoken in certain mystical narratives), any predictions delivered either regarding Judea or Jerusalem, or invasions of any kind, which the sacred histories declare to have happened to Judea or Jerusalem. Whatever, then, is either narrated or predicted of Jerusalem, must, if we accept the words of Paul as those of Christ speaking in him, be understood as spoken in conformity with his opinion regarding that city which he calls the heavenly Jerusalem, and all those places or cities which are said to be cities of the holy land, of which Jerusalem is the metropolis. For we are to suppose that it is from these very cities that the Saviour, wishing to raise us to a higher grade of intelligence, promises to those who have well managed the money entrusted to them by Himself, that they are to have power over ten or five cities. If, then, the prophecies delivered concerning 1 Cf. Heb. xii. 22, 23.

FROM THE GREEK.

oi angels, to the general assembly and to the church of the first-born which are written in heaven." If, then, Israel is among the race of souls, and if there is in heaven a city of Jerusalem, it follows that the cities of Israel have for their metropolis the heavenly Jerusalem, and it consequently is the metropolis of all Judea. Whatever, therefore, is predicted of Jerusalem, and spoken of it, if we listen to the words of Paul as those of God, and of one who utters wisdom, we must understand the Scriptures as speaking of the heavenly city, and of the whole territory included within the cities of the holy land. For perhaps it is to these Heb. xii. 22, 23. iu ipvx, iu ykvu.

from the latin. Judea, and Jerusalem, and Judah, and Israel, and Jacob, not being understood by us in a carnal sense, signify certain divine mysteries, it certainly follows that those prophecies also which were delivered either concerning Egypt, or the Egyptians, or Babylonia and the Babylonians, and Sidon and the Sidonians, are not to be understood as spoken of that Egypt which is situated on the earth, or of the earthly Babylon, Tyre, or Sidon. Nor can those predictions which the prophet Ezekiel delivered concerning Pharaoh king of Egypt, apply to any man who may seem to have reigned over Egypt, as the nature of the passage itself declares. In a similar manner also, what is spoken of the prince of Tyre cannot be understood of any man or king of Tyre. And how could we possibly accept, as spoken of a man, what is related in many passages of Scripture, and especially in Isaiah, regarding Nebuchadnezzar? For he is not a man wdio is said to have ' fallen from heaven," or who was " Lucifer," or who " arose in the morning." But with respect to those predictions which are found in Ezekiel concerning Egypt, such as that it is to be destroyed in forty years, so that the foot of man should not be found within it, and that it should suffer such devas-

FROM THE GREEK.

cities that the Saviour refers us, when to those who have gained credit by having managed their "pounds" well. He assigns the presidency over five or ten cities. If, therefore, the prophecies relating to Judea, and Jerusalem, and Israel, and Judah, and Jacob, not being understood by us in a "'carnal" sense, indicate some such mysteries as already mentioned, it will follow also that the predictions concerning Egypt and the Egyptians, Babylon and the Babylonians, Tyre and the Tyrians, Sidon and the Sidonians, or the other nations, are spoken not only of these " bodily" Egyptians, and Babylonians, and Tyrians, and Sidonians, but also of their " spiritual" counterparts. For if there be " spiritual" Israelites, it follows that there are also "spiritual" Egyptians and Babylonians. For what is related in Ezekiel concerning tation, that throughout the whole land the blood of men should rise to the knees, I do not know that any one possessed of understanding could refer this to that earthly Egypt which adjoins Ethiopia. But let us see whether it may not be understood more fittingly in the following manner: viz. that as there is a heavenly Jerusalem and Judea, and a nation undoubtedly which inhabits it, and is named Israel; so also it is possible that there are certain localities near to these which may seem to be called either Egypt, or Babylon, or Tyre, or Sidon, and that the princes of these places, and the souls, if there be any, that inhabit them, are called Egyptians, Babylonians, Tyrians, and Sidonians. From whom also, according to the mode of life which they lead there, a sort of captivity would seem to result, in consequence of which they are said to have fallen from Judea into Babylonia or Egypt, from a higher and better condition, or to have been scattered into other countries.

23. For perhaps as those who, departing this world in

FROM THE GREEK.

Pharaoh king of Egypt does not at all apply to the case of a certain man who ruled or was said to rule over Egypt, as will be evident to those who give it careful consideration. Similarly, what is said about the ruler of Tyre cannot be understood of a certain man who ruled over Tyre. And what is said in many places, and especially in Isaiah, of Nebuchadnezzar, cannot be explained of that individual. For the man Nebuchadnezzar neither fell from heaven, nor was he the morning star, nor did he arise upon the earth in the morning. Nor would any man of understanding interpret what is said in Ezekiel about Egypt viz. that in forty years it should be laid desolate, so that the footstep of man should not be found thereon, and that the ravages of war should be so great that the blood should run throughout the whole of it, and rise to the knees of that Egypt which is situated beside the Ethiopians whose bodies are blackened by the sun.

23. And perhaps as those here, dying according to the virtue of tliat death wliicli is common to all, are arranged, in conformity Yith their actions and deserts according as they shall be deemed worthy some in the place which is called ' hell," others in the bosom of Abraham, and in different localities or mansions; so also from those places, as if dying there, if the expression can be used, do they come down from the "upper world" to this "hell." For that "hell" to which the souls of the dead are conducted from this world, is, I believe, on account of this distinction, called the " lower hell" by Scripture, as is said in the book of Psalms: " Thou hast delivered my soul from the lowest hell." Every one, accordingly, of those who descend to the earth is, according to his deserts, or agreeably to the position which he occupied there, ordained to be born in this world, in a different country, or among a different nation, or in a different mode of life, or surrounded by infirmities of a different kind, or to be descended from religious parents, or parents who are not religious; so that it may sometimes happen that an Israelite descends among the Scythians, and a poor Egyptian is brought down to Judea. And yet our Saviour came to gather together the lost sheep of the house of Israel; and as many of the Israelites did not accept His teaching, those who 1 Iiifernus.-Yelut illic, si dici potest, morientes.

A superis. Cf. Ps. xxx. 4 and Dent, xxxii. 22.

FROM THE GREEK.

death common to all, are, in consequence of the deeds done here, so arranged as to obtain different places according to the proportion of their sins, if they should be deemed worthy of the place called Hades; so those there dying, so to speak, descend into this Hades, being judged deserving of different abodes better or worse throughout all this space of earth, and of being descended from parents of different kinds," so that an Israelite may sometimes fall among Scythians, and an Egyptian descend into Judea. And yet the Saviour

Tov Kx'hoviii'jov y o)plov ccqov.

2 Kui 'TTCApoi rolaoi, ij rolaos roig txtoxgi.

belonged to the Gentiles were called. From which it will appear to follow, that those prophecies which are delivered to the individual nations ought to be referred rather to the souls, and to their different heavenly mansions. Naj, the narratives of the events which are said to have happened either to the nation of Israel, or to Jerusalem, or to Judea, when assailed by this or that nation, cannot in many instances be understood as having actually occurred, and are much more appropriate to those nations of souls who inhabit that heaven which is said to pass away, or who even now are supposed to be inhabitants of it.

If now any one demand of us clear and distinct declarations on these points out of holy Scripture, we must answer that it was the design of the Holy Spirit, in those portions which appear to relate the history of events, rather to cover and conceal the meaning: in those passages, e. g. j where they are said to go down into Egypt, or to be carried captive to Babylonia, or when in these very countries some are said to be brought to excessive humiliation, and to be placed under bondage to their masters; while others, again, in these very countries of their captivity, were held in honour and esteem, so as to occupy positions of rank and power, and were appointed to the government of provinces; all which things, as we have said, are kept hidden and covered in the narra- Corporaliter.

FROM THE GREEK.

came to gather together the lost sheep of the house of Israel; but many of the Israelites not having yielded to His teaching, those from the, Gentiles were called. And these points, as we suppose, have been concealed in the histories. For " the kingdom of heaven is like a treasure hid in a field; the which when a man hath found, he hideth, and for joy thereof goeth and selleth all that he hath, and buyeth that field." Let us notice, then, whether the apparent and superficial and obvious meaning of Scripture does not resemble a 1 Matt. xii. 44.

tives of holy Scripture, because " the kingdom of heaven is hke a treasure hid in a field; which when a man findeth, he hideth it, and for joy thereof goeth away and selleth all that he hath, and buyeth that field."- By which similitude, consider whether it be not pointed out that the very soil and surface, so to speak, of Scripture that is, the literal meaning is the field, filled with plants and flowers of all kinds; while that deeper and profounder " spiritual" meaning are the very hidden treasures of wisdom and knowledge which the Holy Spirit by Isaiah calls the dark and invisible and hidden treasures, for the finding out of which the divine help is required: for God alone can burst the brazen gates by which they are enclosed and concealed, and break in pieces the iron bolts and levers by which access is prevented to all those things which are written and concealed in Genesis respecting the different kinds of souls, and of those seeds and generations which either have a close connection with Israel" or are widely separated from his descendants; as w ell as what is that descent of seventy souls into Egypt, which seventy souls became in that land as the stars of heaven in multitude.

But as not all of them were the light of this world "for all who are of Israel are not Israel" they

Matt, xiii. 44. propinquitatem pertinent Israel.

2 Rom. ix. 6.

FROM THE GREEK.

field filled with plants of every kind, while the things lying in it, and not visible to all, but buried, as it were, under the plants that are seen, are the hidden treasures of wisdom and knowledge; which the Spirit through Isaiah calls dark and invisible and concealed, God alone being able to break the brazen gates that conceal them, and to burst the iron bars that are upon the gates, in order that all the statements in the book of Genesis may be discovered which refer to the various genuine kinds, and seeds, as it were, of souls, which stand nearly related to Israel, or at a distance from it; and the descent into Eyypt of the seventy souls, that they may there 1 Cf. Isa. xlv. 3.

grow from being seventy souls to be an important people and as the " sand by the sea-shore innumerable."

24. This descent of the holy fathers into Egypt will appear as granted to this world by the providence of God for the illumination of others, and for the instruction of the human race, that so by this means the souls of others might be assisted in the work of enlightenment. For to them was first granted the privilege of converse with God, because theirs is the only race which is said to see God; this being the meaning, by interpretation, of the word "Israel." And now it follows that, agreeably to this view, ought the statement to be accepted aud explained that Egypt was scourged with ten plagues, to allow the people of God to. depart, or the account of what was done with the people in the wilderness, or of the buildino; of the tabernacle bv means of contributions from all the people, or of the wearing of the priestly robes, or of the vessels of the public service, because, as it is written, they truly contain within them the ' shadow and form of heavenly things." For Paul openly says of them, that " they serve unto the example and shadow of heavenlv thino; s."" There are, moreover, contained in this same law the precepts and institutions, according to which men are to live in the holy land. Threatenings also are held out as impending over those who shall transgress the law; different kinds of purifications are moreover prescribed for those who required purification, as being persons who were liable to frequent pollution, that by means of these they may arrive at last at that one purification after which no further pollution is permitted. The very people are num-

Ex ipsis Septuaginta animabus fiunt aliqui.

- Cf. Gen. xxxii. 29. Heb. viii. 5.

FROM THE GREEK.

become as the "stars of heaven in multitude." But since not all who are of them are the light of the world " for not all who are of Israel are Israel" they become from seventy souls as the " sand that is beside the sea-shore innumerable." j L Rom. ix. 6.

bered, though not all; for the souls of children are not yet old enough to be numbered according to the divine command: nor are those souls who cannot become the head of another, but are themselves subordinated to others as to a head, who are called "women," who certainly are not included in that numbering which is enjoined by God; but they alone are numbered who are called " men," by which it might be shown that the women could not be counted separately, but were included in those called men. Those, however, especially belong to the sacred number, wdio are prepared to go forth to the battles of the Israelites, and are able to fight against those public and private enemies whom the Father subjects to the Son, who sits on His right hand that He may destroy all principality and power, and by means of these bands of His soldiery, wdio, being engaged in a warfare for God, do not entangle themselves in secular business, He may overturn the kingdom of His adversary; by wdiom the shields of faith are borne, and the w eapons of wisdom brandished; among whom also the helmet of hope and salvation gleams forth, and the breastplate of brightness fortifies the breast that is filled with God. Such soldiers appear to me to be indicated, and to be prepared for wars of this kind, in those persons who in the sacred books are ordered by God's command to be numbered. But of these, by far the more perfect and distinguished are shown to be those of whom the very hairs of the head are said to be numbered. Such, indeed, as were punished for their sins, whose bodies fell in the wilderness, appear to possess a resemblance to those who had made indeed no little progress, but who could not at all, for various reasons, attain to the end of perfection; because they are reported either to have murmured, or to have worshipped idols, or to have committed fornication, or to have done some evil work which the mind ought not even to conceive. I do not consider the following even to be without some mystical meaning, viz. that certain

Extrinsecus. Hostes iuimicosque.

Ne illud quidem sacramento aliquo vacuum puto. ORIG. Y of the Israelites, possessing many flocks and animals, take possession by anticipation of a country adapted for pasture and the feeding of cattle, which was the very first that the right hand of the Hebrews had secured in war. For, making a request of Moses to receive this region, they are divided off by the waters of the Jordan, and set apart from any possession in the holy land. And this Jordan, according to the form of heavenly things, may appear to water and irrigate thirsty souls, and the senses that are adjacent to it." In connection with which, even this statement does not appear superfluous, that Moses indeed hears from God what is described in the book of Leviticus, while in Deuteronomy it is the people that are the auditors of Moses, and who learn from him what they could not hear from God. For as Deuteronomy is called, as it were, the second law, which to some will appear to convey this signification, that when the first law which was ffiven throufih Moses had come to an end, so a second legislation seems to have been enacted, which was specially transmitted by Moses to his successor Joshua, who is certainly believed to embody a type of our Saviour, by whose second law that is, the precepts of the Gospel all things are brought to pefection.

25. We have to see, however, whether this deeper meaning may not perhaps be indicated, viz. that as in Deuteronomy the legislation is made known with greater clearness and distinctness than in those books which were first written, so also by that advent of the Saviour which He accomplished in His state of humiliation, when He assumed the form of a servant, that more celebrated and renowned second advent in the glory of His Father may not be pointed out, and in it the types of Deuteronomy may be fulfilled, when in the kingdom of heaven all the saints shall live according to the laws of the everlasting gospel; and as in His coming now He fulfilled that law which has a shadow of good things to

Quem primum omnium Israelitici belli dextra defenderat. 2 Rigare et inundare animas sitientes, et sensus adjacentes sibi. " Formam.

come, SO also by that future glorious advent will be fulfilled and brought to perfection the shadows of the present advent. For thus spake the prophet regarding it: " The breath of our countenance, Christ the Lord, to whom we said, that under Thy shadow we shall live among the nations;" at the time, viz., when He will more vorthily transfer all the saints from a temporal to an everlasting gospel, according to the designation, employed by John in the Apocalypse, of "an everlasting gospel."""

26. But let it be sufficient for us in all these matters to adapt our understanding to the rule of religion, and so t(think of the words of the Holy Spirit as not to deem th language the ornate composition of feeble human eloquence but to hold, according to the scriptural statement, that " all the glory of the King is within,"" and that the treasure of divine meaning is enclosed within the frail vessel of the common letter. And if any curious reader were still to ask an explanation of individual points, let him come and hear, along with ourselves, how the Apostle Paul, seeking to penetrate by help of the Holy Spirit, w ho searches even the ", " deep things" of God, into the depths of divine wisdom and knowledge, and yet, unable to reach the end, so to speak, and to come to a thorough knowledge, exclaims in despair and amazement, " Oh the depth of the riches of the knowledge and wisdom of God!" Now, that it was from despair of attaining a perfect understanding that he uttered this exclamation, listen to his own words: " How unsearchable are God's judgments! and His ways, how past finding out!" For he did not say that God's judgments were difficult to discover, but that they were altogether inscrutable; nor that it was simply difficult to trace out His ways, but that they were altogether past finding out. For however far a man 1 Lam. iv. 20.- Cf. Rev. xiv. 6.

2 Omnis gloria regis intrinsecus est. Heb., Sept., and Vulgate all read, "daughter of the king." Probably the omission of "filise" in the t xt may be due to an error of the copyists.

"Rom. xi. 33. Rom. xi. 33.

may advance in his investigations, and how great soever the progress that he may make by unremitting study, assisted even by the grace of God, and with his mind enlightened, he will not be able to attain to the end of those things which are the object of his inquiries. Nor can any created mind deem it possible in any way to attain a full comprehension of things; but after having discovered certain of the objects of its research, it sees again others which have still to be sought out. And even if it should succeed in mastering these, it will see again many others succeeding them which must form the subject of investigation. And on this account, therefore, Solomon, the wisest of men, beholding by his wisdom the nature of things, says, ' I said, I will become wise; and wisdom herself was made far from me, far further than it was; and a profound depth who shall find?" Isaiah also, knowing; that the bemnnino-s of thino; s could not be dis-covered by a mortal nature, and not even by those natures which, although more divine than human, were nevertheless themselves created or formed; knowing then, that by none of these could either the beginning or the end be discovered, says, "Tell the former things which have been, and we know that ye are gods; or announce what are the last things, and then we shall see that ye are gods."

For-my Hebrew teacher also used thus to teach, that as the beginning or end of all things could be comprehended by no one, save only our Lord Jesus Christ and the Holy Spirit, so under the form of a vision Isaiah spake of two seraphim alone, who with two wings cover the countenance of God, and with two His feet, and with two do fly, calling to each other alternately, and saying, " Holy, holy, holy is the Lord God of Sabaoth; the whole earth is full of Thy glory." That the seraphim alone have both their wings over the face of God, and over His feet, we venture to declare as meaning that

The Septuagint reads: Ef-ra '2o(pia7 aof, otr kcci xvtn IfiuKpivsYi dor i , ov' f izkpoiv VTrip V tjv kxi fiotv (2xdos' rig svpyjasi cuvro. The Vulgate translates this literally.

2 Cf. Isa. xli. 22, 23. Isa. vi. 3.

neither the hosts of holy angels, nor the " holy seats," nor the ' dominions," nor the " principalities," nor the " powers," can fully understand the beginning of all things, and the limits of the universe. But we are to understand that those 'saints" whom the Spirit has enrolled, and the "virtues," approach very closely to those very beginnings, and attain to a height which the others cannot reach; and yet whatever it be that these " virtues " have learned throumi revelation from the Son of God and from the Holy Spirit and they will certainly be able to learn very much, and those of higher rank much more than those of a lower nevertheless it is impossible for them to comprehend all things, according ta the statement, ' The most part of the works of God are hid."- And therefore also it is to be desired that every one, according to his strength, should ever stretch out to those things that are before, ' for ettino; the thinojs that are behind," both to better works and to a clearer apprehension and understanding, through Jesus Christ our Saviour, to whom be glory for ever!

27. Let every one, then, w ho cares for truth, be little concerned about words and language, seeing that in every I nation there prevails a different usage of speech; but let him rather direct his attention to the nieanhig,. conveyed by ', the words, than to the nature of the words that convey 1 tlie meaning, especially in matters of such importance and difficulty: as, e. g., when it is an object of investigation whether there is any " substance" in which neither colour, nor form, nor touch, nor magnitude is to be understood as existing visible to the mind alone, which any one names as he pleases; for the Greeks call such aacofiarovy i. e. ' incorporeal," while holy Scripture declares it to be " invisible," for Paul calls Christ the " image of the invisible God," and says again, that by Christ were created all things ' visible and invisible." And by this it is declared that there are, among created things, certain " substances " that are, according to their peculiar nature, invisible. But although these Cf. Ecclus. xvi. 21.

are not themselves " corporeal," they nevertheless make use of bodies, while they are themselves better than any bodily substances. But that " substance" of the Trinity which is the beginning and cause of all things, " from which are all things, and through which are all things, and in which are all things," cannot be believed to be either a body or in a body, but is altogether incorporeal. And now let it suffice to have spoken briefly on these points (although in a digression, caused by the nature of the subject), in order to show that there are certain things, the meaning of which cannot be unfolded at all by any words of human language, but which are made known more through simple apprehension than by any properties of words. And under this rule must be brought also the understanding of the sacred Scripture, in order that its statements may be judged not according to the worthlessness of the letter, but according to the divinity of the Holy Spirit, by whose inspiration they were caused to be written.

SUMMARY of DOCTRINE REGARDING THE FATHER, THE SON, AND THE HOLY SPIRIT, AND THE OTHER TOPICS DISCUSSED IN THE PRECEDING PAGES.

28. It is now" time, after the rapid consideration which to the best of our ability w e have given to the topics discussed, to recapitulate, by way of summing up what w e have said in different places, the individual points, and first of all to restate our conclusions regarding the Father, and the Son, and the Holy Spirit.

Seeing God the Father is invisible and inseparable from the Son, the Son is not generated from Him by " prolation," as some suppose. For if the Son be a " prolation" of the Father (the term " prolation" being used to signify such a generation as that of animals or men usually is), then, of necessity, both He who "prolated" and He who ivas "prolated" are corporeal. For we do not say, as the heretics suppose, that some part of the substance of God was converted into the

Son, or that the Son was procreated by the Father out of things non-existent i, e, beyond His own substance, so tliat there once was a time when He did not exist; but, putting away all corporeal conceptions, we say that the Word and Wisdom was begotten out of the nyisilile. and incorporeal with- out any corporeal feeling, as if it were an act of the will pro- I ceedino; from the understandinix. Nor, seeincr He is called, the Son of His love, will it appear absurd if in this way He be called also the Son of His will. Nay, John also indicates that " God is Light,"' and Paul also declares that the Son is the splendour of everlasting light. As light, accordingly, could never exist without splendour, so neither can the Son be understood to exist without the Father; for He is called the 'express image of His person," and the Word and Wisdom. How, then, can it be asserted that there once was a time when He was not the Son? For that is nothincr else than to say that there was once a time when He was not thei Truth, nor the Wisdom, nor the Life, although in all these He is judged to be the perfect essence of God the Father; for these things cannot be severed from Him, or even be separated from His essence. And although these qualities are said to be many in understanding, yet in their nature and essence they are one, and in them is the fulness of divinity. Now this expression which we employ ' that there neverx was a time when He did not exist" is to be understood with j an allowance. For these very words "when" or "never": have a meaning that relates to time, whereas the statements made regarding Father, Son, and Holy Spirit are to be-understood as transcending all time, all ages, and all eternity.!. For it is the Trinity alone which exceeds the comprehension not only of temporal but even of eternal intelligence; while other things which are not included in it are to be measured by times and ages. This Son of God, then, in respect of the Word being God, which was in the beginning with God, no

Ex nullis substantibus.- 1 Jolin i. 5. Cf. Heb. i. 3.

Quje quidem quamvis intellectu rnulta esse dicantur. Quse sunt extra Trinitatem.

FROM THE LATIN.

one will logically suppose to be contained in any place; nor yet in respect of His being " Wisdom," or " Truth," or the ' " Life," or " Righteousness," or " Sanctification," or " Redemption:" for all these properties do not require space to be able to act or to operate, but each one of them is to be understood as meaning those individuals who participate in His virtue and working.

29. Now, if any one were to say that, through those who i are partakers of the " Word" of God, or of His " Wisdom," I or His " Truth," or His " Life," the Word and Wisdom itself appeared to be contained in a place, we should have to say to him in answer, that there is no doubt that Christ, in respect of being the " Word " or " Wisdom," or all other things, was in Paul, and that he therefore said, "Do you seek a proof of Christ speaking in me? " and again, "I live, yet not I, but Christ liveth in me." Seeing, then. He was in Paul, w ho will doubt that He was in a similar manner in Peter and in John, and in each one of the saints; and not only in those who are upon the earth, but in those also who are in heaven? For it is absurd to say that Christ was in Peter and in Paul, but not in Michael the archangel, nor in Gabriel. And from this it is distinctly shown that the divinity of the Son of God was not shut up in some place; otherwise it would have been in it only, and not in another. But since, in conformity with the majesty of its incorporeal nature, it is confined to no place; so, again, it cannot be understood to be wanting in any. But this is understood to be the sole difference, that although He is in different individuals as we have said as Peter, or Paul, or Michael, or Gabriel He is not in a similar way in all beings wliatever. For He is more fully and clearly, and, so to speak, more openly in archangels than in other holy men. And this is evident from the statement, that when all who are saints have arrived at the summit of perfection, they are said to be made like, 1 Cf. 2 Cor. xiii. 3. 2 Gal. ii. 20.

Quam in aliis Sanctis viris. " Aliis" is found in the mss., but is wanting in many editions.

or equal to, the angels, agi'eeably to the declaration in the Gospels. Whence it is clear that Christ is in each individual in as great a degree as the amount of his deserts allows.

30. Plaving, then, briefly restated these points regarding the nature of the Trinity, it follows that we notice shortly this statement also, that " by the Son " are said to be created " all things that are in heaven, and that are in earth, visible and invisible, whether they be thrones, or dominions, or principalities, or powers: all things were created by Him, and for Him; and He is before all, and all things consist by Him, who is the head." In conformity with which John also in his Gospel says: " All things were created by Him; and without Him was not anything made." And David, intimating that the mystery of the entire Trinity was concerned in the creation of all things, says: " By the Word of the Lord were the heavens made; and all the host of them by the Spirit of His mouth."

After these points we shall appropriately remind the reader of the bodily advent and incarnation of the only-begotten Son of God, with respect to whom we are not to suppose that all the majesty of His divinity is confined within the limits of His slender hodij, so that all the " word" of God, and His " wisdom," and " essential truth," and " life," was either rent asunder from the Father, or restrained and confined within the narrowness of His bodily person, and is not to be considered to have operated anywhere besides; but the cautious acknowledgment of a religious man ought to be between the two, so that it ought neither to be believed that anything of divinity was wanting in Christ, nor that any separation at all was made from the essence of the Father, which is everywhere. For some such meaning seems to be indicated by John the Baptist, when he said to the multitude in the bodily absence of Jesus, "There standeth one among 1 Cf. Matt. xxii. 30 and Luke xx. 36.

2 Unde constat in singulis quibusque tantum effici Christum, quantum ratio indulserit meritorum.

3 Cf. Col. i. 16-18. Jolm i. 3. Ps. xxxiii. 6.

you whom ye know not: He it is who cometh after me, the latchet of whose shoes I am not worthy to unloose." For it certainly could not be said of Him, who was absent, so far as His bodily presence is concerned, that He was standing in the midst of those among whom the Son of God was not bodily present.

31. Let no one, however, suppose that by this we affirm that some portion of the divinity of the Son of God was in Christ, and that the remaining portion was elsewhere or everywhere, which may be the opinion of those who are ignorant of the nature of an incorporeal and invisible essence. For it is impossible to speak of the parts of an incorporeal beinir, or to make any division of them; but He is in all things, and through all things, and above all things, in the manner in which we have spoken above, i. e. in the manner in which He is understood to be either "wisdom " or the r " word," or the " life," or the " truth " by which method of understandino; all confinement of a local kind is un-doubtedly excluded. The Son of God, then, desiring for the salvation of the human race to appear unto men, and to sojourn among them, assumed not only a human body, as some suppose, but also a soul resembling our souls indeed in nature, but in will and power resembling Himself, and such as might unfailingly accomplish all the desires and arrangements of the " word" and " wisdom." Now, that He had a soul, is most clearly shown by the Saviour in the Gospels, when He said, 'No man taketh my life from me, but I lay it down of myself. I have power to lay down my life, and I have power to take it again." And again, ' My soul is sorrowful even unto death." And again, "Now is my soul troubled." For the "Word" of God is not to be understood to be a " sorrowful and troubled" soul, because with the authority of divinity He says, "I have power to lay down my life." Nor yet do we assert that the Son of God 1 Cf. John i. 26, 27. Proposito vero et virtute similem sibi.

s Animam. John x. 18.

Matt. xxvi. 38. John xii. 27.

Chap, i. OBIGEN DE PRINCIPIIS. 347 from the latin.

was in tliat soul as He was in the soul of Paul or Peter and the other saints, in whom Christ is believed to speak as Hb does in Paul. But regarding all these we are to hold, as Scripture declares, "No one is clean from filthiness, not even if his life lasted but a single day." But this soul which was in Jesus, before it knew the evil, selected the good; and because He loved righteousness, and hated iniquity, therefore God " anointed Him with the oil of gladness above His fellows." He is anointed, then, with the oil of gladness when He is united to, the "word" of God in a stainless union, and by this means alone of all souls was incapable of sin, because it was capable of receiving well and fully. the Son of God; and therefore also it is one with Him, and is named by His titles, and is called Jesus Christ, by whom, all things are said to be mad e. Of which soul, seeing it had ' received into itself the whole wisdom of God, and the truth, and the life, I think that the apostle also said this: " Our life is hidden with Christ in God; but when Christ, who is our life, shall appear, then shall we also appear with Him in glory." For what other Christ can be here understood, who is said to be hidden in God, and who is afterwards to appear, except Him who is related to have been anointed with the oil of gladness, i. e. to have been filled with God essentially, in whom He is now said to be hidden? For on this account is Christ proposed as an example to all believers, because as He always, even before He knew evil at all, selected the good, and loved righteousness, and hated iniquity, and therefore God anointed Him with the oil of gladness; so also ought each one, after a lapse or sin, to cleanse himself from his stains, making Him his example, and, taking Him as the guide of his journey, enter upon the steep way of virtue, that so perchance by this means, as far as possible we may, by imitating Him, be made partakers of the divine nature, according to the words of Scripture: " He that saith that he believeth in Christ, ought so to walk, as He also walked."

1 Cf. Job XV. 14. 2 Ps, xlv. 7. 3 cf. Col. iii. 3.

Substantialiter. Cf. 1 John ii. G.

This " word," then, and this " wisdom," by the imitation of which w e are said to be either wise or rational beings, becomes " all things to all men, that it may gain all;" and because it is made weak, it is therefore said of it, "Though He was crucified through weakness, yet He liveth by the power of God."- Finally, to the Corinthians wdio were weak, Paul declares that he "knew nothing, save Jesus Christ, and Him crucified."

32. Some, indeed, would have the following language of the apostle applied to the soul itself, as soon as it had assumed flesh from Mary, viz., "Who, being in the form of. God, thought it not robbery to be equal with God, but divested Himself of His glory, taking upon Himself the form of a servant;" since He undoubtedly restored it to the form of God by means of better examples and training, and recalled it to that fulness of which He had divested Himself.

As now by participation in the Son of God one is adopted as a son, and by participating in that wisdom which is in God is rendered wise, so also by participation in the Holy Spirit is a man rendered holy and spiritual. For it is one and the same thing to have a share in the Holy Spirit, which is the Spirit of the Father and the Son, since the nature of the Trinity is one and incorporeal. And what we have said regarding the participation of the soul is to be understood of angels and heavenly powers in a similar w ay as of souls, because every rational creature needs a participation in the Trinity.

Eespecting also the plan of this visible world seeing one of the most important questions usually raised is as to the manner of its existence we have spoken to the best of our ability in the preceding pages, for the sake of those who are accustomed to seek the grounds of their behef in our religion, and also for those who stir against us heretical questions, and who are accustomed to bandy about the word "matter," which

2 Cor. siii. 4. 1 Cor. ii. 2. De Maria corpus assumsit.

Semet ipsum exinanivit. Vh. ii. G, 7.

6 In filiiun adoptatui'. Ventilare.

FROM THE LATIN.

tliey have not yet been able to understand; of which subject I now deem it necessary briefly to remind the reader.

33. And, in the first place, it is to be noted that we have nowhere found in the canonical Scriptures, up to the present time, the word " matter" used for that substance which is said to underlie bodies. For in the expression of Isaiah, "And he shall devour vxry," i. e. matter, " like hay," when speaking of those who were appointed to undergo their punishments, the word " matter " was used instead of ' sins." And if this word "matter" should happen to occur in any other passage, it will never be found, in my opinion, to have the signification of which we are now in quest, unless perhaps in the book which is called the Wisdom of Solomon, a work which is certainly not esteemed authoritative by all. In that book, however, w e find written as follows: " For Thy almighty hand, that made the world out of shapeless matter, wanted not means to send among them a multitude of bears and fierce lions." Very many, indeed, are of opinion that the matter of which things are made is itself signified in the language used by Moses in the beginning of Genesis: " In the beginning God made heaven and earth; and the earth was invisible, and not arranged:"' for by the words "invisible and not arranged " Moses w ould seem to mean nothing else than shapeless matter. But if this be truly matter, it is clear then that the original elements of bodies are not incapable of change. For those who posited "atoms" either those particles which are incapable of subdivision, or those which are subdivided into equal parts or any one element, as the principles of bodily things, could not posit the word " matter" in the proper sense of the term among the first principles of things. For if they will have it that 1 In Scriptiiris canonicis.

2 Isa. X. 17, x, c(, i (pocyira. i cjasi yjp70v ry, u vt yju, Sept. The Yulgate follows the Masoretic text.

3 Wisd. xi. 17.

Gen. i. 2, " invisibilis et incomposita; " " iuanes et vacua," Vulg. Initia corporum.

matter underlies every body a substance convertible or changeable, or divisible in all its parts they will not, as is proper, assert that it exists without qualities. And with them we agree, for we altogether deny that matter ought to be spoken of as " unbegotten " or " uncreated," agreeably to our former statements, w hen we pointed out that from water, and earth, and air or heat, different kinds of fruits were produced by different kinds of trees; or when we showed that fire, and air, and water, and earth were alternately converted into each other, and that one element was resolved into another by a kind of mutual consanguinity; and also when we proved that from the food either of men or animals the substance of the flesh was derived, or that the moisture of the natural seed was converted into solid flesh and bones; all which go to prove that the substance of the body is changeable, and may pass from one quality into all others.

34. Nevertheless we must not forget that a substance never exists without a quality, and that it is by an act of the understanding alone that this substance which underlies bodies, and which is capable of quality, is discovered to be matter. Some indeed, in their desire to investigate these subjects more profoundly, have ventured to assert that bodily nature is nothing else than qualities. For if hardness and softness, heat and cold, moisture and aridity, be qualities; and if, when these or other qualities of

this sort be cut away, nothing else is understood to remain, then all things will appear to be "qualities." And therefore also those persons who make these assertions have endeavoured to maintain, that since all who say that matter was uncreated will admit that qualities were created by God, it may be in this way shown that even according to them matter was not uncreated; since qualities constitute everything, and these are declared by all without contradiction to have been made by God. Those, again, who would make out that quahties are superimposed from w ithout upon a certain underlying matter, make use of illustrations of this kind: e. g. Paul un- Naturam corpoream.

doubtedly is either silent, or speaks, or watclies, or sleeps, or maintains a certain attitude of body; for he is either in a sitting, or standing, or recumbent position. For these are ' accidents" belonging to men, without which they are almost never found. And yet our conception of man does not lay down any of these things as a definition of liim; but we so understand and regard him by their means, that we do not at all take into account the reason of his particular condition either in watching, or in sleeping, or in speaking, or in keeping silence, or in any other action that must necessarily happen to men. If any one, then, can regard Paul as being without all these things which are capable of happening, he will in the same way also be able to understand this underlying substance without qualities. When, then, our mind puts away all qualities from its conception, and gazes, so to speak, upon the underlying element alone, and keeps its attention closely upon it, without any reference to the softness or hardness, or heat or cold, or humidity or aridity of the substance, then by means of this somewhat simulated process of thought" it will appear to behold matter clear from qualities of every kind.

35. But some one will perhaps inquire whether we can obtain out of Scripture any grounds for such an understanding of the subject. Now I think some such view is indicated in the Psalms, wdien the prophet says, "Mine eyes have seen thine imperfection;" by which the mind of the prophet, examining with keener glance the first principles of things, and separating in thought and imagination only be-

Nee tamen sensus uoster manifeste de eo aliquid horum definit, sed ita eum per haec intelligimiis, vel consideramiis, ut non omniiio rationem status ejus compreliendamus, vel in eo, quod vigilat, vel in eo, quod dormit, aut in quo loquitur, vel tacet, et si qua alia simt, quje accidere necesse est hominibus.

2 Tunc siraulata quodammodo cogitationc.

Ps. cxxxix. 16, TO u-KXTipyocatou jlov i'qo7uu o 6(f:0uxLcoi cov, Sept.; " Imperfectum tuum viderunt oculi tui," Vulg. (same as in the text.) T' " X"! "0?2 " Thine eyes did see my substance, yet being imperfect," auth. vers. Cf. Gesenius and FUrst, s. v. D i- tween matter and its qualities, perceived the imperfection of God, which certainly is understood to be perfected by the addition of qualities. Enoch also, in his book, speaks as follows: "I have walked on even to imperfection;" which expression I consider may be understood in a similar manner, viz. that the mind of the prophet proceeded in its scrutiny and investigation of all visible things, until it arrived at that first beginning in which it beheld imperfect matter existing without " qualities." For it is written in the same book of Enoch, "I beheld the whole of matter;" which is so understood as if he had said: " I have clearly seen all the divisions of matter which are broken up from one into each individual species either of men, or animals, or of the sky, or of the sun, or of all other things in this world." After these points, now, we proved to the best of our power in the preceding pages that all things which exist were made by God, and-Yt that there was nothing which was not made, save the nature of the Father, and the Son, and the Holy Spirit; and that God, who is by nature good, desiring to have those upon whom He might confer benefits, and who might rejoice in receiving His benefits, created creatures worthy of this, i. e. who wera. capable of receiving Him in a worthy manner, who, He says, are also begotten by Him as his sons. He made all things, moreover, by number and measure. For there is nothing before God without either limit or measure. For by His power He comprehends all things, and He Himself is comprehended by the strength of no created thing, because that nature is known to itself alone. For the Father alone knoweth the Son, and the Son alone knoweth the Father, and the Holy Spirit alone searcheth even the deep things of God. All created things, therefore, i. e. either the number of rational beings or the measure of bodily matter, are distinguished by Plim as being within a certain number or measurement; since, as it was necessary for an intellectual nature to employ bodies, and this nature is shown to be

Ambulavi usque ad imperfectum; cf. Book of Enoch, chap. xvii. 2 Universas materias perspexi; cf. Book of Enoch, chap. xvii.

cluingeable and convertible by tlic very condition of its being created (for what did not exist, but began to exist, is said by this very circumstance to be of nuitable nature), it can liave;" neither goodness nor wickedness as an essential, but only as(an accidental attribute of its beinrr. Seein r, then, as we have said, that rational nature was mutable and chanireable, so that it made use of a different bodily coverino- of this or that sort of quality, according to its merits, it was necessarv, as God foreknew there would be diversities in souls or spiritual powers, that He should create also a bodily nature the qualities of which might be changed at the will of the Creator into all that was required. And this bodily nature must last as long as those things which require it as a covering: for there will be always rational natures which need a bodily covering; and there will therefore always be a bodily nature whose coverings must necessarily be used by rational creatures, unless some one be able to demonstrate by arguments that a rational nature can live without a body. But how difficult nay, how almost impossible this is for our imderstanding, we have shown in the preceding pages, in our discussion of the individual topics.

36. It will not, I consider, be opposed to the nature of our undertaking, if we restate with all possible brevltv our opinions on the immortality of rational natures. Every one who participates in anything, is unquestionably of one essence and nature with him who is partaker of the same thing. For example, as all eyes participate in the light, so accordingly all eyes which partake of the light are of one nature; but although every eye partakes of the light, yet, inasmuch as one sees more clearly, and another more obscurely, every eye does not equally share in the light. And again, all hearing receives voice or sound, and therefore all hearing is of one nature; but each one hears more rapidly or more slowly, according as the quality of his hearing is clear and sound. Let us pass now from these sensuous illustrations to the consideration of intellectual

things. Every mind which partakes of intellectual light ought undoubtedly to be of one nature with every mind

OKIG. z which partakes in a similar manner of intellectual light. If the heavenly virtues, then, partake of intellectual light, i. e. of divine nature, because they participate in wisdom and holiness, and if human souls have partaken of the same light and wisdom, and thus are mutually of one nature and of one essence, then, since the heavenly virtues are incorruptible and immortal, the essence of the human soul will also be immortal and incorruptible. And not only so, but because the nature of Father, and Son, and Holy Spirit, of whose Intellectual light alone all created things have a share, is incorruptible and eternal, it is altogether consistent and necessary that every substance which partakes of that eternal nature should last for ever, and be incorruptible and eternal, so that the eternity of divine goodness may be understood also in this respect, that they who obtain its benefits are also eternal. But as, in the instances referred to, a diversity in the participation of the light was observed, when the glance of the beholder was described as being duller or more acute, so also a diversity is to be noted in the participation of Father, Son, and Holy Spirit, varying with the degree of zeal or capacity of mind. If such were not the case, we have to consider whether it would not seem to be an act of impiety to say that the mind which is capable of receiving God should admit of a destruction of its essence; as if the very fact that it is able to feel and understand God could not sufbce for its perpetual existence, especially since, if even through neglect the mind fall away from a pure and complete reception of God, it nevertheless contains within it certain seeds of restoration and renewal to a better understanding, seeing the "inner," which is also called the "rational" man, is renewed after " the image and likeness of God, who created him." And therefore the prophet says, "All the ends of the earth shall remember, and turn unto the Lord; and all the kindreds of the nations shall worship before Thee.""

37. If any one, indeed, venture to ascribe essential corruption to him who was made after the image and likeness 1 Alioquin.- Substantialem interitiira. Ps. xxii. 27.

of Gvid, then, in my opinion, this impious cliarge extends even to the Son of God Himself, for He is called in Scripture the image of God. Or he who holds this opinion would certainly impugn the authority of Scripture, which says that man was n. ade in the image of God; and in him are manifestly to be discovered traces of the divine image, not by any appearance of the bodily frame, which is corruptible, but by mental wisdom, by justice, moderation, virtue, wisdom, discipline; in fine, by the whole band of virtues, which are innate in the essence of God, and which may enter into man by diligence and imitation of God; as the Lord also intimates in the Gospel, when He says, " Be ye therefore merciful, as your Father also is merciful;""" and, "Be ye perfect, even as your Father also is perfect." From which it is clearly shown that all these virtues are perpetually in God, and that they can never approach to or depart from Him, whereas by men they are acquired only slowly, and one by one. And hence also by these means they seem to have a kind of relationship with God; and since God knows all things, and none of things intellectual in themselves can elude His notice" (for God the Father alone, and His only-begotten Son, and the Holy Spirit, not only possess a knowledge of those things which they have created, but also of themselves), a rational understanding also, advancing from small things to great, and from things visible to things invisible, may attain to a more perfect knowledge. For it is placed in the body, and advances from sensible things themselves, which are corporeal, to things that are intellectual. But lest our statement that things intellectual are not cognisable by the senses should appear unbecoming, we shall employ the instance of Solomon, who says, "You will find also a divine sense;" by which he shows that those thinf s which are intellectual are to be

Cf. Col. i. 15 and 2 Cor. iv. 4. 2 mke vi. 36.

3 Matt. V. 48.

Nihil eum rernm intellectualium ex se lateat.

Cf. Prov. ii. 5, 7: iyvuni'j Qiov ivpviaug Sept. Scientiam Dei invcnies, souo-lit out not by means of a bodily sense, but by a crtain other which he calls " divine." And with this sensj must we look on each of those rational beings w hich ye have enumerated above; and with this sense are to be jnderstood those words which we speak, and those statements to be weimied which we commit to writing. For the divij-ie nature knows even those thoughts which we revolve withn us in silence. And on those matters of wdiich we have spoken, or on the others which follow from them, according to thv rule above laid down, are our opinions to be formed.

II. INDEX OF TEXTS.

PACK 106, 325 237, 238 125,.346 jkEETIXG, my lord and son, most worthy Origen, from Africanus. In your sacred discussion with Agnomon you referred to that prophecy of Daniel wliich is related of his youth. This at that time, as was meet, I accepted as genuine. Now, however, I cannot understand how ib escaped you that this part of the book is spurious. For, in sooth, this section, although apart from this it is elegantly written, is plainly a more modern forgery. There are many proofs of this. When Susanna is condemned to die, the prophet is seized by the Spirit, and cries out that the sentence is unjust. Now, in the first place, it is always in some other way that Daniel prophesies by visions, and dreams, and an angel appearing to him, never by prophetic inspiration. Then, after crying out in this extraordinary fashion, he detects them in a way no less incredible, which not even Philistion the play-writer would have resorted to. For, not satisfied with rebuking them through the Spirit, he placed them apart, and asked them severally where they saw her committing adultery. And when the one said, Under a holm-tree" (prinos), he answered that the angel would saw him asunder (prisein); and in a similar fashion menaced the other who said, '- Under a mastich-tree" (schinos), with being-rent asunder (schisthenai). Now, in Greek, it liappens that "holm-tree" and "saw asunder," and "rend"' and "mastich-tree " sound alike; but in Hebrew they are quite distinct. But all the books of the Old Testament have been translated from Hebrew into Greek.

2. Moreover, liow Is it tliat they who were captives among the Chaklgeans, lost and won at play, thrown out unburied on the streets, as w as prophesied of the former captivity, their sons torn from them to be eunuchs, and their daughters to be concubines, as had been prophesied; how is it that such could pass sentence of death, and that on the wife of their king Joakim, whom the king of the Babylonians had made partner of his throne? Then if it was not this Joakim, but some other from the common people, whence had a captive such a mansion and spacious garden? But a more fatal objection is, that this section, along with the other two at the end of it, is not contained in the Daniel received amonoj the Jews. And add that, among all the many prophets who had been before, there is no one who has quoted from another word for w ord. For they had no need to go a-begging for words, since their own were true; but this one, in rebuking one of those men, quotes the words of the Lord: " The innocent and righteous shalt thou not slay." From all this I infer that this section is a later addition. Moreover, the style is different. I have struck the blow; do you give the echo; answer, and instruct me. Salute all my masters. The learned all salute thee. With all my heart I pray for your and your circle's health.

Nolte would change vjarpccyocxoif iuoi (or a. arpaya. T uusvoi, as Wetsten. has it), which is a utra flpyixsvoy, into (jrpxyyx'huy. iuoi or 'iarpccyycc?-f."Auoi, " strangled." He compares Tob. ii. 3.

RIGEN to Afrlcanus, a beloved brother in God the Father, through Jesus Christ, His holy child, greeting. Your letter, from which I learn what you think of the Susanna in the book of Daniel, which is used in the churches, although apparently somewhat short, presents in its few words many problems, each of which demands no common treatment, but such as oversteps the character of a letter, and reaches the limits of a discourse. And I, when I consider, as best I can, the measure of my intellect, that I may know myself, am aware that I am wanting in the accuracy necessary to reply to your letter; and that the more, that the few days I have spent in Nico-media have been far from sufficient to send you an answer to all your demands and queries even after the fashion of the present epistle. Wherefore pardon my little ability, and the little time I had, and read this letter with all indulgence, supplying anything I may omit.

2. You begin by saying, that when, in my discussion with our friend Bassus, I used the Scripture Avhicli contains the prophecy of Daniel when yet a young man in the affair of Susanna, I did this as if it had escaped me that this part of the book was spurious. You say that you praise this passage as elegantly written, but find fault with it as a more modern composition, and a forgery; and you add that the forger has had recourse to something which not even Philistion the play-writer would have used in his puns between prinos and priseiny scldnos and scjiisis, which words as they sound in Greek can be used in this way, but not in Hebrew. In ans Yer to this, I have to tell you what it be- lioves us to do in the cases not only of tlie History of Susanna, which is found in every church of Christ in that Greek copy which the Greeks use, but is not in the Hebrew, or of the two other passages you mention at the end of the book containing the history of Bel and the Dragon, which likewise are not in the Hebrew copy of Daniel; but of thousands of other passages also which I found in many places when with my little strength I was collating the Hebrew copies with ours. For in Daniel itself I found the word "- bound " followed in our versions by very many verses

which are not in the Hebrew at all, beginning (according to one of the copies which circulate in the churches) thus: " Ananias, and Azarias, and Misael prayed and sang unto God," down to " O, all 3'e that worship the Lord, bless ye the God of gods. Praise Him, and say that His mercy endureth for ever and ever. And it came to pass, when the king heard them singing, and saw them that they were alive." Or, as in another co jy, from "And they walked in the midst of the fire, praising God and blessing the Lord," down to " O, all ye that worship the Lord, bless ye the God of gods. Praise Him, and say that His mercy endureth to all generations." But in the Hebrew copies the words, "And these three men, Sedrach, Misach, and Abdenego fell down bound into the midst of the fire," are immediately followed by the verse. "'Nabouchodo-nosor the king was astonished, and rose up in haste, and spake, and said unto his counsellors." For so Aquila, following the Hebrew reading, gives it, who has obtained the credit among the Jews of having interpreted the Scriptures with no ordinary care, and whose version is most commonly used by those who do not know Hebrew, as the one which has been most successful. Of the copies in my possession whose readings I gave, one follows the Seventy, and the other Theodotion; and just as the History of Susanna which you call a forgery is found in both, together with the passages at the end of Daniel, so they give also these passages, amounting, to make a rough guess, to more than two hundred verses.

3. And in many other of the sacred books I found some-1 The Song of the Three Holy Children in the Apocrypha.

times more In our copies than in the Hebrew, sometimes less. I shall adduce a few examples, since it is impossible to give them all. Of the book of Esther neither the prayer of lar-dochaios nor that of Esther, both fitted to edify the reader, is found in the Hebrew. Neither are the letters; nor the one written to Amman about the rooting up of the Jewish nation, nor that of Mardochaios in the name of Artaxerxes delivering the nation from death. Then in Job, the words from " It is written, that he shall rise a ain with those whom the Lord raises," to the end, are not in the Hebrew, and so not in Aquila's edition; while they are found in the Septuagint and in Theodotion's version, agreeing with each other at least in sense. And many other places I found in Job where our copies have more than the Hebrew ones, sometimes a little more, and sometimes a great deal more: a little more, as when to the words, "Eising up in the morning, he offered burnt-offerings for them according to their number," they add, ' one heifer for the sin of their soul;" and to the words, ' The angels of God came to present themselves before God, and the devil came with them," " from going to and fro in the earth, and from walking up and down in it." Again, after " The Lord gave, the Lord has taken away," the Hebrew has not, "It was so, as seemed good to the Lord." Then our copies are very much fuller than the Hebrew, when Job's wafe speaks to him, from " How long wilt thou hold out? And he said, Lo, I wait yet a little while, looking for the hope of my salvation," down to " that I may cease from my troubles, and my sorrows which compass me." For they have only these words of the woman, "But say a word against God, and die."

4. Again, through the whole of Job there are many passages in the Hebrew which are wanting in our copies, generally four or five verses, but sometimes, however, even fourteen, and nineteen, and sixteen. But why should I enumerate all the instances I

collected with so much labour, to prove that the difference between our copies and those of the Jews did

This should probably be corrected, with Pat. Jmi., into, "Nor are the letters, neither,"' etc.

not escape me? In Jeremlali I noticed many instances, and indeed in that book I found much transposition and variation in the readings of tlie prophecies. Again, in Genesis, the words, "God saw that it was good," when the firmament was made, are not found in the Hebrew, and there is no small dispute among them about this; and other instances are to be found in Genesis, which I marked, for the sake of distinction, with the sio n the Greeks call an obelisk, as on the other hand I marked with an asterisk those passages in our copies which are not found in the Hebrew. What needs tliere speak of Exodus, where there is such diversity in what is said about the tabernacle and its court, and the ark, and the garments of the high priest and the priests, that sometimes the meaning even does not seem to be akin? And, forsooth, when we notice such things, we are forthwith to reject as spurious the copies in use in our churches, and enjoin the brotherhood to put away the sacred books current among them, and to coax the Jews, and persuade them to give us copies which shall be untampered with, and free from forgery! Are we to suppose that that Providence which in the sacred Scriptures has ministered to the edification of all the churches of Christ, had no thought for those bought with a price,- for whom Christ died; whom, although his Son, God who is love spared not, but gave Him up for us all, that with Him He might freely give us all things?

5. In all these cases consider whether it would not be well to remember the words, "Thou shalt not remove the ancient landmarks which thy fathers have set." " Nor do I say this because I shun the labour of investigating the Jewish Scriptures, and comparing them with ours, and noticing their various readings. This, if it be not arrogant to say it, I have already to a great extent done to the best of my ability, labouring hard to get at the meaning in all the editions and various readings; while I paid particular attention to the interpre- 1 1 Cor. vi. 20; Rom. xiv. 15.

2 Rom. viii. 32. Prov. xxii. 28.

Origen's most important contribution to biblical literature was his elaborate attempt to rectify the text of the Septuagint by collating it tetion of the Seventy, lest I might be found to accredit anj-forgery to the churches which are under heaven, and give an occasion to those who seek such a starting-point for gratifying their desire to slander the common brethren, and to bring some accusation against those who shine forth in our community. And I make it my endeavour not to be ignorant of their various readings, lest in my controversies w ith the Jews I should quote to them wliat is not found in their copies, and that I may make some use of what is found there, even although it should not be in our Scriptures. For if we arc so prepared for them in our discussions, they will not, as is their manner, scornfully laugh at Gentile believers for their ignorance of the true readino; as thev have them. So far as to the History of Susanna not being found in the Hebrew.

6. Let us now look at the things you find fault with in the story itself. And here let us begin with what would probably make any one averse to receiving the history: I mean the play of words between lyrincs and j risfs, schinos and scjiisis. You say that

you can see how this can be in Greek, but that in Hebrew the words are altogether distinct. On this point, however, I am still in doubt; because, when I was considering this passage (for I myself saw this difficulty), I consulted not a few Jews about it, asking them the Ilebrew w ords for j ’i ios and iirisein and how they would translate schinos the tree, and how schisis. And they said that they did not know these Greek words j ’ os and schinos. and asked me to show them the trees, that they might see what they called them. And I at once (for the truth's dear sake))ut before them pieces of the different trees. One of them

Y.-ith the Hebrew original and other Greek versions. On this he sj ent twenty-eight years, during which he travelled through the East collecting materials. The form in which he first issued the result of his labours was that of the Tetrapla, which presented in four columns the texts of the LXX., Aquila, Symmachus, and Theodotion. He next issued the Hexapla, in which the Hebrew text was given, first in Hebrew and then in Greek letters. Of some books he gave two additional Greek versions, whence the title Octapla; and there was even a seventh Greek version added for some books. Unhappily this great work, which extended to nearly fifty volumes, was never transcribed, and so perished (Kitto, Cycl).

then said, that he could not with any certainty give the Hebrew name of anything not mentioned in Scriptare, since, if one was at a loss, he was prone to use the Syriac word instead of the Hebrew one; and he went on to say, that some words the very wisest could not translate. " If, then," said he, " you can adduce a passage in any Scripture where the schinos is mentioned, or the prinos you will find there the words you seek, together with the words which have the same sound; but if it is nowhere mentioned, we also do not know it." This, then, being what the Hebrews said to whom I had recourse, and who were acquainted with the history, I am cautious of affirming whether or not there is any correspondence to this play of words in the Hebrew. Your reason for affirming that there is not,-you yourself probably know.

7. Moreover, I remember hearing from a learned Hebrew, said among themselves to be the son of a wise man, and to have been specially trained to succeed his father, with whom I had intercourse on many subjects, the names of the. se elders, just as if he did not reject the History of Susanna, as they occur in Jeremia as follows: " The Lord make thee like Zedekias and Achiab, whom the king of Babylon roasted in the fire, for the iniquity they did in Israel." How, then, could the one be sawn asunder by an angel, and the other rent in pieces? The answer is, that these things were prophesied not of this world, but of the judgment of God, after the departure from this world. For as the lord of tliat wicked servant who says, "My lord delayeth his coming," and so gives himself up to drunkenness, eating and drinking with drunkards, and smiting his fellow-servants, shall at his coming " cut him asunder, and appoint him his portion with the unbelievers," even so the angels appointed to punish v."ili accomplish these things (just as they will cut asunder the wicked steward of that passage) on these men, who were called indeed elders, but who administered their stewardship wickedly. One will saw asunder him who was waxen old in wicked days, who had pronounced false judgment, condemning the innocent, and letting the guilty go free; and 1 Jer. xxix. 22. 2 1 j. xii. 45, 46. Susanna 52, 53.

another will rend in pieces him of the seed of Chanaan, and not of Judah, whom beauty had deceived, and whose heart lust had perverted.

8. And I knew another Hebrew, who told about these elders such traditions as the following: that they pretended to the Jews in captivity, who were hoping by the coming of Christ to be freed from the yoke of their enemies, that they could explain clearly the things concerning Christ,. and that they so deceived the wives of their countrymen. Wherefore it is that the prophet Daniel calls the one " waxen old in wicked days," and says to the other, ' Thus have ye dealt with the children of Israel; but the daughters of Juda would not abide your wickedness."

9. But probably to this you will saiy, Why then is the "History" not in their Daniel, if, as you say, their wise men hand down by tradition such stories? The answ er is, that they hid from the knowledge of the people as many of the passages which contained any scandal against the elders, rulers, and judges, as they could, some of which have been preserved in uncanonical writings (Apocrypha). As an example, take the story told about Esaias, and guaranteed by the Epistle to the Hebrews, which is found in none of their public books. For the author of the Epistle to the Hebrews, in speaking of the prophets, and what they suffered, says, "They were stoned, they were sawn asunder, they w ere slain with the sword." To whom, I ask, does the " sawn asunder" refer (for by an old idiom, not peculiar to Hebrew, but found also in Greek, this is said in the plural, although it refers to but one person)? Now we know very well that tradition says that Esaias the prophet was sawn asunder; and this is found in some apocryphal work, which probably the Jews have pur-

Susanna 5G.

2 Et utrumque sigillatim in quamcunque mulierem incidebat, et ciii vitium afferre cupiebat, ei secreto afrrmasse sibi a Deo datum gignere Cbristum. Hinc spe gignendi Christum decepta mulier, sui copiam decipienti faciebat, et sic civium uxores stuprabant seniores Achib et Sedekias, 3 Heb. xi. 38.

posely tampered with, introducing some phrases manifestly incorrect, that discredit might be thrown on the whole.

Plowever, some one hard pressed by this argument may have recourse to the opinion of those who reject this epistle as not being Paul's; against whom I must at some other time use other arguments to prove that it is Paul's. At present I shall adduce from the Gospel what Jesus Christ testifies concerning the prophets, together with a story which He refers to, but which is not found in the Old Testament, since in it also there is a scandal against unjust judges in Israel. The words of our Saviour run thus: " Woe unto you, scribes and Pharisees, hypocrites! because ye build the tombs of the prophets, and garnish the sepulchres of the righteous, and say. If we had been in the days of our fathers, we would not have been partakers with them in the blood of the prophets. Wherefore ye be witnesses unto yourselves, that ye are the children of them which killed the prophets. Fill ye up then the measure of your fathers. Ye serpents, ye generation of vipers, how can ye escape the damnation of Gehenna? Wherefore, behold, I send unto o prophets, and wise men, and scribes; and some of them ye shall kill and crucify; and some of them shall ye scourge in your synagogues, and persecute them from city to city: that upon you may come all the rigliteous blood shed upon the earth, from the blood of righteous Abel unto the blood of Zacharias, son of Barachias, whom ye slew between the temple and the altar. Verily I say unto you, All these things shall come upon this generation." And what follows is of the same tenor: " O Jerusalem, Jerusalem, thou that killest the prophets, and stonest them which are sent unto thee, how often would I have gathered thy children together, even as a hen gathereth her chickens under her wings, and ye would not! Behold, your house is left unto you desolate."

Let us see now if in these cases we are not forced to the conclusion, that while the Saviour gives a true account of them, none of the Scriptures which could prove what He tells are to be found. For they who build the tombs of the 1 Matt. xxiii. 29-36.

propliets and garnish the sepulchres of the righteous, con-clemnino; the crimes their fathers committed against the righteous and the propliets, say, If we had been in the days of our fathers, we would not have been partakers with them in the blood of the prophets." In the blood of what prophets, can any one tell me? For where do w e find anything like this written of Esaias, or Jeremias, or any of the twelve, or Daniel? Then about Zacharias the son of Bara-chias, who was slain between the temple and the altar, we learn from Jesus only, not knowing it otherwise from any Scripture. Wherefore I think no other supposition is possible, than that they who had the reputation of wisdom, and the rulers and elders, took away from the people every passage which might bring them into discredit among the people. We need not wonder, then, if this history of the evil device of the licentious elders against Susanna is true, but was concealed and removed from the Scriptures by men themselves not very far removed from the counsel of these elders.

In the Acts of the Apostles also, Stephen, in his other testimony, says, "Which of the prophets have not your fathers persecuted? And they have slain them which showed before of the coming of the Just One; of whom ye liave been now the betrayers and murderers." That Stephen speaks the truth, every one will admit who receives the Acts of the Apostles; but it is impossible to show from the extant books of the Old Testament how with any justice he throws the blame of having persecuted and slain the prophets on the fathers of those who believed not in Christ. And Paul, in the first Epistle to the Thessalonians, testifies this concerning the Jews: " For ye, brethren, became followers of the churches of God which in Judea are in Christ Jesus: for ye also have suffered like things of your own countrymen, even as they have of the Jews; who both killed the Lord Jesus and their own prophets, and have persecuted us; and they please not God, and are contrary to all men." What I have said is, I think, sufficient to prove that it would be nothing wonderful if this history were true, and the licentious and cruel attack was 1 Matt. xxiii. 30. cts vii. 52. 3 i Thess. ii. 14-16.

actually made on Susanna by those who were at that time elders, and written down by the wisdom of the Spirit, but removed by these rulers of Sodom,- as the Spirit would call them.

10. Your next objection is, that in this writing Daniel is said to have been seized by the Spirit, and to have cried out that the sentence was unjust; while in that writing of his which is universally received he is represented as prophesying in quite another manner, by visions and dreams, and an angel appearing to him, but never by prophetic inspiration. You seem to me to pay too little heed to the words, "At sundry times, and in divers manners, God spake in time past unto the fathers by the prophets."" This is

true not only in the general, but also of individuals. For if you notice, you will find that the same saints have been favoured with divine dreams and angelic appearances and direct inspirations. For the present it will suffice to instance what is testified concerning Jacob. Of dreams from God he speaks thus: " And it came to pass, at the time that the cattle conceived, that I saw them before my eyes in a dream, and, behold, the rams and he-goats which leajoed upon the sheep and the goats, white-spotted, and speckled, and grisled. And the angel of God spake unto me in a dream, saying, Jacob. And I said, What is it? And he said. Lift up thine eyes and see, the goats and rams leaping on the goats and sheep, white-spotted, and speckled, and grisled: for I have seen all that Laban doeth unto thee. I am God, who appeared unto thee in the place of God, where thou anointedst to me there a pillar, and vowed a vow there to me: now arise, get thee out from this land, and return unto the land of thy kindred."

And as to an appearance (which is better than a dream), he speaks as follows about himself: " And Jacob was left alone; and there wrestled a man with him until the breaking of the day. And he saw that he prevailed not against him, and he touched the breadth of his thigh; and the breadth of Jacob's thigh grew stiff while he was wrestling with him. And he said to him. Let me go, for the day breaketh. And 1 Isa. i. 10. 2 Heb. i. 1. Gen. xxxi. 10.

he said, I will not let thee go, except thou bless me. And he said, unto him. What is thy name? And he said, Jacob. And he said to him, Thy name shall be called no more Jacob, but Israel shall be thy name: for thou hast prevailed with God, and art powerful with men. And Jacob asked him, and said. Tell me thy name. And he said. Wherefore is it that thou dost ask after my name? And he blessed him there. And Jacob called the name of the place Vision of God: for I have seen God face to face, and my life is preserved. And the sun rose, when the vision of God passed by." And that he also prophesied by inspiration, is evident from this passage: " And Jacob called unto his sons, and said. Gather yourselves together, that I may tell you wdiat shall befall you in the last days. Gather yourselves together, and hear, ye sons of Jacob; and hearken unto Israel your father. Eeuben, my first-born, my might, and the beginning of my children, hard to be born, hard and stubborn. Thou wert wanton, boil not over like water; because thou wentest up to thy father's bed; then defiledst thou the couch to which thou wentest up." And so with the rest: it was by inspiration that the prophetic blessings were pronounced. We need not wonder, then, that Daniel sometimes prophesied by inspiration, as when he rebuked the elders sometimes, as you say, by dreams and visions, and at other times by an angel appearing unto him.

11. Your other objections are stated, as it appears to me, somewhat irreverently, and without the becoming spirit of piety. I cannot do better than quote your very words:- Then, after crying out in this extraordinary fashion, he detects them in a way no less incredible, which not even Pliilistion the play-writer would have resorted to. For, not satisfied with rebuking them through the Spirit, he placed them apart, and asked them severally where they saw her committing adultery; and when the one said, ' Under a holm-tree' d rinos), he answered that the angel would saw him asunder (prisein); and in a similar fashion threatened the other, who said, ' Under a mastich-tree' (schinos), with being rent asunder." 1 Gen. xxxii. 24. 2 q j lix. 1.

You might as reasonably compare to Phillstion the play-writer, a story somewhat like this one, which is found in the third book of Kings, which you yourself will admit to be well written. Here is what we read in Kincrs:

"Then there appeared two women that were harlots before the king, and stood before him. And the one woman said, To me, my lord, I and this woman dwell in one house; and we were delivered in the house. And it came to pass, the third day after that I was delivered, that this w oman was delivered also: and we were together; there is no one in our house except us two. And this woman's child died in the night; because she overlaid it. And she arose at midnight, and took my son from my arms. And thine handmaid slept. And she laid it in her bosom, and laid her dead child in my bosom. And I arose in the morning to give my child suck, and he was dead; but wdien I had considered it in the morning, behold, it was not my son which I did bear. And the other woman said, Nay; the dead is thy son, but the living is my son. And the other said. No; the living is my son, but the dead is thy son. Thus they spake before the king. Then said the king. Thou sayest. This is my son that liveth, and thy son is the dead: and thou sayest. Nay; but thy son is the dead, and my son is the living. And the king said. Bring me a sword. And they brought a sword before the king. And the king said, Divide the living child in two, and give half to the one, and half to the other. Then spake the woman whose the living child was unto the king (for her bowels yearned after her son), and she said. To me, my lord, give her the living child, and in no wise slay it. But the other said. Let it be neither mine nor thine, but divide it. Then the king answered and said. Give the child to her which said, Give her the living child, and in no wise slay it: for she is the mother of it. And all Israel heard of the judgment which the king had judged; and they feared the face of the king: for they saw that the wisdom of God was in him to do judgment."

For if we were at liberty to speak in this scoffing way of the Scriptures in use in the churches, we should rather com-1 1 Kiugsiii. lg-28.

pare this story of the two harlots to the play of Philistion than that of the chaste Susanna. And just as the people would not have been persuaded if Solomon had merely said, "Give this one the living child, for she is the mother of it;" so Daniel's attack on the elders would not have been sufficient had there not been added the condemnation from their own mouth, when both said that they liad seen her lying with the young man under a tree, but did not agree as to what kind of tree it w as. And since you have asserted, as if you knew for certain, that Daniel in this matter judged by inspiration (which may or may not have been the case), I would have you notice that there seem to me to be some analogies in the story of Daniel to the judgment of Solomon, concerning whom the Scripture testifies that the people saw that the wisdom of God was in him to do judgment This might be said also of Daniel, for it was because wisdom was in him to do judgment that the elders were judged in the manner described.

12. I had nearly forgotten an additional remark I have to make about the prino-prisein and scliino-schisein difficulty; that is, that in our Scriptures there are many etymological fancies, so to call them, which in the Hebrew are perfectly suitable, but not in the Greek. It need not surprise us, then, if the translators of the History of Susanna contrived it so that they found out some Greek words, derived from the same

root, which either corresponded exactly to the Hebrew-form (though this I hardly think possible), or presented some analogy to it. Here is an instance of this in our Scripture. When the woman w as made by God from the rib of the man, Adam says, "She shall be called woman, because she was taken out of her husband." Now the Jews say that the w oman was called " Essa ' and that "taken" is a translation of this word, as is evident from " clios isouoth essa, which means, "I have taken the cup of salvation;" and that ' w" means "man," as we see from Ilesre ais," which is, "Blessed is the man."' According to the Jews, then, "zs" is "man," and " es a " " woman," because she was taken out of her husband is). It need not then surprise us if some interpreters 1 1 Kiii s iii. 28. 2 pg. cxv. 13. s pg, i 1, of the Hebrew " Susanna," whicli had been concealed among them at a very remote date, and had been preserved only by the more learned and honest, should have either given the Hebrew word for word, or hit upon some analogy to the Hebrew forms, that the Greeks might be able to follow them. For in many other passages we can find traces of this kind of contrivance on the part of the translators, whicli I noticed when I was collating the various editions.

13. You raise another objection, which I give in your own words: " Moreover, how is it that they, who were captives among the Chaldabans, lost and won at play, thrown out unburied on the streets, as was prophesied of the former captivity, their sons torn from them to be eunuchs, and their daughters to be concubines, as had been prophesied; how is it that such could pass sentence of death, and that on the wife of their king Joakim, whom the king of the Babylonians had made partner of his throne? Then, if it was not this Joakim, but some other from the common people, whence had a captive such a mansion and spacious garden?"

Where you get your " lost and won at play, and thrown out unburied on the streets," I know not, unless it is from Tobias; and Tobias (as also Judith), we ought to notice, the Jews do not use. They are not even found in the Hebrew Apocrypha, as I learned from the Jews themselves. However, since the churches use Tobias, you must know that even in the captivity some of the captives were rich and well to do. Tobias himself says, "Because I remembered God with all my heart; and the Most High gave me grace and beauty in the eyes of Nemessarus, and I was his purveyor; and I went into Media, and left in trust with Gabael, the brother of Gabrias at Kagi, a city of Media, ten talents of silver." And he adds, as he were a rich man, " In the days of Nemessarus I gave many alms to my brethren. I gave my bread to the hungry, and my clothes to the naked: and if I saw any of my nation dead, and cast outside the walls of Nineve, I buried him; and if king Senachereim had slain any when he came fleeing from Judea, I buried them privily (for in his wrath he killed i Tob. i. 12.

many)." Think wlietlier this great catalogue of Tobias' good deeds does not betoken great wealth and much property, especially when he adds, ' Understanding that I was sought for to be put to death, I withdrew myself for fear, and all my goods were forcibly taken away."

And another captive, Dachiacharus, the son of Ananiel, the brother of Tobias, was set over all the exchequer of the kingdom of king Acherdon; and we read, "Now Achiacharus was cup-bearer and keeper of the signet, and steward and overseer of the accounts.""

Mardochaios, too, frequented the court of the king, and liad such boldness before him, that he was inscribed among the benefactors of Artaxerxes.

Again we read in Esdras, that Neemias, a cup-bearer and eunuch of the king, of Hebrew race, made a request about the rebuilding of the temple, and obtained it; so that it was granted to him, with many more, to return and build the temple again. Why then should we wonder that one Joakim had garden, and house, and property, whether these were very expensive or only moderate, for this is not clearly told us in the writing?

14. But you say, "How could they who were in captivity pass sentence of death? " asserting, I know not on wliat grounds, that Susanna was the wife of a king, because of the name Joakim. The answer is, that it is no uncommon thing, when great nations become subject, that the king should allow tiie captives to use their own laws and courts of justice. Now, for instance, that the Romans rule, and the Jews pay the half-shekel to them, how great power by the concession of Caesar the ethnarch has; so that we, who have had experience of it, know that he differs in little from a true kino! Private trials are held according to the law, and some are condemned to death. And though there is not full licence for this, still it is not done without the knowledge of the ruler, as we learned and were convinced of when we spent much time in the country of that people. And yet the Eomans only take account of two tribes, while at that time 1 Toid. i. 19. 2 xob. i. 22.

ORIG. 2 B besides Juda there were the ten tribes of Israel. Probably the Assyrians contented themselves with holding them in subjection, and conceded to them their own judicial processes.

15. I find in your letter yet another objection in these words: " And add, that among all the many prophets who had been before, there is no one who has quoted from another word for word. For they had no need to go a-begging for words, since their own were true. But this one, in rebuking one of these men, quotes the words of the Lord, ' The innocent and righteous shalt thou not slay."" I cannot understand how, with all your exercise in investigating and meditating on the Scriptures, you have not noticed that the prophets continually quote each other almost word for word. For who of all believers does not know the words in Esaias? " And in the last days the mountain of the Lord shall be manifest, and the house of the Lord on the top of the mountains, and it shall be exalted above the hills; and all nations shall com e unto it. And many people shall go and say. Come ye, and let us go up to the mountain of the Lord, unto the house of the God of Jacob; and He will teach us His way, and we will walk in it: for out of Zion shall go forth a law, and a word of the Lord from Jerusalem. And He shall judge among the nations, and shall rebuke many people; and they shall beat their swords into ploughshares, and their spears into pruning-hooks: nation shall not lift up sword against nation, neither shall they learn war any more."

But in Micah we find a parallel passage, which is almost word for word: " And in the last days the mountain of the Lord shall be manifest, established on the top of the mountains, and it shall be exalted above the hills; and people shall hasten unto it. And many nations shall come, and say. Come, let us go up to the mountain of the Lord, to the house of the God of Jacob; and they will teach us His way, and we will walk in His paths: for a law shall go forth from Zion, and a word of the Lord from Jerusalem.

And He shall judge among many people, and rebuke strong nations; and they shall beat their swords into ploughshares, and their spears 1 Isa. ii. 2.

into pruning-hooks: nation shall not lift up a sword against nation, neither shall they learn war any more."'

Again, in First Chronicles, the psalm which is put in the hands of Asaph and his brethren to praise the Lord, beginning, "Give thanks unto the Lord, call upon His name,"" is in the beginning almost identical with Ps. civ., down to ' and do my prophets no harm;" and after that it is the same as Ps. xcv., from the beginning of that psalm, which is something Hke this, "Praise the Lord all the earth," down to " For He Cometh to judge the earth." (It w ould have taken up too much time to quote more fully; so I have given these short references, which are sufficient for the matter before us.) And you wdll find the law about not bearing a burden on the Sabbath-day in Jeremia, as well as in Moses. And the rules about the passover, and the rules for the priests, are not only in Moses, but also at the end of Ezekiel. I would have quoted these, and many more, had I not found that from the shortness of my stay in Nicomedia my time for writing you was already too much restricted.

Your last objection is, that the style is different. This 1 cannot see.

This, then, is my defence. I might, especially after all these accusations, speak in praise of this history of Susanna, dwelling on it word by word, and expounding the exquisite nature of the thoughts. Such an encomium, perhaps, some of the learned and able students of divine things may at some other time compose. This, however, is my answer to your strokes, as you call them. Would that I could instruct you! But I do not now arrogate that to myself. My lord and dear brother Ambrosius, who has written this at my dictation, and has, in looking over it, corrected as he pleased, salutes you. His faithful spouse, Marcella, and her children, also salute you. Also Anicetus. Do you salute our dear father Apol-linarius, and all our friends.

1 Mic. iv. 1. 2 1 Chron. xvi. 8.

2 Ex. XXXV. 2; Num. xy. 32; Jer. xvii. 21-24. 111 Levit. passim; Ezek. xliii. xliv. xlv. xlvi.

REETING ill God, my most excellent sir, and venerable son Gregory, from Origen. A natural readiness of comprehension, as you well know, may, if practice be added, contribute somewhat to the contingent end, if I may so call it, of that which any one wishes to practise. Thus, your natural good parts might make of you a finished Roman lawyer or a Greek philosopher, so to speak, of one of the schools in high reputation. But I am anxious that you should devote all the strength of your natural good parts to Christianity for your end; and in order to this, I wish to ask you to extract from the philosophy of the Greeks what may serve as a course of study or a preparation for Christianity, and from geometry and astronomy what will serve to explain the sacred Scriptures, in order that all that the sons of the philosophers are wont to say about geometry and music, grammar, rhetoric, and astronomy, as fellow-helpers to philosophy, we may say about philosophy itself, in relation to Christianity.

2. Perhaps something of this kind is shadowed forth in what is written in Exodus from the mouth of God, that the children of Israel were connnanded to ask from their neighbours, and those who dwelt with them, vessels of silver and gold, and raiment, in order that, by spoiling the Egyptians, they might have material for the preparation

of the things which pertained to the service of God. For from the things which the children of Israel took from the Egyptians the vessels in the holy of holies were made, the ark with its lid, and the cherubim, and the mercy-seat, and the golden coffer, where

1 This Gregory, styled the Wonder-worker, was afterwards bishop of Neo-Csesarea.

was tlie manna, the angels' bread. These things were probably made from the best of the Egyptian gold. An inferior kind would be used for the solid golden candlestick near the inner veil, and its branches, and the golden table on which were the pieces of shewbread, and the golden censer between them. And if there was a third and fourth quality of gold, from it would be made the holy vessels; and the other things would be made of Egyptian silver. For when the children of Israel dwelt in Egypt, they gained this from their dwelling there, that they had no lack of such precious material for the utensils of the service of God. And of the Egyptian raiment were probably made all those things which, as the Scripture mentions, needed sewed and embroidered work, sewed with the wisdom of God, the one to the other, that the veils might be made, and the inner and the outer courts. And why should I go on, in this untimely digression, to set forth how useful to the children of Israel were the things brought from Egypt, which the Egyptians had not put to a proper use, but which the Hebrews, guided by the wisdom of God, used for God's service? Now the sacred Scripture is wont to represent as an evil the going down from the land of the children of Israel into Egypt, indicating that certain persons get harm from sojourning among the Egyptians, that is to say, from meddling with the knowledge of this world, after they have subscribed to the law of God, and the Israelitish service of Him. Ader at least, the Idumsean, so long as he was in the land of Israel, and had not tasted the bread of the Egyptians, made no idols. It was when he fled from the wise Solomon, and went down into Egypt, as it were flying from the wisdom of God, and was made a kinsman of Pharaoh by marrying his wife's sister, and begetting a child, wdio was brought up with the children of Pharaoh, that he did this. Wherefore, although he did return to the land of Israel, he returned only to divide the people of God, and to make them say to the golden calf, "These be thy gods, O Israel, which brought thee up from the land of Egypt. And I may tell you from

Origen evidently confounds Hadad the Edomite, of 1 Kings xii. 14, with Jeroboam.

my experience, that not many take from Egypt only the useful, and go away and use it for the service of God; while Ader the Idumsean has many brethren. These are they who, from their Greek studies, produce heretical notions, and set them up, like the golden calf, in Bethel, which signifies " God's house." In these words also there seems to me an indication that they have set up their own imaginations in the Scriptures, where the word of God dwells, which is called in a figure Bethel. The other figure, the word says, was set up in Dan. Now the borders of Dan are the most extreme, and nearest the borders of the Gentiles, as is clear from what is written in Joshua, the son of Nun. Now some of the devices of these brethren of Ader, as we call them, are also very near the borders of the Gentiles.

3. Do you then, my son, diligently apply yourself to the reading of the sacred Scriptures. Apply yourself, I say. For we who read the things of God need much application, lest we should say or think anything too rashly about them. And applying yourself thus to the study of the things of God, with faithful prejudgments such as

are well, pleasing to God, knock at its locked door, and it will be opened to you by the porter, of whom Jesus says,- To him the porter opens." And applying yourself thus to the divine study, seek aright, and with unwavering trust in God, the meaning of the holy Scriptures, which so many have missed. Be not satisfied with knocking and seeking; for prayer is of all things indispensable to the knowledge of the things of God. For to this the Saviour exhorted, and said not only, "Knock, and it shall be opened to you; and seek, and ye shall find," but also, ' Ask, and it shall be given unto you." My fatherly love to you has made me thus bold; but whether my boldness be good, God will know, and His Christ, and all partakers of the Spirit of God and the Spirit of Christ. May jow also be a partaker, and be ever increasing your inheritance, that you may say not only, "We are become partakers of Christ,"' but also partakers of God.

1 John X. 3. Matt. vii. 7.

s Luke xi. 9. "" Heb. iii. 14.

1. ifek' Aife lhEN false witnesses testified against our Lord and Saviour Jesus Christ, He remained silent; and when unfounded charo es were brought against Him, He returned no answer, believing that His whole life and conduct among the Jews were a better refutation than any answer to the false testimony, or than any formal defence against the accusations. And I know not, my pious xvmbrosius, why you wished me to write a reply to the false charges brought by Celsus against the Christians, and to his accusations directed against the faith of the churches in his treatise; as if the facts themselves did not furnish a manifest refutation, and the doctrine a better answer than any writing, seeing it both disposes of the false statements, and does not leave to the accusations any credibility or validity. Now, with respect to our Lord's silence when false witness was borne against Him, it is sufficient at present to quote the words of Matthew, for the testimony of Mark is to the same effect. And the words of Matthew are as follow: " And the high priest and the council sought false witness against Jesus to put Him to death, but found none, although many false witnesses came forward. At last two false witnesses came and said, This fellow said, I am able to destroy the temple of God, and after three days to

This individual is mentioned by Eusebius Eccles. Hist. b. vi. c. 18) as having been converted from the heresy of Yalentinus to the faith of the church by the efforts of Origen.

build it up. And tlie high priest arose, and said to Hiiii, Answerest thou nothing to wliat these witness against thee? But Jesus held His peace." And that He returned no answer when falsely accused, the following is the statement: " And Jesus stood before the governor; and he asked Him, saying. Art thou the king of the Jews? And Jesus said to him, Thou sayest. And. when He was accused of the chief priests and elders. He answered nothing. Then said Pilate unto Him, Hearest thou not how many things they witness against thee? And He answered him to never a word, insomuch that the governor marvelled greatly." '"

2. It was, indeed, matter of surprise to men even of ordinary intelligence, that one who was accused and assailed by false testimony, but who was able to defend Himself, and to show that He was guilty of none of the charges alleged, and who might have enumerated the praiseworthy deeds of His own life, and His miracles wrought by

divine power, so as to give the judge an opportunity of delivering a more honourable judgment regarding Him, should not have done this, but should have disdained such a procedure, and in the nobleness of His nature have contemned His accusers. That the judge would, without any hesitation, have set Him at liberty if He had offered a defence, is clear from what is related of him when he said, ' Which of the two do ye wish that I should release unto you, Barabbas or Jesus, who is called Christ? " and from what the Scripture adds, "For he knew that for envy they had delivered Him." Jesus, however, is at all times assailed by false witnesses, and, while wickedness remains in the world, is ever exposed to accusation. And yet even now He continues silent before these things, and makes no audible answer, but places His defence in the lives of His genuine disciples, which are a pre-eminent testimony, and one that rises superior to all false witness, and refutes and overthrows all unfounded accusations and charges.

3. I venture, then, to say that this ' ' apology " which you 1 Cf. Matt. xxvi. 59-62. 2 cf. Matt, xxvii. 11-14.

Msyctaoipy Jj' VTirspsapcucivut tcl'; zcr' yopovg.

4 Cf. Matt, xxvii. 17. Cf. Matt, xxvii. 18.

require me to compose will somewhat weaken that defence of Christianity which rests on facts, and that power of Jesus which is manifest to those who are not altogether devoid of perception. Notwithstanding, that we may not have the appearance of being reluctant to undertake the task which you have enjoined, we have endeavoured, to the best of our ability, to suggest, by way of answer to each of the statements advanced by Celsus, what seemed to us adapted to refute them, although his arguments have no power to shake the faith of any true believer. And forbid, indeed, that any one should be found who, after having been a partaker in such a love of God as was displayed in Christ Jesus, could be shaken in his purpose by the arguments of Celsus, or of any such as he. For Paul, when enumerating the innumerable causes which generally separate men from the love of Christ and from the love of God in Christ Jesus (to all of which, the love that was in himself rose superior), did not set down argument among the grounds of separation. For observe that he says, firstly: ' Who shall separate us from the love of Christ? Shall tribulation, or distress, or persecution, or famine, or nakedness, or peril, or sword? (as it is written. For Thy sake we are killed all the day long; we are accounted as sheep for the slaughter.) Nay, in all these things we are more than conquerors through Him that loved us." ' And secondly, when laying down another series of causes which naturally tend to separate those who are not firmly grounded in their religion, he says: " For I am persuaded that neither death, nor life, nor angels, nor principalities, nor powers, nor things present, nor things to come, nor height, nor depth, nor any other creature, shall be able to se: parate us from the love of God, which is in Christ Jesus our Lord."' 4. Now, truly, it is proper that ice should feel elated because afflictiohS, or those other causes enumerated by Paul, do not separate us from Christ; but not that Paul and the other apostles, and any other resembling them, should entertain that feeling, because they were far exalted above such 1 Eom. viii. S5-37. 2. yiii. 38, 39.

things when they said, "In all these things we ai'e more than conquerors through Him that loved us," which is a stronger statement than that they are simply "conquerors." But if it be proper for apostles to entertain a feeling of elation in not being separated from the love of God that is in Christ Jesus our Lord, that feeling will be entertained by them because neither death, nor life, nor angels, nor principalities, nor any of the things that follow, can separate them from the love of God which is in Christ Jesus our Lord. And therefore I do not congratulate that believer in Christ whose faith can be shaken by Celsus who no longer shares the common life of men, but has long since departed or by any apparent plausibility of argument." For I do not know in what rank to place him who has need of arguments written in books in answer to the charo es of Celsus ae ainst the Christians, in order to prevent him from being shaken in his faith, and confirm him in it. But nevertheless, since in the multitude of those wdio are considered believers some such persons miojht be found as would have their faith shaken and over-thrown by the writings of Celsus, but who might be preserved by a reply to them of such a nature as to refute his statements and to exhibit the truth, we have deemed it right to yield to your injunction, and to furnish an answer to the treatise which you sent us, but which I do not think that any one, although only a short way advanced in philosophy, will allow to be a "True Discourse," as Celsus has entitled it.

5. Paul, indeed, observing that there are in Greek philosophy certain things not to be lightly esteemed, which are plausible in the eyes of the many, but which represent falsehood as truth, says with regard to such: " Beware lest any man spoil you through philosophy and vain deceit, after the tradition of men, after the rudiments of the world, and not after Christ." And seeing that there was a kind of greatness manifest in the words of the world's wisdom, he said that the words of the philosophers w ere " according to

Rom. viii. 37, VTnpvikoiiai'j. n ' i og T idavori roi T oyov.

3 Col. ii. 8.

the rudiments of the workl." No man of sense, however, would say that those of Celsus were according to the rudiments of the world." Now those words, which contained some element of deceitfulness, the apostle named vain deceit," prohably by way of distinction from a deceit that was not "vain;" and the prophet Jeremiah observing this, ventured to say to God, "O Lord, Thou hast deceived me, and I was deceived; Thou art stronger than I, and hast prevailed." But in the language of Celsus there seems to me to be no deceitfulness at all, not even that which is 'Wain;" such deceitfulness, viz., as is found in the language of those who have founded philosophical sects, and who have been endowed with no ordinary talent for such pursuits. And as no one v, ould say that any ordinary error in geometrical demonstrations was intended to deceive, or would describe it for the sake of exercise in such matters; so those opinions which are to be styled " vain deceit," and the " tradition of m. en," and " according to the rudiments of the world," must have some resemblance to the views of those who have been the founders of philosophical sects, if such titles are to be appropriately applied to them.

6. After proceeding with this work as far as the place where Celsus introduces the Jew diq uting with Jesus, I resolved to prefix this preface to the beginning of the treatise, in order that the reader of our reply to Celsus nn'ght fall in with it first, and see that this book has been composed not for those wdio are thorough believers, but for such as are either wdiolly unacquainted with the Christian faith, or for those who,

as the apostle terms them, are " weak in the faith;" regarding whom he says, "Him that is weak in the faith receive ye."' And this preface must be my apology for beginning my answ er to Celsus on one plan, and carrying it on on another. For my first intention was to indicate 1 Cf. Jer. XX. 7.

Kfiti uatirsp ou ro tv ou ruu Jy Voo usucjj lu yiuy. zrpikfji; io)py: f ocat i vshoypa,(povf. ivo! J ri; ecu T syoi, ij kui ccvccypx ot yvy. vualov hizi'j rov dito Toiovroyj. Cf. note of Ruseus in loc,

Rom. xiv. 1.

Ills principal objections, and then briefly the answers that were returned to them, and subsequently to make a systematic treatise of the whole discourse. But afterwards, circumstances themselves susjcjested to me that I should be economical of my time, and that, satisfied with what I had already stated at the commencement, I should in the following part grapple closely, to the best of my ability, with the charges of Celsus. I have therefore to ask indulgence for those portions which follow the preface towards the beginning of the book. And if you are not impressed by the powerful arguments which succeed, then, asking similar indulgence also with respect to them, I refer you, if you still desire an argumentative solution of the objections of Oelsus, to those men who are wiser than myself, and who are able by words and treatises to overthrow the charges which he brings against us. But better is the man who, although meeting with the work of Celsus, needs no answer to it at all, but who despises all its contents, since they are contemned, and with good reason, by every believer in Christ, through the Spirit that is in him.

Chaptee I.

The first point which Celsus brings forward, in his desire to throw discredit upon Christianity, is, that the Christians entered into secret associations with each other contrary to law, saying, that " of associations some are public, and that these are in accordance with the laws; others, again, secret, and maintained in violation of the laws." And his wish is to bring into disrepute what are termed the ove-feasts" of the Christians, as if they had their origin in the common danger, and were more binding than any oaths. Since, then, he babbles about the public law, alleging that the associations of the Christians are in violation of it, we have to reply, that if a man were placed among Scythians, whose laws were unholy, and having no opportunity of escape, were compelled to live among them, such an one would with good reason, for the sake of the law of truth, which the Scythians would regard as wickedness, enter into associations contrary to tlicir laws, with those Hke-minded with himself; so, if truth is to decide, the laws of tlie heathens which relate to images, and an atheistical polytheism, are ' Scythian" laws, or more impious e en than these, if there be any such. It is not irrational, then, to form associations in opposition to existing laws, if done for the sake of the truth. For as those persons would do well who should enter into a secret association in order to put to death a tyrant who had seized upon the liberties of a state, so Christians also, when tyrannized over by him who is called the devil, and by falsehood, form leagues contrary to the laws of the devil, against his power, and for the safety of those others whom they may succeed in persuading to revolt from a government which is, as it were, ' Scythian, ' and despotic.

Chapter it.

Celsus next proceeds to say, that the system of doctrine, viz. Judaism, upon which Christianity depends, was barbarous in its origin. And with an appearance of fairness, he does not reproach Christianity because of its origin among barbarians, but gives the latter credit for their ability in discovering such doctrines. To this, however, he adds the statement, that the Greeks are more skilful than any others in judging, establishing, and reducing to practice the discoveries of barbarous nations. Now this is our answer to his allegations, and our defence of the truths contained in Christianity, that if any one were to come from the study of Grecian opinions and usages to the gospel, he would not only decide that its doctrines were true, but would by practice establish their truth, and supply whatever seemed wanting, from a Grecian point of view, to their demonstration, and thus confirm the truth of Christianity. We have to say, moreover, that the gospel has a demonstration of its own, more divine than any established by Grecian dialectics. And this diviner method is called by the apostle the " manifestation of the Spirit and of power:" of ' the Spirit," on account of the prophecies, which are sufficient to produce faith in any one who reads them, especially in those things which relate to Christ; and of ' power," because of the signs and wonders which we must believe to have been performed, both on many other grounds, and on this, that traces of them are still preserved among those who regulate their lives by the precepts of the gospel.

Chapter hi.

After this, Celsus proceeding to speak of the Christians teaching and practising their favourite doctrines in secret, and saying that they do this to some purpose, seeing they escape the penalty of death which is imminent, he compares their dangers with those which were encountered by such men as Socrates for the sake of philosophy; and here he might have mentioned Pythagoras as well, and other philosophers. But our answer to this is, that in the case of Socrates the Athenians immediately afterwards repented; and no feeling of bitterness remained in their minds regarding liim, as also happened in the history of Pythagoras. The followers of the latter, indeed, for a considerable time established their schools in that part of Italy called Magna Grsecia; but in the case of the Christians, the Koman Senate, and the princes of the time, and the soldiery, and the people, and the relatives of those who had become converts to the faith, made war upon their doctrine, and would have prevented its progress, overcoming it by a confederacy of so powerful a nature, had it not, by the help of God, escaped the danger, and risen above it, so as finally to defeat the whole world in its conspiracy against it.

Chapter iy.

Let us notice also how he thinks to cast discredit upon our system of morals, alleging that it is only common to us with other philosophers, and no venerable or new branch of in-

TOV 7l6lk0V roTTOV.

stiniction. In reply to Yllicll we have to say, that unless all men had naturally impressed upon their minds sound ideas of morality, the doctrine of the punishment of sinners would liave been excluded by those who bring upon themselves the righteous judgments of God. It is not therefore matter of surprise that the same God should have sown in the hearts of all men those truths which He taught by the prophets and the Saviour, in order that at the divine judgment every man may be without excuse, having the " requirements of the law written upon his heart," a truth obscurely alluded to by the Bible" in what the Greeks regard as a myth, where it represents God as having with His own finger written down the connnandments, and given them to Moses, and which the wickedness of the worshippers of the calf made him break in pieces, as if the flood of wickedness, so to speak, had swept them away. But Moses having again hewn tables of stone, God wrote the commandments a second time, and gave them to him; the prophetic word preparing the soul, as it were, after the first transgression, for the writing of God a second time.

Chapter v.

Treating of the regulations respecting idolatry as being peculiar to Christianity, Celsus establishes their correctness, saying that the Christians do not consider those to be gods that are made with hands, on the ground that it is not in conformity with right reason to suppose that images, fashioned by the most worthless and depraved of workmen, and in many instances also provided by wicked men, can be regarded as gods. In what follows, however, wishing to show that this is a common opinion, and one not first discovered by Christianity, he quotes a saying of Heraclitus to this effect: " That those who draw near to lifeless images, as if they were gods, act in a similar manner to those who would enter into conversation with houses." Kespecting this, then, we have to say, that ideas were implanted in the minds

TO 3ovxj t406 Ty yoy QV. 6.6yog.

OKIG. 2 O of men like the principles of morality, from-which not only Heraclitus, but any other Greek or barbarian, might by reflection have deduced the same conclusion; for he states that the Persians also were of the same opinion, quoting Herodotus as his authority. We also can add to these Zeno of Citium, who in his Politi says: ' And there will be no need to build temples, for nothing ought to be regarded as sacred, or of much value, or holy, which is the w ork of builders and of mean men." It is evident, then, with respect to this opinion as well as others, that there has been engraven upon the hearts of men by the finger of God a sense of the duty that is required.

Chapter yi.

After this, through the influence of some motive which is unknown to me, Celsus asserts that it is by the names of certain demons, and by the use of incantations, that the Christians appear to be possessed of miraculous power; hinting, I suppose, at the practices of those who expel evil spirits by incantations. And here he manifestly appears to malign the gospel. For it is not by incantations that Christians seem to prevail over evil spirits, but by the name of Jesus, accompanied by the announcement of the narratives which relate to Him; for the repetition of these has frequently been the means of driving demons out of men, especially when those who repeated them did so in a sound and genuinely believing spirit. Such power, indeed, does the name of Jesus possess over evil spirits, that there have been instances where it was effectual, when it was pronounced even by bad men, which Jesus Himself taught would be the case, when He said: "Many shall say to me in that day, In Thy name we have cast out devils, and done many wonderful works."- Whether Celsus omitted this from intentional malignity, or from ignorance, I do not know. And he next proceeds to bring a charge against the Saviour Himself, alleging that it was by means of sorcery that He was able to 1 Cf. Matt. vii. 22.

accomplish the-svoiiders which He performed; and that foreseeing that others would attain the same knowledge, and do the same things, making a boast of doing them by help of the power of God, He excludes such from His kingdom. And his accusation is, that if they are justly excluded, while He Himself is guilty of the same practices, He is a wicked man; but if He is not guilty of wickedness in doing such things, neither are they who do the same as He. But even if it be impossible to show by what power Jesus wrought these miracles, it is clear that Christians employ no spells or incantations, but the simple name of Jesus, and certain other w ords in which they repose faith, according to the Holy Scriptures.

CliArtER VII.

Moreover, since he frequently calls the Christian doctrine a secret system of belief, we must confute him on this point also, since almost the entire world is better acquainted with what Christians preach than with the favourite opinions of philosophers. For who is ignorant of the statement that Jesus was born of a virgin, and that He was crucified, and that His resurrection is an article of faith among many, and that a general judgment is announced to come, in which the wicked are to be punished according to their deserts, and the righteous to be duly rew arded? And yet the mystery of the resurrection, not being understood, is made a subject of ridicule among unbelievers. In these circumstances, to speak of the Christian doctrine as a secret system, is altogether absurd. But that there should be certain doctrines, not made known to the multitude, which are revealed after the exoteric ones have been taught, is not a peculiarity of Christianity alone, but also of philosophic systems, in which certain truths are exoteric and others esoteric. Some of the hearers of Pythagoras were content with his ijpse dixit; while others

The words, as they stand in the text of Lommatzsch, are, d."ha. x. al f Tj'j uori iu TO 'TTspl T' j uvotatKaio); f. v(jtjp: ou. Riid3US would read fzvi instead of 'jy. This emendation has been adopted in the translation.

were tauglit in secret those doctrines wliicli were not deemed fit to be communicated to profane and insufficiently prepared ears. Moreover, all the mysteries that are celebrated everywhere throughout Greece and barbarous countries, although held in secret, have no discredit thrown upon them, so that it is in vain that he endeavours to calumniate the secret doctrines of Christianit, seeing he does not correctly understand its nature.

Chapter viii.

It is with a certain eloquence, indeed, that he appears to advocate the cause of those who bear witness to the truth of Christianity by their death, in the following words: " And I do not maintain that if a man, who has adopted a system of good doctrine, is to incur danger from men on that account, he should either apostatize, or feign apostasy, or openly deny his opinions." And he condemns those who, while holding the Christian views, either pretend that they do not, or deny them, saying that ' he who holds a certain opinion ought not to feign recantation, or publicly disown it." And here Celsus must be convicted of self-contradiction. For from other treatises of his it is ascertained that he was an Epicurean; but here, because he thou fht that he could assail Christianitv with better effect by not professing the opinions of Epicurus, he pretends that there is a something better in man than the earthly part of his nature, which is akin to God, and says that " they in whom this element, viz. the soul, is in a healthy condition, are ever seeking after their kindred nature, meaning God, and are ever desiring to hear something about Him, and to call it to remembrance." Observe now the insincerity of his character! Having said a little before, that " the man who had embraced a system of good doctrine ought not, even if exposed to danger on that account from men, to disavow it, or pretend that he had done so, nor yet openly disown it," he now involves himself in all manner of contradictions. For he knew that if he acknowledged himself an

Epicurean, lie would not obtain any credit when accusing those whoj in any degree, introduce the doctrine of Providence, and who place a God over the world. And we have heard that there were two individuals of the name of Celsus, both of whom were Epicureans; the earlier of the two having lived in the time of Nero, but this one in that of Adrian, and later.

Chapter ix.

Pie next proceeds to recommend, that in adopting opinions we should follow reason and a rational guide, since he who assents to opinions without following this course is very liable to be deceived. And he compares inconsiderate believers to Metragyrt e, and soothsayers, and Mithrab, and Sabbadians, jmd to anything else that one may fall in with, and to the phantoms of Hecate, or any other demon or demons. For as amongst such persons are frequently to be found wicked men, who, taking advantage of the ignorance of those who Lire easily deceived, lead them away whither' they will, so also, he says, is the case among Christians. And he asserts that certain persons who do not wish either to give or receive a reason for their belief, keep repeating, "Do not examine, but believe!" and, "Your faith will save you!" And he alleges that such also say, "The wisdom of this life is bad, but that foolishness is a good thing!" To which we have to answer, that if it were possible for all to leave the business of life, and devote themselves to philosophy, no other method ought to be adopted by any one, but this alone. For in the Christian system also it will be found that there is, not to speak at all arrogantly, at least as much of investigation into articles of belief, and of explanation of dark sayings, occurring in the prophetical writings, and of the parables in the Gospels, and of countless other things, which either were narrated or enacted with a symbolical signification," as is the case with other systems. But since the course alluded to is impossible, partly on account of the necessities of life, partly on account of the weakness of men, as only a very few individuals devote themselves earnestly to study, what better method could be devised with a view of assisting the multitude, than that which was delivered by Jesus to the heathen? And let us inquire, with respect to the great multitude of believers, who have washed away the mire of wickedness in which they formerly wallowed, whether it were better for them to believe without a reason, and so to have become reformed and improved in their habits, through the belief that men are chastised for sins, and honoured for good works; or not to have allowed themselves to be converted on the strength of mere faith, but to have waited until they could give themselves to a thorough examination of the necessary reasons. For it is manifest that, on such a plan, all men, with very few exceptions, would not obtain this amelioration of conduct which they have obtained through a simple faith, but would continue to remain in the practice of a wicked life. Now, wdiatever other evidence can be furnished of the fact, that it was not without divine intervention that the philanthropic scheme of Christianity was introduced among men, this also must be added. For a pious man will not believe that even a physician of the body, who restores the sick to better health, could take up his abode in any city or country without divine permission, since ro good happens to men without the help of God. And if he who has cured the bodies of many, or restored them to better health, does not effect his cures without the help of God, how much more He who has healed the souls of many, and has turned them to virtue, and improved their nature, and attached them to God who is over all things, and tauglit them to refer every action to His good pleasure, and to shun all that is displeasing to Him, even to the least of their words or deeds, or even of the thoughts of their hearts?

acpohpa ohiyoiv itrl rot 7jyou arrovrav.

CltAPTEP. X.

In the next place, since our opponents keep repeating tliose statments about faith, we must say that, considering it as a useful thing for the multitude, we admit that ye teach those men to believe without reasons, who are unable to abandon all other employments, and give themselves to an examination of arguments; and our opponents, although they do not acknowledge it, yet practically do the same. For who is there that, on betaking himself to the study of philosophy, and throwing himself into the ranks of some sect, either by chance, or because he is provided with a teacher of that school, adopts such a course for any other reason, except that he believes his particular sect to be superior to any other? For, not waitino; to hear the arguments of all the other philosophers, and of all the different sects, and the reasons for condemning one system and for supporting another, he in this way elects to become a Stoic, e. g., or a Platonist, or a Peripatetic, or an Epicurean, or a follower of some other school, and is thus borne, although they will not admit it, by a kind of irrational impulse to the practice, say of Stoicism, to the disregard of the others; despising either Platonism, as being marked by greater humility than the others; or Peri-pateticism, as more human, and as admitting with more fairness" than other systems the blessings of human life. And some also, alarmed at first sight "' about the doctrine of providence, from seeing what happens in the world to the vicious and to the virtuous, have rashly concluded that there is no divine providence at all, and have adopted the views of Epicurus and Celsus.

Chapter xi.

Since, then, as reason teaches, we must repose faith in some one of those who have been the introducers of sects among the Greeks or barbarians, why should we not rather believe in God who is over all things, and in Him who teaches that worship is due to God alone, and that other things are to be passed by, either as non-existent, or as existing indeed, and worthy of honour, but not of worship and reverence? And respecting these things, he who not only beheves, but who contemplates things with the eye of reason, will state the demonstrations that occur to him, and which are the result of careful investigation. And why should it not be more reasonable, seeing all human things are dependent upon faith, to believe God rather than them? For who enters on a voyage, or contracts a marriage, or becomes the father of children, or casts seed into the ground, without believing that better things will result from so doing, although the contrary might and sometimes does happen? And yet the belief that better things, even agreeably to their wishes, will follow, makes all men venture upon uncertain enterprises, which may turn out differently from what they expect. And if the hope and belief of a better future be the support of life in every uncertain enterprise, vvliy shall not this faith rather be rationally accepted by him who believes on better grounds than he who sails the sea, or tills the ground, or marries a wife, or engages in any other human pursuit, in the existence of a God who was the Creator of all these things, and in Him who with surpassing wisdom and divine greatness of mind dared to make known this doctrine to men in every part of the world, at the cost of great danger, and of a death considered infamous, which He underwent for the sake of the human race; having also taught those who were persuaded to embrace His doctrine at the first, to proceed, under the peril of every danger, and of ever impending death, to all quarters of the world to ensure the salvation of men?

Chapter xii.

In the next place, when Celsus says in express words, ' If they would answer me, not as if I were asking for information, for I am acquainted with all their opinions, but because I take an equal interest in them all, it would be well. And if they Yill not, but will keep reiterating, as they generally do, Do not investigate," etc., they must, he continues, explain to me at least of what nature these things are of which they speak, and whence they are derived," etc. Now, with regard to his statement that he " is acquainted with all our doctrines," we have to say that this is a boastful and daring assertion; for if he had read the prophets in particular, which are full of acknowledged difficulties, and of declarations that are obscure to the multitude, and if he had perused the parables of the Gospels, and the other writings of the law and of the Jewish history, and the utterances of the apostles, and had read them candidly, with a desire to enter into their meaning, he would not have expressed himself with such boldness, nor said that he ' was acquainted with all their doctrines." Even we ourselves, who have devoted much study to these writings, would not say that ' we were acquainted with everything," for we have a regard for truth. Xot one of us will assert, "I know all the doctrines of Epicurus," or will be confident that he knows all those of Plato, in the knowledge of the fact that so many differences of opinion exist among the expositors of these systems. For who is so daring as to say that he knows all the opinions of the Stoics or of the Peripatetics? Unless, indeed, it should be the case that he has heard this boast, '-1 know them all," from some ignorant and senseless individuals, who do not perceive their own ignorance, and should thus imagine, from having had such persons as his teachers, that he w'as acquainted with them all. Such an one appears to me to act very much as a person would do who had visited Egypt (where the Egyptian savans, learned in their country's literature, are greatly given to philosophizing about those things which are regarded among them as divine, but where the vulgar, hearing certain myths, the reasons of which they do not understand, are greatly elated because of their fancied knowledge), and who should imagine that he is acquainted with the whole circle of Egyptian knowledge, after having been a disciple of the ignorant alone, and without having associated with any of the priests, or having learned the mysteries of the Egyptians from any other source. And what I have said regarding the learned and ignorant among the Egyptians, I might have said also of the Persians; among whom there are mysteries, conducted on rational principles by the learned among them, but understood in a symbolical sense by the more superficial of the multitude. And the same remark applies to the Syrians, and Indians, and to all those who have a literature and a mythology.

Chapter xiii.

But since Celsus has declared it to be a saying of many Christians, that " the wisdom of this life is a bad thing, but that foolishness is good," we have to answer that he slanders the gospel, not giving the words as they actually occur in the writings of Paul, where they run as follow: " If any one among you seemeth to be wise in this world, let him become a fool, that he may become wise. For the wisdom of this w orld is foolishness with God." The apostle, therefore, does not say simply that " wisdom is foolishness with God," but " the wisdom of tjiis luorldr And again, not, "If any one among you seemeth to be wise, let him become a fool universally;" but, "let him become a fool in this luorld, that he may become wise." We term, then, " the wisdom of this world," every false system of philosophy, which, according to the Scriptures, is brought to nought; and we call foolishness good, not without restriction, but when a man becomes foolish as to this ivorld. As if we were to say that the Platonist, who believes in the immortality of the soul, and in the doctrine of its metempsychosis, incurs the charge of folly with the Stoics, who discard this opinion; and with the Peripatetics, who babble about the subtleties of Plato; and with the Epicureans, who call it superstition to introduce a providence, and to place a God over all things. Moreover, that it is in agreement with the spirit of

Ucip' olg ilai rsyxsrocl, Trpsaievo csuai fJu 'hoymug vtto roiu. rcx. p' uvrol; 'Aoyiau, av ufiokix-ug os yiv6y. ivo(, i vtto ruu Trap' aiirolg iztikhcdu x. ui i'mtro'Kcx. to–ripoyj. For yivo i'ja, i Riiseus prefers yivo)uk6 ivut which is adopted in the transhition.

2 1 Cor. iii. 18, 19.

Christianity, of much more importance to give our assent to doctrines upon grounds of reason and wisdom than on that of faith merely, and that it was only in certain circumstances that the latter course was desired by Christianity, in order not to leave men altogether without help, is shown by that genuine disciple of Jesus, Paul, when he says: " For after that, in the wisdom of God, the world by wisdom knew not God, it pleased God by the foolishness of preaching to save them that believe." Now by these words it is clearly shown that it is by the wisdom of God that God ought to be known. But as this result did not follow, it pleased God a second time to save them that believe, not by " folly" universally but by such foolishness as depended on preaching. For the preaching of Jesus Christ as crucified is the " foolishness" of preaching, as Paul also perceived, when he said, ' But we preach Christ crucified, to the Jews a stumbling-block, and to the Greeks foolishness; but to them who are called, both Jews and Greeks, Christ the po yer of God, and wisdom of God."

Chapter xiv.

Celsus, being of opinion that there is to be found among many nations a general relationship of doctrine, enumerates all the nations which gave rise to such and such opinions; but for some reason, unknown to me, he casts a slight upon the Jews, not including them amongst the others, as having either laboured along with them, and arrived at the same conclusions, or as having entertained similar opinions on many subjects. It is propei", therefore, to ask him why lie gives credence to the histories of barbarians and Greeks respecting the antiquity of those nations of whom he speaks, but stamps the histories of this nation alone false. For ' Er OS otl Kui Kccroi ro ra "Koya dpiakOVi ttoaAw oict(pipst (. sroc. 'Koyov xai Go! pia ovKccruridiadui roig ooyy-ctaiv Titrtp y iroi pi'Krjg TTjg Trianag' Kcil on y. circi "Triplaretatv, a, l rovr sjsqvt tisyi 6 Ao'yo?, I'- ci y TrautYi diiaipi-"kug iasv Toug ccudpatrovg' Zn'hol 6 70u ' Imov yyiaiog y, ci9rit'; g, etc.

2 1 Cor. i. 23, 2-1.

if the respective writers related the events which are found in these works in the spirit of truth, why should we distrust the prophets of the Jews alone? And if Moses andjthe prophets have recorded many things in their history from a desire to favour their own system, why should we not say the same of the historians of other countries? Or, when the Egyptians or their histories speak evil of the Jews, are they to be believed on that point; but the Jews, when saying the same things of the Egyptians, and declaring that they had suffered great injustice at their hands, and that on this account they had been persecuted by God, are to be charged with falsehood? And this applies not to the Egyptians alone, but to others; for we shall find that there was a connection between the Assyrians and the Jews, and that this is recorded in the ancient histories of the Assyrians. And so also the Jewish historians (I avoid using the word " prophets," that I may not appear to prejudge the case) have related that the Assyrians were enemies of the Jews. Observe at once, then, the arbitrary procedure of this individual, who believes the histories of these nations on the ground of their being learned, and condemns others as being wholly ignorant. For listen to the statement of Celsus: ' There is," he says, ' an authoritative account from the very beginning, respecting which there is a constant agreement among ail the most learned nations, and cities, and men." And yet will not call the Jews a learned nation in the same way in which he does the Egyptians, and Assyrians, and Indians, and Persians, and Odrysians, and Samothracians, and Eleusinians.

Chapter xv.

How much more impartial than Celsus is Numenius the Pythagorean, who has given many proofs of being a very eloquent man, and who has carefully tested many opinions, and collected together from many sources what had the appearance of truth; for, in the first book of his treatise On the Good, speaking of those nations who have adopted the opinion that God is incorporeal, he enumerates the Jews also among those who hold this view; not showing any reluctance to use even the language of their prophets in his treatise, and to give it a metaphorical signification. It is said, moreover, that Hermippus has recorded in his first book, Oil Laicgivers, that it was from the Jewish people that Pythagoras derived the philosophy which he introduced among the Greeks. And there is extant a work by the historian Hecatseus, treating of the Jews, in which so high a character is bestowed upon that nation for its learning, that Herennius Philo, in his treatise on the Jews, has doubts, in the first place, whether it is really the composition of the historian; and says, in the second place, that if really his, it is probable that he was carried away by the plausible nature of the Jewish history, and so yielded his assent to their system.

Chapter xvi.

I must express my surprise that Celsus should class the Odrysians, and Samothracians, and Eleusinians, and Hyperboreans among the most ancient and learned nations, and should not deem the Jews worthy of a place among such, either for their learning or their antiquity, although there are: nany treatises in circulation among the Egyptians, and Pha; nicians, and Greeks, which testify to their existence as, n. n Micient people, but which I have considered it unnecessary to quote. For any one who chooses may read what Flavins Josephus has recorded in his two books. On the Antiquity of the Jews, where he brings together a great collection of writers, who bear witness to the antiquity of the Jewish people; and there exists the Discourse to the Greeks of Tatian the younger, in which with very great learning he enumerates those historians who have treated of the antiquity of the Jewish nation and of Moses. It seems, then, to be not from a love of truth, but from a spirit of hatred, that Celsus makes these statements, his object being to asperse the origin of Christianity, which is connected with Judaism. Nay, he styles the Galactophagi of Homer, and the Druids of the Gauls, and the Getaj, most learned and ancient tribes, on account of the resemblance between their traditions and those of the Jews, although I know not whether any of their histories survive; but the Hebrews alone, as far as in him lies, he deprives of the honour both of antiquity and learning. And again, when making a list of ancient and learned men who have conferred benefits upon their contemporaries by their deeds, and upon posterity by their writings, he excluded Moses from the number; while of Linus, to whom Celsus assigns a foremost place in his list, there exist neither laws nor discourses which produced a change for the better among any tribes; whereas a whole nation, dispersed throughout the entire world, obey the laws of Moses. Consider, then, whether it is not from open malevolence that he has expelled Moses from his catalogue of learned men, while asserting that Linus, and Musgeus, and Orpheus, and Pherecydes, and the Persian Zoroaster, and Pythagoras, discussed these topics, and that their opinions were deposited in books, and have thus been preserved down to the present time. And it is intentionally also that he has omitted to take notice of the myth, embellished chiefly by Orpheus, in which the gods are described as affected by human weaknesses and passions.

Chapter xvii.

Li what follows, Celsus, assailing the Mosaic history, fimls fault with those who give it a tropical and allegorical si nifi-i cation. And here one might say to this great man, vvho inscribed upon his own work the title of a True Discouyse " Why, good sir, do you make it a boast to have it recorded that the gods should engage in such adventures as are described by your learned poets and philosophers, and be guilty of abominable intrigues, and of engaging in wt 'S against their own fathers, and of cutting off their secret partys, and should dare to commit and to suffer such enormitiesi; while Moses, who gives no such accounts respecting ioixl, nou-even regarding the holy angels, and who relates deeds-of fai less atrocity regarding men (for in his writings no one ever ventured to commit such crimes as Kronos did against Uranus, or Zeus against lils father, or that of the father of men and gods, who had intercourse with his own daughter), should be considered as having deceived those who were placed under his laws, and to have led them into error?" And here Celsus seems to me to act somewhat as Thrasymachus the Platonic philosopher did, wdien he would not allow Socrates to answer regarding justice, as he wished, but said, " Take care not to say that utility is justice, or duty, or anything of that kind." For in like manner Celsus assails (as he thinks) the Mosaic histories, and finds fault with those who understand them allegorically, at the same time bestowing also some praise upon those wdio do so, to the effect that they are more impartial than those who do not; and thus, as it were, he prevents by his cavils those wdio are able to show the true state of the case from offering such a defence as they would wish to offer.

Chapter xviii.

And challenging a comparison of book with book, I would say, "Come now, good sir, take down the poems of Linus, and of Mus eus, and of Orpheus, and the writings of Pherecydes, and carefully compare these with the laws of Closes histories with histories, and ethical discourses with laws and commandments and see wdiich of the two are the better fitted to change the character of the hearer on the very spot, and which to harden him in his wickedness; and observe that your series of writers display little concern for those readers who are to peruse them at once unaided, but have composed their philosophy (as you term it) for those who are able to comprehend its metaphorical and allegorical signification;

Oiovtl Ku'hviza. i Kctt'iyooyidct: a; (iout STcci d'Trot oyiig xt rov; ovucc-ya'jovg 0); TicPvkSu e csiu tcc itrpuyf xrcc. Wc have taken KOhintcti as middle. Some propose Ka'Kvu. And we have read 3oj Ac!r , a lection which is given byv a second hand in one MS.

'E'7rirprpcii." Other readmgs are k-Tna-ps-ipcci and cctroarps-' xi, which convey the opposite meaning.

"ccvrohi.

whereas Moses, like a distinguished orator who meditates some figure of Rhetoric, and who carefully introduces in every part language of twofold meaning, has done this in his five books: neither affording, in the portion which relates to morals, any handle to his Jewish subjects for committing evil; nor yet giving to the few individuals who were endowed with greater wisdom, and Avho were capable of investigating his meaning, a treatise devoid of material for speculation. But of your learned poets the very writings would seem no longer to be preserved, although they would have been carefully treasured up if the readers had perceived any benefit likely to be derived from them; whereas the works of Moses have stirred up many, who were even aliens to the manners of the Jews, to the belief that, as these writings testify, the first who enacted these laws and delivered them to Moses, was the God who was the Creator of the world. For it became the Creator of the universe, after laying down laws for its government, to confer upon His words a power which might subdue all men in every part of the earth. And this I maintain, having as yet entered into no investigation regarding Jesus, but still demonstrating that Moses, who is far inferior to the Lord, is, as the Discourse will show, greatly superior to your wise poets and philosophers."

Chapter xix.

After these statements, Celsus, from a secret desire to cast discredit upon the Mosaic account of the creation, which teaches that the world is not yet ten thousand years old, but very much under that, while concealing his wish, intimates his aorreement with those who hold that the world is uncreated. For, maintaining that there have been, from all eternity, many conflagrations and many deluges, and that the flood which lately took place in the time of Deucalion is comparatively modern, he clearly demonstrates to those who are able to understand him, that, in his opinion, the world was uncreated. But let this assailant of the Christian faith tell us by what arguments he was compelled to accept the statement that there have been many conflagrations and many cataclysms, and that the flood which occnrred in the time of Deucalion, and the conflagration in that of Phagthon, were more recent than any others. And if he should put forward the dialogues of Plato as evidence on these subjects, we shall say to him that it is allowable for us also to believe that there resided in the pure and pious soul of Moses, who ascended above all created things, and united himself to the Creator of the universe, and who made known divine things with far greater clearness than Plato, or those other wise men who lived among the Greeks and Pomans, a spirit wdilcli was divine. And if he demand of us our reasons for such a belief, let him first give grounds for his own unsupported assertions, and then we shall show that this view of ours is the correct one.

Chapter xx.

And yet, against his will, Celsus is entangled into testifying that the w orld is comparatively modern, and not yet ten thousand years old, when he says that the Greeks consider those things as ancient, because, owing to the deluges and conflagrations, they have not beheld or received any memorials of older events. But let Celsus have, as his authorities for the myth regarding the conflagrations and inundations, those persons who, in his opinion, are the most learned of the Egyptians, traces of whose wisdom are to be found in the worship of irrational animals, and In arguments which prove that such a worship of God is in conformity with reason, and of a secret and mysterious character. The Egyptians, then, when they boastfully give their own account of the divinity of animals, are to be considered wise; but if any Jew, who has signified his adherence to the law and the lawgiver, refer everything to the Creator of the universe, and the only God, he is, In the opinion of Celsus and those like him, deemed inferior to him who degrades the Divinity not only to the level of rational and mortal animals, but even to that of irrational also! a view which goes far beyond the OFJG. 2 D mythical doctrine of transmigration, according to wliicli the soul falls down from the summit of heaven, and enters into the body of brute beasts, both tame and savage! And if the Egyptians related fables of this kind, they are believed to convey a philosophical meaning by their enigmas and mysteries; but if Moses compose and leave behind him histories and laws for an entire nation, they are to be considered as empty fables, the language of which admits of no allegorical meaning!

Chapter xxi.

The following is the view of Celsus and the Epicureans: " Moses having," he says, ' learned the doctrine which is to be found existing among wise nations and eloquent men. obtained the reputation of divinity." Now, in answer to this we have to say, that it may be allowed him that Moses did indeed hear a somewhat ancient doctrine, and transmitted the same to the Hebrews; that if the doctrine which he heard was false, and neither pious nor venerable, and if notwithstanding, he received it and handed it down to those under his authority, he is liable to censure; but if, as you assert, he gave his adherence to opinions that were wise and true, and educated his people by means of them, what, pray, has he done deserving of condemnation? Would, indeed, that not only Epicurus, but Aristotle, whose sentiments regarding providence are not so impious as those of the former, and the Stoics, who assert that God is a body, had heard such a doctrine! Then the world would not have been filled with opinions which either disallow or enfeeble the action of providence, or introduce a corrupt corporeal principle, according to which the god of the Stoics is a body, with respect to whom they are not afraid to say that he is capable of change, and may be altered and transformed in all his parts, and, generally, that he is capable of corruption, if there be any one to corrupt him, but that he has the good fortune to escape corruption, because there is none to corrupt. Whereas the doctrine of the Jews and Christians, which preserves the immutability and unalterableness of the divine nature, is stigmatized as impious, because it does not partake of the profanity of those whose notions of God are marked by impiety, but because it says in the supplication addressed to the Divinity, "Thou art the same," it being, moreover, an article of faith that God has said, "I change not.""

Chapter xxii.

After this, Celsus, without condemning circumcision as practised by the Jews, asserts that this usage was derived from the Egyptians; thus believing the Egyptians rather than Moses, who says that Abraham was the first among men who practised the rite. And it is not Moses alone who mentions the name of Abraham, assigning to him great intimacy with God; but many also of those who give themselves to the practice of the conjuration of evil spirits, employ in their spells the expression " God of Abraham," pointing out by the very name the friendship that existed between that just man and God. And yet, while making use of the phrase " God of Abraham," they do not know who Abraham is! And the same remark applies to Isaac, and Jacob, and Israel; which names, although confessedly Hebrew, are frequently introduced by those Egyptians who profess to produce some wonderful result by means of their knowledge. The rite of circumcision, however, which began with Abraham, and was discontinued by Jesus, who desired that His disciples should not practise it, is not before us for explanation; for the present occasion does not lead us to speak of such things, but to make an effort to refute the char2: es brou fht aojainst the doctrine of the Jews by Celsus, who thinks that he will be able the more easily to establish the falsity of Christianity, if, by assailing its origin in Judaism, he can show that the latter also is untrue.

1 Ps. cii. 27. 2 Mai. iii. 6.

Chapter xxiii.

After this, Celsus next asserts that " Those herdsmen and shepherds who followed Moses as their leader, had their minds deluded by vulgar deceits, and so supposed that there was one God." Let him show, then, how, after this irrational departure, as he regards it, of the herdsmen and shepherds from the worship of many gods, he himself is able to establish the multiplicity of deities that are found amongst the Greeks, or among those other nations that are called Barbarian. Let him establish, therefore, the existence of Mnemosyne, the mother of the Muses by Zeus; or of Themis, the parent of the Hours; or let him prove that the ever naked Graces can have a real, substantial existence. But he will not be able to show, from any actions of theirs, that these

fictitious representations of the Greeks, which have the appearance of being invested
with bodies, are really gods. And why should the fables of the Greeks regarding the
gods be true, any more than those of the Egyptians for example, who in their language
know nothing of a Mnemosyne, mother of the nine Muses; nor of a Themis, parent of
the Hours; nor of a Euphros ne, one of the Graces; nor of any other of these names?
How much more manifest (and how much better than all these inventions!) is it that,
convinced by what we see, in the admirable order of the world, we should worship the
Maker of it as the one Author of one effect, and which, as being wholly in harmony
with itself, cannot on that account have been the work of many makers; and that
we should believe that the whole heaven is not held together by the movements of
many souls, for one is enough, wdiich bears the whole of the non-wandering" sphere
from east to west, and embraces within it all things which the world requires, and
which are not self-existing! For all are parts of the world, while God is no part of tlie
wdiole. But God cannot be imperfect, as a part is imperfect. And perhaps profounder
consideration will show, that as God is not a part, so neither is He properly the whole,
since the whole is com. posed of parts; and 2 rviv sitct xuv.

reason will not allow us to believe that the God who is over all is composed of
parts, each one of which cannot do what all the other parts can.

Chapter xxiv.

After this he continues: " These herdsmen and shepherds concluded that there was
but one God, named either the Highest, or Adonai, or the Heavenly, or Sabaoth, or
called by some other of those names which they delight to give this world; and they
knew nothing beyond that." And in a subsequent part of his work he says, that " It
makes no difference whether the God who is over all things be called by the name of
Zeus, which is current among the Greeks, or by that, e. g., wdiich is in use among the
Indians or Egyptians." Now, in answer to this, we have to remark that this involves
a deep and mysterious subject that, viz., respecting the nature of names: it being a
question whether, as Aristotle thinks, names were bestowed by arrangement, or, as
the Stoics hold, by nature; the first words being imitations of things, agreeably to
which the names were formed, and in conformity wath which they introduce certain
principles of etymology; or whether, as Epicurus teaches (differing in this from the
Stoics), names were given by nature, the first men having uttered certain words varying
with the circumstances in which they found themselves. If, then, we shall be able to
establish, in reference to the preceding statement, the nature of powerful names, some
of wdiich are used by the learned amongst the Egyptians, or by the Magi among the
Persians, and by the Indian philosophers called Brahmans, or by the Saman ans, and
others in different countries; and shall be able to make out that the so-called magic is
not, as the followers of Epiearns and Aristotle suppose, an altogether uncertain thing,
but is, as those skilled in it prove, a consistent system, having w ords wdiich are known
to exceedingly few; then we say that the name Sabaoth, and Adonai, and the other
names treated with so much reverence amons the Hebrews, are not applicable to any
ordinary created things, but belong to a secret theology which refers to the Frainer
of all things. These names, accordingly, when pronounced with that attendant train
of circumstances which is appropriate to their nature, are possessed of great power;
and other names, again, current in the Egyptian tongue, are efficacious against certain

demons who can only do certain things; and other names in the Persian language have corresponding power over other spirits; and so on in every individual nation, for different purposes. And thus it will be found that, of the various demons upon the earth, to whom different localities have been assigned, each one bears a name appropriate to the several dialects of place and country. He, therefore, who has a nobler idea, however small, of these matters, will be careful not to apply differing names to different things; lest he should resemble those who mistakenly apply the name of God to lifeless matter, or who drag down the title of " the Good" from the First Cause, or from virtue and excellence, and apply it to blind Plutus, and to a healthy and well-proportioned mixture of flesh and blood and bones, or to what is considered to be noble birth.

Chapter xxv.

And perhaps there is a danger as great as that which degrades the name of ' God," or of " the Good," to improper objects, in changing the name of God according to a secret system, and applying those which belong to inferior beings to greater, and vice versa. And I do not dwell on this, that when the name of Zeus is uttered, there is heard at the same time that of the son of Kronos and Rhea, and the husband of Hera, and brother of Poseidon, and father of Athene, and Artemis, who was guilty of incest with his own daughter Persephone; or that Apollo immediately suggests the son of Leto and Zeus, and the brother of Artemis, and half-brother of Hermes; and so with all the other names invented by these wise men of Celsus, who are the parents of these opinions, 'Ea'tti tou rv(p7 6u 'K'hovrov jcmi S'tti rviv aap- oiu y. ai ai. ccarojy icoct 6artc)'j and the ancient theologians of tlie Greeks. For what are the rounds for decidin j that he should on the one hand be properly called Zeus, and yet on the other should not have Kronos for his father and Eliea for his mother? And the same argument applies to all the others that are called gods. But this charge does not at all apply to those who, for some mysterious reason, refer the word Sabaoth, or Adonai, or any of the other names to the true God. And when one is able to philosophize about the mystery of names, he will find much to say respecting the titles of the angels of God, of whom one is called Michael, and another Gabriel, and another Kaphael, appropriately to the duties which they discharge in the world, according to the will of the God of all things. And a similar philosophy of names applies also to our Jesus, whose name has already been seen, in an unmistakeable manner, to have expelled myriads of evil spirits from the souls and bodies of men, so great was the power which it exerted upon those from whom the spirits were driven out. And while still upon the subject of names, we have to mention that those who are skilled in the use of incantations, relate that the utterance of the same incantation in its proper language can accomplish what the spell professes to do; but when translated into any other tongue, it is observed to become inefficacious and feeble. And thus it is not the things signified, but the qualities and peculiarities of words, which possess a certain power for this or that purpose. And so on such grounds as these we defend the conduct of the Christians, when they struggle even to death to avoid calling God by the name of Zeus, or to give Him a name from any other language. For they either use the common name God indefinitely, or with some such addition as that of the " Maker of all things," " the Creator of heaven and earth" He who sent down to the human race those good men, to whose names that of

God being added, certain mi htv works are wroumit amono; men. And much more besides might be said on the subject of names, against those who think that we ought to be indifferent as to our use of them. And if the remark of Plato in the Philehus should surprise us, when he says, "My fear, O Protagoras, about the names of the gods is no small one," seeing Philebus in his discussion with Socrates had called pleasure a " god," how shall we not rather approve the piety of the Christians, who apply none of the names used in the mythologies to the Creator of the world? And now enough on this subject for the present.

Chapter xxyi.

But let us see the manner in which this Celsus, who professes to know everything, brings a false accusation against the Jews, when he alleges that " they worship angels, and are addicted to sorcery, in which Moses was their instructor." Now, in what part of the writings of Moses he found the lawgiver laying down the worship of angels, let him tell, who professes to know all about Christianity and Judaism; and let him show also how sorcery can exist among those who have accepted the Mosaic law, and read the injunction, "Neither seek after wizards, to be defiled by them." Moreover, he promises to show afterwards "how it was through ignorance that the Jews were deceived and led into error." Now, if he had discovered that the ignorance of the Jews reo; ardincj Christ was the effect of their not having heard the prophecies about Him, he would show with truth how the Jews fell into error. But without any wish whatever that this should appear, he views as Jewish errors what are no errors at all. And Celsus having promised to make us acquainted, in a subsequent part of his work, with the doctrines of Judaism, proceeds in the first place to speak of our Saviour as liaving been the leader of our generation, in so far as we are Christians, and says that " a few years ago he began to teach this doctrine, being regarded by Christians as the Son of God." Now, with respect to this point His prior existence a few years ago we have to remark as follows. Could it have come to pass without divine assistance, that Jesus, desiring during these. years to spread abroad His words and teaching, should have Lev. xix. 31.

been so successful, that everywhere throughout the worhl, not a few persons, Greeks as well as Barbarians, learned as well as ignorant, adopted His doctrine, so that. they struggled even to death in its defence, rather than deny it, which no one is ever related to have done for any other system? I indeed, from no wish to flatter Christianity, but from a desire thoroughly to examine the facts, would say that even those who are eii Tao; ed in the healino of numbers of sick persons, do not attain their object the cure of the body without divine help; and if one were to succeed in delivering souls from a flood of wickedness, and excesses, and acts of injustice, and from a contempt of God, and were to show, as evidence of such a result, one hundred persons improved in their natures (let us suppose the number to be so large), no one would reasonably say that it was without divine assistance that he had implanted in those hundred individuals a doctrine capable of removing so many evils. And if any one, on a candid consideration of these things, shall admit that no improvement ever takes place among men without divine help, how much more confidently shall he make the same assertion regarding Jesus, when he compares the former lives of many converts to His doctrine with their after conduct, and reflects in what acts of licentiousness and injustice and covetousness they formerly indulged, until, as Celsus, and they who think wdth him, allege, " they were deceived," and accepted a doctrine which, as these individuals assert, is destructive of the life of men; but who, from the time that they adopted it, have become in some way meeker, and more religious, and more consistent, so that certain among them, from a desire of exceeding chastity, and a wish to worship God with greater purity, abstain even from the permitted indulgences of lawful love.

ChaPTEK XXVII.

Any one who examines the subject will see that Jesus attempted and successfully accomplished works beyond the

O'J KO'hoc. KivCJil.

reach of human power. For although, from the very beginning, all things opposed the spread of His doctrine in the world, both the princes of the times, and their chief captains and generals, and all, to speak generally, who were possessed of the smallest influence, and in addition to these, the rulers of the different cities, and the soldiers, and the people, yet it proved victorious, as being the Word of God, the nature of which is such that it cannot be hindered; and becoming more powerful than all such adversaries, it made itself master of the whole of Greece, and a considerable portion of barbarian lands, and converted countless numbers of souls to His religion. And although, among the multitude of converts to Christianity, the simple and ignorant necessarily outnumbered the more intelligent, as the former class always does the latter, yet Celsus, unwilling to take note of this, thinks that this philanthropic doctrine, which reaches to every soul under the sun, is vulgar, and on account of its vulgarity and its want of reasoning power, obtained a hold only over the ignorant. And yet he himself admits that it was not the simple alone who were led by the doctrine of Jesus to adopt His religion; for he acknowledges that there were amongst them some persons of moderate intelligence, and gentle disposition, and possessed of understanding, and capable of comprehending allegories.

Chapter xxviii.

And since, in imitation of a rhetorician training a pupil, he introduces a Jew, who enters into a personal discussion with Jesus, and speaks in a very childish manner, altogether unworthy of the grey hairs of a philosopher, let me endeavour, to the best of my ability, to examine his statements, and show that he does not maintain, throughout the discussion, the consistency due to the character of a Jew. For he represents him disputing with Jesus, and confuting Him, as he thinks, on many points; and in the first place, he accuses Him of having " invented his birth from a virgin,"

- ihiomy."iiu.

and upbraids Him with being born in a certain Jewish village, of a poor woman of the country, who gained her subsistence by spinning, and who was turned out of doors by her husband, a carpenter by trade, because she was convicted of adultery; that after being driven away by her husband, and wandering about for a time, she disgracefully gave birth to Jesus, an illegitimate child, who having hired himself out as a servant in Egypt on account of his poverty, and having there acquired some miraculous powers, on which the Egyptians greatly pride themselves, returned to his own country, highly elated on account of them, and by means of these proclaimed himself a God." Now, as I cannot allow anything said by unbelievers to remain unexamined, but must investigate everything from the beginning, I give it as my opinion J: hat all these things worthily harmonize w ith the predictions that Jesus is the Son of God.

Chapter xxix.

For birth is an aid towards an individual's becoming famous, and distinguished, and talked about; viz., when a man's parents happen to be in a position of rank and influence, and are possessed of wealth, and are able to spend it upon the education of their son, and when the country of one's birth is great and illustrious; but when a man having all these things against him is able, notwithstanding these hindrances, to make himself known, and to produce an impression on those who hear of him, and to become distinguished and visible to the whole world, which speaks of him as it did not do before, how can we help admiring such a nature as being both noble in itself, and devoting itself to great deeds, and possessing a courage which is not by any means to be despised? And if one were to examine more fully the history of such an individual, why should he not seek to know in what manner, after being reared up in frugality and poverty, and without receiving any complete education, and without having studied systems and opinions by means of which he might have acquired confidence to associate with multitudes, and play the demagogue, and attract to himself many hearers, he nevertheless devoted himself to the teaching of new opinions, introducing among men a doctrine which not only subverted the customs of the Jews, while preserving due respect for their prophets, but which especially overturned the established observances of the Greeks regarding the Divinity? And how could such a person one who had been so brought up, and who, as his calumniators admit, had learned nothing great from men have been able to teach, in a manner not at all to be despised, such doctrines as he did regarding the divine judgment, and the punishments that are to overtake wickedness, and the rewards that are to be conferred upon virtue; so that not only rustic and ignorant individuals were won by his words, but also not a few of those who were distinguished by their wisdom, and who were able to discern the hidden meaning in those more common doctrines, as they were considered, which were in circulation, and which secret meaning enwrapped, so to speak, some more recondite signification still? The Seriphian, in Plato, who reproaches Themistocles after he had become celebrated for his military skill, saying that his reputation was due not to his own merits, but to his good fortune in having been born in the most illustrious country in Greece, received from the good-natured Athenian, who saw that his native country did contribute to his renown, the following reply: " Neither would I, had I been a Seriphian, have been so distinguished as I am, nor would you have been a Themistocles, even if you had had the good fortune to be an Athenian!" And now, our Jesus, who is reproached with being born in a village, and that not a Greek one, nor belonging to any nation widely esteemed, and being despised as the son of a poor labouring woman, and as having on account of his poverty left his native country and hired himself out in Egypt, and being, to use the instance already quoted, not only a Seriphian, as it were, a native of a very small and undistinguished island, but even, so to speak, the meanest of the Seriphians, has yet been able to shake the whole inhabited world not only to a decri'ee far above what Themistocles tlie

Athenian ever did, but beyond what even Pytliagoras or Plato, or any other wise man in any part of the world whatever, or any prince or general, ever succeeded in doing.

Chapter xxx.

Now would not any one who investigated with ordinary care the nature of these facts, be struck with amazement at this man's victory? with his complete success in surmounting by his reputation all causes that tended to bring him into disrepute, and with his superiority over all other illustrious individuals in the w orld? And yet it is a rare thing for distinguished men to succeed in acquiring a reputation for several things at once. For one man is admired on account of his wisdom, another for his military skill, and some of the barbarians for their marvellous powers of incantation, and some for one quality, and others for another; but not many have been admired and acquired a reputation for many things at the same time; whereas this man, in addition to his other merits, is an object of admiration both for his wisdom, and for his miracles, and for his power of government. For he persuaded some to withdraw themselves from their laws, and to secede to him, not as a tyrant w ould do, nor as a robber, who arms his followers against men; nor as a rich man, who bestows help upon those who come to him; nor as one of those who confessedly are deserving of censure; but as a teacher of the doctrine retrardinff the God of all tilings, and of the worship which belongs to Him, and of all moral precepts which are able to secure the favour of the Supreme God to him who orders his life in conformity therewith. Now, to Themistocles, or to any other man of distinction, nothing happened to prove a hindrance to their reputation; whereas to this man, besides what we have already enumerated, and wdiich are enough to cover with dishonour the soul of a man even of the most noble nature,

Gelenins reads 6z-?. i au (instead of u'Keipcou), which has been adopted in the translation.

there was that apparently infamous death of crucifixion, which was enough to efface his previously acquired glory, and to lead those who, as they who disavow his doctrine assert, were formerly deluded by him to abandon their delusion, and to pass condemnation upon their deceiver.

Chapter xxxi.

And besides this, one may well wonder how it happened that the disciples if, as the calumniators of Jesus say, they did not see him after his resurrection from the dead, and were not'persuaded of his divinity were not afraid to endure the same sufferings with their master, and to expose themselves to danger, and to leave their native country to teach, according to the desire of Jesus, the doctrine delivered to them by him. For I think that no one who candidly examines the facts would say that these men devoted themselves ta-a life of danger for the sake of the doctrine of Jesus, without a profound belief which he had wrought in their minds of its truth, not only teaching them to conform to his precepts, but others also, and to conform, moreover, when manifest destruction to life impended over him who ventured to introduce these new opinions into all places and before all audiences, and who could retain as his friend no human being who adhered to the former opinions and usages. For did not the disciples of Jesus see, when they ventured to prove not only to the Jews from their prophetic Scriptures that this is he who w as spoken of by the prophets, but also to the other heathen nations, that he who was crucified yesterday or the day before underwent this death voluntarily on behalf of the human race, that this was analogous to the case of those who have died for their country in order to remove pestilence, or barrenness, or tempests? For it is probable that there is in the nature of things, for certain mysterious reasons which are difficult to be understood by the multitude, such a virtue that one just man, dying a voluntary death for the common good, might be the means of removing wicked spirits, which are the cause of plagues, or barrenness, or tempests, or similar calamities. Let those, therefore, who would disbelieve the statement that Jesus died on the cross on behalf of men, say whether they also refuse to accept the many accounts current both among Greeks and Barbarians, of persons who have laid down their lives for the public advantage, in order to remove those evils which had fallen upon cities and countries? Or will they say that such events actually happened, but that no credit is to be attached to that account which makes this so-called man to have died to ensure the destruction of a mighty evil spirit, the ruler of evil spirits, who had held in subjection the souls of all men upon earth? And the disciples of Jesus, seeing this and much more (which, it is probable, they learned from Jesus in private), and being filled, moreover, with a divine power (since it was no mere poetical virgin that endowed them with strength and courage, but the true wisdom and understanding of God), exerted all their efforts ' to become distinguished among all men," not only among the Argives, but among all the Greeks and Barbarians alike, and " so bear away for themselves a irlorious renown."

Chapter xxxit.

But let us now return to where the Jew is introduced speaking of the mother of Jesus, and saying that " when she was pregnant she was turned out of doors by the carpenter to whom she had been betrothed, as having been guilty of adultery, and that she bore a child to a certain soldier named Panthera;" and let us see whether those who have blindly concocted these fables about the adultery of the virgin with Panthera, and her rejection by the carpenter, did not invent these stories to overturn His miraculous conception by the Holy Ghost: for they could have falsified the history in a different manner, on account of its extremely miraculous character, and not have admitted, as it were against their will, that Jesus was born of no ordinary human marriage. Cf. Homer's Iliad book v. 2, 3.

It was to be expected, indeed, that those who would not believe the miraculous birth of Jesus would invent some falsehood. And their not doing this in a credible manner, but their preserving the fact that it was not by Joseph that the Virgin conceived Jesus, rendered the falsehood very palpable to those who can understand and detect such inventions. Is it at all agreeable to reason, that he who dared to do so much for the human race, in order that, as far as in him lay, all the Greeks and Barbarians, who were looking for divine condemnation, might depart from evil, and regulate their entire conduct in a manner pleasing to the Creator of the world, should not have had a miraculous birth, but one the vilest and most diso-raceful of all? And I will ask of them as Greeks, and particularly of Celsus, who either holds or not the sentiments of Plato, and at any rate quotes them, whether He who sends souls down into the bodies of men, degraded Him who was to dare such mighty acts, and to teach so many men, and to reform so many from the mass of wickedness in the world, to a birth more disgraceful than any other, and did not rather introduce Him into the world throumi a lawful marriao; e? Or is it not more in conformitv with reason, that every soul, for certain mysterious reasons (I speak now according to the opinion of Pythagoras, and Plato, and Empedocles, whom Celsus frequently names), is introduced into a body, and introduced according to its deserts and former actions? It is probable, therefore, that this soul also which conferred more benefit by its residence in the flesh than that of many men (to avoid prejudice, I do not say "all"), stood in need of a body not only superior to others, but invested with all excellent qualities.

Chapter xxxiii.

Now if a particular soul, for certain mysterious reasons, is not deserving of being placed in the body of a wholly irrational being, nor yet in that of one purely rational, but is clothed with a monstrous body, so that reason cannot discharge its functions in one so fashioned, which has the head disproportioned to the other parts, and altogether too short; and another receives such a body tliat the soul is a little more rational than the other; and another still more so, the nature of the body counteracting to a greater or less degree the reception of the reasoning principle; why should there not be also some soul which receives an altogether miraculous body, possessing some qualities common to those of other men, so that it may be able to pass through life with them, but possessing also some quality of superiority, so that the soul may be able to remain untainted by sin? And if there be any truth in the doctrine of the physiognomists, wdiether Zopyrus, or Loxus, or Polemon, or any other who wrote on such a subject, and who profess to know in some wonderful way that all bodies are adapted to the habits of the souls, must there have been for that soul which was to dwell with miraculous power among men, and work mighty deeds, a body produced, as Celsus thinks, by an act of adultery between Panthera and the Virgin?! Why, from such unhallowed intercourse there must rather have been brought forth some fool to do injury to mankind, a teacher of licentiousness and wickedness, and other evils; and not of temperance, and righteousness, and the other virtues.!

Chapter xxxiv.

But it was, as the prophets also predicted, from a virgin that there was to be born, according to the promised sign, one who was to give His name to the fact, showing that at His birth God was to be with man. Now it seems to me appropriate to the character of a Jew to have quoted the prophecy of Isaiah, which says that Emmanuel was to be born of a virgin. This, however, Celsus, who professes to know everything, has not done, either from ignorance or from an unwillingness (if he had read it and voluntarily passed it by in silence) to furnish an argument which might defeat his purpose. And the prediction runs thus: And the Lord spake again unto Ahaz, saying, Ask thee a sign of the Lord thy God; ask it either in the depth or in the height above.

OEIG. 2 E

But Ahaz said, I will not ask, neither will I tempt the Lord. And. he said, Hear ye now, O house of David; is it a small thing for you to weary men, but will ye weary my God also? Therefore the Lord Himself shall give you a sign. Behold, a virgin shall conceive, and bear a son, and shall call His name Immanuel, which is, being interpreted, God with us." And that it was from intentional mahce that Celsus did not quote this prophecy, is clear to me from this, that although he makes numerous quotations from the Gospel according to Matthew, as of the star that appeared at the birth of Christ, and other miraculous occurrences, he has made no mention at all of this. Now, if a Jew should split words, and say that the words are not, "Lo, a virgin," but, "Lo, a young woman," we reply that the word " Olmah" which the Septuagint have rendered by " a virgin," and others by " a young woman" occurs, as they say, in Deuteronomy, as applied to a ' virgin," in the following connection: "If a damsel that is a virgin be betrothed unto an husband, and a man find her in the city, and lie with her; then ye shall bring them both out unto the gate of that city, and ye shall stone them with stones that they die; the damsel, because she cried not, being in the city; and the man, because he humbled his neighbour's wife." And again: " But if a man find a betrothed damsel in a field, and the man force her, and lie with her: then the man only that lay with her shall die: but unto the damsel ye shall do nothing; there is in her no sin worthy of death."

Chapter xxxv.

But that we may not seem, because of a Hebrew word, to endeavour to persuade those who are unable to determine whether they ought to beheve it or not, that the prophet spoke of this man being born of a virgin, because at his birth these words, "-God with us," were uttered, let us make good our point from the words themselves. The Lord is related to have spoken to Ahaz thus: " Ask a sign for thyself from 1 Cf. Isa. vii. 10-14 with Matt. i. 23.- vistvig.

viuviv.- Cf. Deut. xxii. 23, 24. rri viuvilt.

tlie Lord thy God, either in the deptli or height above;" and afterwards the sign is given, "Behokl, a virgin shall conceive, and bear a son."- What kind of sign, then, woukl that have been a young woman who was not a virgin giving birth to a chikl? And which of the two is the more appropriate as the mother of Immanuel i. e. "God with us"), whether a woman who has had intercourse with a man, and who has conceived after tlie manner of women, or one who is still a pure and holy virgin? Surely it is appropriate only to the latter to produce a being at whose birth it is said, "God with us."' And shoukl he be so captious as to say that it is to Ahaz that the command is addressed, "Ask for thyself a sign from the Lord thy God," we shall ask in return, who in the times of Ahaz bore a son at whose birth the expression is made use of, "Immanuel," i. e. " God with us?" x nd if no one can be found, then manifestly what was said to Ahaz was said to the house of David, because it is written that the Saviour was born of the house of David accordino; to the flesh; and this sign is said to be " in the depth or in the heifrht," since " He that descended is the same also that ascended up far above all heavens, that He might fill all things." And these arguments I employ as against a Jew who believes in prophecy. Let Celsus now tell me, or any of those who think with him, with what mxcaning the prophet utters either these statements about the future, or the others which are contained in the prophecies? Is it with any foresight of the future or not? If with a foresight of the future, then the prophets were divinely inspired; if with no foresight of the future, let him explain the meaning of one who speaks thus boldly regarding the future, and who is an object of admiration among the Jews because of his prophetic powers.

Chapter xxxvr.

And now, since we have touched upon the subject of the prophets, what we are about to advance will be useful not only to the Jews, who believe that they spake by divine 1 Cf. Isa. vii. 11. 2 isa. vii. U. cf Eph. iv. 10.

inspiration, but also to the more candid among the Greeks. To these we say that we must necessarily admit that the Jews had prophets, if they were to be kept together under that system of law which had been given them, and were to believe in the Creator of the world, as they had learned, and to be without pretexts, so far as the law was concerned, for apostatizing to the polytheism of the heathen. And we establish this necessity in the following manner. " For the nations," as it is written in the law of the Jews itself, " shall hearken unto observers of times, and diviners; " but to that people it is said: " But as for thee, the Lord thy God hath not suffered thee so to do." And to this is subjoined the promise: " A prophet shall the Lord thy God raise up unto thee from among thy brethren." Since, therefore, the heathen employ modes of divination either by oracles or by omens, or by birds, or by ventriloquists, or by those who profess the art of sacrifice, or by Chaldean genealogists all which practices were forbidden to the Jews this people, if they had no means of attaining a knowledge of futurity, being led by the passion common to humanity of ascertaining the future, would have despised their own prophets, as not having in them any particle of divinity; and' would not have accepted any prophet after Moses, nor committed their words to writing, but would have spontaneously betaken themselves to the divining usages of the heathen, or attempted to establish some such practices amongst themselves. There is therefore no absurdity in their prophets having uttered predictions even about events of no importance, to soothe those who desire such things, as when Samuel prophesies regarding three she-asses which were lost, or when mention is made in the third book of Kings respecting the sickness of a king's son. And why should not those who desired to obtain auguries from idols be severely rebuked by the administrators of the law among the Jews? as Elijah is found rebuking Ahaziah, and saying, "Is it because there is not a God in Israel that ye go to inquire of Baalzebub, god of Ekron?"

1 Cf. Dent, xviii. 14. 2 cf. Deut. xviji. 14. Cf. Deut. xviii. 15. Cf. 1 Sam. ix. 10. Cf. 1 Kings xiv. 12. e Cf. 2 Kings i. 3.

Chapter xxxvii.

I tliink, then, that it has been pretty well established not only that our Saviour was to be born of a virgin, but also that there were prophets among the Jews who uttered not merely general predictions about the future, as e. g. regarding Christ and the kingdoms of the world, and the events that were to happen to Israel, and those nations which were to believe on the Saviour, and many other things concerning Him, but also prophecies respecting particular events; as, for instance, how the asses of Kish, which were lost, were to be discovered, and regarding the sickness which had fallen upon the son of the king of Israel, and any other recorded circumstance of a similar kind. But as a further answer to the Greeks, who do not believe in the birth of Jesus from a virgin, we have to say that the Creator has shown, by the generation of several kinds of animals, that what Pie has done in the instance of one animal. He could do, if it pleased Him, in that of others, and also of man himself. For it is ascertained that there is a certain female animal which has no intercourse with the male (as writers on animals say is the case with vultures), and that this animal, without sexual intercourse, preserves the succession of race. What incredibility, therefore, is there in supposing that, if God wished to send a divine teacher to the human race, He caused Him to be born in some manner different from the common? Nay, according to the Greeks themselves, all men were not born of a man and woman. For if the world has been created, as many even of the Greeks are pleased to admit, then the first men must have been produced not from sexual intercourse, but from the earth, in which spermatic elements existed; which, however, I consider more incredible than that Jesus was born like other men, so far as regards the half of his birth. And there is no absurdity in employing Grecian histories to answer Greeks, with the view of showing that we are not the only persons who have recourse to miraculous narratives of this kind. For some have thought fit, not in regard to ancient and heroic narratives, but in regard to events of very recent occurrence, to relate as a possible thing that Plato was the son of Amphictione, Ariston being prevented from having marital intercourse with his wife until she had given birth to him with whom she was pregnant by Apollo. And yet tliese are veritable fables, which have led to the invention of such stories concerning a man whom they regarded as possessing greater wisdom and power than the multitude, and as having received the beginning of his corporeal substance from better and diviner elements than others, because they thought that this was appropriate to persons who were too great to be human beings. And since Celsus has introduced the Jew disputing with Jesus, and tearing in pieces, as he imagines, the fiction of His birth from a virgin, comparing the Greek fables about Danae, and Melanippe, and Auge, and Antiope, our answer is, that such language becomes a buffoon, and not one who is writing in a serious tone.

Chapter xxxviii.

But, moreover, taking the history, contained in the Gospel according to Matthew, of our Lord's descent into Egypt, he refuses to believe the miraculous circumstances attending it, viz. either that the angel gave the divine intimation, or that our Lord's quitting Judea and residing in Egypt was an event of anv sio; nificance; but he invents somethino; altoo ether different, admitting somehow the miraculous w orks done by Jesus, by means of which He induced the multitude to follow Him as the Christ. And yet he desires to throw discredit on them, as being done by help of magic and not by divine power; for he asserts " that he (Jesus), having been brought up as an illegitimate child, and having served for hire in Egypt, and then coming to the knowledge of certain miraculous powers, returned from thence to his own country, and by means of those powers proclaimed himself a God." Now I do not understand how a magician should exert himself to teach a doctrine wdiich persuades us always to act as if God were to judge every man for lils deeds; and sliould. have trained liis disciples, whom he was to employ as the ministers of his doctrine, in the same belief. For did the latter make an impression upon their hearers, after they had been so taught to work miracles; or was it without tlie aid of these? The assertion, therefore, that they did no miracles at all, but that, after yielding their belief to arguments which were not at all convincing, like the wisdom of Grecian dialectics, they gave themselves up to the task of teaching the new doctrine to those persons among whom they happened to take up their abode, is altogether absurd. For in what did they place their confidence when thev taucrht the doctrine and disseminated the new opinions? But if they indeed wrought miracles, then how can it be believed that magicians exposed themselves to such hazards to introduce a doctrine which forbade the practice of magic?

Chapter xxxix.

I do not think it necessary to grapple with an argument advanced not in a serious but in a scoffing spirit, such as the following: " If the mother of Jesus was beautiful, then the God whoso nature is not to love a corruptible body, had intercourse with her because she was beautiful;" or, "It was improbable that the God would entertain a passion for her, because she was neither rich nor of royal rank, seeing no one, even of her neighbours, knew her."' And it is in the same scoffing spirit that he adds: " When hated by her husband, and turned out of doors, she was not saved by divine power, nor was her story believed. Such things, he says, have no connection with the kingdom of lieaven." In what respect does such language differ from that of those who pour abuse on others on the public streets, and whose words are unworthy of any serious attention?

1 This difficult passage is rendered in the Latin translation: " but tliat, after they had believed in Christ, they with no adequate supply of arguments, such as is furnished by the Greek dialectics, gave themselves up," etc.

Chapter xl.

After these assertions, he takes from the Gospel of Matthew, and perhaps also from the other Gospels, the account of the dove alighting upon our Saviour at His baptism by John, and desires to throw discredit upon the statement, alleging that the narrative is a fiction. Having completely disposed, as he imagined, of the story of our Lord's birth from a virgin, he does not proceed to deal in an orderly manner with the accounts that follow it; since passion and hatred observe no order, but angry and vindictive men slander those whom they hate, as the feeling comes upon them, being prevented by their passion from arranging their accusations on a careful and orderly plan. For if he had observed a proper arrangement, he would have taken up the Gospel, and, with the view of assailing it, would have objected to the first narrative, then passed on to the second, and so on to the others. But now, after the birth from a virgin, this Celsus, who professes to be acquainted with all our history, attacks the account of the appearance of the Holy Spirit in the form of a dove at the baptism. He then, after that, tries to throw discredit upon the prediction that our Lord was to come into the woi'ld. In the next place, he runs away to what immediately follows the narrative of the birth of Jesus the account of the star, and of the wise men who came from the east to worship the child. And you yourself may find, if you take the trouble, many confused statements made by Celsus throughout his whole book; so that even in this account he may, by those who know how to observe and require an orderly method of arrangement, be convicted of great rashness and boasting, in having inscribed upon his work the title of A True Discourse, a thing which is never done by a learned philosopher. For Plato says, that it is not an indication of an intelligent man to make strong assertions respecting those matters which are somewhat uncertain; and the celebrated Chrysippus even, who frequently states the reasons by which he is decided, refers us to those whom we shall find to be abler speakers than himself. This man, however, who is wiser than those already named, and than all the other Greeks, agreeably to his assertion of being acquainted with everything, inscribed upon his book the words, A True Discourse!

Chapter xli.

But, that we may not have the appearance of intentionally passing by his charges through inability to refute them, we liave resolved to answer each one of them separately according to our ability, attending not to the connection and sequence of the nature of the things themselves, but to the arrangement of the subjects as they occur in his book. Let us therefore notice what he has to say by way of impugning the bodily appearance of the Holy Spirit to our Saviour in the form of a dove. And it is a Jew who addresses the following language to Him vhom w'e acknowledge to be our Lord Jesus: ' When you were bathing," says the Jew, " beside John, you say that wdiat had the appearance of a bird from the air alighted upon you." And then this same Jew of his, continuing his interrogations, asks, "What credible witness beheld this appearance? or who heard a voice from heaven declaring you to be the Son of God? What proof is there of it, save your own assertion, and the statement of another of those individuals who have been punished along with you?"

Chapter xlii.

Before we begin our reply, we have to remark that the endeavour to show, with regard to almost any history, however true, that it actually occurred, and to produce an intelligent conception regarding it, is one of the most difficult undertakings that can be attempted, and is in some instances an impossibility. For suppose that some one were to assert that there never had been any Trojan war, chiefly on account of the impossible narrative interwoven therewith, about a certain Achilles being the son of a sea-goddess Thetis and of a man Peleus, or Sarpedon being the son of Zeus, or Ascalaphus and lalmenus tlie sons of Ares, or xeneas that of Aphrodite, how should we prove that such was the case, especially under the weight of the fiction attached, I know not how, to the universally prevalent opinion that there was really a war in Ilium between Greeks and Trojans? And suppose, also, that some one disbelieved the story of QLdipus and Jocasta, and of their two sons Eteocles and Polynices, because the sphinx, a kind of half-virgin, was introduced into the narrative, how should we demonstrate the realitv of such a thinoj? And in like manner also with the history of the Epigoni, althoumi there is no such marvellous event interwoven with it, or with the return of the Heracleida, or countless other historical events. But he who deals candidly with histories, and would wish to keep himself also from being imposed upon by them, will exercise his judgment as to what statements he will give his assent to, and what he will accept figuratively, seeking to discover the meaning of the authors of such inventions, and from what statements he will withhold his belief, as havino been written for the ratification of certain individuals. And we have said this by way of anticipation respecting the whole history related in the Gospels concerning Jesus, not as inviting men of acuteness to a simple and unreasoning faith, but wishing to show that there is need of candour in those who are to read, and of much investigation, and, so to speak, of insight into the meaning of the writers, that the object with which each event has been recorded may be discovered.

Chapter xliii.

We shall therefore say, in the first place, that if he who disbelieves the appearance of the Holy Spirit in the form of a dove had been described as an Epicurean, or a follower of Democritus, or a Peripatetic, the statement would have been in keeping witli the character of such an objector. But now even this Celsus, wisest of all men, did not perceive that it is to a Jew, who believes more incredible things contained in the writings of the prophets than the narrative of the ap- pearance of the dove, that he attributes such an objection! For one might say to the Jew, when expressing his disbehef of the appearance, and thinking to assail it as a fiction, ' How are you able to prove, sir, that the Lord spake to Adam, or to Eve, or to Cain, or to Noah, or to Abraham, or to Isaac, or to Jacob, those words which He is recorded to have spoken to these men?" And, to compare history with history, I would say to the Jew, "Even your own Ezekiel writes, saying, The heavens were opened, and I savv a vision of God." After relating which, he adds, ' This was the appearance of the likeness of the glory of the Lord; and He said to me,""- etc. Now, if what is related of Jesus be false, since we cannot, as you suppose, clearly prove it to be true, it being seen or heard by himself alone, and, as you appear to have observed, also by one of those who were punished, why should we not rather say that Ezekiel also was dealing in the marvellous when he said, "The heavens were opened," etc.? Nay, even Isaiah asserts, "I saw the Lord of hosts sitting on a throne, high and lifted up; and the seraphim stood round about it: the one had six winors, and the other had six winos."' How can we tell whether he really saw them or not? Now, O Jew, you have believed these visions to be true, and to have been not only shown to the prophet by a diviner Spirit, but also to have been both spoken and recorded by the same. And who is the more worthy of belief, when declaring that the heavens were opened before him, and that he heard a voice, or beheld the Lord of Sabaoth sitting upon a throne high and lifted up, whether Isaiah and Ezekiel or Jesus? Of the former, indeed, no work has been found equal to those of the latter; whereas the good deeds of Jesus have not been confined solely to the period of His tabernacling in the flesh, but up to the present time His power still produces conversion and amelioration of life in those who believe in God through Him. And a manifest proof that these things are done by His power, is the fact that, although, as He Himself said, and as is admitted, there are not labourers enough to gather in the harvest of souls, there really is nevertheless 1 Cf. Ezek. i. 1. cf. Ezek. i. 28 and ii. 1. Cf. Isa. vi. 1, 2.

such a great harvest of those who are gathered together and conveyed into the everywhere existing threshing-floors and churches of God.

Chapter xliv.

And with these arguments I answer the Jew, not disbelieving, I who am a Christian, Ezekiel and Isaiah, but being very desirous to show, on the footing of our common belief, that this man is far more worthy of credit than they are when He says that He beheld such a sight, and, as is probable, related to His disciples the vision which He saw, and told them of the voice which He heard. But another party might object, that not all those who have narrated the appearance of the dove and the voice from heaven heard the accounts of these things from Jesus, but that that Spirit which taught Moses the history of events before his own time, beginning with the creation and descending down to Abraham his father, taught also the writers of the Gospel the miraculous occurrence which took place at the time of Jesus' baptism. And he who is adorned with the spiritual gift, called the " word of wisdom," will explain also the reason of the heavens opening, and the dove appearing, and why the Holy Spirit appeared to

Jesus in the form of no other living thing than that of a dove. But our present subject does not require us to explain this, our purpose being to show that Celsus displayed no sound judgment in representing a Jew as disbelieving, on such grounds, a fact which has greater probability in its favour than many events in which he firmly reposes confidence.

Chapter xlv.

And I remember on one occasion, at a disputation held with certain Jews who were reputed learned men, having employed the following argument in the presence of many judges: " Tell me, sirs," I said, " since there are two indivi- duals who have visited the human race, regarding whom are related marvellous works surpassing human power Moses, viz., your own legislator, who wrote about himself, and Jesus our teacher, who has left no writings regarding Himself, but to whom testimony is borne by the disciples in the Gospels what are the grounds for deciding that Moses is to be believed as speaking the truth, although the Egyptians slander him as a sorcerer, and as appearing to have wrought his mighty works by jugglery, while Jesus is not to be believed because you are His accusers? And yet there are nations which bear testimony in favour of both: the Jews to Moses; and the Christians, who do not deny the prophetic mission of Moses, but proving from that very source the truth of the statement regarding Jesus, accept as true the miraculous circumstances related of Him by His disciples. Now, if ye ask us for the reasons of our faith in Jesus, give yours first for believing in Moses, who lived before Him, and then we shall give you ours for accepting the latter. But if you draw back, and shirk a demonstration, then we, following your own example, decline for the present to offer any demonstration likewise. Nevertheless, admit that ye have no proof to offer for Moses, and then listen to our defence of Jesus derived from the law and the prophets. And now observe what is almost incredible! It is shown from the declarations concerning Jesus, contained in the law and the prophets, that both Moses and the prophets were truly prophets of God."

Chapter xlyi.

For the law and the prophets are full of marvels similar to those recorded of Jesus at His baptism, viz. regarding the dove and the voice from heaven. And I think the wonders wrought by Jesus are a proof of the Holy Spirit's having then appeared in the form of a dove, although Celsus, from a desire to cast discredit upon them, alleges that He performed only what He had learned among the Egyptians. And I shall refer not only to His miracles, but, as is proper, to those also of the apostles of Jesus. For they could not without the help of miracles and wonders have prevailed on those who heard their new doctrines and new teachings to abandon their national usages, and to accept their instructions at the danger to themselves even of death. And there are still preserved among Christians traces of that Holy Spirit which appeared in the form of a dove. They expel evil spirits, and perform many cures, and foresee certain events, according to the will of the Logos. And although Celsus, or the Jew whom he has introduced, may treat with mockery what I am going to say, I shall say it nevertheless, that many have been converted to Christianity as if against their will, some sort of spirit having suddenly transformed their minds from a hatred of the doctrine to a readiness to die in its defence, and having appeared to them either in a waking vision or a dream of the night. Many such instances have we knowui, which, if we were to commit to writing, although they w ere seen and witnessed by ourselves, w e should afford great occasion for ridicule to unbelievers, who would imagine that we, like those whom they suppose to have invented such things, had ourselves also done the same. But God is witness of our conscientious desire, not by false statements, but by testimonies of different kinds, to establish the divinity of the doctrine of Jesus. And as it is a Jew wdio is perplexed about the account of the Holy Spirit having descended upon Jesus in the form of a dove, we would say to him, "Sir, who is it that says in Isaiah, And now the Lord hath sent me and His Spirit?"" Li wdiich sentence, as the meaning is doubtful viz. whether the Father and the Holy Spirit sent Jesus, or the Father sent both Christ and the Holy Spirit the latter is correct. For, because the Saviour was sent, afterwards the Holy Spirit was sent also, that the prediction of the prophet might be fulfilled; and as it was necessary that the fulfilment of the prophecy should. be known to posterity, the disciples of Jesus for that reason committed the result to writing, i Cf. Isa. xlviii. IC.

Chapter xlvit.

I would like to say to Celsus, who represents the Jew as accepting somehow John as a Baptist, who baptized Jesus, that the existence of John the Baptist, baptizing for the remission of sins, is related by one who lived no great length of time after John and Jesus. For in the 18th book of his Antiquities of the Je? ys, Josephus bears witness to John as having been a Baptist, and as promising purification to those who underwent the rite. Now this writer, although not believing in Jesus as the Christ, in seeking after the cause of the fall of Jerusalem and the destruction of the temple, whereas he ought to have said that the conspiracy against Jesus was the cause of these calamities befalling the people, since they put to death Christ, who was a prophet, says nevertheless being, although against his will, not far from the truth that these disasters happened to the Jews as a punishment for the death of James the Just, who was a brother of Jesus (called Christ), the Jews having put him to death, although he was a man most distinguished for his justice. Paul, a genuine disciple of Jesus, says that he regarded this James as a brother of the Lord, not so much on account of their relationship by blood, or of their being brought up together, as because of his virtue and doctrine."" If, then, he says that it was on account of James that the desolation of Jerusalem was made to overtake the Jews, how should it not be more in accordance with reason to say that it happened on account of the death of Jesus Christ, of whose divinity so many churches are witnesses, composed of those who have been converted from a flood of sins, and who have joined themselves to the Creator, and who refer all their actions to His good pleasure?

CliArtER XLVIII.

Although the Jew, then, may offer no defence for himself in the instances of Ezekiel and Isaiah, when we com-1 Cf. Joseph. Aiitiq. book xviii. c. x. sec. 2.- Cf. Gal. L 19.

pare tlie opening of the heavens to Jesus, and the voice that was heard by Him, to the similar cases which we find recorded m Ezekiel and Isaiah, or any other of the prophets, we nevertheless, so far as we can, shall support our position, maintaining that, as it is a matter of belief that in a dream impressions have been brought before the minds of many, some relating to divine things, and others to future events of this life, and this either with clearness or in an enigmatic manner, a fact which is manifest to all who accept the doctrine of providence; so how is it absurd to say that the mind which could receive impressions in a dream should be impressed also in a waking vision, for the benefit either of him on whom the impressions are made, or of those who are to hear the account of them from him? And as in a dream we fancy that we hear, and that the organs of hearing are actually impressed, and that we see with our eyes although neither the bodily organs of sight nor hearing are affected, but it is the mind alone which has these sensations so there is no absurdity in believing that similar things occurred to the prophets, when it is recorded that they witnessed occurrences of a rather wonderful kind, as when they either heard the words of the Lord or beheld the heavens opened. For I do not suppose that the visible heaven was actually opened, and its physical structure divided, in order that Ezekiel might be able to record such an occurrence. Should not, therefore, the same be believed of the Saviour by every intelhgent hearer of the Gospels? although such an occurrence may be a stumbling-block to the simple, who in their simplicity would set the whole world in movement, and split in sunder the compact and mighty body of the whole heavens. But he who examines such matters more profoundly will say, that there being, as the Scripture calls it, a kind of general divine perception which the blessed man alone knows how to discover, according to the saying of Solomon, "Thou slialt find the knowledge of God;"" and as there are various forms of this perceptive power, such as a faculty of vision which can naturally see things that are better than 1 Cf. Prov. ii. 5.

bodies, among wlilcli arc ranked the cherubim and seraphim; and a faculty of hearing Avhich can perceive voices-which liave not their being in the air; and a sense of taste which can make use of living bread that has come down from heaven, and that giveth life unto the world; and so also a sense of smelhng, which scents such things as leads Paul to say that he is a sweet savour of Christ unto God; and a sense of touch, by which John says that he " handled wdth his hands of the Word of life; "- the blessed prophets having discovered this divine perception, and seeing and hearing in this divine manner, and tasting likewise, and smelling, so to speak, with no sensible organs of perception, and laying hold on the Logos by faith, so that a healing effluence from it comes upon them, saw in this m. anner what they record as having seen, and heard wdiat they say they heard, and w ere affected in a similar manner to what they describe when eating the roll of a book that was given them. And so also Isaac smelled the savour of his son's divine garments," and added to the spiritual blessing these words: ' See, the savour of my son is as the savour of a full field which the Lord blessed."' And similarly to this, and more as a matter to be understood by the mind than to be perceived by the senses, Jesus touched the leper, to cleanse him, as I think, in a twofold sense, freeing him not only, as the multitude heard, from the visible leprosy by visible contact, but also from that other leprosy, by His truly divine touch. It is in this way. accordingly, that John testifies when he says, " 1 beheld the Spirit descending from heaven like a dove, and it abode upon Him. And I knew Him not; but He that sent me to baptize w ith water, the same said to me, Upon whom you will see the Spirit descending, and abiding on Him, the same is He that baptizeth with the Holy Ghost. And I saw, and bear witness, that this is the Son of God." " Now it was to Jesus that the heavens were opened; and on that occasion no one except John is recorded to have seen them opened. But 1 Cf. 2 Cor. ii. 15. "- Cf. 1 John i. 1. cf Ezek. iii. 2, 3.

' ni7(pa. ud- T'? i; oaavi; ruu rov vlov d-ioripuu iaxttoiv. 5 Cf. Gen. xxvii. 27. cf. Matt. viii. 3. ' Cf. John i. 32-34.

ORIG. 2 F with respect to this opening of tlie heavens, the Saviourj foreteuing to His disciples that It wouki happen, and that they would see it, says, "Verily, verily, I say unto you. Ye shall see the heavens opened, and the angels of God ascending and descending upon the Son of man." And so Paul was carried away into the third heaven, having previously seen it opened, since he was a disciple of Jesus. It does not, however, belong to our present object to explain why Paul says, "Whether in the body, I know not; or whether out of the body, I know not: Qod knoweth." But I shall add to my argument even those very points which Celsus Imagines, viz. that Jesus Himself related the account of the opening of the heavens, and the descent of the Holy Spirit upon Him at the Jordan in the form of a dove, although the Scripture does not assert that He said that He saw it. For this great man did not perceive that it was not In keeping with Him who commanded His disciples on the occasion of the vision on the mount, "Tell what ye have seen to no man, until the Son of man be risen from the dead," to have related to His disciples what was seen and heard by John at the Jordan. For It may be observed as a trait of the character of Jesus, that He on all occasions avoided unnecessary talk about Himself; and on that account said, "If I speak of myself, my witness Is not true." And since He avoided unnecessary talk about Himself, and preferred to show by acts rather than words that He was the Christ, the Jews for that reason said to Him, "If thou art the Christ, tell us plainly." And as it is a Jew who. In the work of. Celsus, uses the language to Jesus regarding the appearance of the Holy Spirit in the form of a dove, " This Is your own testimony, unsupported save by one of those who vere sharers of your punishment, whom you adduce," it is necessary for us to show him that such a statement is not appropriately placed in the mouth of a Jew. For the Jews do not connect John with Jesus, nor the punishment of John with that of Christ. And by this Instance, this man who boasts of universal knowledge 1 Cf. John i. 52. 2 cf. 2 Cor. xii. 2. cf. Matt. xvii. 9.

John V. 31. 5 John x. 24.

is convicted of not knowing Yhat words he ought to ascribe to a Jew engaged in a disputation Avith Jesus.

Chapter xltx.

After this he wilfully sets aside, I know not why, the strongest evidence in confirmation of the claims of Jesus, viz. that His coming was predicted by the Jewish propliets Moses, and those who succeeded as well as preceded that legislator from iuabihty, as I think, to meet the argument that neither the Jews nor any other heretical sect refuse to believe that Christ was the subject of prophecy. But perhaps he was unacquainted with the prophecies relating to Christ. For no one who was acquainted with the statements of the Christians, that many prophets foretold the advent of the Saviour, would have ascribed to a Jew sentiments which it would have better befitted a Samaritan or a Sadducee to utter; nor would the Jew in the dialogue have expressed himself in language like the following: " But my prophet once declared in Jerusalem, that the Son of God will come as the Judge of the righteous and the Punisher of the wicked." Now it is not one of the prophets merely who predicted the advent of Christ. But although the Samaritans and Sadducees, who receive the books of Moses alone, would say that there w ere contained in them predictions regarding Christ, yet certainly not in Jerusalem, which is not even mentioned in the times of Moses, was the prophecy uttered. It were indeed to bo desired, that all the accusers of Christianity were equally ignorant with Celsus, not only of the facts, but of the bare letter of Scripture, and would so direct their assaults against it, that their aro-uments mimit not have the least available influence in shaking, I do not say the faith, but the little faith of unstable and temporary believers. A Jew, however, would not admit that any prophet used the expression, "The Son of God' will come;" for the term whicli they employ is, "' The ' Christ of God' will come." And many a time indeed do they directly interrogate us about the ' Son of God," saying that no such being exists, or was made the subject of prophecy. We do not of course assert that the " Son of God" is not the subject of prophecy; but we assert that he most inappropriately attributes to the Jewish disputant, who would not allow that He vras, such language as, "My prophet once declared in Jerusalem that the ' Son of God' will come."

Chapter l.

In the next place, as if the only event predicted were this, that He was to be ' the Judge of the righteous and the Punisher of the wicked," and as if neither the place of His birth, nor the sufferings which He was to endure at the hands of the Jews, nor His resurrection, nor the wonderful works which He was to perform, had been made the subject of prophecy, he continues: " Why should it be you alone, rather than innumerable others, who existed after the prophecies were published, to whom these predictions are applicable? " And desiring, I know not how, to suggest to others the possibility of the notion that they themselves were the persons referred to by the prophets, he says that " some, carried away by enthusiasm, and others having gathered a multitude of followers, give out that the Son of God is come down from heaven." Now we have not ascertained that such occurrences are admitted to have taken place among the Jews. We have to remark then, in the first place, that many of the prophets have uttered predictions in all kinds of ways regarding Christ; some by means of dark sayings, others in allegories or in some other manner, and some also in express words. And as in what follows he says, in the character of the Jew addressing the converts from his own nation, and repeating emphatically and malevolently, that " the prophecies referred to the events of his life may also suit other events as well," we shall state a few of them out of a greater number; and with respect to these, any one who chooses may say what he thinks fitted to ensure a refutation of them, and which may turn a Yay intelligent believers from the faith.

Chapter li.

Now the Scripture speaks, respecting the place of tlso Saviour's birth that the Euler was to come forth from Bethlehem in the following manner: " And thou Bethlehem, liouse of Ephrata, art not the least among the thousands of Judah: for out of thee shall He come forth unto me who is to be Ruler in Israel; and His goings forth have been of old, from everlasting." Now this prophecy could not suit aiy one of those who, as Celsus' Jew says, were fanatics and mob-leaders, and who gave out that they had come

from heaven unless it were clearly shown that He had been b orn in Bethlehem, or, as another might say, had come forth from Bethlehem to be the leader of the people. With respect to the birth of Jesus in Bethlehem, if any one desires, after the prophecy of Micah and after the history recorded in the Gospels by the disciples of Jesus, to have additional evidence from other sources, let him know that, in conformity with the narrative in the Gospel regarding His birth, there is shown at Bethlehem the cave where He was born, and the manger in the cave where He was wrapped in swaddling-clothes. And this sight is greatly talked of in surrounding places, even among the enemies of the faith, it being said that in this cave was born that Jesus who is worshipped and reverenced by the Christians. Moreover, I am of opinion that, before the advent of Christ, the chief pnests and scribes of the people, on account of the distinctness and clearness of this prophecy, taught that in Bethlehe L-the JQhrist vas to be born. And this opinion had prevailed also extensively among the Jews; for which reason it is related that Herod, on inqufring at the chief priests and scribes of the people, heard from them that the Christ was to be born in Bethlehem of Judea, ' whence David was." It is stated also in the Gospel according to John, that the Jews declared that the Christ was to be born in Bethlehem, " whence David was."'"' But after our Lord's coming, those who busied themselves with overthrowing the belief that the place of His birth
1 Cf. Mic. V. 2 and Matt. ii. G. 2 Cf. Jf; iin vii. 42.

had been the subject of prophecy from the beginning, withheld such teaching from the people; acting in a similar manner to those individuals who won over those soldiers of the suard stationed around the tomb who had seen Him arise from the dead, and who instructed these eye-witnesses to report as follows: " Say that his disciples, while we slept, came and stole him away. And if this come to the governor's ears, we shall persuade him, and secure you."

Chapter lii.

Strife and prejudice are powerful instruments in leading men to disregard even those things wdiich are abundantly clear; so that they who have somehow become familiar with certain opinions, which have deeply imbued their minds, and stamped them with a certain character, will not give them up. For a man w ill abandon his habits in respect to other things, although it may be difficult for him to tear himself from them, more easily than he will surrender his opinions. Nay, even the former are not easily put aside by those who have become accustomed to them; and so neither houses, nor cities, nor villages, nor intimate acquaintances, are willingly forsaken when w e are prejudiced in their favour. Tl i j therefore, w as a reason why many of the Jews at that time disregarded the clear testimony of the prophecies, and miracles which Jesus wrought, and of the sufferings which He is related to have endured. And that human nature is thus affected, will be manifest to those who observe that those who have once been prejudiced in favour of the most contemptible and paltry traditions of their ancestors and fellow-citizens, with difficulty lay them aside. For example, no one could easily persuade an Egyptian to despise what he had learned from his fathers, so as no longer to consider this or that irrational animal as a god, or not to guard against eating, even under the penalty of death, of the flesh of such an animal. Now, if in carrying our examination of this subject to a considerable length, we have enumerated the 1 Cf. Matt, xxviii. 13, 14.

points respecting Bethlehem, and the prophecy regarding it, we consider that we were obliged to do this, by way of defence against those who would assert that if the prophecies current amonoj the Jews re ardino; Jesus were so clear as we represent them, why did they not at His coming give in thieir'adhesion to His doctrine, and betake themselves to the better life pointed out by Him? Let no one, however, bring such a reproach against believers, since he may see that reasons of no light weight are assigned by those who have learned to state them, for their faith in Jesus.

Chapter liii.

And if we should ask for a second prophecy, which may appear to us to have a clear reference to Jesus, we would quote that which was written by Moses very many years before the advent of Christ, when he makes Jacob, on his departure from this life, to have uttered predictions regard-incr each of his sons, and to have said of Judah alonor with the others: " The ruler will not fail from Judah, and the governor from his loins, until that which is reserved for him come." Now, any one meeting with this prophecy, which is in reality much older than Moses, so that one who was not a believer might suspect that it was nofwritten hj Tnrn would be surprised that Moses should be able to predict that thcprinces of the Jews, seeing there are among them twelve tribes, should be born of the tribe of Judah, and should be the rulers of the people; for which reason also the whole nation are called Jews, deriving their name from the ruling tribe. And, in the second place, one who candidly considers the prophecy, would be surprised how, after declaring that the rulers and governors of the people were to proceed from the tribe of Judah, he should determine also the limit of their rule,

Cf. Gen. xlix. 10, tag uv 'i'Ky to, d'Trokily. vjcc ccvtu. This is one of the passages of the Septuagint whicli Justin Martyr charges the Jews with corrupting; the true reading, according to him, being sug ecu 'ixdvi a cctroksircci. Cf. Ju? tin Martyr, Dialogue with Tripho, Ante-Nicene Lib.

p. 251, saying that " the ruler should not fail from Juclah, nor the governor from his loins, until there should come that which was reserved for him, and that He is the expectation of the Gentiles." For Pie came for whom these things were reserved, viz. the Christ of God, the ruler of the promises of God. And manifestly He is the only one among those who preceded, and, I might make bold to say, among those also who followed Him, who was the expectation of the Gentiles; for converts from among all the Gentile nations have believed on God through Him, and that in conformity with the prediction of Isaiah, that in His name the Gentiles had hoped: " In Thy name shall the Gentiles hope." And this man said also to those who are in prison, as every man is a captive to the chains of his sins, "Come forth;" and to the ignorant, "Come into the light:" these things also having been thus foretold: " I have given Thee for a covenant of the people, to establish the earth, to cause to inherit the desolate heritage; saying to the prisoners, Go forth; and to them that are in darkness, Show yourselves." And we may see at the appearing of this man, by means of those who everywhere throughout the world have reposed a simple faith in Him, the fulfilment of this prediction: " They shall feed in the ways, and their pastures shall be in all the beaten tracks."

Chapter liv.

And since Celsus, although professing to know all about the Gospel, reproaches the Saviour because of His sufferings, saying that He received no assistance from the

Father, or was unable to aid Himself; ve have to state that His sufferings w ere the subject of prophecy, along with the cause of them; because it w as for the benefit of mankind that He should die on their account, and should suffer stripes because of His condemnation. It was predicted, moreover, that some from among the Gentiles would come to the knowledge of Him (among whom the prophets are not included); and 1 Of. Gen. xlix. 10. 2 ig. xlii. 4. cf. Isa. xlix. 8, 0.

Isa. xlix. 9.

it had been declared that He would be seen in a form svhich is deemed dishonourable amonf men. The words of prophecy run thus: " Lo, my Servant shall have understanding, and shall be exalted and glorified, and raised exceedingly high. In like manner, many shall be astonished at Thee; so Thy form shall be in no reputation among men, and Thy glory among the sons of men. Lo, many nations shall marvel because of Him; and kings shall close their mouths: because they, to whom no message about Him was sent, shall see Ilim; and they who have not heard of Him, shall have knowledge of Him." " Lord, who hath believed our report? and to whom was the arm of the Lord revealed? We have reported, as a child before Him, as a root in a thirsty ground. He has no form nor glory; and we beheld Plim, and He had not any form nor beauty: but His appearance was without honour, and deficient more than that of all men. He was a m. an under suffering, and wdio knew how to bear sickness: because His countenance was averted, He was treated with disrespect, and was made of no account. This man bears our sins, and suffers pain on our behalf; and we regarded Him as in trouble, and in suffering, and as ill-treated. But He was wounded for our sins, and bruised for our iniquities. The chastisement of our peace was upon Him; by His stripes we w ere healed. We all, like sheep, wandered from the way. A man wandered in his way, and the Lord delivered Him on account of our sins; and He, because of His evil treatment, opens not His mouth. As a sheep was He led to slaughter; and as a lamb before her shearer is dumb, so He opens not His mouth. In His humiliation His judgment was taken away. And who shall describe His generation? because His life is taken away from the earth; because of the iniquities of my people was He led unto death."

Chapter lv.

Now I remember that, on one occasion, at a disputation 1 Cf. Isa. lii. 13-15 in the Scptuagint version (Roman text).

2 Cf. Isa. liii. 1-8 in the Septuagint version (Roman text).

held with certain Jews, who were reckoned wise men, I q uoted these prophecies; to which my Jewish opponent replied, that these predictions idore reference to the whole people, regarded as one individual, and as being in a state of dispersion and suffering, in order that many proselytes might be gained, on account of the dispersion of the Jews among numerous heatlien nations. And in this way he explained the w ords, "Thy form shall be of no reputation among men; " and then, "They to wdiom no message was sent respecting him shall see;" and the expression, "A man under suffering." Many arguments w ere employed on that occasion during the discussion to prove that these predictions regarding one particular person wxre not rightly applied by them to the whole nation. And I asked to what character the expression would be appropriate, "Tliis man bears our sins, and suffers pain on our behalf;" and this,

"But he was wounded for our sins, and bruised for our iniquities;" and to whom the expression properly belonged, "By his stripes were w e healed." For it is manifest that it is they who had been sinners, and had been healed by the Saviours sufferings (whether belonging to tlie Jewish nation or converts from the Gentiles), who use such language in the writings of the prophet who foresaw these events, and who, under the influence of the Holy Spirit, applied these words to a person. But we seemed to press them hardest with the expression, "Because of the iniquities of my people was he led away unto death." For if the people, according to them, are the subject of the prophecy, how is the man said to be led away to death because of the iniquities of the people of God, unless he be a different person from that people of God? And who is this person save Jesus Christ, by whose stripes they wdio believe on Him are healed, when " He had spoiled the principalities and powers (that Avere over us), and had made a show of them openly on His cross?" At another time we may explain the several parts of the prophecy, leaving none of them unexamined. But these matters have been treated at greater length, necessarily as I think, on account of the language of the Jew, as quoted in the work of Celsus.

Chapter lvi.

Now it escaped the notice of Celsus, and of the Jew whom he has introduced, and of all who are not believers in Jesus, that the prophecies speak of two advents of Christ: th e form er characterized by human suffering and humility, in order that Christ, being with men, might make known the way that leads to God, and might leave no man in this life a ground of excuse, in saying that he knew not of the judgment to come; and the latter, distinguished only by glory and divinity, having no element of human infirmity intermingled with its divine greatness. To quote the prophecies at length would be tedious; and I deem it sufficient for the present to quote a part of the forty-fifth Psalm, which has this inscription, in addition to others, "A Psalm for the Beloved," where God is evidently addressed in these words: ' Grace is poured into Thy lips: therefore God will bless Thee for ever and ever. Gii'd Thy sword on Thy thigh, O mighty One, with Thy beauty and Thy majesty. And stretch forth, and ride prosperously, and reign, because of Thy truth, and meekness, and righteousness; and Thy right hand shall lead Thee marvellously. Thine arrows are pointed, O mighty One; the people will fall under Thee in the heart of the enemies of the Kin." But attend carefully to what follows, where He is called God: " For Thy throne, O God, is for ever and ever: a sceptre of righteousness is the sceptre of Thy kingdom. Thou hast loved righteousness, and hated iniquity: therefore God, even Thy God, hath anointed Thee with the oil of gladness above Thy fellows."'" And observe that the prophet, speaking familiarly to God, whose " throne is for ever and ever," and " a sceptre of righteousness the sceptre of His kingdom," says that this God has been anointed by a God who was His God, and anointed, because more than His fellows He had loved righteousness and hated iniquity. And I remember that I pressed the. Jew who was deemed a learned man, very hard with this passage; and he, being perplexed about it, gave such an answer as was in keeping with his Judaistic views, saying that the words.

"l Ps. xlv. 2-5. "' ' " 2 Ps. xlv. G, 7.

' Thy throne, O God, is for ever and ever: a sceptre of righteousness is the sceptre of Thy kingdom," are spoken of the God of all things; and these, "Thou hast loved righteousness and hated iniquity, therefore Thy God hath anointed Thee," etc., refer to the Messiah.

Chapter lvii.

The Jew, moreover, in tlie treatise, addresses the Saviour thus: "If you say that every man, born according to tlie decree of Divine Providence, is a son of God, in what respect should you differ from another?" In reply to whom we say, that every man who, as Paul expresses it, is no longer under fear, as a schoolmaster, but who chooses good for its own sake, is "a son of God;" but this man is distinguished far and wide above every man who is called, on account of his virtues, a son of God, seeing He is, as it were, a kind of source and beginning of all such. The words of Paul are as follow: "For ye have not received the spirit of bondage again to fear; but ye have received the spirit of adoption, whereby we cr, Abba, Father." But, according to the Jew of Celsus, " countless individuals will convict Jesus of falsehood, alleging that those predictions which were spoken of him were intended of them." We are not aware, indeed, whether Celsus knew of any who, after coming into this world, and having desired to act as Jesus did, declared themselves to be also the " sons of God," or the "power" of God. But since it is in the spirit of truth that we examine each passage, we shall mention that there Avas a certain Theudas among the Jews before the birth of Christ, who gave himself out as some great one, after whose death his deluded followers were completely dispersed. And after him, in the days of the census, when Jesus appears to have been born, one Judas, a Galilean, gathered around him many of the Jewish people, saying he was a wise man, and a teacher of certain new doctrines. And when he also had paid the penalty of his rebellion, his doctrine was overturned, having taken hold 'Trpoi Tou Xpiarou. Rom. viii. 16.

of very few persons indeed, and tliese of tlie very liumblest condition. And after the times of Jesus, Dositlieus the Samaritan also Yished to persuade the Samaritans that he was the Christ predicted by Moses; and he appears to Iiave gained over some to his views. But it is not absurd, in quoting the extremely wise observation of that Gamaliel named in the book of Acts, to show how those persons above mentioned were strangers to the promise, being neither " sons of God" nor "powers" of God, v hereas Christ Jesus was truly the Son of God. Now Gamaliel, in the passage referred to, said: ' If this counsel or this work be of men, it will come to nought" (as also did the designs of those men already mentioned after their death); " but if it be of God, ye cannot overthrow this doctrine, lest haply ye be found even to fight against God." There was also Simon the Samaritan magician, who wished to draw away certain by his magical arts. And on that occasion he was successful; but now-a-days it is impossible to find, I suppose, thirty of his followers in the entire world, and probably I have even overstated the number. There are exceedingly few in Palestine; while in the rest of the world, through which he desired to spread the glory of his name, you find it nowhere mentioned, x nd where it is found, it is found quoted from the Acts of the Apostles; so that it is to Christians that he owes this mention of himself, the unmistakeable result having proved that Simon was in no respect divine.

Chapter lviit.

After these matters this Jew of Celsus, instead of the Mam mentioned in tlie Gospel, says that ' Chaldeans are spoken of bv Jesus as havino; been induced to come to him at his birth, and to worship him while yet an infant as a God, and to have made this known to Herod the tetrarch; and that the latter sent and slew all the infants that had been born about the same time, thinking that in this way he would ensure his death among the others; and that he was led to do this 1 Cf. Acts V. 38, 39.

tliroufvli fear that, if Jesus lived to a sniiicient age, he would obtain the throne." See now in this instance the blunder of one who cannot distinguish between Magi and Chaldeans, nor perceive that what they profess is different, and so has falsified the Gospel narrative. I know not, moreover, why he has passed by in silence the cause which led the Magi to come, and why he has not stated, according to the scriptural account, that it was a star seen by them in the east. Let us see now what answer we have to make to these statements. The star that was seen in the east we consider to have been a new star, unlike any of the other well-known planetary bodies, either those in the firmament above or those among the lower orbs, but partaking of the nature of those celestial bodies which appear at times, such as comets, or those meteors which resemble beams of wood, or beards, or wine jars, or any of those other names by wdiich the Greeks are accustomed to describe their varying appearances. And we establish our position in the following manner.

Chapter lix.

It has been observed that, on the occurrence of great events, and of mighty changes in terrestrial things, such stars are wont to appear, indicating either the removal of dynasties or the breaking out of wars, or the happening of such circumstances as may cause commotions upon the earth. But we have read in the Treatise on Comets by Chaeremon the Stoic, that on some occasions also, when good was to happen, comets made their appearance; and he gives an account of such instances. If, then, at the commencement of new dynasties, or on the occasion of other important events, there aris ST' a comet so called, or any similar celestial body, why should it be matter of wonder that at the birth of Him who was, to introduce a new doctrine to the human race, and to make known His teaching not only to Jews, but also to Greeks, and to many of tlie barbarous nations besides, a star should have arisen Now I would say, that with respect to comets there is no prophecy in circulation to the effect that such and sncli a comet was to arise in connection witli a particular kingdom or a particular time; but with respect to the appearance of a star at the birth of Jesus there is a prophecy of Balaam recorded by Moses to this effect: " There shall arise a star out of Jacob, and a man shall rise up out of Israel." And now, if it shall be deemed necessary to examine the narrative about the Magi, and the appearance of the star at the birth of Jesus, the following is what we have to say, partly in answer to the Greeks, and partly to the Jews.

CHArtER LX.

To the Greeks, then, I have to say that the Magi, being on familiar terms with evil spirits, and invoking them for such purposes as their knowledge and wishes extend to, bring about such results only as do not appear to exceed the superhuman power and strength of the evil spirits, and of the spells which invoke them, to accomplish; but should some greater manifestation of divinity be made, then the powers of the evil spirits are overthrown, being unable to resist the light of divinity. It is probable, therefore, that since at the birth of Jesus " a multitude of the heavenly host," as Luke records, and as I believe, "praised God, saying. Glory to God in the highest, and on earth peace, good-will towards men," the evil spirits on that account became feeble, and lost their strength, the falsity of their sorcery being manifested, and their power being broken; this overthrow being brought about not only by the angels having visited the terrestrial regions on account of the birth of Jesus, but also by the power of Jesus Himself, and His innate divinity. The Magi, accordingly, wishing to produce the customary results, which formerly they used to perform by means of certain spells and sorceries, sought to know the reason of their failure, conjecturing the cause to be a great one; and beholding a divine sign in the heaven, they desired to learn its signification. I am therefore of opinion that, possessing as they did the prophecies of Balaam, which Moses also records, inasmuch as 1 Cf. Num. xxiv. 17 (Septuag.).

Balaam was celebrated for siicli predictions, and finding among them tlie prophecy about the star, and the words, ' I shall show him to him, but not now; I deem him happy, although lie will not be near,"- they conjectured that the man whose appearance had been foretold along with that of tlie star, had actually come into the w orld; and having predetermined that he was superior in power to all demons, and to all common appearances and powers, they resolved to offer him homage. They came, accordingly, to Judea, persuaded that some king had been born; but not knowing over what kingdom he was to reign, and being ignorant also of the place of his birth, bringing gifts, which they offered to him as one whose nature partook, if I may so speak, both of God and of a mortal man, gold, viz., as to a king; myrrh, as to one who w as mortal; and incense, as to a God; and they brought these offerings after they had learned the place of His birth. But since He was a God, the Saviour of the human race, raised far above all those angels which minister to men, an angel rewarded the piety of the Magi for their worship of Him, by making known to them that they were not to go back to Herod, but to return to their own homes by another way.

Chapter lxi.

That Herod conspired against the child (although the Jew of Celsus does not believe that this really happened), is not to be wondered at. For wickedness is in a certain sense blind, and would desire to defeat fate, as if it were stronger than it. And this being Herod's condition, he both believed that a king of the Jews had been born, and yet cherished a purpose contradictory of such a belief; not seeing that the child is assuredly either a king and will come to the throne, or that he is not to be a king, and that his death, therefore, will be to no purpose. He desired accordingly to kill Him, his mind being agitated by contending passions on account of his wickedness, and being instigated by the blind and wicked devil who from the very beginning plotted against the Saviour, 1 Cf. Num. xxiv. 17 (Septuag.).

imagining that He was and would become some migliry one. An angel, liowever, perceiving the course of events, intimated to Joseph, although Celsus may not believe it, that he was to withdraw with the child and His mother into Egypt, while Herod slew all the infants that were in Bethlehem and the surrounding borders, in the hope that he would thus destroy Him also who had been born King of tlie Jews. For he saw not the sleepless guardian power that is around those who deserve to be protected and preserved for the salvation of men, of whom Jesus is the first, superior to all others in honour and excellence, who was to be a King indeed, but not in the sense that Herod supposed, but in that in which it became God to bestow a kingdom, for the benefit, viz., of those who were to be under His sway, who was to confer no ordinary and unimportant blessings, so to speak, upon His subjects, but who was to train them and to subject them to laws that were truly from God. And Jesus, knowing this well, and denying that He was a king in the sense that the multitude expected, but declaring the superiority of His kingdom, says: "If my kingdom were of this world, then would my servants fight, that I should not be delivered to the Jews: but now is my kingdom not of this world." Now, if Celsus had seen this, he would not have said: "But if, then, this was done in order that you might not reign in his stead when you had grown. to man's estate; why, after you did reach that estate, do you not become a king, instead of you, the Son of God, wandering about in so mean a condition, hiding yourself through fear, and leading a miserable life up and down? " Now, it is not dishonourable to avoid exposing one's self to dangers, but to guard carefully against them, when this is done, not through fear of death, but from a desire to benefit others by remaining in life, until the proper time come for one who has assumed human nature to die a death that will be useful to mankind. And this is plain to him who reflects that Jesus died for the sake of men, a point of which we have spoken to the best of our ability in the preceding pages.

Cf. John xviii. 36. ORIG. 2 G

Chapter lxii.

And after sucli statements, showing his ignorance even of the number of the apostles, he proceeds thus: " Jesus having gathered around him ten or eleven persons of notorious character, the very wickedest of tax-gatherers and sailors, fled in company vith them from place to place, and obtained his living in a shameful and importunate manner." Let us to the best of our power see what truth there is in such a statement. It is manifest to us all who possess the Gospel narratives, which Celsus does not appear even to have read, thcit Jesus selected twelve apostles, and that of these Matthew alone was a tax-o-atherer; that when he calls them indiscri-minately sailors, he probably means James and John, because they left their ship and their father Zebedee, and followed Jesus; for Peter and his brother Andrew, who employed a net to gain their necessary subsistence, must be classed not as sailors, but as the Scripture describes them, as fishermen. The Lebes also, who was a follower of Jesus, may have been a tax-gatherer; but he was not of the number of the apostles, except according to a statement in one of the copies of Mark's Gospel. And we have not ascertained the employments of the remaining disciples, by wdiich they earned their livelihood before becoming disciples of Jesus. I assert, therefore, in answer to such statements as the above, that it is clear to all who are able to institute an intelligent and candid examination into the history of the apostles of Jesus, that it was by help of a divine power that these men taught Christianity, and succeeded in leading others to embrace the word of God. For it was not any power of speaking, or any orderly arrangement of their message, according to the arts of Grecian dialectics or rhetoric, which was in them the effective cause of converting their hearers. Nay, I am of opinion that if Jesus had selected some individuals who w ere wise according to the apprehension of the multitude, and who were fitted both to think and speak so as to please them, and had used such as the ministers of His 1 A 3)9?. 2 Qi; ij p j iii, 18 with Matt. x. 3.

doctrine, He would most justly have been suspected of employing artifices, like those philosophers who are the leaders of certain sects, and consequently the promise respecting the divinity of His doctrine would not have manifested itself; for had the doctrine and the preaching consisted in the persuasive utterance and arrangement of words, then faith also, like that of the philosophers of the world in their opinions, would have been through the wisdom of men, and not through the power of God. Now, who is there, on seeing fishermen and tax-gatherers, who had not acquired even the merest elements of learning (as the Gospel relates of them, and in respect to which Celsus believes that they speak the truth, inasmuch as it is their own ignorance which they record), discoursing boldly not only among the Jews of faith in Jesus, but also preaching Him with success among other nations, would not inquire whence they derived this power of persuasion, as theirs w as certainly not the common method followed by the multitude? And who would not say that the promise, "Follow me, and I will make you fishers of men," had been accomplished by Jesus in the history of His apostles by a sort of divine power? And to this also, Paul, referring in terms of commendation, as we have stated a little above, says: "And my speech and my preaching was not with enticing words of man's wisdom, but in demonstration of the Spirit and of power; that your faith should not stand in the wisdom of men, but in the power of God." '- For, according to the predictions in the prophets, foretelling the preaching of the gospel, " the Lord gave the word in great power to them wdio preached it, even the King of the powders of the Beloved," in order that the prophecy might be fulfilled which said, "His word shall run very swiftly." And we see that " the voice of the apostles of Jesus has gone forth into all the earth, and their words to the end of the world." On this account are they who hear the word powerfully proclaimed filled with power, which they manifest both by their dispositions and their lives, and by stru ri!; lin T even to death on behalf of the 1 Matt. iv. 19. CLl Cor. ii. 4-, 5.

s Cf. Ps. Ixviii. 11 (Septu. ag.). T. cxh'ii. 15. Fs. xix. 4.

truth; while some are altogether empty, although they profess to believe in God through Jesus, inasmuch as, not possessino-any divine power, they have the appearance only of bein converted to the word of God. And although I have previously mentioned a Gospel declaration uttered by the Saviour, I shall nevertheless quote it again, as appropriate to the present occasion, as it confirms both the divine manifestation of our Saviour's foreknowledge regarding the preaching of His gospel, and the power of His word, which without the aid of teachers gains the mastery over those who yield their assent to persuasion accompanied with divine power; and the words of Jesus referred to are, "The harvest is plenteous, but the labourers are few; pray ye therefore the Lord of the harvest, that He will send forth labourers into His harvest."

Chapter Ixiii.

And since Celsus has termed the apostles of Jesus men of Infamous notoriety, saying that they were tax-gatherers and sailors of the vilest character, we have to remark, with respect to this charge, that he seems, in order to bring an accusation against Christianity, to believe the Gospel accounts only where he pleases, and to express his disbelief of them, in order that he may not be forced to admit the manifestations of Divinity related in these same books; whereas one who sees the spirit of truth by which the writers are influenced, ought, from their narration of things of inferior importance, to believe also the account of divine things. Now in the general Epistle of Barnabas, from which perhaps Celsus took the statement that the apostles were notoriously wicked men, it is recorded that " Jesus selected His own apostles, as persons who were more guilty of sin than all other evil-doers." And in the Gospel according to Luke, Peter says to Jesus, "Depart from me, O Lord, for I am a sinful man." Moreover, Paul, who himself also at a later time became an apostle of Jesus, says in his 1 Matt. ix. 37, 38.

2 Epistle of Barnabas, chap. v. (Cf. Ante-Nicene Library, vol. Apos-touc Fathers, p. 108.) Luks v. 8.

Epistle to Timotliy, ' This is a faithful saying, that Jesus Christ came into the world to save sinners, of whom I am the chief." And I do not know how Celsus should have forgotten or not have thought of saying something about Paul, the founder, after Jesus, of the churches that are in Christ. He saw, probably, that anything he might say about that apostle would require to be explained, in consistency with the fact that, after being a persecutor of the church of God, and a bitter opponent of believers, who went so far even as to deliver over the disciples of Jesus to death, so great a change afterwards passed over him, tliat he preached the gospel of Jesus from Jerusalem round about to Illyricum, aud was ambitious to carry the glad tidings where he needed not to build upon another man's foundation, but to places where the gospel of God in Christ had not been proclaimed at all What absurdity, therefore, is there, if Jesus, desiring to manifest to the human race the power which He possesses to heal souls, should have selected notorious and wicked men, and should have raised them to such a degree of moral excellence, that they became a pattern of the purest virtue to all who were converted by their instrumentality to the gospel of Christ?

Chapter lxiv.

But if we were to reproach those who have been converted with their former lives, then we would have occasion to accuse Ph edo also, even after he became a philosopher; since, as the history relates, he was drawn aw y by Socrates from a house of bad fame to the pursuits of philosophy. Nay, even the licentious life of Polemo, the successor of Xeno-crates, will be a subject of reproach to philosophy; whereas even in these instances we ought to regard it as a ground of praise, that reasoning was enabled, by the persuasive power of these men, to convert from the practice of such vices those 1 Cf. 1 Tim. i. 15.

2 d-Tro oik'ifixTo;. Sucli is the reading in the text of Lommatzscb. Hoeschel and Spencer read cctto ou-! ucctog huov, and Ruseus proposes

STCCtpioV.

who had been formerly entangled by them. Now among the Greeks there was only one Phcedo, I know not if there were a second, and one Polemo, who betook themselves to philosophy, after a licentious and most wicked life; while with Jesus there were not only at the time we speak of, the twelve disciples, but many more at all times, who, becoming a band of temperate men, speak in the following terms of their former lives: " For we ourselves also were sometimes foolish, disobedient, deceived, serving divers lusts and pleasures, living in malice and envy, hateful, and hating one another. But after that the kindness and love of God our Saviour towards man appeared, by the washing of regeneration, and renewing of the Holy Ghost, which

He shed upon us richly,"- we became such as we are. For " God sent forth His Word and healed them, and delivered them from their destructions," as the prophet taught in the book of. Psalms. And in addition to what has been already said, I would add the following: that Chrysippus, in his treatise on the Cure of the Passions, in his endeavours to restrain the passions of the human soul, not pretending to determine what opinions are the true ones, says that according to the principles of the different sects are those to be cured who have been brought under the dominion of the passions, and continues: " And if pleasure be an end, then by it must the passions be healed; and if there be three kinds of chief blessings, still, according to this doctrine, it is in the same way that those are to be freed from their passions who are under their dominion;" whereas the assailants of Christianity do Y 6t see in how many persons the passions have been brought under restraint, and the flood of wickedness checked, and savage manners softened by means of jhe gospel. So that it well became those who are ever boasting of their zeal for the public good, to make a public acknowledgment of their thanks to that doctrine which by a new method led men to abandon many vices, and to bear their testimony at least to it, that even though not the truth, it has at all events been productive of benefit to the human race. 1 Cf. Tit. iii. 3-6. " Cf. Ps. cvii. 20.

Chapter lxy.

And since Jesus, in teaching His disciples not to be guilty of rashness, gave them the precept, "If they persecute you in this city, flee ye into another; and if they persecute you in the other, flee again into a third," to which tcacliing lie added the example of a consistent life, acting so as not to expose Ilimself to danger rashly, or imseasonably, or Yithout good grounds; from this Celsus takes occasion to bring a malicious and slanderous accusation, the Jew whom he brings forward saying to Jesus, "In company with your disciples you go and hide yourself in different places." Now similar to what has thus been made the ground of a slanderous charge against Jesus and His disciples, do we say was the conduct recorded of Aristotle. This philosopher, seeing that a court was about to be summoned to ivy him, on the ground of his being guilty of impiety on account of certain of his philosophical tenets which the Athenians regarded as impious, withdrew from Athens, and fixed his school in Chalcis, defending his course of procedure to his friends by saying, 'Let us depart from Athens, that we may not give the Athenians a handle for incurring guilt a second time, as formerly in the case of Socrates, and so prevent them from committing a second act of impiety against philosophy." He further says, ' that Jesus v'ent about with his disciples, and obtained his livelihood in a disgraceful and importunate manner." Let him show wherein lay the disgraceful and importunate element in their manner of subsistence. For it is related iii the Gospels, that there were certain women who had been healed of their diseases, among whom also was Susanna, who from their own possessions afforded the disciples the means of support. And who is there among philosophers, that, when devoting himself to the service of his acquaintances, is not in the habit of receiving from them what is needful for his wants? Or is it only in them that such acts are proper and becoming; but when the disciples of Jesus do the same, they are accused by Celsus of obtaining their livelihood by disgraceful importunity t 1 Cf. Matt. X. 23.

Chapter lxvi.

And in addition to the above, this Jew of Celsus afterwards addresses Jesus: " What need, moreover, was there that yon, while still an infant, should be conveyed into Egypt? Was it to escape being murdered? But then it was not likely that a God should be afraid of death; and yet an angel came down from heaven, commanding you and your friends to flee, lest ye should be captured and put to death! And was not the great God, who had already sent two angels on your account, able to keep you, His only Son, there in safety?" From these words Celsus seems to think that there was no element of divinity in the human body and soul of Jesus, but that His body was not even such as is described in the fables of Homer; and with a taunt also at the blood of Jesus which was shed upon the cross, he adds that it was not

"Iclior, such as flows in the veins of the blessed gods."

We now, believing Jesus Himself, when He says respecting His divinity, 'I am the way, and the truth, and the life," and employs other terms of similar import; and when He says respecting His being clothed with a human body, "And now ye seek to kill me, a man that hath told you the truth,"' conclude that He w as a kind of compound being. And so it became Him who was making provision for His sojourning in the world as a human being, not to expose Himself unseasonably to the danger of death. And in like manner it was necessary that He should be taken away by His parents, acting under the instructions of an ano'el from heaven, who communicated to them the divine will, saying on the first occasion, "Joseph, thou son of David, fear not to take unto thee Mary thy wife; for that which is conceived in her is of the Holy Ghost;" and on the second, "Arise, and take the young child, and His mother, and flee into Egypt; and be thou there until I bring thee word: for Herod will seek the young child to destroy Him." Now, what is recorded in 1 Cf. Iliad, V. 340. John xiv. 6. Cf. John viii. 40.

4 Cf. Matt. i. 20. Cf. Matt. ii. 13.

these words appears to me to be not at all marvellous. For in either passage of Scripture it is stated that it was in a dream that the angel spoke these words; and that in a dream certain persons may have certain things pointed out to them to do, is an event of frequent occurrence to many individuals, the impression on the mind being produced either by an angel or by some other thing. Where, then, is the absurdity in believing that He who had once become incarnate, should be led also by human guidance to keep out of the way of dangers? Not indeed from any impossibility that it should be otherwise, but from the moral fitness that ways and means should be made use of to ensure the safety of Jesus. And it was certainly better that the child Jesus should escape the snare of Herod, and should reside with His parents in Egypt until the death of the conspirator, than that Divine Providence should hinder the free will of Herod in his wish to put the child to death, or that the fabled poetic helmet of Hades should have been employed, or anything of a similar kind done with respect to Jesus, or that they who came to destroy Him should have been smitten with blindness like the people of Sodom. For the sending of help to Him in a very miraculous and unnecessarily public manner, would not have been of any service to Him who wished to show that as a man, to whom witness was borne by God, He possessed within that form which was seen by the eyes of men some higher element of divinity, that which was properly the Son of God God the Word the power of God, and the wisdom of

God He who is called the Christ. But this is not a suitable occasion for discussing the composite nature of the incarnate Jesus; the investigation into such a subject being for believers, so to speak, a sort of private question.

Chapter lxvii.

After the above, this Jew of Celsus, as if he were a Greek who loved learning, and were well instructed in Greek literature, continues: " The old mythological fables, which attributed a divine origin to Perseus, and Amphion ani acus, and Minos, were not believed bj us. Nevertheless, that they might not appear unworthy of credit, they represented the deeds of these personages as great and wonderful, and truly beyond the power of man; but what hast thou done that is noble or wonderful either in deed or in word? Thou hast made no manifestation to las, although they challenged you in the temple to exhibit some unmistakeable sign that you were the Son of God." In reply to which we have to say: Let the Greeks show to us, among those who have been enumerated, any one whose deeds have been marked by a utility and splendour extending to after generations, and which have been so great as to produce a belief in the fables which represented them as of divine descent. But these Greeks can show us nothing regarding those men of whom they speak, which is even inferior by a great degree to what Jesus did; unless they take us back to their fables and histories, wishing us to believe them without any reasonable grounds, and to discredit the Gospel accounts even after the clearest evidence. For we assert that the whole habitable world contains evidence of the works of Jesus, in the existence of those churches of God which have been founded through Him by those who have been converted from, the practice of innumerable sins. And the name of Jesus can still remove distractions from the minds of men, and expel demons, and also take away diseases; and produce a marvellous meekness of spirit and complete change of character, and a humanity, and goodness, and gentleness in those individuals who do not feign themselves to be Christians for the sake of subsistence or the supply of any mortal wants, but who have honestly accepted the doctrine concerning God and Christ, and the judgment to come.

Chapter lxviii.

But after this, Celsus, having a suspicion that the great works performed by Jesus, of which we have named a few out of a great number, would be brought forward to view, affects to grant that those statements may be true which are made refrardlnn: His cures, or His resurrection, or the feeclinir of a multitude with a few loaves, from which many fragments remained over, or those other stories which Celsus thinks the disciples have recorded as of a marvellous nature; and he adds: " Well, let us believe that these vrere actually wrought by you." But then he immediately compares them to the tricks of jugglers, who profess to do more wonderful things, and to the feats performed by those who have been taught by Egyptians, who in the middle of the market-place, in return for a few obols, will impart the knowledge of their most venerated arts, and will expel demons from men, and dispel diseases, and invoke the souls of heroes, and exhibit expensive banquets, and tables, and dishes, and dainties having no real existence, and who will put in motion, as if alive, what are not really living animals, but which have only the appearance of life. And he asks, "Since, then, these persons can perform such feats, shall we of necessity conclude that they are 'sons of God," or must we admit that they are the proceedings of wicked men under the influence of an evil spirit?" You see that by these expressions he allows, as it w ere, the existence of magic. I do not know, however, if he is the same who wrote several books against it. But, as it helped his purpose, he compares the miracles related of Jesus to the results produced by magic. There would indeed be a resemblance between them, if Jesus, like the dealers in magical arts, had performed His works only for show; but now there is not a single juggler who, by means of his proceedings, invites his spectators to reform their manners, or trains those to the fear of God who are amazed at what they see, nor who tries to persuade them so to live as men who are to be justified- by God. And jugglers do none of these things, because they have neither the power nor the will, nor any desire to busy themselves about the reformation of men, inasmuch as their own lives are full of the grossest and most notorious sins. But how should not He who, by the miracles which He did, induced those wdio beheld the excellent results to undertake the reformation of their characters, manifest u; Oikcciad'iaouivov;.

Himself not onh to His genuine disciples, but also to others as a pattern of most virtuous life, in order that His disciples raio; ht devote themselves to the work of instructino; men in the will of God, and that the others, after being more fully-instructed by His word and character than by His miracles, as to how they were to direct their lives, might in all their conduct have a constant reference to the good pleasure of the universal God? And if such were the life of Jesus, how could any one with reason compare Him with the sect of impostors, and not, on the contrary, believe, according to the promise, that He was God, who appeared in human form to do good to our race?

Chapter lxix.

After this, Celsus, confusing together the Christian doctrine and the opinions of some heretical sect, and bringing them forward as charges that w ere applicable to all who believe in the divine word, says: " Such a body as yours could not have belonged to God." Now, in answer to this, we have to say that Jesus, on entering into the world, assumed, as one born of a woman, a human body, and one which was capable of suffering a natural death. For which reason, in addition to others, we say that He was also a great wrestler;- having, on account of His human body, been tempted in all respects like other men, but no longer as men, with sin as a consequence, but being altogether without sin. For it is distinctly clear to us that " He did no sin, neither was guile found in His mouth; and as one who knew no sin," God delivered Him up as pure for all who had sinned. Then Celsus says: 'The body of God would not have been so generated as you, O Jesus, were." He saw, besides, that if, as it is written, it had been born. His body somehow might be even more divine than that of the multitude, and in a certain sense a body of God. But he disbelieves the accounts of His conception by the Holy Ghost, and believes that He was begotten by one Panthera, who corrupted the Virgin,

"because a God's body would not have been so generated as you were." But we have spoken of these matters at greater length in the preceding pages.

Chapter lxx.

He asserts, moreover, that " the body of a god is not nourished with such food as was that of Jesus," since he is able to prove from the Gospel narratives both that He partook of food, and food of a particular kind. Well, be it so. Let him assert that He ate the passover with His disciples, when He not only used the words, "With desire have I desired to eat this passover with you," but also actually partook of the same. And let him say also, that He experienced the sensation of thirst beside the well of Jacob, and drank of the water of the well. In what respect do these facts militate against what w6 have said respecting the nature of His body? Moreover, it appears indubitable that after His resurrection He ate a piece of fish; for, according to our view, He assumed a true body, as one born of a woman. " But," objects Celsus, " the body of a god does not make use of such a voice as that of Jesus, nor employ such a method of persuasion as he." These are, indeed, trifling and altogether contemptible objections. For our reply to him will be, that he who is believed among the Greeks to be a god, viz. the Pythian and Didymean Apollo, makes use of such a voice for his Pythian priestess at Delphi, and for his prophetess at Miletus; and yet neither the Pythian nor Didymean is charged by the Greeks with not being a god, nor any other Grecian deity whose worship is established in one place. And it was far better, surely, that a god should employ a voice which, on account of its being uttered with power, should produce an indescribable sort of persuasion in the minds of the hearers.

Chapter lxxi.

Continuing to pour abuse upon Jesus as one who, on account of his impiety and wicked opinions, was, so to speak, hated by God, he asserts that "these tenets of his were those of a Avicked and God-hated sorcerer." And yet, if the name and the thing be properly examined, it will be found an impossibility that man should be hated by God, seeing God loves all existing things, and " hateth nothino; of what He has made," for He created nothing in a spirit of hatred. And if certain expressions in the prophets convey such an impression, they are to be interpreted in accordance with the general principle by which Scripture employs such language with regard to God as if He were subject to human affections. But what reply need be made to him who, wdiile professing to bring forward credible statements, thinks himself bound to make use of calumnies and slanders against Jesus, as if He were a wicked sorcerer? Such is not the procedure of one who seeks to make good his case, but of one who is in an ignorant and unphilosophic state of mind, inasmuch as the proper course is to state the case, and candidly to investigate it; and, according to the best of his ability, to bring forward what occurs to him with regard to it. But as the Jew of Celsus has, with the above remarks, brought to a close his charges against Jesus, so we also shall here bring to a termination the contents of our first book in reply to him. And if God bestow the gift of that truth which destroys all falsehood, agreeably to the words of the prayer, ' Cut them off in thy truth," we shall, begin, in what follows, the consideration of the second appearance of the Jew, in which he is represented by Celsus as addressing those who have become converts to Jesus.

1 Ps. liv. 5.

Lightning Source UK Ltd.
Milton Keynes UK
10 February 2010

149848UK00002B/56/P